Numismatics and Greek Lexicography

Numismatics and Greek Lexicography

Michael P. Theophilos

LONDON • NEW YORK • OXFORD • NEW DELHI • SYDNEY

T&T CLARK
Bloomsbury Publishing Plc
50 Bedford Square, London, WC1B 3DP, UK
1385 Broadway, New York, NY 10018, USA
29 Earlsfort Terrace, Dublin 2, Ireland

BLOOMSBURY, T&T CLARK and the T&T Clark logo
are trademarks of Bloomsbury Publishing Plc

First published in Great Britain 2020
Paperback edition first published 2021

Copyright © Michael P. Theophilos, 2020

Michael P. Theophilos has asserted his right under the Copyright,
Designs and Patents Act, 1988, to be identified as Author of this work.

For legal purposes the Acknowledgements on p. xi constitute
an extension of this copyright page.

Cover image: Sellwood 27.2. Silver drachm. Obverse: Mithradates II, long-bearded bust
facing left; reverse: archer seated holding bow. 123-88 BCE (© Michael P. Theophilos)

All rights reserved. No part of this publication may be reproduced or
transmitted in any form or by any means, electronic or mechanical,
including photocopying, recording, or any information storage or retrieval
system, without prior permission in writing from the publishers.

Bloomsbury Publishing Plc does not have any control over, or responsibility for,
any third-party websites referred to or in this book. All internet addresses given
in this book were correct at the time of going to press. The author and publisher
regret any inconvenience caused if addresses have changed or sites have
ceased to exist, but can accept no responsibility for any such changes.

A catalogue record for this book is available from the British Library.

A catalog record for this book is available from the Library of Congress.

ISBN: HB: 978-0-5676-7436-4
PB: 978-0-5677-0197-8
ePDF: 978-0-5676-7437-1
eBook: 978-0-5676-9022-7

Typeset by Integra Software Services Pvt. Ltd.

To find out more about our authors and books visit
www.bloomsbury.com and sign up for our newsletters.

Contents

List of Figures	vii
List of Tables	x
Acknowledgements	xi
List of Abbreviations	xii

Part One

1	Introduction	3
	Nomenclature and definitions	16
2	The History of Coinage	19
	Introduction	19
	The inception and evolution of coinage	20
	Conclusion	42
3	The Study of Coinage	43
	Introduction	43
	Sources	43
	Conclusion	70
4	Critical Issues in the Appeal to Coinage	71
	Introduction	71
	Coins as propaganda: Can we trust them?	71
	Coins as currency: Did people notice them?	76
	Coins as witnesses: A truncated view?	77
	Strengths of coinage as evidence	78
	Conclusion	91

Part Two

5	ΦΙΛΟΣ	105
	Introduction	105
	ΦΙΛ–lexeme	105
	The Greco-Roman context	107
	The numismatic evidence	109
	Conclusion	113
6	ΚΑΡΠΟΦΟΡΟΣ	115
	Introduction	115

	Definition of καρποφόρος in the literature and lexicons	116
	The Roman context	119
	Conclusion	126
7	ΝΕΩΚΟΡΟΣ	127
	Introduction	127
	Context and background	128
	Numismatic evidence	133
	Implications for the 'νεωκόρος' of Acts 19:35	140
	Conclusion	142
8	ΘΕΟΣ, ΕΛΕΥΘΕΡΙΑ, ΕΙΡΗΝΗ ΚΑΙ ΑΣΦΑΛΕΙΑ, ΚΑΒΕΙΡΟΣ	143
	Introduction	143
	Thessalonian coinage	143
	Case studies	146
	Conclusion	163
9	ΧΑΡΑΚΤΗΡ	165
	Introduction	165
	Historical context of Hebrews	165
	The literary context of Hebrews 1:3	166
	Numismatic material on ΧΑΡΑΚΤΗΡ and related terms	167
	Conclusion	173
10	ΚΤΙΣΤΗΣ	175
	Introduction	175
	The historical and literary context of 1 Peter 4:19	175
	Numismatic material on Κτίστης and related terms	176
	New Testament lexeme	184
	Conclusion	191
11	ΒΑΣΙΛΕΥΣ ΒΑΣΙΛΕΩΝ	193
	Introduction	193
	The history of ΒΑΣΙΛΕΥΣ ΒΑΣΙΛΕΩΝ	194
	Numismatic evidence	195
	Interpretive implications for the book of Revelation	209
	Conclusion	214
12	Conclusion	217
	Bibliography	222
	Index of Modern Authors	259
	Index of Scripture References and Other Ancient Sources	266

List of Figures

1	SNG Ashmolean 760	23
2	Carradice I	24
3	Carradice II	25
4	Carradice IIIa	26
5	Carradice IIIb (early)	26
6	Carradice IIIb (late)	26
7	Carradice IVa	27
8	Carradice IVb	27
9	Carradice IVc	27
10	SNG Paris 1.1544	28
11	SNG Copenhagen 32	29
12	Ravel 619	29
13	SNG Keckman 544	30
14	Dewing 1508	31
15	SNG Ashmolean 648	32
16	SNG Ashmolean 728	32
17	SNG Ashmolean 1671	33
18	SNG ANS 807	33
19	SNG Ashmolean 2891	34
20	SNG Ashmolean 3756	35
21	SNG Copenhagen 70	35
22	Crawford 20.1	37
23	Crawford 72.3	38
24	Crawford 295.1	38
25	Crawford 480.13	39
26	RIC *Aug.* 210	40
27	RIC *Nero* 181	79
28	RPC 1.4967	87
29	RPC 1.4968	88
30	RPC 1.4969	88
31	RPC 1.4982	111
32	RPC 1.3031	112

33	RPC 1.3056	113
34	RPC 1.4949	120
35	RPC 1.3540	123
36	RPC 1.3538	123
37	SNG Ashmolean 3300	144
38	AMNG III/2, 41	145
39	SNG Ashmolean 3301	145
40	SNG Copenhagen 369	145
41	RPC 1.1554	147
42	RPC 1.1552	147
43	RPC 1.1555	148
44	RPC 1.5421	149
45	CNG 75.2007.798	150
46	RPC 1.1563	150
47	RPC 1.1427	151
48	RPC 1.1551	153
49	RPC 1.1552	154
50	RPC 1.1553	155
51	RIC *Claud.* 16	158
52	RIC *Claud.* 96	159
53	RPC 2.327	161
54	RPC 2.328	162
55	RPC 2.330	162
56	Youroukova 145	168
57	RPC 1.2049	177
58	RPC 1.2017	178
59	RPC 1.1363	179
60	RPC 1.2495	180
61	RPC 1.2991	181
62	RPC 1.2511	182
63	RPC 1.2512	182
64	RPC 1.3601	183
65	RPC 1.4948	184
66	Sellwood 27.2	195
67	Sellwood 41.8	196
68	Sellwood 42.2	197
69	Sellwood 51.9	197
70	Crawford 543.1	201

71	Pharn 1	202
72	MIG 5.681	203
73	MIG 5.694	204
74	MIG 6.737	205
75	MIG 6.740	206
76	MIG 8.1070	207

List of Tables

1	Aes grave denominations	36
2	Majority composition of Roman provincial coinage	37
3	Published volumes of the *Sylloge Nummorum Graecorum*	48
4	Numismatic basis for RPC series	64
5	Roman provincial coinage volumes: Status and contributors	65
6	Electronic resources for numismatics	66
7	First-century Tribunicia Potestas dates	80
8	Collated first-century dates for abbreviated titulature	81
9	Ancient Greek numerals	87
10	Augustan values 27 BCE–301 CE	93
11	Egyptian denominations	94
12	Conversion rate between Egypt and the provincial denominations	94
13	Documented price transactions	96
14	Coinage and related terminology in the New Testament	100
15	Sample of relevant material for ΦΙΛ–lexeme	109
16	Attestations of the adjective καρποφόρος and verb καρποφορέω in the New Testament	115
17	Numismatic evidence for ΝΕΩΚΟΡΟΣ	134
18	New Testament examples of κτίζω	185
19	New Testament examples of κτίσις	185
20	New Testament examples of κτίσμα	186
21	New Testament example of κτίστης	186
22	LXX examples of κτίστης	186
23	Selective table of numismatic inscriptional evidence for ΒΑΣΙΛΕΥΣ ΒΑΣΙΛΕΩΝ	208

Acknowledgements

This volume began as a tangential footnote in a draft of my doctoral dissertation at Oxford University in 2004. That footnote has cascaded into what is now a monograph-length investigation on one aspect of the relationship between numismatics and New Testament Studies. There have been many dialogue partners in helping formulate an argument that attempts to do justice to the marrying of two fields of research which have had difficulty being integrated in the past.

I wish to acknowledge Professor Christopher Howgego, keeper of the Heberden coin room at the Ashmolean Museum, for his forbearance in the several years of numismatic instruction at Oxford University while I was a doctoral student in 2004–2007. His patient and careful guidance, together with the most exhaustive reading lists in the field, provided a staggering breadth of exposure. During my extracurricular pursuits during my doctoral studies in Oxford, one of my enduring memories of participating in Michael Kim's lectures on Greek numismatics (Ashmolean Museum, Faculty of Classics, Oxford University) was his weekly challenge for the class to request a viewing of a coin that he could *not* produce from the vast Ashmolean collection. What made this challenge even more exhilarating was the setting: twelve eager disciples sitting on the numbing concrete floor of the numismatic vault, before the recent renovations of the Ashmolean Museum. Needless to say, his challenge was never overcome.

I owe a steadily increasing debt to John Lee (Macquarie University, Sydney), who has generously given of time and effort to help refine my own thoughts on the way new primary sources should be integrated as the discipline of Greek lexicography evolves. His vast experience within the discipline of Greek lexicography has influenced my own approach to the discipline more than I can express. I also wish to express immense gratitude to Anne Thomson for her erudite and insightful comments throughout. I was humbled and honoured when I was invited to be the 2015 Senior Research Fellow at the Australian Centre for Ancient Numismatic Study (Sydney, Australia). The director (Associate Professor Ken Sheedy), staff and board provided the most invigorating and robust numismatic discussion I have experienced, and this volume is better for it. On multiple occasions, Colin Pitchfork (Noble Numismatics, Sydney) was willing to obtain obscure bibliographic items that were unavailable in any public or university libraries. My debt of gratitude is great.

tantus labor non sit cassus

List of Abbreviations

ABS   Archaeology and Biblical Studies

AJA   *American Journal of Archaeology*

AJP   *American Journal of Philology*

ANF   *Ante-Nicene Fathers*. Edited by Alexander Roberts and James Donaldson. 1885–1887. 10 vols. Repr., Peabody: Hendrickson, 1994.

ANRW   *Aufstieg und Niedergang der römischen Welt*

ANS   American Numismatic Society

BA   *The Biblical Archaeologist*

BAG   Arndt, William F. and F. Wilbur Gringrich. *A Greek-English Lexicon of the New Testament and Other Early Christian Literature: A Translation and Adaptation of Walter Bauer's Griechisch-Deutches Wöterbuch zu den Schriften des Neuen Testaments und der übrigen urchristlichen Literatur, fourth revised and augmented edition*, 1952.

BAGD   Arndt William F. and F. Wilbur Gingrich. *A Greek-English Lexicon of the New Testament and Other Early Christian Literature: A Translation and Adaptation of the Fourth Revised and Augmented Edition of Walter Bauer's Griechisch-Deutsches Wörterbuch zu den Schriften des Neuen Testaments und der übrigen urchristlichen Literatur*, 1979.

BCH   *Bulletin de Correspondance Hellénique*

BDAG   Danker, Frederick W., Walter Bauer, William F. Arndt and F. Wilbur Gingrich. *Greek-English Lexicon of the New Testament and Other Early Christian Literature*. 3rd ed. Chicago: University of Chicago Press, 2000.

BICS   *Bulletin of the Institute of Classical Studies*

BJRL   *Bulletin of the John Rylands University Library of Manchester*

CQ   *Classical Quarterly*

DDbDP   Duke Databank of Documentary Papyri (http://www.papyri.info/ddbdp)

EAH   Bagnall, Roger S., Kai Brodersen, Craige B. Champion, Andrew Erskine and Sabine R. Huebner. *The Encyclopedia of Ancient History*, 13 vols. v.1. Ab-An; v.2. An-Be; v. 3. Be-Co; v. 4. Co-Ec; v. 5. Ec-Ge; v. 6. Ge-In; v. 7.

Io-Li; v. 8. Li-Ne; v. 9. Ne-Pl; v. 10. Pl-Ro; v. 11. Ro-Te; v. 12. Te-Zy; v. 13. Index (Malden: Wiley-Blackwell, 2013).

EEC	Furguson, E. *Encyclopedia of Early Christianity*. Chicago: St. James Press, 1990.
HTR	*Harvard Theological Review*
IG	*Inscriptiones Graecae*
ISBE	*The International Standard Bible Encyclopedia*
JBL	*Journal of Biblical Literature*
JETS	*Journal of the Evangelical Theological Society*
JHS	*Journal of Hellenic Studies*
JJS	*Journal of Jewish Studies*
JNG	*Jahrbuch für Numismatik und Geldgeschichte*
JRA	*Journal of Roman Archaeology*
JRS	*Journal of Roman Studies*
JSJ	*Journal for the Study of Judaism*
JTS	*Journal of Theological Studies*
LCL	Loeb Classical Library
LSJ	Liddell, Henry George, Robert Scott and Henry Stuart Jones. *A Greek-English Lexicon*. 9th ed. with revised supplement. Oxford: Clarendon, 1996.
L&N	Louw, Johannes P. and Eugene A. Nida, eds. *Greek-English Lexicon of the New Testament: Based on Semantic Domains*, 2nd ed.; 2 vols. New York: United Bible Societies, 1988–1989.
MIG	Mitchiner, Michael. Indo-Greek and Indo-Scythian Coinage, 9 vols. London: Hawkins Publications, 1975.
MM	Moulton, James Hope, and George Milligan. *The Vocabulary of the Greek Testament*. London: Hodder and Stoughton, 1930.
NA27	*Novum Testamentum Graece*, Nestle-Aland, 27th ed.
NA28	*Novum Testamentum Graece*, Nestle-Aland, 28th ed.
NC	*Numismatic Chronicle*
NIDNTTE	Silva, Moisés, ed. *New International Dictionary of New Testament Theology and Exegesis*, 5 vols. Grand Rapids: Zondervan, 2014.
NovT	*Novum Testamentum*

OLD	Glare, P. G. W. *Oxford Latin Dictionary*. 2nd ed. Oxford: Clarendon, 2012.
RBN	*Revue Belge Numismatique*
ResQ	*Restoration Quarterly*
RIC	Roman Imperial Coinage
RN	*Review Numismatique*
RPC	Roman Provincial Coinage
RTR	*Reformed Theological Review*
SBL	Society of Biblical Literature
SEG	*Supplementum Epigraphicum Graecum*
SNG	*Sylloge Nummorum Graecorum*
TDNT	*Theological Dictionary of the New Testament*. Edited by Gerhard Kittel and Gerhard Friedrich. Translated by Geoffrey W. Bromiley. 10 vols. Grand Rapids: Eerdmans, 1964–1976.
TLZ	*Theologische Literaturzeitung*
WTJ	*Westminster Theological Journal*

Part One

1

Introduction

The Russian novelist Ivan Turgenev wrote in 1862, 'Рисунок наглядно представит мне то, что в книге изложено на целых десяти страницах' (trans. 'the drawing shows me at one glance what might be spread over ten pages in a book'),[1] and this is particularly relevant for numismatics where physical space on the surface of the coin is extremely limited, and thus generally reserved for iconographic depictions with short epigraphic inscriptions. The goal of this volume is to bring two distinct areas of historical enquiry, namely numismatics and post-classical Greek lexicography, into a more fruitful dialogue. In so doing, the volume aims to cover new methodological ground as well as application of the theory to New Testament (NT) studies.[2] As a corollary, it is hoped that our present discussion will directly expand the material culture that is considered by NT specialists in general and Greek lexicographers in particular, beyond normative recourse to papyrological, epigraphic and related literary traditions.[3]

Numismatic material has, at times, been drawn upon for contributing to clues which illuminate the iconographic and symbolic world of the NT period.[4] A strong case has been put forward by R. Oster who advocates for the inclusion of numismatic material by NT academicians at the *conceptual symbolic* level (rather than, per se, the

---

[1] Ivan Sergeevich Turgenev, *Fathers and Sons*, trans. Richard Freeborn (Oxford: Oxford University Press, 1998), §16. Turgenev's attestation of this phrase pre-dates the modern English idiom, 'a picture is worth a thousand words' by half a century. While debated, the English idiom is thought to have derived from Tess Flanders, a newspaper editor who is quoted as saying, 'Use a picture. It's worth a thousand words' ('Speakers Give Sound Advice', *Syracuse Post Standard*, 28 March 1911, page 18). A related phrase occurs in 1913 in the form of 'One Look Is Worth a Thousand Words', in the context of a newspaper advertisement for Piqua Auto Supply House of Piqua, Ohio ('One Look Is Worth a Thousand Words', *Piqua Leader-Dispatch*, 15 August 1913, 2).

[2] For the contribution of coins and seals to the study of the Old Testament, see Meir Lubetski and Edith Lubetski, eds., *New Inscriptions and Seals Relating to the Biblical World*, ABS 19 (Atlanta, GA: SBL Press, 2012). Somewhat surprisingly only one of the eighteen chapters has anything more than a paragraph on the linguistic connections, see Matthew Morgenstern, 'Mandaic Magic Bowls in the Moussaie Collection: A Preliminary Survey', in *New Inscriptions and Seals Relating to the Biblical World*, ed. Meir Lubetski and Edith Lubetski (Atlanta, GA: SBL Press, 2012), 165–169.

[3] Although numismatics has traditionally involved coins, medals, stamps, tokens, seals and bullae, our present study will focus exclusively on coinage. For a discussion on definitions, see John William Betlyon, 'Guide to Artefacts: Numismatics and Archaeology', *BA* (1985): 162.

[4] Michael Stone has noted that iconography is 'underexploited for the study of ancient Judaism', Michael Stone, *Ancient Judaism: New Visions and Views* (Grand Rapids, MI: Eerdmans, 2011), 23.

lexicographic level as proposed in the current volume). Oster's 'Numismatic Windows into the Social World of Early Christianity',[5] among other achievements, admirably explores the apotheosis of the Roman emperor, the appearance of the comet at the commemorative games and the relationship of these images to the so-called 'nativity comet' of Matthew's Gospel, specifically in light of the coinage subsequently produced by Octavian in the late first century BCE.[6] The narrative of Oster's article more broadly is the general neglect of numismatic evidence for ancient history in general and NT studies in particular.[7] In Oster's analysis, coins are to be seen as a valid 'source for ancient economics, art, political science, history of religions, and general history',[8] yet he fails to make any mention of the serious and substantial contribution of numismatics to Greek lexicography, which strikes at the very heart of the discipline. Nonetheless, Oster is accurate when he states, 'historians of earliest Christianity have repeatedly failed to give appropriate and significant attention to the analysis and application of data preserved on ancient coins'.[9]

Since 1982, when Oster penned this critique, little has changed. The use of coins in the secondary literature of NT studies has typically been haphazard and generally employed for non-related aesthetic purposes of only tenuous connection or mere decorative value. There are, of course, several valuable exceptions to this rather pessimistic assessment but I note the phenomenon here as a genuine cause for concern more broadly on how the material has been applied. Nonetheless, the studies noted above, and indeed several others noted below provide ample evidence that the iconographic dimension of incorporating numismatic material into NT studies has significant exegetical implications.

For example, as I have argued elsewhere,[10] Roman imperial coins were minted under state contracts and paid, first and foremost to the soldiers, whose loyalty the emperors were constantly seeking to secure, the coins of the emperors are themselves valuable documents. By way of further illustration, one of the primary indications that the reality which Matthew 24 describes is that of 70 CE and not a cataclysmic end to the space–time continuum is the proverbial-like saying of verse 28, 'Wherever the corpse is, there the eagles will gather'. Nonetheless, commentators (Luz, Davies

---

[5] Richard Oster, 'Numismatic Windows into the Social World of Early Christianity', *JBL* 101 (1982): 195–223.

[6] A second profitable example of the employment of iconographic numismatic study and the NT is Larry J. Kreitzer's collection of essays (Larry J. Kreitzer, *Striking New Images: Roman Imperial Coinage and the New Testament World*, JSNTSup 134 (Sheffield: Sheffield Academic, 1996)), which contains eight studies on how the study of Roman numismatics can contribute to the understanding of the NT in its world, including among others, the emperor's apotheosis, Roman triumph imagery and the imperial *adventus* coinage. This comparative iconographic numismatic approach, while constructive for the field of NT studies more generally, is not the approach or purpose of this volume.

[7] See also Richard Oster, '"Show Me a Denarius": Symbolism of Roman Coinage and Christian Beliefs', *ResQ* 28 (1986): 107–115; Marius Reiser, 'Numismatik und Neues Testament', *Biblica* 81 (2000): 457–488.

[8] Oster, 'Numismatic', 195.

[9] Oster, 'Numismatic', 195.

[10] Michael P. Theophilos, *The Abomination of Desolation in Matthew 24:15* (London: T&T Clark International, 2012), 127–133.

Introduction 5

and Allison, Mühlethaler[11]) have often taken this phrase in reference to the 'second coming' of Jesus, and related it to his visibility and obvious heavenly descent. However, a strong connection between 'eagles' and '(Roman) military troops' is able to be established on the basis of the numismatic record. Representations of eagles (and their association with Jupiter, the chief god of the Roman state) were common on coins which functioned as tangible propaganda, demonstrably so in the case of Nero, Galba, Otho, Vespasian and Domitian. In confirmation of this Josephus regularly refers to the events surrounding Herod's erection of an eagle on the temple in Jerusalem as a sign of political dominion (*War.* 1.648-655; 2.5; *Ant.* 17.151-152, 155, 206). The focus of this volume, however, is not the iconographic exegetical dimension but the lexicographic contribution to NT studies, that is, where inscriptions on coins can help to refine the relevant semantic domains of key or debated terminology.[12]

One of the early modern scholarly endeavours to grapple with, and incorporate, critical numismatic material into the emerging discipline of Greek lexicography was that of F. Passow's *Wörterbuch der griechischen Sprache* (1825–1831).[13] A century later, the pioneering linguistic work by F. Preisigke and E. Kiessling, *Wörterbuch der griechischen Papyrusurkunden mit Einschluss der griechischen Inschriften, Ausschriften, Ostraka, Mumienschilder usw. aus Ägypten* also drew on numismatic material, as did the work's revisions and supplements.[14] Although later studies have occasionally drawn on the material evidence of the numismatic record, characteristically this material is neglected in technical discussions of Greek lexicography.

The trajectory of this project explores the implications of the numismatic material for contributions to lexicography, particularly as it pertains to linguistic features of post-classical Greek. The working aim and methodology adopted can be summarized as follows: To employ dated and geographically legitimate comparative numismatic

---

[11] See discussion in U. Luz, *Matthew 21–28: A Commentary*, trans. J. E. Crouch (Minneapolis, MN: Fortress Press, 2005), 199.

[12] This, however, does not preclude the possibility of discussion of relevant iconography where such representations mutually reinforce or are contrasted with the epigraphic material on coinage. Although both may require our attention, the focus in this project squarely remains on the linguistic contribution of the inscriptions on coinage to particular linguistic questions related to the NT.

[13] Appropriately acknowledged as precursor to LSJ (1845); Franz Passow, *Handwörterbuch der griechischen Sprache* (Leipzig: F. C. W. Vogel, 1825–1831). Upon Passow's death in 1833, work continued on the project by V. Rost and F. Palm with a two-volume revision published in 1841 and 1857. See also Wilhelm Crönert, *Passow's Wörterbuch der griechischen Sprache* (Göttingen: Vandenhoeck and Ruprecht, 1912–1914).

[14] F. Preisigke and Emil Kiessling, *Wörterbuch der griechischen Papyrusurkunden mit Einschluss der griechischen Inschriften, Ausschriften, Ostraka, Mumienschilder usw. aus Ägypten*, 3 vols. (Berlin: Erbe, 1925–1931); Emil Kiessling, *Wörterbuch der griechischen Papyrusurkunden mit Einschluss der griechischen Inschriften, Ausschriften, Ostraka, Mumienschilder usw. aus Ägypten, Bande IV* (Berlin: Bersasser, 1944–1971); Emil Kiessling, *Wörterbuch der griechischen Papyrusurkunden mit Einschluss der griechischen Inschriften, Ausschriften, Ostraka, Mumienschilder usw. aus Ägypten, Supplement 1 (1940-1966)* (Amsterdam: Hakkert, 1971); Hans-Albert Rupprecht and Andrea Jördens, *Wörterbuch der griechischen Papyrusurkunden mit Einschluss der griechischen Inschriften, Ausschriften, Ostraka, Mumienschilder usw. aus Ägypten, Supplement 2 (1967-1976)* (Wiesbaden: Otto Harrassowitz, 1991); Hans-Albert Rupprecht and Andrea Jördens, *Wörterbuch der griechischen Papyrusurkunden mit Einschluss der griechischen Inschriften, Ausschriften, Ostraka, Mumienschilder usw. aus Ägypten, Supplement 3 (1977-1988)* (Wiesbaden: Otto Harrassowitz, 2000).

data to refine, illuminate and clarify the relevant semantic domains of NT vocabulary, with a particular interest in NT *cruces interpretationis*.

There are, of course, many other dimensions and possibilities for the contribution of numismatics to NT studies, including economics,[15] social customs,[16] archaeology[17] and semiotics, but as noted I am concerned in this study exclusively with the linguistic. This is the distinctive approach of the current volume, and where it seeks to make its most original and significant contribution. The simple supposition is that the linguistic material on coins should be included as one part of the primary source materials for NT Greek lexicography. The hope is that when the current array of ancient Greek dictionaries proceed through the next iteration of revision, our current discussion might provide some impetus for further considering the inclusion of coins as primary sources of documented Greek linguistic use in the Mediterranean world. As noted above, the current monograph is by no means a definitive discussion on the contribution, but it is hoped that the response in this volume goes some way to bridge the deficit and open up many possibilities for further examination. Similar to many branches of knowledge that flourished in the nineteenth and twentieth centuries, numismatics is as guilty as any other for operating within an academic silo. Several modern commentators have highlighted this phenomenon. Nathan T. Elkins readily identifies the discipline of numismatics as one which has been 'an inward-looking and isolated discipline, much like the early study of Greek painted vases, with its own specialised methodologies and applications'.[18] The hope is that there might be further cross-pollination between related disciplines that might truly open up new interpretive vistas.

This work is written for colleagues in NT studies as encouragement to incorporate the linguistic inscriptions on coinage into discussions of NT Greek lexicography. Focus is particularly upon the numismatic linguistic data rather than the iconographic (as noted above), which of course could easily fill several more volumes. As a secondary goal the volume seeks to address a significant lacuna in graduate NT curricula, and indeed more broadly, that lack any serious programmes in numismatics. This is not surprising given the rarity of numismatic programmes offered in tertiary education, even within those universities that have active and well-published numismatists or large numismatic holdings. An exception to this general observation however is Macquarie University's Australian Centre for Ancient Numismatic Study (ACANS) which promotes research in the field of ancient numismatics to advance the study of

---

[15] On the contribution of economics and NT interpretation, see Peter Oakes, 'Methodological Issues in Using Economic Evidence in Interpretation of Early Christian Texts', in *Engaging Economics: New Testament Scenarios and Early Christian Reception*, ed. B. W. Longenecker and K. D. Liebengood (Grand Rapids, MI: Eerdmans, 2009), 9–36.

[16] Cynthia L. Thomson, 'Hairstyles, Head-Coverings, and St. Paul: Portraits from Roman Corinth', *BA* 51.2 (1988): 99–115.

[17] P. J. Casey, *Understanding Ancient Coins: An Introduction for Archaeologists* (London: Batsford, 1986); P. J. Casey and R. Reece, *Coins and the Archaeologist* (London: Seaby, 1988).

[18] Nathan T. Elkins, 'The Trade in Fresh Supplies of Ancient Coins: Scale, Organisation, and Politics', in *All the King's Horses: Essays on the Impact of Looting and the Illicit Trade on Our Knowledge of the Past*, ed. P. K. Lazarus and A. W. Baker (Washington, DC: Society for American Archaeology Press, 2012), 94.

Introduction 7

ancient history.[19] Although ACANS is not the only dedicated numismatic research centre connected to a university, such a thorough integration of numismatics within a tertiary environment offering programmes in classics and ancient history is admirable. Yet the rarity of such a phenomenon does perhaps explain why research graduates and future scholars, especially within the discipline of NT studies do not have equal opportunity to develop the significant expertise required to beneficially employ numismatic material within their research.

This volume is divided into two parts. Part One offers a prolegomena, of sorts, to the employment of numismatic material in historical research. Topics covered aim to orientate the NT scholar who might be familiar with the generic foreground of the Greco-Roman world but unfamiliar with the intricacies and complexities of numismatics and its employment as a historical and linguistic source. Chapter 1 will provide a diachronic framework for the historical origin and evolution of coinage. Chapter 2 will then sketch the development of the study of coinage to put into perspective where, why and how the current volume contributes to the long history of numismatics. Chapter 3 will offer a methodological discussion on the pertinent issues in attempting to use coinage for Greek lexicography, and will attempt to offer some tentative guidelines for future and further engagement. Chapter 4 will introduce the main sources and collections of coins, and indeed how these can be accessed and used by NT scholars and others who see value in doing so.

On the basis of this prior discussion, Part Two will then offer a series of case studies that cogently illustrate the value of taking into consideration the numismatic material for issues in Greek lexicography and NT studies. The subsequent discussion attempts to make an original, direct and significant advance in the related fields of NT studies and Greek lexicography. Perhaps unsurprisingly, I assure the reader that this effort, although systematic, does not seek to offer an exhaustive account of the contributions of numismatics. Rather, this work is offered as a *prolegomenon* to a method and application of numismatics to Greek lexicography within NT studies.

Lexicography involves the arrangement and classification of the meanings and usages of words as attested in the history of a language.[20] Such a pursuit naturally draws on a variety of interconnected disciplines, including linguistics, philology, lexicology, semantics, and cultural studies.[21] No area within the discipline of biblical studies is more prone to assumption by the end user than that of lexicography. Consider the

---

[19] I was humbled and honoured when I was invited to be the 2015 Senior Research Fellow at the Australian Centre for Ancient Numismatic Study (Sydney, Australia). The director (Ken Sheedy), staff and board provided an invigorating and robust context for numismatic discussion, this volume is better for it.

[20] For a regularly updated bibliography on Greek lexicography, see *Repertorio Bibliográfico de la Lexicografía Griega*, ed. Rodríguez Somolinos, Juan and Mónica Elias, http://dge.cchs.csic.es/blg/blg-s.htm.

[21] For a history of Greek lexicography, see J. R. Fishlake, 'Article VII', *Quarterly Review* 51 (1834): 144–177; J. R. Fishlake, 'Article I', *Quarterly Review* 75 (1845): 293–324; Robert Lewis Collison, *A History of Foreign-Language Dictionaries* (London: André Deutsch, 1982); August A. Imholtz Jr., "'Liddell and Scott": Precursors, Nineteenth-Century Editions, and the American Contributions', in *Oxford Classics: Teaching and Learning 1800–2000*, ed. Christopher Stray (London: Duckworth, 2007), 117–134; Ladislav Zgusta, *Lexicography Then and Now: Selected Essays* (Tübingen: Niemeyer, 2006).

8 Numismatics and Greek Lexicography

following scenario: a reader comes across an unfamiliar word, proceeds to look it up in a Greek lexicon, selects the gloss that makes the most sense and then feels confident that they know the meaning of the word.[22] For example, Acts 25:23 reads Τῇ οὖν ἐπαύριον ἐλθόντος τοῦ Ἀγρίππα καὶ τῆς Βερνίκης μετὰ πολλῆς φαντασίας καὶ εἰσελθόντων εἰς τὸ ἀκροατήριον σύν τε χιλιάρχοις καὶ ἀνδράσιν τοῖς κατ' ἐξοχὴν τῆς πόλεως καὶ κελεύσαντος τοῦ Φήστου ἤχθη ὁ Παῦλος.[23] A modern reader of the Greek NT may not be familiar with the *hapax legomenon* ἀκροατήριον and hence is prompted to look up the word in one of the standard Greek lexicons. Etymologically one might naturally assume something to do with a place and the idea of listening, and the context of the passage indicates some sort of judicial scenario, v.26 ὅπως τῆς ἀνακρίσεως γενομένης (trans. 'after we have examined him' [NRSV]; 'so that as a result of this investigation' [NIV]). The term seems to indicate something more specific, but it is not immediately apparent what this might be. BDAG (2000) has the following:

> ἀκροατήριον, ου, τό *audience hall* (Lat. auditorium) of the procurator, in which hearings were held and justice was privately dispensed (Mommsen, Röm. Strafrecht 1899, 362) *hall of justice* Ac 25:23. Otherwise gener. *auditorium, chamber, lecture-hall* (Philo, Congr. Erud. Grat. 64; Tat. 22, 2; Dio Chrys. 15 [32], 8; Plut., Mor. 45f; Epict. 3, 23, 8). – DELG s.v. ἀκροάομαι.

BDAG recognizes two meanings. The first, apparently a technical term, is equivalent to the Latin auditorium for judicial proceedings, namely a 'hall of justice', despite the absence of Greek evidence. The second, a general term, is not necessarily associated with a legal context, 'hall'. Lee insightfully traces the history of the debate and notes 'the long-term persistence of doubtful material in the tradition, the problems caused by a paucity of evidence, and the effect of using Latin as a medium and treating Latin and Greek as one and the same thing'.[24] The result of Lee's analysis is that there is no firm foundation for reading ἀκροατήριον as a technical term for a courtroom or hall of justice. What is even more surprising is that the entry in the OLD (1982) does not have any one of its meanings of auditorium which would support the specificity claimed by the vast majority of the Latin tradition: Betuleius, *Conc.* (1546), Stephanus, *Conc.* (1594), Pasor (1619, 1639), Leigh (1639), Lucius (1640) and Pasor-Schöttgen (1717).[25] It is rather a sad irony that present in the modern Ancient Greek lexicons is 'a meaning that had no right to be there in the first place'.[26]

The most recent iteration of BDAG (third edition, 2000) contains fifty-four references to coins and/or numismatics.[27] Only five of these references have any bearing whatsoever upon the meaning of the lexemes themselves. The majority of references are used in

---

[22] David M. Schaps, *Handbook for Classical Research* (London: Routledge, 2011), 92.

[23] This example is drawn from John A. L. Lee, *A History of New Testament Lexicography* (New York: Peter Lang, 2003), 213–223. For a fuller discussion of this example, and several others, the reader is directed to Lee's erudite analysis.

[24] Lee, *Lexicography*, 220.

[25] Cited in Lee, *Lexicography*, 218.

[26] Lee, *Lexicography*, 220.

[27] This includes the following terms: numismatic, coin, coins, coinage and coinages.

Introduction 9

relation to (a) *terms directly related to money* (ἀργύριον [silver], ἀσσάριον [assarion], δηνάριον [denarius], δίδραχμον [two-drachma piece], δραχμή [drachma], ἵστημι [set], κέρμα [piece of money], κερματιστής [money-changer], κῆνσος [tax], κοδράντης [quadrans], κόλλυβος [small coin], νόμισμα [coin], στατήρ [stater], τάλαντον [talent], χαλκός [brass, bronze]), (b) *generic literary references with only the most tangential relevance* (ἄσημος [insignificant], ἀποδοκιμάζω [reject], εἰκών [image], ἐκχέω [pour out], ἐπιγραφή [inscription], ἐπίκειμαι [lie upon/be on], ἕως [until], καινός [new], λαμβάνω [remove], τράπεζα [table], φοῖνιξ/φοίνιξ [palm tree], χάραγμα [mark], χαρακτήρ [representation]), (c) *personal names or proper nouns* which although relevant for etymological investigation some, but limited lexicographic value (Ἀγρίππας [Agrippa], Βάσσος [Bassus], Ζμύρνα [Smyrna], Κάρπος [Carpus], Κεγχρεαί [Cenchreae], Μαγνησία [Magnesia], Πέργη [Perga], Πιλᾶτος [Pilate],[28] Τέρτουλλος [Tertullus]).[29]

The five entries that do refer to coins in some constructive lexicographic manner are insufficient in several regards. First, the entry for ἐθνάρχης (head of an ethnic community), does not specifically state the numismatic contribution but only refers readers to a secondary reference, which upon investigation does not attest any lexicographic advance. Second, εὐεργέτης (benefactor) mentions coins in the summary and then proceeds to cite Deissmann as secondary literature,[30] but does not indicate what contribution, if any, the numismatic materials make to the semantic domain of the lexeme itself. Third, ἡμέρα (ἀνθρωπίνη) is glossed as 'a day appointed by a human court' apparently on the basis of a coin amulet. On the anachronistic use of this numismatic evidence see discussion below. Fourth, in the entry on νεωκόρος (temple keeper) it is noted that the lexeme appears 'also on coins', yet does not note any of the requisite detail that can contribute to our understanding of this lexeme. For further investigation of this, see the case study in Part Two: Case Studies below. Fifth, νίκη (victory) is noted as being an attribute of the emperor on coinage, but again, no further detail is given lexicographically on the extent or definition of the semantic domain. We will have the opportunity to broaden and deepen this observation in the case studies below. Wenkel notes that BDAG does 'reference numismatic material, but these studies are mostly dated'.[31] This, it seems, is a considerable understatement, and in light of our survey above of BDAG is far too optimistic of the achievements of the lexicon.

An example of how fraught the appeal to numismatic evidence can be is illustrated by a letter dated 11 March 1949 by Henri Seyrig (Director of the French Archaeological Institute at Beyroth) who sent a copy of a Greek amulet text incised upon a Roman silver denarius (smoothed over for the re-inscription) to Campbell Bonner.[32] What makes this example particularly interesting is the suggestion that 'the poorer people

---

[28] Cf. E. Bammel, 'Syrian Coinage and Pilate', JJS 2 (1950/1): 108–110.

[29] For a more positive assessment of the contribution of personal names for lexicography see A. Thomson, 'Ancient Greek Personal Names', in *A History of Ancient Greek: From Beginnings to Late Antiquity*, ed.A.-F. Christidis (New York, NY: Cambridge University Press, 2001), 677–692.

[30] Adolf Deissmann, *Light from the Ancient East: The New Testament Illustrated by Recently Discovered Texts of the Greco-Roman World*, trans. Lionel R. M. Strachan (New York: Harper & Brothers, 1922), 249.

[31] David H. Wenkel, *Coins as Cultural Texts in the World of the New Testament* (London: Bloomsbury, 2017), xix.

[32] C. Bonner, 'A Reminiscence of Paul on a Coin Amulet', HTR 43 (1950): 165–168.

10   *Numismatics and Greek Lexicography*

often made amulets out of small coins'.[33] This particular inscription provides a numismatic snapshot of the non-elite, although hardly sufficient to address the social stratification critique mentioned above, it does provide an alternative avenue to pursue the question.[34] The letter shapes of the inscription itself are dated to Larfeld's Period XVII (120–210 CE).[35] The obverse reads, ἐπικαλοῦμ{ε}[αι] τὸ ἅγιον κ{ὲ} [αι] μέγιστον ὄνομα ἵνα μοι συνεργῇ πάντα ὅσα θέλω (trans. 'I invoke the holy and greatest name, that it may help me all that I wish'). The reverse reads, ἵνα μοι ὑποτάσ{ι} [ση] πᾶσαν ἀνθρωπίνην ἡμέραν, (trans. 'that it may give me the upper hand in every human judgment'). Bonner argues that πᾶσαν ἀνθρωπίνην ἡμέραν is reminiscent of 1 Corinthians 4:3, ἐμοὶ δὲ εἰς ἐλάχιστόν ἐστιν, ἵνα ὑφ᾽ ὑμῶν ἀνακριθῶ ἢ ὑπὸ ἀνθρωπίνης ἡμέρας (trans. 'But with me it is a very small thing that I should be judged by you or by any human court').[36] LSJ includes, in their fifth definition of the term, 'a fixed day' in reference to a 'human tribunal',[37] yet the source cited in support of such a definition is from Pamphylia (Beiblatt 93), and within the context of the inscription ἡμέρα refers to 'days of festivity'. Bonner notes that the Preisigke cites several spurious examples of ἡμέρα as 'a human court' per se, other than the term being used in conjunction with legal proceeding, but there is nothing further to suggest that the term alone was understood in this manner.[38]

What then can we conclude in relation to the amulet and the biblical text? It seems readily apparent that, although initially promising, this coin amulet does not provide a contemporaneous (or earlier) attestation of a term or phrase that appears in the NT. Rather, the direction of influence is reversed, that is, from biblical text to amulet, not vice versa. The writer of the amulet was presumably accustomed with the juxtaposition of a human court and divine court, as per 1 Corinthians 4:3, and chose to echo this phraseology in the inscribed coin amulet. A. D. Nock suggests that there is, in fact, a second allusion in the short text of the amulet from Romans 8:28, Οἴδαμεν δὲ ὅτι τοῖς ἀγαπῶσιν τὸν θεὸν πάντα συνεργεῖ εἰς ἀγαθόν, τοῖς κατὰ πρόθεσιν κλητοῖς οὖσιν (trans. 'We know that all things work together for good for those who love God, who are called according to his purpose'). Nock draws attention to πάντα as the object of συνεργεῖ and θεός as its subject, and that ἵνα μοι συνεργῇ πάντα on the obverse of the

---

[33] Bonner, 'A Reminiscence', 165.

[34] Among other examples we can note H. Mattingly, 'A Mithraic Tessera from Verulam', *Numismatic Chronicle* 12 (1932): 54–57, who refers to a denarius of Augustus (BMC 29) which had the reverse inscription erased leaving only the portrayal of Tarpeia half buried under shields as a representation of the birth of Mithras from the rock. The obverse was smoothed over and re-inscribed with, 'ΜΙΘΡΑΣ ΩΡΟΜΑΣ{D}[Δ]ΗΣ ΦΡΗΝ', a tripartite combination of Mithra, the Persian supreme god and the Egyptian sun god. Although thought to have been an amulet, the absence of a hole for suspension, cause Mattingly to suggest it functioned as a σύμβολον (trans. 'pass') 'used to obtain admission to the Mithraic worship or to show membership of one of the Mithraic degrees' (p. 57).

[35] W. Larfeld, *Handbuch der griechischen Epigraphik* (Leipzig: O. R. Reisland, Hildashelm, 1898–1907), III, 490–495.

[36] Commentators have noted that ἡμέρα here is included in contrast to 1 Corinthians 3:13 where it refers to the 'Day of the Lord'. See A. Plummer and A. T. Robinson, *1 Corinthians* (London: T&T Clark, 1911), 76.

[37] LSJ, 770.

[38] Bonner, 'A Reminiscence', 167.

Introduction 11

coin echoes the Pauline phrase.[39] There is no doubt as to the nature of the dependence (NT to amulet or amulet to NT) given the dates of the respective texts. The coin on which the amulet is inscribed seems to be a denarius of Hadrian (125–128 CE),[40] and no doubt one would have chosen a well-worn example that had been circulating for some time, rather one with high relief or freshly minted.

Part of the problem is that many lexicons provide only glosses and not true definitions, and when a definition is provided it is often so brief that the actual meaning is far from obvious. Photographs or archaeological plans of an ἀκροατήριον would be most welcome. But BDAG like all its contemporaries is not adorned with images, a luxury, it seems, which is reserved for longer entries in topical encyclopaedias.[41] But the far more pernicious problem is that no gloss can ever do justice to a word in another language, even less so when the problems are compounded when the lexicon provides an apparent equivalent in Latin. Henri Estienne had precisely this matter in mind when he protested against sixteenth-century lexica:

> Even if a single Greek word could be translated by so many Latin ones … still, what would this be but to overwhelm the reader with an unclear and confused assortment of meanings? … Here is the word βαίνω, which struck my eye first when I opened the dictionary, with twenty-two interpretations listed under it in uninterrupted succession, namely: I hurry, I walk calmly, I go, I make to go, I approach, I come forth, I enter, I aim, I stroll, I enter upon, I set foot upon, I walk, I approach, I bring in, I go in, I follow upon, I march along, I go up, I make to go up, I go down, I love, I flatter. Most of these interpretations are either wrong or certainly inappropriate; but even if all of them were right, shouldn't they rather have been placed individually, that is, each one with appropriate examples?[42]

Add to this the regular and apparently accepted practice of the derivative nature of lexicons as is evident in LSJ's birth as a translation of Passow's *Handwörterbuch der griechischen Sprache*, which was itself a reworking of Johann Gottlob Schneider's *Griechisch-Deutsches Wöterbuch*, and the problems are plainly evident.[43] Many of

---

[39] A. D. Nock, cited in Bonner, 'A Reminiscence', 168.

[40] H. Mattingly, *Coins of the Roman Empire in the British Museum*, 6 vols. (London: British Museum, 1923–1976), plates 3.68, 3.19.

[41] Rare exceptions to the norm are Robert P. Keep, *A Homeric Dictionary for Schools and Colleges* (New York: Harper and Brothers, 1895) which includes 130 images directly related to and illustrating lexical entries, and F. Gaffiot, *Dictionnaire* (Paris: Hachette, 1934) which contains over 500.

[42] Stephanus, Henricus, "Excerpta ex H. Stephani Epistola a. 1569 Edita Qua ad multas multorum Amicorum respondet, de suae Typographiae Statu, nominatimque de suo Thesauro Linguae Graecae," in *Thesaurus Graecae Linguae*, ed. Henricus Stephanus (London: A. J. Valpy, 1816–28), xxix–xxxvi (in the appendix to the Paris edition, Vol. 8, XXXVII–L), cited in Schaps, *Handbook*, 71.

[43] At the Biblical Lexicography session at the Annual Meeting of the Society of Biblical Literature, held in 2014 in San Diego, Jim Aitken (Cambridge) a colleague whom I hold in the highest esteem, boldly declared (with tongue firmly planted in cheek) a fifty-year moratorium on the production of ancient Greek dictionaries, which might allow scholars the time to address many of these issues, and perhaps produce a dictionary that was a genuine step forward in the field of Greek lexicography. It is no small irony that in the following year, I chaired a review session at the annual meeting of a new Greek dictionary. For a discussion with specific examples of the over-reliance on previous lexicons, see John A. L. Lee, 'Hebrews 5:14 and ἕξις: A History of Misunderstanding', *Novum Testamentum* 39 (1997): 151–176.

these difficulties are discussed and weighed by John Chadwick[44] who was to become the founder of the Cambridge Greek Lexicon project.[45] Chadwick's justification for a new dictionary of ancient Greek was predicated on the deficiencies of LSJ which he observed being (1) incorrect and misleading etymological notes,[46] (2) the choice of lemmata for principal parts of irregular verbs, in particular non-existent lemmata,[47] (3) the treatment of dialect inscriptions,[48] (4) the lack of consistency with proper names,[49] (5) failure to provide a clear account of the range of meanings,[50] (6) the provision of a proper definition[51] and among other issues (7) failure to recognize various spellings of a single word which has resulted in multiple entries.[52] Furthermore, John A. L. Lee validly highlighted a flawed methodological assumption of LSJ in its inclusion of material related to the LXX, namely that when the authors of the LXX used a certain Greek word to translate the Hebrew, the Greek word had the same meaning as what modern scholars attribute to the Hebrew.[53] Lee copiously demonstrated the shortcomings of this approach. Chadwick has provided several further studies of particular Greek words in the application of historical lexicography for ordering senses,[54] but still, much fertile work remains to be done.[55]

---

[44] John Chadwick, 'The Case for Replacing Liddell and Scott', *Bulletin of the Institute of Classical Studies* 39 (1994): 1–11.

[45] For an outline of the nature and distinctive contribution of the Cambridge Lexicon Project including the importance of newly discovered literary texts and advances in philology, lexicography and digital technologies, see Pauline Hire, 'The Cambridge New Greek Lexicon Project', *Classical World* 98 (2005): 179–185; B. L. Fraser, 'Beyond Definition: Organising Semantic Information in Bilingual Dictionaries', *International Journal of Lexicography* 21 (2008): 69–93; B. L. Fraser, 'Lexicographic Slips: Gathering and Organising Contextual Data for Dictionary Entries', in *Lexicografía e semántica lexical: Caminhos para a feitura de um dicionário de Grego: Colóquio Internacional – ACTAS (Lisboa, 24–25 de Novembro de 2006)*, ed. Manuel Alexander Junior (Lisbon: Centro de Estudos Clássicos, 2008), 53–72.

[46] Chadwick, 'Case', 2.

[47] Chadwick, 'Case', 2.

[48] Chadwick, 'Case', 2, 9.

[49] Chadwick, 'Case', 3.

[50] Chadwick, 'Case', 3.

[51] Chadwick, 'Case', 4.

[52] Chadwick, 'Case', 8.

[53] John A. L. Lee, 'A Note on Septuagint Material in the Supplement to Liddell and Scott', *Glossa* 47 (1969): 234–242.

[54] John Chadwick, 'The Semantic History of Greek ἐσχάρα', in *O-o-pe-ro-si: Festschrift für Ernst Risch zum 75. Geburtstag*, ed. Annemarie Etter (Berlin: De Gruyter, 1986), 515–523, primarily drawing on Mycenaean textual evidence and noting the over-reliance of lexicographers on ancient grammarians; John Chadwick, 'Semantic History and Greek Lexicography', in *La langue et les textes en grec ancien: Actes du Colloque Pierre Chantraine (Grenoble, 5–8 Septembre 1989)*, ed. Françoise Létoublon (Amsterdam: J. C. Gieben, 1992), 281–288, arguing for the historical principle of sense order, as per OLD but not LSJ; John Chadwick, *Lexicographica Graeca: Contributions to the Lexicography of Ancient Greek* (Oxford: Clarendon, 1996) on lexicographic methodology. For an explanation of the various approaches of sense arrangement as logical, historical and empirical, see F. Hiorth, 'Arrangements of Meanings in Lexicography', *Lingua* 4 (1954–55): 413–424.

[55] The lexicographer is also faced with the question of extent; should the dictionary include *all* the words in the language? LSJ famously, although somewhat controversially, included a made-up tongue twister of 171 characters from Aristophanes (Eccl. 1169–75), λοπᾰδοτεμᾰχοσελᾰ χογᾰλεοκρανιολειψᾰνοδρῑμῠποτριμμᾰτοσιλφῐοκαρᾰβομελῐτοκᾰτ ᾰκεχῠμενοκιχλεπῐκοσσῠφοφαττοπεριστερᾰλεκτρῠονοπτοκεφαλλῑ

Introduction

One subset of the broader discipline of Greek lexicography is that of a NT lexicon. The standard reference work in this respect is BDAG which seeks to cover the NT, apostolic Fathers, early apocryphal texts and select Jewish texts in Greek. The acronym derives from its own composition and revisional history. The 2000 edition is based on Walter Bauer's *Griechischen-deutsches Wörterbuch zu den Schriften des Neuen Testaments und der frühchristlichen Literatur*, edited by Kurt Aland and Barbara Aland, and on previous English editions by W. F. Arndt, F. W. Gingrich, and F. W. Danker. The alphabetical arrangement is typical and provides both definitions and glosses.[56]

Louw and Nida[57] groups words into ninety-three semantic domains based on the UBS dictionary by Barclay Newman. These domains can be grouped as follows: Domains 1–12: Objects and Entities; Domains 13–57: Events; Domains 58–91: Abstracts; and Other (consisting of discourse referentials and unique referentials). The rationale is provided by the editors, 'the principal reason for a new type of Greek New Testament lexicon is the inadequacy of most existing dictionaries, which for the most part are limited in indicating meanings, since they depend principally on a series of glosses'.[58] Although most would consider the exclusion of non-NT evidence a weakness, the project received a generally positive reception mainly due to the innovative linguistic approach.[59] In review, M. Silva comments, 'this work has to be regarded as a prodigious step forward in the field of lexicography generally, and in the study of NT vocabulary specifically'.[60]

The discoveries of vast quantities of Greek documentary texts (300 BCE–300 CE) in the late nineteenth and early twentieth century from Egypt (papyri, parchment, ostraca, inscriptions, wooden tablets, mummy labels, etc.) have provided an extensive body of Hellenistic linguistic material that has the potential to significantly contribute to NT studies in general and lexicography in particular. One of the first systematic attempts to incorporate this material was that of Friedrich Preisigke, whose passing in 1924 meant that another individual, Emil Kiessling, completed

---

ο κ ι γ κ λ ο π ε λ ε ι ο λ ᾰ γ ῳ ο σ ῑ ρ α ι ο β ᾰ φ η τ ρ ᾰ γ ᾰ ν ο π τ ε ρ ύ γ ω ν, and we are informed that this is the name of a dish compounded of various kinds of dainties, fish, flesh, fowl and sauces. In Aristophanes, Jeffrey Henderson translates the word as, 'limpets and saltfish and sharksteak and dogfish and mullets and oddfish with savory pickle sauce and thrushes with blackbirds and various pigeons and roosters and pan-roasted wagtails and larks and nice chunks of hare marinated in mulled wine and all of it drizzled with honey and silphium and vinegar, oil, and spices galore'. Jeffrey Henderson, trans. *Aristophanes. Frogs. Assembly Women. Wealth* (LCL 180; Cambridge, MA: Harvard University Press, 2002), 411.

[56] Frederick William Danker and Kathryn Krug, *The Concise Greek-English Lexicon of the New Testament* (Chicago, IL: University of Chicago Press, 2009) is neither an abridgement of BDAG nor a revision of another dictionary, rather, it attempts to offer definitions of vocabulary in the NA27 and select textual variants.

[57] Johannes P. Louw and Eugene A. Nida, eds., *Greek-English Lexicon of the New Testament: Based on Semantic Domains*, 2nd edn.; 2 vols. (New York: United Bible Societies, 1988–1989).

[58] L&N, viii.

[59] H. Boers, review of *Greek-English Lexicon of the New Testament: Based on Semantic Domains*, ed. Johannes P. Louw and Eugene A. Nida, *JBL* 108 (1989): 705–707; J. K. Elliott, review of *Greek-English Lexicon of the New Testament: Based on Semantic Domains*, ed. Johannes P. Louw and Eugene A. Nida, *NovT* 31 (1989): 379–380.

[60] M. Silva, review of *Greek-English Lexicon of the New Testament: Based on Semantic Domains*, ed. Johannes P. Louw and Eugene A. Nida, *WTJ* 5 (1989), 165.

14   *Numismatics and Greek Lexicography*

the first phase of the project initiated by Preisigke.[61] These volumes drew heavily on Preisigke's previous scholarship on the reconstruction of financial and administrative system in Egypt under Roman control.[62] A later revision by Kiessling in 1971 included references to documents published after the publication of the 1925–1931 edition, specifically for entries for α to ἐπικόπτω.[63] A further three supplements were produced in the following decades, which in addition to the inclusion of words published since the previous edition, including a number of word lists for Latin loan words, magistrates and titles, weights and measures, calendrical terminology and topography.[64]

In the years leading up to the 1930 release of J. H. Moulton and G. Milligan's one-volume lexicon,[65] three instalments were released (1914, 1915 and 1919) which were effectively reprinted in the one-volume edition with the addition of a single page of supplementary notes and a small number of corrections. It is helpful to be mindful of this timeline, as it helps clarify that the first parts of Preisigke's *Wörterbuch der griechischen Papyrusurkunden* postdate Moulton and Milligan's by more than a decade. In the lead up to the release of the first instalment of Moulton and Milligan in 1914, a series of articles were published in *The Expositor* initially by Moulton (1901–1903) and then jointly by Moulton and Milligan (1908–1912) which sought to introduce the English-speaking world to the application of the evidence of papyri to the study of NT lexicography.[66] The initial instalments of the initiative

---

[61] Preisigke and Kiessling, *Wörterbuch*.

[62] Friedrich Preisigke, *Girowesen im griechischen Ägypten, enthaltend Korngiro, Geldgiro, Girobanknotariat mit Einschluss des Archivwesens: ein Beitrag zur Geschichte des Verwaltungsdienstes im Altertume* (Strassburg im Elsass: Schlesier & Schweikhardt, 1910).

[63] Kiessling, *Wörterbuch*.

[64] Kiessling, *Wörterbuch: Supplement 1 (1940–1966)*; Rupprecht and Jördens, *Wörterbuch Supplement 2 (1967–1976)*; Rupprecht and Jördens, *Wörterbuch Supplement 3 (1977–1988)*.

[65] J. H. Moulton and G. Milligan, *Vocabulary of the Greek Testament: Illustrated from the Papyri and Other Non-Literary Sources* (London: Hodder and Stoughton, 1930).

[66] J. H. Moulton, 'Notes from the Papyri. I', *Expositor* 6.3.4 (1901): 271–282; J. H. Moulton, 'Notes from the Papyri. II', *Expositor* 6.7.2 (1903): 104–121; J. H. Moulton, 'Notes from the Papyri. III', *Expositor* 6.8.6 (1903): 423–439; J. H. Moulton and G. Milligan, 'Lexical Notes from the Papyri. IV', *Expositor* 7.5.1 (1908): 51–60; J. H. Moulton and G. Milligan, 'Lexical Notes from the Papyri. V', *Expositor* 7.5.2 (1908): 170–185; J. H. Moulton and G. Milligan, 'Lexical Notes from the Papyri. VI', *Expositor* 7.5.3 (1908): 262–277; J. H. Moulton and G. Milligan, 'Lexical Notes from the Papyri. VII', *Expositor* 7.6.1 (1908): 84–93; J. H. Moulton and G. Milligan, 'Lexical Notes from the Papyri. VIII', *Expositor* 7.6.2 (1908): 183–192; J. H. Moulton and G. Milligan, 'Lexical Notes from the Papyri. IX', *Expositor* 7.6.3 (1908): 273–281; J. H. Moulton and G. Milligan, 'Lexical Notes from the Papyri. X', *Expositor* 7.6.4 (1908): 370–384; J. H. Moulton and G. Milligan, 'Lexical Notes from the Papyri. XI', *Expositor* 7.6.6 (1908): 562–568; J. H. Moulton and G. Milligan, 'Lexical Notes from the Papyri. XII', *Expositor* 7.7.1 (1909): 88–95; J. H. Moulton and G. Milligan, 'Lexical Notes from the Papyri. XIII', *Expositor* 7.7.3 (1909): 282–285; J. H. Moulton and G. Milligan, 'Lexical Notes from the Papyri. XIV', *Expositor* 7.7.4 (1909): 375–384; J. H. Moulton and G. Milligan, 'Lexical Notes from the Papyri. XV', *Expositor* 7.7.5 (1909): 470–480; J. H. Moulton and G. Milligan, 'Lexical Notes from the Papyri. XVI', *Expositor* 7.7.6 (1909): 559–568; J. H. Moulton and G. Milligan, 'Lexical Notes from the Papyri. XVII', *Expositor* 7.9.3 (1910): 284–288; J. H. Moulton and G. Milligan, 'Lexical Notes from the Papyri. XVIII', *Expositor* 7.10.1 (1910): 89–96; J. H. Moulton and G. Milligan, 'Lexical Notes from the Papyri. XVIII', *Expositor* 7.10.3 (1910): 282–288; J. H. Moulton and G. Milligan, 'Lexical Notes from the Papyri. XIX', *Expositor* 7.10.5 (1910): 477–480; J. H. Moulton and G. Milligan, 'Lexical Notes from the Papyri. XX', *Expositor*

Introduction 15

were enthusiastically received, with one reviewer asking, 'have you ever read the *Vocabulary* for the joy of reading it? That is the best way with all great books of the kind … For the present reviewer began at the beginning of this part [III] and pulled himself up after many pages with the surprise of much time spent and many things to do'.[67] Moulton and Milligan's collaboration was tragically cut short by the untimely death of Moulton during his return from India in April 1917 when the boat he was travelling in was torpedoed while crossing the Mediterranean. Milligan brought the initial phase of the lexicon project to completion with the publication of the single volume.

Despite the great illumination and linguistic context the papyri demonstrably provided, the speed at which papyrus discoveries were made and published in the twentieth century meant that entries in the lexicon were quickly outdated. Formal plans for a replacement rather than revision of Moulton and Milligan have been proposed, with most traction being gained by G. H. R. Horsley and John A. L. Lee's collaborative efforts.[68] We can only look forward to further developments in this area.[69]

7.10.6 (1910): 563–568; J. H. Moulton and G. Milligan, 'Lexical Notes from the Papyri. XXI', *Expositor* 8.1.3 (1911): 284–288; J. H. Moulton and G. Milligan, 'Lexical Notes from the Papyri. XXI', *Expositor* 8.1.4 (1911): 380–384; J. H. Moulton and G. Milligan, 'Lexical Notes from the Papyri. XXII', *Expositor* 8.1.5 (1911): 475–480; J. H. Moulton and G. Milligan, 'Lexical Notes from the Papyri. XXIII', *Expositor* 8.1.6 (1911): 561–568; J. H. Moulton and G. Milligan, 'Lexical Notes from the Papyri. XXIV', *Expositor* 8.2.3 (1911): 275–288; J. H. Moulton and G. Milligan, 'Lexical Notes from the Papyri. XXV', *Expositor* 8.4.6 (1912): 561–568.

[67] Editor, 'Literature', *The Expository Times* 30.11 (1919): 493, cited in C. J. Hemer, 'Towards a New Moulton and Milligan', *NovT* 24 (1982): 102–103.

[68] For a description of the proposed methodology, see G. H. R. Horsley and John A. L. Lee, 'A Lexicon of the New Testament with Documentary Parallels: Some Interim Entries, 1', *Filología Neotestamentaria* 10 (1997): 55–84; G. H. R. Horsley and John A. L. Lee, 'A Lexicon of the New Testament with Documentary Parallels: Some Interim Entries, 2', *Filología Neotestamentaria* 11 (1998): 57–84.

[69] Although the series has now shifted focus somewhat, the project initiated by G. Horsley in the form of *New Documents Illustrating Early Christianity* has compiled and collated relevant material for several hundred potential lexical entries, G. H. R. Horsley, *New Documents Illustrating Early Christianity, Volume 1: A Review of the Greek Inscriptions and Papyri Published in 1976* (North Ryde: Ancient History Documentary Research Centre, 1981); G. H. R. Horsley, *New Documents Illustrating Early Christianity, Volume 2: A Review of the Greek Inscriptions and Papyri Published in 1977* (North Ryde: Ancient History Documentary Research Centre, 1982); G. H. R. Horsley, *New Documents Illustrating Early Christianity, Volume 3: A Review of the Greek Inscriptions and Papyri Published in 1978* (North Ryde: Ancient History Documentary Research Centre, 1983); G. H. R. Horsley, *New Documents Illustrating Early Christianity, Volume 4: A Review of the Greek Inscriptions and Papyri Published in 1979* (North Ryde: Ancient History Documentary Research Centre, 1987); G. H. R. Horsley, *New Documents Illustrating Early Christianity, Volume 5: Linguistic Essays* (North Ryde: Ancient History Documentary Research Centre, 1989); S. R. Llewelyn, *New Documents Illustrating Early Christianity, Volume 6: A Review of the Greek Inscriptions and Papyri Published in 1980–81* (North Ryde: Ancient History Documentary Research Centre, 1992); S. R. Llewelyn, *New Documents Illustrating Early Christianity, Volume 7: A Review of the Greek Inscriptions and Papyri Published in 1982–83* (North Ryde: Ancient History Documentary Research Centre, 1994); S. R. Llewelyn, *New Documents Illustrating Early Christianity, Volume 8: A Review of the Greek Inscriptions and Papyri Published 1984–85* (Grand Rapids, MI: Eerdmans, 1998); S. R. Llewelyn, *New Documents Illustrating Early Christianity, Volume 9: A Review of the Greek Inscriptions and Papyri Published in 1986 and 1987* (Grand Rapids, MI: Eerdmans, 2002); S. R. Llewelyn and J. R. Harrison, *New Documents Illustrating Early Christianity, Volume 10: A Review of the Greek and Other Inscriptions and Papyri Published between 1988 and 1992* (Grand Rapids, MI: Eerdmans, 2012).

The current project under investigation, *Numismatics and Greek Lexicography*, is born out of the methodological desire to incorporate, rather than exclude, relevant Greek material in the lexicographer's task. As the above short review has made clear, newly discovered and incorporated linguistic material can significantly enhance the manner in which lexicographers delineate senses for a lexical item, define the relationships between polysemous lexemes and inform how one represents the multi-dimensionality of these relationships within a dictionary entry. This is not to suggest that we propose that numismatic evidence will necessarily provide the same volume of insight as the papyri or inscriptions. The measure of contribution is intangible at this stage, as the discipline of numismatic incorporation into Greek lexicography is in its infancy. But if more than 20,000 Greek inscriptions on Roman provincial (and related) coins are anything to go by, the prospect of finding relevant material for consideration and inclusion seems promising. The series of extended case studies in Part Two of this study will attempt to provide cogent examples of the theory in practice.

Nomenclature and definitions

The following list of fundamental definitions relating to numismatics is provided in order to assist readers who have more limited experience of handling or interpreting coins. Consultation of the following will facilitate a more fluid interaction with both the source material and the present analysis in this volume. The glossary is provided to further assist in familiarization with the nomenclature that will be assumed in the remainder of the volume.

Alignment	A method of striking in which the obverse and reverse are aligned in some fashion
Alliance coinage	Coins minted by two or more cities or states in cooperation
Alloy	Mixture of two or more elements, where the resulting compound has metallic properties, commonly electrum (gold and silver) or bronze (copper and tin)
Anepigraphic	Without an inscription
Annealing	Heating and cooling metal in order to relieve stresses, often done with coin blanks to make the metal less brittle before striking
Attribution	Identification of a coin by such as date, mint, denomination or variety
Base metal	Non-precious metal or alloy containing no gold or silver, e.g. copper
Beading	Raised border of dots on perimeter of coin
Blank	Prepared disc of metal on which the coin design will be stamped. Also referred to as a 'planchet' or 'flan'
Brass	Copper-based alloy with zinc
Brockage	Coin struck when the previous coin remained stuck to a die, creating an incuse impression in the next struck coin
Bronze	Copper-based alloy with tin

Cast coins	Coins produced by pouring metal into a mould. Used for the first Ancient Roman bronze "As" coins, and many renaissance copies or modern forgeries of ancient coins
Collar	The outer ring of the die chamber that holds the blank in place while the obverse and reverse are being stamped
Countermark	Over-stamping of a portion of a coin's surface in order to change its value, issuing authority, or to display a political slogan or symbol
Cud	A defect from a damaged die
Debase	Reducing the purity of the coin, often by lowering the gold or silver content
Die	Metal engraved with the design used for stamping the coin
Die alignment	Relationship of alignment between the obverse and reverse (also called die axis or coin rotation). Most often expressed in degrees, clock face hour or arrows. Most Roman coins have consistent die alignment of 0 or 180 degrees, Athenian tetradrachms almost always have a die alignment of 270 degrees
Die clash	When a blank is not placed between two dies during the minting process. Often a cause for damaged or cracked dies
Edge	Rim of a coin
Electrotype	Reproduction made by electrodeposition
Electrum	Artificial or naturally occurring mixture of gold and silver
Engraver	The person who cuts the image of a design onto a die
Exergue	Section of the coin separated by a line (usually indicating the ground in the design) in which a legend is often inscribed
Field	Background area of a coin not used for a design or inscription
Flan	Blank metal piece before striking, also called a planchet or blank
Grade	The condition of a coin. Common terms include: Poor (Po), Fair (Fr), About Good (AG), Good (G), Very Good (VG), Fine (F), Very Fine (VF), Extremely Fine (EF or XF), Almost Uncirculated (AU), Uncirculated (UNC) and Brilliant Uncirculated (BU)
Hammered	A coin that has been struck by hand, using dies and a hammer
High Relief	A coin with the raised design high above the field
Incuse	Impression below the surface (opposite of relief)
Inscription	Lettering or wording on a coin
Laureate	Head crowned with a laurel wreath
Legend	The inscription on the coin excluding mint characters. The legend typically is placed on the perimeter of the coin, but there are exceptions, more commonly on the obverse
Milled coinage	Machine-struck coinage
Mint/control marks	A sequence of letters, symbols and/or abbreviations indicating further information about the coin, often who or where it was produced
Mule Coin	Struck from two dies not normally seen together

Obverse	The side of the coin that bears the 'heads' or principal design. From the Latin *obvertere* (trans. 'turn towards'), hence 'turned toward the observer'. Roman coins are relatively consistent and it is generally a simple task to determine the obverse by simple observation. Determining the obverse of other coins can sometimes be more difficult due to the variety of images regularly depicted
Orichalcum	Alloy of copper and zinc
Overstrike	Impression with new dies on a previously struck coin
Patina	Surface film caused by oxidation. Colours vary based on metal, conditions and other factors but include (from most to least common) green, brown, earthen red or blue
Pedigree	Record of previous owners of a rare coin
Relief	Coin design that is raised above the field, opposite of incuse
Reverse	The opposite side to the obverse
Type	Distinguishing design

2

The History of Coinage

Introduction

Money has taken various shapes and forms over human history. Varieties include feather money of the Solomon Islands (twentieth century CE), Chinese Cowrie shells (thirteenth century BCE), Chinese spade money (fifth century BCE), Chinese knife money (fourth century BCE), and Kissi pennies, consisting of iron twisted and hammered into points, from Liberia and Sierra Leone (nineteenth century CE).[1] Not only has the form varied over the course of societal interactions, but also the purpose and use, encompassing such functions as a medium of exchange, storage of wealth, means of payment or even units of account.[2] So complex is the definition of 'money' that S. M. Stuard praises P. Sufford because he 'wisely avoids beginning his study with any attempt at defining money'.[3] The German political economist Max Weber noted much earlier in the twentieth century that physical objects, other than coins, did function as money throughout history.[4] A much earlier commentator, Hermogenianus, is quoted in Justinian's sixth-century CE encyclopaedic *Digest* 50.16.222: '"Pecuniae" nomine non solum numerata pecunia, sed omnes res tam soli quam mobiles et tam corpora quam iura continentur' (trans. 'In the designation of "pecunia" is included not only coinage but everything whether immobile or mobile and whether it is an object or a claim'). Several contemporary scholars have been sensitive to this nuanced definition, yet the old consensus of Roman money = coins unfortunately persists in

---

[1] J. Cribb, *Money: From Cowrie Shells to Credit Cards* (London: British Museum, 1986).

[2] See further David B. Hollander, *Money in the Late Roman Republic* (Leiden: Brill, 2007), 1–14.

[3] S. M. Stuard, review of *Money and Its Uses in Medieval Europe*, by P. Spufford, *Journal of Economic History* 49 (1989): 207. See P. Spufford, *Money and Its Uses in Medieval Europe* (Cambridge: Cambridge University Press, 1988).

[4] M. Weber, *General Economic History* (New York: Greenberg, 1927), 236–241. On the function of coinage, see C. J. Howgego, 'Why Did Ancient States Strike Coins?' *NC* 150 (1990): 1–27; T. R. Martin, 'Why Did the Greek Polis Originally Need Coins?' *Historia* 45 (1996): 257–283; K. Shipton and A. Meadows, eds., *Money and Its Uses in the Ancient Greek World* (Oxford: Oxford University Press, 2001); D. Schaps, *The Invention of Coinage and the Monetization of Ancient Greece* (Ann Arbor: University of Michigan Press, 2004).

some quarters.[5] Without entering into that foray of scholarly debate,[6] we will proceed attentively to the insight of C. Howgego that 'purchases on credit could allow many monetary transactions to take place with little actual use of coin.'[7]

The inception and evolution of coinage

The form of money that has been most common from the seventh to sixth century BCE onwards is that of a coin. However, despite its popularity, the production of coinage for economic transactions by individual states may well cease in the next century or sooner. Such a bold prediction is based on at least three factors. First, in the information age, physical coin-currency is cumbersome and unnecessary. The same, more convenient transactions can occur electronically without the burden of the production of coinage, nor the obligation for the user to carry (often heavy) metal discs of limited value on their person for purchases. For some time, modern states have been moving towards a cashless society. Second, coins are a vector for disease and may be a public health risk, especially when associated with the handling of food. Given that most pathogens are able to survive on coin surfaces, they pose a significant risk in the transmission of infection. In a recent illuminating study, it was found that although coins exhibit a lower bacterial load than paper currency, they 'have been found to carry opportunistic bacterial pathogens',[8] including *Staphylococcus, Bacillus and Corynebacterium*. 13 per cent of coinage analysed by Berel L. Abrams and Norton G. Waterman from Europe, North America, Asia, Australia and the Middle East contained multiple varieties of pathogens.[9] Third, add to this the cost to the public sector for the production of coins, the burden businesses bear in handling and transferring cash, the benefits of limiting illegal activities, including tax evasion, stolen goods and violent crime, and the case against modern coinage is overwhelming. Inevitably coinage will cease, but it has played a significant part in human history over the last two and a half millennia.

---

[5] K. Verboven, *The Economy of Friends: Economic Aspects of Amicitia and Patronage in the Late Republic* (Brussels: Latomus, 2002), states, for example 'a very inelastic money supply, consisting almost exclusively of state minted coins with a chronic lack of small denominations, supplemented by a limited supply of bullion, most of which was tied up in decorative objects' (166); E. Lo Cascio, 'State and Coinage in the Late Republic and Early Empire', *JRS* 71 (1981): 76–86, states that Roman 'money was coinage' (76); M. I. Finley, *The Ancient Economy* (Berkeley: University of California Press, 1973) writes, 'Money was hard coin, mostly silver, and a fair amount of that was hoarded, in strong-boxes, in the ground, often in banks as non-interest-bearing deposits. Payments were in coin, only under special conditions by a transfer within a particular bank or within the coffers of a Roman tax-farming corporation' (141).

[6] For an exposition of a view which correlates closely with my own, see W. V. Harris, 'A Revisionist View of Roman Money', *JRS* 96 (2006): 1–24.

[7] C. Howgego, 'The Supply and Use of Money in the Roman World 200 B.C. to A.D. 300', *JRS* 82 (1992): 13.

[8] Emmanouil Angelakis, Esam I. Azhar, Fehmida Bibi, Muhammad Yasir, Ahmed K. Al-Ghamdi, Ahmad M. Ashshi, Adel G. Elshemi, and Didier Raoult, 'Paper Money and Coins as Potential Vectors of Transmissible Disease', *Future Microbiology* 9, no. 2 (2014): 253.

[9] B. L. Abrams and N. G. Waterman, 'Dirty Money', *Journal of the American Medical Association* 219, no. 9 (1972): 1202–1203.

The History of Coinage   21

Ancient writers do not provide any kind of systematic investigation into the origins or philosophical nature of coinage. However, at a critical junction of Plato's *Republic* (II, 371b), Socrates leads Adeimantus to the idea that an ideal city will have coinage to facilitate local trade, "'Well then; in the city itself how will they exchange with one another what they make? It was, after all, for this purpose that we created a community and founded a city." "Clearly," he said, "by buying and selling." "And from this there will come into being a market, and coinage as a token for the purpose of exchange." "Certainly"'.[10]

There are certain historical hints and fragments from the ancient authors which do invite brief comment. We will restrict ourselves to two ancient quotations which have a direct bearing on our forgoing discussion. In Herodotus's notes on the Lydians (1.94) he observes that they were the 'first people of whom we have knowledge who struck coinage of gold and silver (νόμισμα χρυσοῦ καὶ ἀργύρου), and were the first who became small scale retailers (κάπηλοι)'. If Herodotus saw a connection between the former (minters of first coinage) and the latter small-scale retailers (κάπηλοι) he was almost certainly mistaken, as the first coins were far too large a denomination and too valuable to be used for goods in small-scale purchases.[11] Furthermore, the phrase νόμισμα χρυσοῦ καὶ ἀργύρου is ambiguous.[12] It could refer to the production of coins from electrum, an alloy of gold and silver, such as the coinage of the Lydians which depicts a lion and bull engaged in confrontation on the obverse, and incuse punch on the reverse (on which, see further below). Melville Jones suggests the phrase could refer to the introduction of pure gold and pure silver coinages individually.[13]

Alternatively, in a collection of statements Ἐκ τῶν Ἡρακλείδου περὶ πολιτείας (trans. 'from the work of Heracleides on the Constitution of the Athenians'), a section typically attributed to Heracleidas Poniticus (fourth century BCE, Athens),[14] but commonly recognized as a quotation from Aristotle's *Constitutions*, clearly draws on the myth of King Midas who turned everything he touched into gold: Ἑρμοδίκην δὲ γυναῖκα τοῦ Φρυγῶν βασιλέως Μίδα φασὶ κάλλει διαφέρειν, ἀλλὰ καὶ σοφὴν {εἶναι} καὶ τεχνικὴν καὶ πρώτην νόμισμα κόψαι Κυμαίοις (trans. 'and they say that Hermodice the wife of Midas the king of the Phrygians was exceptionally beautiful, and clever as well, and skilled in the crafts, and that she was the first to strike coinage for the Cumaeans').[15] Although Herodotus seems to preserve a kernel of historical memory of the origin of

---

[10] Cited in J. Melville Jones, *Testimonia Numaria, Greek and Latin Texts Concerning Ancient Greek Coinage, Volume I: Texts and Translations* (London: Spink and Son, 1993), 3.

[11] J. Melville Jones, *Testimonia Numaria, Greek and Latin Texts Concerning Ancient Greek Coinage, Volume II: Addenda and Commentary* (London: Spink and Son, 2007), 3.

[12] P. Gardner notes that 'to say that the Lydians first struck coins in gold and silver is not the same thing as to say that they first issued money of mixed gold and silver or electrum'. P. Gardner, *A History of Ancient Coinage* (Oxford: Clarendon Press, 1918), 68.

[13] See further Melville Jones, *Testimonia II*, 3–4, who favours the latter.

[14] Melville Jones argues for the re-attribution to the later Heracleidas Lembus (second century BCE, Alexandria), Melville Jones, *Testimonia II*, 4.

[15] Heracleides Ponticus, *De Rebus Publicis* XI, 3 (Aristotle fragment 611 Rose, §37), cited in Melville Jones, *Testimonia II*, 4. See full text in Mervin R. Dilts, *Heraclidis Lembi excerpta Politiarum* (Durham, NC: Duke University, 1971), §37.

coinage, the quotation commonly attributed as a quote from Aristotle has no historical value beyond tracing the reception of such an idea in antiquity.[16]

Precious metals in the form of weighed ingots had long been in use for monetary purposes, and archaeological evidence indicates that coinage was first introduced in the mid-seventh century BCE in Asia Minor (see further below). Moray Kornuk notes that the first coins were almost certainly minted in the Lydian capital Sardis in western Asia Minor, with electrum (an alloy of gold and silver, with small amounts of other elements, including copper, tin, lead and iron).[17] Deposits of naturally occurring electrum were common in the rivers (Hermus and Pactolus) that flowed through Sardis.[18] The gold content of alluvial electrum varied significantly. Two hoards analysed from Samos demonstrate a wide range of 46 to 84 per cent.[19] This inconsistency was problematic for valuation, so much so that Kornuk suggests 'coinage was invented precisely because of the varying intrinsic value of electrum, which could not readily circulate without a guarantee'.[20] If precious metal were to serve as the basis for trade, it would need to be accurately weighed and the metal composition confirmed before any transaction could take place. Given this impractical need, the development of a standard 'minted coinage', where the weight and metal were certified by a governmental authority, was a natural and necessary development. Although, obviously, from a later period than seventh-century Asia Minor, Plato's *Laws* XI, 918a-b highlights the theoretical necessity of coinage:

> Retail trade has by its nature come into existence universally throughout the state not for any harmful purpose, but for quite the opposite reason. For surely one who makes equal and similar the nature of goods of any kind, when it is dissimilar and unequal, does good; and we must agree that this is what the power of coinage also achieves, and it must be said that the merchant was put in place for this purpose.[21]

---

[16] The following passage is attributed to Aristotle, *Economics* 1345.b20, where it is said 'πρῶτον μὲν τοίνυν τὴν βασιλικὴν ἴδωμεν. ἔστι δὲ αὕτη δυναμένη μὲν τὸ καθόλου, εἴδη δὲ ἔχουσα τέσσαρα: περὶ νόμισμα, περὶ τὰ ἐξαγώγιμα, περὶ τὰ εἰσαγώγιμα, περὶ τὰ ἀναλώματα. τούτων δὲ ἕκαστον μὲν περὶ... τὸ νόμισμα' (trans. 'taking first the royal administration, we see that while theoretically its power is unlimited, it is in practice concerned with four departments, namely currency, exports, imports, and expenditure. Taking these severally, I assign to that of currency'). Other passages which regard minting a royal prerogative include 1 Maccabees 15:6, 'καὶ ἐπέτρεψά σοι ποιῆσαι κόμμα ἴδιον, νόμισμα τῇ χώρᾳ σου' (trans. 'I give you permission to coin money for your country with your own stamp'), where a letter sent by the Syrian king Antiochus VII (138–129 BCE) to his subject the Jewish prince Simon Maccabeeus, records an instance of a grant of coinage made by one such king.

[17] Koray Konuk, 'Asia Minor to the Ionian Revolt', in *The Oxford Handbook of Greek and Roman Coinage*, ed. William E. Metcalf (Oxford: Oxford University Press, 2012), 43.

[18] A. Ramage, 'Golden Sardis', in *King Croesus' Gold: Excavations at Sardis and the History of Gold Refining*, ed. A. Ramage and P. Craddock (Cambridge, MA: Harvard University Arts Museums, 2000), 14–26.

[19] H. Nicole-Pierre and J.-N. Barrandon, 'Monnaies d'électrum archaïques. Le trésor de Samos de 1894 (IGCH 1158) conservé à Paris', *RN* 152 (1997): 130; Koray Konuk, 'The Electrum Coinage of Samos in Light of a Recent Hoard', in *Neue forschungen zu Ionien*, ed E. Schwertheim and E. Winter (Bonn: Habelt, 2005), 49.

[20] Konuk, 'Asia Minor', 44.

[21] Melville Jones, *Testimonia I*, 46.

We now turn specifically to the archaeological record to determine the date of the introduction of coinage. The British Museum's sponsored excavations under the direction of D. G. Hogarth of the Temple of Artemis at Ephesus in 1904–1905 yielded ninety-three coins among the foundations of the archaic temple, the majority of which were the lion head type.[22] The dating of these coins has been vigorously debated. Some have opted for an earlier date of 700–675 BCE,[23] while others settle on the later date of c. 600 BCE.[24] Most numismatists have accepted a date of approximately 630 BCE.[25] More recent research into ceramic stratigraphy, particularly the pot in which one of the hoards was discovered, suggests a date between 650 and 630 BCE.[26]

While electrum was the composition of choice in the earliest coinage in western Asia Minor, given the scarcity of alluvial deposits and the difficulties noted above regarding the determination of metallic content, this discouraged the broader use of electrum. A century later, partly due to these concerns, Croesus (561–546 BCE), King of Lydia, replaced electrum coinage with issues in pure gold and pure silver. An example of this is SNG Ashmolean 760 (Figure 1), a silver stater minted in Sardes,

Figure 1 SNG Ashmolean 760 (used with permission).

[22] E. S. G. Robinson, 'The Coins from the Ephesian Artemision Reconsidered', *JHS* 71 (1951): 156–167; Konuk, 'Asia Minor', 48.
[23] L. Weidauer, *Probleme der Frühen Elektronprägung* (Freiburg: Office du livre, 1975); A. Furtwängler, 'Neue Beobachtungen zur frühesten Munzprägung', *Schweizerische Numismatische Rundschau* 65 (1986): 153–165.
[24] M. J. Price, 'Thoughts on the Beginnings of Coinage', in *Studies in Numismatic Method Presented to Philip Grierson*, ed. B. H. I. Stewart, Christopher N. L. Brooke, J. G. Pollard, and T. R. Volk (Cambridge: Cambridge University Press, 1983), 4.
[25] I. Carradice and M. Price, *Coinage in the Greek World* (London: Seaby, 1988), 30; Robinson, 'Coins'; C. M. Kraay, *Archaic and Classical Greek Coins* (London: Methuen, 1976), 21–22; R. W. Wallace, 'The Origin of Electrum Coinage', *AJA* 91 (1987): 385.
[26] D. Williams, 'The Pot Hoard from the Archaic Artemision of Ephesus', *BICS* 38 (1991–1993): 98–103.

which depicts the typical foreparts of lion and bull facing on the obverse, and two incuse squares on the reverse.

Persian conquest of Asia Minor in 546 BCE saw Cyrus continue minting in the same style in both gold and silver issues at Sardis down to 520 BCE with little iconographic variation.[27] With the arrival of Darius I (521–486) coinage underwent a significant shift both in terms of representation and weight standard.[28] The Persian coinage is characterized by a more dynamic style, which Konuk refers to as encapsulating a 'vivid sense of movement'.[29] The unit of currency, the daric, derived from the name of Darius and was known by Greek authors more commonly as the daric stater. The daric of 8.4 grams was heavier than the previous standard of 8.1 grams, but the silver siglos remained at 5.4 grams. The established standard of exchange between gold and silver was 1:13, and the exchange rate between the daric and siglos was 1:20.[30] There is some sub-variation in representational type over time.[31] Type I (Figure 2: Carradice I) (Darius I, 521–505 BCE) portrays a bearded figure of the king from the waist up facing right, crowned, with two arrows in right hand and bow in left (5.30–5.39 grams). Type II (Figure 3: Carradice II) (Darius I, 510–486 BCE) depicts a bearded kneeling/

Figure 2 Carradice I (used with permission).

---

[27] I. Carradice, 'The "Regal" Coinage of the Persian Empire', in *Coinage and Administration in the Athenian and Persian Empires*, ed. I. Carradice (Oxford: BAR Publishing, 1987), 73–108.

[28] Theodore V. Buttrey's excavation report on the coins found on the site of the Lydian capital is relevant for the advent of coinage in the Persian period, Roman control from 133 BCE and the nature of Jewish colonies and subsequent Christian communities in the first century, Theodore V. Buttrey, *Greek, Roman, and Islamic Coins from Sardis* (Cambridge, MA: Harvard University Press, 1981).

[29] Konuk, 'Asia Minor', 33.

[30] Konuk, 'Asia Minor', 51.

[31] For the following, see Carradice, '"Regal" Coinage'.

Figure 3 Carradice II (used with permission).

running figure of the king facing right, drawing bow, who is crowned and has a quiver at his shoulder (5.30–5.39 grams). Type III (Darius I – Artaxerxes II, 490–375 BCE) also has a crowned bearded kneeling/running figure of the king facing right, but with transverse spear with point downward in right, and also a bow in left (Type IIIa [Figure 4: Carradice IIIa] has a lighter weight of 5.30–5.39; Type IIIb [Figure 5: Carradice IIIb (early)] has a fold in drapery over the advanced left knee, 5.55–5.60; Type IIIb[late] [Figure 6: Carradice IIIb (late)] has a semi-circular sweep of folds in the drapery, 5.55–5.60). Type IV (Artaxerxes I – Darius III, 450–340 BCE) has a crowned bearded kneeling/running figure of the king facing right, with a dagger in his right hand and bow in left (Type IVa [Figure 7: Carradice IVa] has a shapeless with no waist and cartoon-like portrait, 450–420 BCE [Artaxerxes I – Darius II]; Type IVb [Figure 8: Carradice IVb] has an uncharacteristically large eye and shorter beard, 420–375 BCE [Darius II – Artaxerxes II]; Type IVc [Figure 9: Carradice IVc] has three or four pellets on chest and a long beard, 375–340 BCE [Artaxerxes II – Darius III]). All types have a variety of the incuse oblong punch on the reverse of which G. F. Hill enumerated 187 and varieties.[32]

The Greeks seem to have adopted coinage during the time of Cyrus the Persian in the mid to late sixth century BCE. An early example is SNG Paris 1.1554[33] (Figure 10) issued by the island city Aegina in 550–500 BCE in the Saronic Gulf off the northeast

---

[32] G. F. Hill, *Catalogue of the Greek Coins in the British Museum: Arabia, Mesopotamia and Persia* (London: British Museum, 1922), cxxxvii; G. F. Hill, 'Notes on the Imperial Persian Coinage', *Journal of Hellenic Studies* 39 (1919): 116–129.

[33] H. Nicolet-Pierre, J. Delepierre, M. Delepierre, and G. Le Rider, *Sylloge Nummorum Graecorum: France 1. Bibliothèque Nationale de France: Collection Jeanet Marie Delepierre* (Paris: Bibliothèque Nationale de France, 1983).

Figure 4 Carradice IIIa (used with permission).

Figure 5 Carradice IIIb (early) (used with permission).

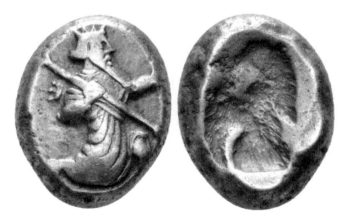

Figure 6 Carradice IIIb (late) (used with permission).

The History of Coinage

Figure 7 Carradice IVa (used with permission).

Figure 8 Carradice IVb (used with permission).

Figure 9 Carradice IVc (used with permission).

Figure 10 SNG Paris 1.1544 (used with permission).

coast of the Peloponnesus. The coin features a sea turtle on the obverse and a decorative form of the incuse punch on the reverse. The depiction of a turtle is probably due to the influence of the inhabitants of the island as a significant sea power, but could also be drawing on the topographical similarity of the symmetrical convex shape of the island, viewed from the surrounding region, and the profiled depiction of the turtle.[34]

The Athenian Tetradrachm was the most significant and influential coin produced during the sixth to first centuries BCE. There is a noticeable evolution of iconography from their Persian and Anatolian predecessors, where generic depictions of animals or nature are replaced with specific symbols of the city responsible for their minting. SNG Copenhagen 32 (Figure 11) (454–414 BCE), as is typical, displays on the obverse the head of Athena facing right with a large almond-shaped eye with lips drawn back in a tight smile. Athena wears the crested Attic helmet with three laurel leaves and a vine scroll. The reverse has AΘE with an owl, the sacred animal of Athena, standing right, head facing, and an olive sprig and crescent moon behind. The standard weight of tetradrachm was set at 17.28 grams (drachm 4.32 grams; obol 0.72 grams) and remained in effect for centuries, a feat which J. Elsen rightly considers remarkable given the political changes during the period.[35]

Coinage spread rapidly to other Greek city states that used the iconography to express aspects of their identity. Corinth produced a stater from *c.* 400 BCE onwards (cf. Ravel 619[36] [Figure 12]) which depicted the head of Athena on the obverse wearing

---

[34] H. H. Miller, *Greece through the Ages, as Seen by Travelers from Herodotus to Byron* (New York: Funk & Wagnalls, 1972), 162.

[35] J. Elsen, 'La Stabilité Du Système Pondéral et Monétaire Attique (Vie-IIe s. avant notre ére)', *RBN* 148 (2002): 1–32.

[36] Oscar E. Ravel, *Les 'Poulains' de Corinthe: Monographie Des Stateres Corinthiens* (2 vols; London: Spink, 1948).

Figure 11 SNG Copenhagen 32 (used with permission).

Figure 12 Ravel 619 (used with permission).

an uncrested Corinthian helmet pushed back on head, with EYΘ in retrograde above. The reverse depicted a Pegasus flying right and had the archaic Greek letter qoppa (Ϙ) below. Greek mythology tells of Pegasus, born from the blood of Medusa, who was an untameable and wild creature. This was, however, only until Athena granted a golden girdle to Bellerophon who was able to tame the horse and later is related in myth as becoming the King of Corinth.[37] Hence the comment in Theocritus, *Idylls*

---

[37] Pausanias, *Description of Greece* 2.4.1.

15.92 in the third century BCE, 'If you must know, we are Corinthian women by extraction, like Bellerophontes himself.'[38]

The centuries that followed saw many city states issue coins with their particular local iconography. In the third century BCE Rhodes minted a tetradrachm (SNG Keckman 544 [Figure 13]) which on the obverse depicted Helios the sun god with radiate wreath and a rose on the reverse. The connection between Helios and Rhodes is well established. The fifth-century BCE Greek poet Pindar refers to the awarding of the island of Rhodes to Helios.[39] Similarly, four centuries later the Greek historian Diodorus Siculus relates a story of Helios' infatuation with Rhodes, and how the Rhodians 'made it their practice to honour Helios above all the other gods, as the ancestor and founder from whom they were descended'.[40] The representation of Helios on the coinage of Rhodes reflects the Colossus of Rhodes, a bronze statue erected in the early third century BCE as a thank offering to Helios for protection against the Macedonians in 305 BCE.[41]

Distinctive coin types effectively functioned as badges of identity for the city state producing them. Coinage of Thebes typically displays a Boeotian shield. Dewing 1508[42] (Figure 14) is a silver hemidrachm (13 mm; 2.67 grams; 395–340 BCE) featuring the Boeotian shield, oval in shape with semi-circular openings at either side on the obverse.

Figure 13 SNG Keckman 544 (used with permission).

---

[38] See further Homer, *Iliad* 6.144–221; Homer, *Iliad* 16.327; Hesiod, *Theogony* 319; Hesiod, *Catalogues of Women* Fragment 7; Pindar, *Olympian Ode* 13.60; Pindar, *Isthmian Ode* 7.44.
[39] Pindar, *Olympian Ode* 7.54–74.
[40] Diodorus Siculus, *Library of History* 5.56.3. Cf. Ovid, *Metamorphoses* 7. 365 who refers to Rhodes as Helios' favourite.
[41] Pindar, *Olympian Ode* 7.54; Pliny, *Natural History* 34.7.17.
[42] Silvia Hurter and Leo Mildenberg, *The Arthur S. Dewing Collection of Greek Coins* (New York: American Numismatic Society, 1985).

Figure 14 Dewing 1508 (used with permission).

The reverse has a Kantharos club above and an ivy leaf in the right field. Despite the prominence and popularity of the imagery of the shield, which is assumed to relate to a deity, there is no literary or other evidence linking this symbol to a specific deity. Among other possibilities it may be the shield of Athena Itonia whose temple was the place the Boeotians celebrated their national festivals, or it could be the shield of Ares who played a role in the popular Boeotian games.[43]

City states west of Athens also began minting coinage with relevant emblems of their identity. Metapontum in Magna Graecia (the middle point of the arch of the foot in the 'boot' of Italy) produced coinage from an early period (540–510 BCE) celebrating its main agricultural product, grain. The obverse of SNG Ashmolean 648 (Figure 15) displays a head of grain and MET in the left field. The relief design of the obverse is repeated intaglio on the reverse. There are several hundred types and variations of this iconography including variations in the legend form, style and location, the number of pellets on the grain head, and its width and many other features. It is uncertain whether these differences relate to specific engraving styles or developments which enhance coin production.[44] A later coin of Metapontum SNG Ashmolean 728 (Figure 16), minted mid to late fourth century BCE, depicts on the obverse the bearded head of Leukippos, the reputed founder of the city facing right wearing a Corinthian helmet with cross-torch in left field. The reverse has the usual symbol of grain with inscription META.

---

[43] On the Boeotian League, see B. V. Head, *On the Chronological Sequence of the Coins of Boeotia* (Cambridge: Cambridge University Press, 1895); J. Ducat, 'La confédération béotienne et l'expansion thébaine à l'époque archaïque', *BCH* 97 (1973): 59–73; R. Étienne and Denis Knoepfler, 'Le monnayage d'Hyettos à l'époque archaïque', *BCH Suppl.* 3 (1976): 383–390, 400.

[44] Kraay, *Archaic*, 170–171.

32   *Numismatics and Greek Lexicography*

Figure 15 SNG Ashmolean 648 (used with permission).

Figure 16 SNG Ashmolean 728 (used with permission).

The city of Akragas in Sicily produced coinage in the fifth century BCE depicting an eagle with closed wings on the obverse with inscription AKPAC-ANTOC partially in retrograde. The reverse of SNG Ashmolean 1671 (Figure 17) has a striking depiction of a crab above a lotus flower on double spiral vine. One assumes that these crabs were plentiful in the nearby river, or the twin symbols of eagle and crab represent Zeus and Poseidon.

The next major development in the Greek was instigated by the Macedonians who transformed the multiplicity of city states into a unified kingdom under Alexander III.

Figure 17 SNG Ashmolean 1671 (used with permission).

Figure 18 SNG ANS 807 (used with permission)

The Macedonians transferred imagery on coins from civic emblems, to honouring prominent men by specific inscriptional reference. The obverse of SNG ANS 807 (Figure 18) depicts the laureate head of Zeus facing right with beading. The reverse displays a youth riding a horse towards the right holding a palm frond. The inscription clearly identifies the coin as belonging not to a city but an individual, ΦΙΛΙΠΠΟΥ (trans, 'of Philip').

Similarly, a tetradrachm of Alexander III, SNG Ashmolean 2891 (Figure 19), displays the head of the youthful Herakles in lion skin headdress facing right on

Figure 19 SNG Ashmolean 2891 (used with permission).

the obverse. The reverse depicts Zeus seated to the left on a throne with his feet on a footstool, holding an eagle with closed wings on his outstretched right hand and long sceptre in his left. The prominence of Zeus and Herakles can be attributed to the Macedonian kings who traced their descent to Herakles, and even made sacrifices to him at Vergina and Pella.[45] In the right field is the inscription ΑΛΕΞΑΝΔΡΟΥ (trans. 'of Alexander'), which like the genitive noun ΦΙΛΙΠΠΟΥ identifies an individual who sponsors coinage rather than the state.[46]

The successors of Alexander's empire relied on their links with Alexander to legitimate their own rule. This is clearly evidenced in the numismatic record. Lysimachus (323–281 BCE) for example, minted coins with the diademed head of the deified Alexander with the horn of Ammon on the obverse (SNG Ashmolean 3756 [Figure 20]). The reverse has Athena Nikephoros seated to the left with the inscription ΒΑΣΙΛΕΩΣ ΛΥΣΙΜΑΧΟΥ.[47] In a radical development in numismatic portraiture, Alexander's successors eventually appeared on coinage during their own lifetimes. SNG Copenhagen 70 (Figure 21) is a tetradrachm of Ptolemy Soter I (323–284 BCE) minted in Alexandria. The obverse depicts the diademed head of the living Ptolemy wearing an aegis around his neck. The reverse has an eagle with closed wings standing facing left on a thunderbolt, with the inscription ΒΑΣΙΛΕΩΣ ΠΤΟΛΕΜΑΙΟΥ (trans. 'of King Ptolemy') around top

---

[45] Paul Christesen and Sarah Murray, 'Macedonian Religion', in *A Companion to Ancient Macedonia*, ed. Joseph Roisman and Ian Worthington (Oxford: Wiley-Blackwell, 2010), 430.

[46] On the coinage of Alexander III, see A. R. Bellinger, *Essays in the Coinage of Alexander the Great* (New York: S.J. Durst, 1963); M. J. Price, *The Coinage in the Name of Alexander the Great and Philip Arrhidaeus: A British Museum Catalogue* (London: British Museum Press, 1991), 24–40, 79–80.

[47] Otto Mørkholm, *Early Hellenistic Coinage: From the Accession of Alexander to the Peace of Apamea (336–188 B.C.)* (Cambridge: Cambridge University Press, 1991), 81.

Figure 20 SNG Ashmolean 3756 (used with permission).

Figure 21 SNG Copenhagen 70 (used with permission).

perimeter.[48] Hereafter, Hellenistic kings would routinely replace depictions of deities which had been the norm up until this point in numismatic history.[49]

---

[48] On coinage of Lysimachus, see Mørkholm, *Early*, 63–96; M. Thompson, 'The Mints of Lysimachus', in *Essays in Greek Coinage Presented to Stanley Robinson*, ed. C. M. Kraay and G. K. Jenkins (Oxford: Clarendon, 1968), 163–182.

[49] The initial coinage of the Hellenistic successors imitated Alexander's coinage closely. Later each kingdom evolved its own typology and imagery to suit their political and historical circumstances. On the coinage of the Seleucids, see Arthur Houghton's extensive catalogue, Arthur Houghton,

Within the Roman sphere, the earliest money produced seems to have rough cast bronze in the fifth century BCE or earlier, and is referred to as aes rude (trans. 'rough bronze').[50] But weighing anywhere between 10 grams and 500 grams, its practicality was limited. The concept, however, paved the way for the large, rectangular cast currency bars made to a specific weight standard, aes signatum (trans. 'stamped bronze'). But again, due to the cumbersome nature of the bars, it was relatively short lived. This was replaced by the aes grave (trans. 'heavy bronze'), which despite its name was more portable and usable than its predecessor. The aes grave was cast rather than struck and circular in shape. The unit of currency for cast bronze was based on the as (pl. asses), originally 1 Roman pound equated to approximately 329 grams,[51] and was divided into 12 ounces (unciae). Each uncia is represented by a raised dot (see Tables 1 and 2).

The earliest struck Roman coinage displays similarities with both the coinage of free Greek city states (civic emblems and political statements) and philhellenic aspects. Crawford 20.1 (Figure 22) is a didrachm minted after 276 BCE with the diademed head of Hercules facing right with club and lion skin over shoulder on the obverse, which clearly seeks to borrow imagery (especially hair and diadem) from the coinage of Alexander. The reverse has the she-wolf suckling the twins Romulus and Remus, with inscription ROMANO(RUM) (trans. '[a coin] of the Romans'). The association with Alexander as conqueror and the expanding Roman as depicted on Crawford 20.1 sought to make a political statement of the Roman rise to dominance in the region.

Table 1 Aes grave denominations

Denomination	Division of As	Denomination mark
As	One	I
Semis	half an as	S
Triens	third of an as	••••
Quadrans	quarter of an as	•••
Sextans	sixth of an as	••
Uncia	twelfth of an as	•

Catharine Lorber, and O. Hoover, *Seleucid Coins: A Comprehensive Catalogue*, 2 vols. (New York: American Numismatic Society, 2002–2008). On the coinage of the Ptolemaic dynasty, see J. N. Svoronos, *Τὰ Νομίσματα τοῦ Κράτους τῶν Πτολεμαίων* (Athens: P. D. Sakellarios, 1904). A more popular, but updated, discussion is found in R. A. Hazzard, *Ptolemaic Coins: An Introduction for Collectors* (Toronto: Kirk and Bentley, 1995). Georges Le Rider, and Françoise de Callataÿ's French study on the Seleucids and Ptolemies, Georges Le Rider, and Françoise de Callataÿ, *Les Séleucides et les Ptolémées* (Paris: Éd. du Rocher, 2006), provides a comparative study of the coinages and fiscal policies of the two competing kingdoms. Commentators on Hellenistic coinage often draw a distinction between 'civic' and 'royal' coinages. A. Meadows questions this strict classification primarily on the basis that the former may be impressed into royal service, A. Meadows, 'The Eras of Pamphylia and the Seleucid Invasions of Asia Minor', *American Journal of Numismatics* 21 (2009): 51–88.

50 Pliny the Elder, *Natural History* 33.13.43.

51 Ronald Edward Zupko, *British Weights and Measures: A History from Antiquity to the Seventeenth Century* (Madison: University of Wisconsin Press, 1977), 7.

Figure 22 Crawford 20.1 (used with permission).

Table 2 Majority composition of Roman provincial coinage

Copper	Pure copper
Copper and lead	copper alloyed with at least 10% lead
Bronze	copper alloyed with about 5–30% tin, sometimes including up to 10% lead
Leaded bronze	copper alloyed with tin and with > 10% lead
Brass	copper alloyed with about 10–30% zinc, sometimes including up to 5% lead

The Second Punic War (against Hannibal's Carthaginian army) caused economic hardship for Rome and effectively resulted in the establishment of the Roman monetary standard based on the silver denarius in 211 BCE.[52] Typical in this regard is Crawford 72.3 (Figure 23), which on the obverse portrays the helmeted head of Roma facing right personifying the city, with X behind signifying the value of 10 asses.[53] The reverse generally depicted a scene from Greco-Roman mythology, in this case the Dioscuri, the divine twins, Castor and Pollux riding right armed with spears, with a corn-ear below. This was potentially a challenge to the Brutti, Hannibal's allies in southern Italy who had issued coins with the Dioscuri for several generations. The inscription 'Roma' is in exergue.

---

[52] Eric Sjöqvist and Theodore V. Buttrey's volume on Morgantina (east central Sicily) is critical for the chronology of the early Roman denarius and early iconography. Eric Sjöqvist and Theodore V. Buttrey, *Morgantina Studies: Results of the Princeton University Archaeological Expedition to Sicily, Vol. 2: The Coins* (Princeton, NJ: Princeton University Press, 1989).

[53] There were rarer denominations such as the quinarius (5 asses, marked V) and sestertius (2.5 asses, marked IIS) but these were generally only issued during times of crisis in the Republican period. In 141 BCE the denarius was re-valued at 16 asses, for a short period of time the denarius was marked with XVI to signify this change, but eventually X was retained as the traditional mark of the denarius on both coinage and inscriptions despite the discrepancy in value pre/post 141 BCE.

Figure 23 Crawford 72.3 (used with permission).

Figure 24 Crawford 295.1 (used with permission).

As with their Hellenistic counterpart, Roman coinage became more than conduits of civic emblems, but associated with living persons or families. In this regard moneyers began to inscribe their names and symbols on coins.[54] The one who designed and minted the coin became an important office in the Roman state. The individuality of the moneyer became much more prominent during the years 140 BCE and following, a time when intense political rivalry wrestled to use the coinage as a form of propaganda. Eventually, civic emblems give way to personal references,

---

[54] For the evolution from state iconography to the family-inspired designs, see Anna Serena Fava, *I Simboli Nelle Monete Argentee Repubblicane e la Vita dei Romani* (Turin: Museo Civico, 1969).

inscriptions and ancestors.⁵⁵ Crawford 295.1 (Figure 24) is a silver denarius of Lucius Manlius Torquatus minted in Rome in 113–112 BCE. The obverse has the head of Roma, and inscription ROMA downwards behind, and an X below chin. The reverse depicts Titus Manlius Torquatus, a famous ancestral warrior who defeated a Gaul of enormous size in single combat in 361 BCE.⁵⁶ He is depicted on horseback charging to the left holding spear and shield.

The first living Roman to be portrayed on the obverse of Roman coinage was Julius Caesar. In an act that would recall the Hellenistic monopoly of power, traditionally minded Romans would have been deeply suspicious, if not outraged by the centralization of power and loyalty to Caesar which was reminiscent of kingship.⁵⁷ Crawford 480.13 (Figure 25) has on the obverse a wreathed head of Caesar facing right, with inscription CAESAR in right field downward, and DICT PERPETUO left and upwards, trans. 'Caesar, Dictator for life'. The reverse has Venus standing facing left holding victory in her right hand and long sceptre in left hand, with P SEPULLIUS behind downwards and MACER in front downwards, all within a border of dots. In only a matter of a few months after the issuing of this coin, Caesar had been stabbed twenty-three times by various individuals eager to eliminate him.⁵⁸ Plutarch highlights the enthusiasm of

Figure 25 Crawford 480.13 (used with permission).

---

[55] From at least the first century BCE moneyers were responsible for the minting of coinage. These are referred to as 'triumviri auro argento aere flando feriundo' (trans. 'three men responsible for casting and striking gold, silver and bronze'). On coinage the common abbreviation is IIIVIRAAAFF.

[56] See further Livy, *The History of Rome from Its Foundations*, 6–10.

[57] For the evolution of iconography into dynastic portraiture under Caesar, see Andreas Alföldi, *Caesar in 44 v. Chr. Vol. 2, Das Zeugnis der Münzen. Antiquitas 3.17* (Bonn: R. Habelt, 1974).

[58] For discussion of the gold coinage of Octavian, Mark Antony and Marcus Lepidus in 42 BCE with the specific purpose of casting the triumvirs as legitimate heirs to Caesar, see Theodore Vern Buttrey, *The Triumviral Portrait Gold of the Quattuorviri Monetales of 42 B.C.* (New York: American Numismatic Society, 1956).

participants, 'many of the conspirators were wounded by one another, as they struggled to plant all those blows in one body'.[59] There may not be a direct correlation between the issuing of the coin and Caesar's death, but the correlations between contemporary political tensions and imagery captured on the coin are striking.

The coinage of Augustus is vast, complicated, and intensely personal and political. Although Caesar was the first to put his own living image on a coin, Augustus took up the mandate with such enthusiasm that his efforts in numismatic representation far surpass any other in the first century CE. During his fifty-six years of operation, first as Octavian then as Augustus, he put millions of coins into circulation in gold, silver and bronze. There are at least 48 types of imperial obverse portraits, accompanied by a variety of at least 127 different obverse inscriptions, 216 different reverse inscriptions and 202 different reverse types. The imperial coinage of Augustus was minted in at least thirteen locations (Africa, Antioch, Berytos, Colonia Patricia, Emerita, Ephesus, Greece, Lugdunum, Nemausus, Nicomedia, Pergamum, Roma and Spain), excluding his portable mints which could accompany an army. A significant evolution in iconography is evident on the Augustan coinage, in that he not only portrays himself, contemporaries or illustrious ancestors, but younger members of his family, namely the next generation of rulers. RIC Aug. 210 (Figure 26) is a silver denarius minted at Lugdunum in 2 BCE. The obverse has the laureate head of Augustus facing right with the inscription, CAESAR AVGVSTVS DIVI F PATER P[ATRIA]E (trans. 'Caesar Augustus, divine son, father of the fatherland'). The reverse has Gaius and Lucius Caesars togate, standing facing, supporting between them on the ground honorary

Figure 26 RIC Aug. 210 (used with permission).

[59] Plutarch, *Life of Caesar* 66 in *Lives, Volume VII: Demosthenes and Cicero. Alexander and Caesar*, trans. Bernadotte Perrin. Loeb Classical Library 99 (Cambridge, MA: Harvard University Press, 1919), 599.

The History of Coinage 41

shields and spears. Above are the instruments for sacrifice, a lituus (curved staff of augurs) and a simpulum (earthenware ladle or pouring vessel) turned inward. The inscription reads C L CAES[ARES AVGVSTI F COS D]ESIG PRINC IVVENT, (Caius et Lucius Caesares Augusti Filii Consules Designati Principes Juventutis [trans. 'Caius and Lucius Caesars, Sons of Caesar Augustus consul elect and leaders of youth']). Because Augustus had no male heirs of his own, he formally adopted his two grandsons, Gaius and Lucius, the children of his friend and general M. Agrippa and his only child, his daughter Julia. Both were groomed as heirs, but neither survived him, Lucius dying in Gaul in 2 BCE and Gaius in Lycia in 4 CE. With their deaths Augustus was forced to consider another suitable candidate to succeed him, eventually his stepson, Tiberius. Nonetheless, this focusing on youth and future generations was a distinct evolution in the way in which imagery on coinage had been used within a Roman context.

Roman provincial coinage is remarkably rich. One can estimate up to one hundred thousand types, from over five hundred cities from Caesar to Diocletian.[60] That said, typically provincial coinage portrayed the portrait and titles of the emperor on the obverse and the name of the community and its symbols on the reverse, mostly traditional civic gods. There was only very limited provincial gold coinage produced, it was an exception for a select few client kingdoms (Bosporus, Mauretania). Silver coinage was slightly more common,[61] but by far the normal type of provincial coinage was of based metal. The most common were copper (pure copper); copper and lead (copper alloyed with at least 10 per cent lead); bronze (copper alloyed with about 5–30 per cent tin, sometimes including up to 10 per cent lead); Leaded bronze (copper alloyed with tin and with >10 per cent lead) and brass (copper alloyed with about 10–30 per cent zinc, sometimes including up to 5 per cent lead).

Roman provincial coinage attests to one part of how the identity of the inhabitants of a city was cultivated and articulated in a particular historical context. Indeed, Fergus Millar suggests that 'the most explicit symbols of a city's identity and status were its coins'.[62] However, as Millar concedes, 'behind that statement lies a multitude of problems'.[63] One complication is what one means by a 'mint', and whether these where permanent entities or episodic. Another difficulty is that a single workshop could produce coinage for multiple cities.[64] Cognizant of these, and other, limitations Christopher Howgego considers the overall pattern of the evidence in five categories: (1) religion, where polytheism left room for localism, specifically polis-religion not private-religion; (2) the use of monumentality, namely the practice of putting buildings on coins, which was essentially a Roman innovation;[65] (3) the representation of the

---

[60] Volker Heuchert, 'The Chronological Development of Roman Provincial Coin Iconography', in *Coinage and Identity in the Roman Provinces*, ed. Christopher Howgego, Volker Heuchert, and Andrew Burnett (Oxford: Oxford University Press, 2005), 29–56.

[61] See D. R. Walker, *The Metrology of the Roman Silver Coinage: Part I, from Augustus to Domitian* (Oxford: British Archaeological Reports, 1976).

[62] Fergus Millar, *The Roman Near East 31 BC–AD 337* (London: Harvard University Press, 1993), 257.

[63] Millar, *Roman*, 257.

[64] K. Kraft, *Das System der kaiserzeitlichen Münzprägung in Kleinasien* (Berlin: Mann, 1972).

[65] A. Meadows and J. H. C. Williams, 'Moneta and the Monuments: Coinage and Politics in Republican Rome', *JRS* 91 (2001): 27–49.

past, both mythological and historical, in so far as it could locate and historically parse the relationship between the issuing city and with other cities, especially so, given the realities of increasing Roman power; (4) the choice of language, Latin in the west and Greek in the east, the only exception being Roman coloniae using Latin in the east in recognition of their Roman status and (5) the degree of identity/connectedness with the imperial power, i.e. so-called 'Romanness'.[66] Howgego helpfully highlights that 'coins were a *deliberate* advertisement of *public* identity',[67] in the sense that they are self-identified (deliberate) and widely publicized/broadcast (public). We will have ample opportunity in Part Two of this volume to explore specific case studies of the manner in which these characteristics are employed by local communities to articulate their identity, in regard to both the apparent continuity and discontinuity with Roman ideals.

Conclusion

This chapter has sought to highlight the critical moments and historical developments in the history of coinage in order to briefly sketch the evolution of the medium, and contextualize our following discussion. The beauty and rich variety of the numismatic record is captured well in Frank Sherman Benson's poem entitled 'A Cabinet of Greek Coins':[68]

Behold portrayed in miniature, yet clear,
The changing seasons of Hellenic art;
Fair spring-time, when dim haunting visions start
Forth into life, and forms divine appear;
Full, radiant summer, when a heaven-born skill
Achieves such height as man ne'ermore can gain;
Dear autumn of decay, wherein remain
Mere phantoms which a glimmering twilight fill.
Here too the Olympic pantheon displays
Pure, grand ideals of each dreaded god,
Or cherished goddess, or loved nymph enshrined.
With likeness too of many a king whose nod
Could empires shake. Thus various-hued we find
A rich emblazonry of ancient days.

The basic tenet of our ensuing discussion is that numismatic inscriptions have demonstrable value for the study of Hellenistic Greek lexicography in general, and the application of this method specifically to NT studies.

---

[66] Christopher Howgego, 'Coinage and Identity in the Roman Provinces', in *Coinage and Identity in the Roman Provinces*, ed. Christopher Howgego, Volker Heuchert, and Andrew Burnett (Oxford: Oxford University Press, 2005), 1–17.

[67] Howgego, 'Coinage and Identity', 1, italics original.

[68] The poem was printed in the opening to a volume of Benson's self-published work in 1901–1902 on Greek numismatics simply titled *Ancient Greek Coins*.

3

The Study of Coinage

Introduction

The academic discipline of numismatics challenges traditional monolithic field of research classifications, as coins can be studied from polyvalent approaches. They can be appreciated for their aesthetic value as pieces of art and design, considered for their contribution to resolving historical or linguistic questions, analysed metallurgically for investigating technological innovation, or appraised for the economic function within their original or later context. These multifaceted disciplines, specializations and associated questions, in addition to the archaeological problems of association within the assemblage, are often an impenetrable wall for other historians or scholars seeking to incorporate numismatic evidence into their discipline or enquiry. Although commentators regularly state sentiments indicating the relative ease and availability of numismatic materials, 'coins or photos of coins are readily accessible in museums, libraries, and on the internet',[1] rarely is any specific advice or direction given as to how these can actually be accessed, used, and referenced in a consistent and accurate manner. This chapter will survey the most important primary and secondary sources for studying and understanding coinage in antiquity, with a particular emphasis on the topic under discussion, namely, numismatic evidence for its contribution to Greek lexicography, with the addition of select additional material which provides needed context.[2]

Sources

By far the most exhaustive collection of bibliographic material is E. E. Clain-Stefanelli's *Numismatic Bibliography*, which includes 18,311 listings of articles and monographs.[3] It is the most extensive published collection of numismatic bibliography in print.

---

[1]   David H. Wenkel, *Coins as Cultural Texts in the World of the New Testament* (London: Bloomsbury, 2017), xix.

[2]   On the subject of the whole chapter, see the bibliographic overview presented by Oliver D. Hoover, *Greek and Roman Numismatics* (Oxford: Oxford University Press, 2011), from which I have drawn for the discussion below.

[3]   E. E. Clain-Stefanelli, *Numismatic Bibliography* (Munich: Battenberg, 1985).

Although now it is somewhat dated, it can be used in conjunction with two periodicals, *Numismatic Literature*, the American Numismatic Society's quarterly then semi-annual bibliography of publications relevant to numismatics, and *Survey of Numismatic Research*, the numismatic bibliographical publication of the International Numismatic Commission, published on the occasion of the International Numismatic Congress with a focus on methodology, new discoveries and critical discussion of works cited.[4] W. E. Daehn's bibliographic volume on Greek numismatics, *Ancient Greek Numismatics*,[5] is useful in its clear structure into discrete sub-disciplines within the field of numismatics: artistic aspects including types and representations, art, engravers and stylistic trends, portraiture; technical aspects regarding the minting process and issues pertaining to metallurgy (properties of metals) and metrology (measurement), and also significant numismatic collections arranged by geographical region and country. Daehn however, as the sub-title indicates, excludes items written in languages other than English, and is thus significantly, and unhelpfully, truncates bibliographic material on almost every area of numismatics. A helpful counter to the preferential collection of English material is the volume by Philip Grierson which has a significant collection of material on ancient numismatics, but as a whole the volume is superseded by Clain-Stefanelli's work.[6]

Evidence from coins is most regularly employed in archaeological contexts for dating archaeological sites and strata. John Casey and Richard Reece's volume, *Coins and the Archaeologist*, provides a robust discussion and overview of archaeological numismatic methodology, appropriately nuanced and balanced in regard to the actual use of coin evidence in dating.[7] Giovanni Gorini's Italian volume, *I ritrovamenti monetali nel mondo antico: Problemi e metodi* (trans. 'The Monetary Finds in the Ancient World: Problems and Methods'), includes a thorough discussion on the methodological challenges in using numismatic material for interpreting archaeological features within a site.[8]

---

[4] Nils Ludvig Rasmusson, Carsten Svarstad, and Lars O. Lagerqvist, *A Survey of Numismatic Research, 1960–1965* (Copenhagen: International Numismatic Commission, 1967); Paul Naster. J.-B Colbert de Beaulieu, Joan M. Fagerlie, Jacques Yvon, and Helen W. Mitchell Brown, *A Survey of Numismatic Research, 1966–1971* (New York: International Numismatic Commission, 1973); Peter Berghaus, Robert A. G. Carson, and Nicholas M. Lowick, *A Survey of Numismatic Research, 1972–1977* (Berne: International Association of Professional Numismatists, 1979); Martin Price, *A Survey of Numismatic Research, 1978–1984* (London: International Numismatic Commission, 1986); Tony Hackens, *A Survey of Numismatic Research, 1985–1990* (Brussels: International Numismatic Commission, 1991); John Kleeberg, Hermann Maué, Lutz Ilisch, Bernd Kluge, Wolfgang Steguweit, Andrew Burnett, and Cécile Morrisson, *A Survey of Numismatic Research, 1990–1995* (Berlin: International Association of Professional Numismatists, 1997); Carmen Alfaro and Andrew Burnett, *A Survey of Numismatic Research, 1996–2001* (Madrid: Madrid International Numismatic Commission 2003); Michel Amandry and Philip Attwood, *A Survey of Numismatic Research, 2002–2007* (Glasgow: International Association of Professional Numismatists, 2009); Carmen Arnold-Biucchi and Maria Caccamo-Caltabiano, *A Survey of Numismatic Research, 2008–2013* (Taormina: International Association of Professional Numismatists, 2015).

[5] William E. Daehn, *Ancient Greek Numismatics: A Guide to Reading and Research; A Bibliography of Works Written in English with Summaries of Their Contents* (London: Classical Numismatic Group Inc., 2012).

[6] Philip Grierson, *Bibliographie Numismatique*, 2nd ed. (Brussels: Cercle d'Études Numismatiques, 2001).

[7] John Casey and Richard Reece, *Coins and the Archaeologist* (Oxford: British Archaeological Reports, 1974).

[8] Giovanni Gorini, *I ritrovamenti monetali nel mondo antico: Problemi e metodi* (Padua, Italy: Esedra, 2003).

The Study of Coinage 45

Several specific studies have been published which are more akin to excavation reports but which focus on the numismatic material. Kevin Butcher's volume on ancient Berytus (Beirut) is an ideal example of a well-documented publication of emergency archaeology, that is, a site threatened by modern development.[9]

Single or multi-volume surveys or introductions to the field are quite common, but a select few stand out. On methodology C. Howgego[10] (in English) and F. Rebuffat[11] (in French) are indispensable, and should be the starting point for an introduction to the field. E. Babelon[12] (in French) provides a most helpful history of the study of ancient coinage from the sixteenth to the nineteenth centuries,[13] and a general survey of Greek and Roman coins in antiquity. Despite its age it offers a comprehensive survey of relevant material, especially on the development of coinage. Barclay V. Head's *Historia Numorum*[14] is one of the most popular and regularly reprinted surveys of Greek and Roman coinage in English. Colin M. Kraay's *Archaic and Classical Greek Coins*[15] is a reputable and popular introduction to early Greek coinage from the sixth to the fourth centuries BCE. It has value despite some of his conclusions challenged by recent discoveries and new interpretations. Despite its title, Otto Mørkholm posthumously published survey, *Early Hellenistic Coinage: From the Accession of Alexander to the Peace of Apamea (336–188 B.C.)*,[16] is useful for material into the first century BCE. However, the most up to date, thorough and extensive introduction is William Metcalf's *Oxford Handbook of Greek and Roman Coinage* which includes extensive bibliographies for all essays in chapters addressing Archaic and Classical, Hellenistic and Roman coinage.[17] Matthew J. Ponting's chapter (pp. 12–32) on 'The Substance of Coinage: The Role of Scientific Analysis in Ancient Numismatics' is particularly illuminating. Andrew Burnett's introductory volume provides a succinct and articulate account of the coinages of the Roman Republic and Empire as well as to their use as historical and economic evidence.[18] Kevin Butcher offers a brief overview of the coinages produced outside Rome and the official imperial mints in the Roman provinces, and provides relevant historical and geographical context, while highlighting the various methodological problems associated with their interpretation.[19] Michael H. Crawford's

---

[9]   Kevin Butcher, *Small Change in Ancient Beirut: The Coin Finds from bey 006 and bey 045, Persian, Hellenistic, Roman, and Byzantine Periods* (Beirut: American University, 2002).

[10] C. Howgego, *Ancient History from Coins* (London: Routledge, 1995).

[11] F. Rebuffat, *La Monnaie dans L'antiquité* (Paris: Picard, 1996).

[12] Ernest Babelon, *Traité de Monnaies Grecques et Romaines*, 4 vols. (Paris: E. Leroux, 1901–1933).

[13] On the history of numismatics, see E. E. Clain-Stefanelli, 'Numismatics – An Ancient Science. A Survey of Its History', in *Contributions from the Museum of History and Technology*, ed. Vladimir Clain-Stefanelli and E. E Clain-Stefanelli (Washington, DC: Smithsonian Institution, 1970), paper 32, 1–102.

[14] Barclay V. Head, *Historia Numorum*, 2nd ed. (London: Clarendon, 1911).

[15] C. M. Kraay, *Archaic and Classical Greek Coins* (London: Methuen, 1976), 21–22.

[16] Otto Mørkholm, *Early Hellenistic Coinage: From the Accession of Alexander to the Peace of Apamea (336–188 B.C.)* (Cambridge: Cambridge University Press, 1991), 81.

[17] William Metcalf, *Oxford Handbook of Greek and Roman Coinage* (Oxford: Oxford University Press, 2012).

[18] Andrew Burnett, *Coinage in the Roman World* (London: Seaby, 1987).

[19] Kevin Butcher, *Roman Provincial Coins: An Introduction to the 'Greek Imperials'* (London: Seaby, 1988).

one-volume survey distils the complex issues around Roman coin production and circulation in connection with the expansion of Roman military.[20] Harold Mattingly offers a broad survey of the republican and imperial coinages.[21] Kenneth W. Harl's introduction provides a survey of the development of Roman coinage from the fourth century BCE to the fifth century CE.[22] Theodor Mommsen's early German study, while outdated, is regularly cited in contemporary secondary literature.[23]

Although Republican coinage most typically refers to coinage produced during the period of the fourth century BCE to 27 BCE, where Romans adopted and adapted Greek coinage for their own distinctive expression.[24] There have been various attempts to catalogue republican coinage according to the family of the issuing moneyer such as the early endeavour by Ernest Babelon's French work of 1885,[25] *Description Historique et Chronologique de monnaies de la République Romaine*, where material is organized by gens. More recent works by E. A. Sydenham in 1952, *Coinage of the Roman Republic*,[26] and M. H. Crawford in 1974, *Roman Republican Coinage*,[27] are commonly referred to in secondary literature. Crawford, in particular, incorporates new dating evidence and archaeological material excavated in the 1960s. Françoise De Callataÿ's monograph, *L'histoire des Guerres Mithridatiques vue par les Monnaies*,[28] used a quantitative approach to assess coinage produced during the period of the Mithridatic Wars (89–63 BCE) and to calculate the number of dies originally used per issue, and then multiplies by an estimate of coin production per die and determine the coinage total. Although there are some valid observations noted in this discussion, Callataÿ's conclusions should be read in light of Buttrey and Buttrey,[29] who outline a range of methodological concerns regarding the quantification of ancient coin production through the use of mathematical formulas when other considerations such as the treasury orders which the production filled are almost completely unknown, they conclude that 'there is no way to calculate coin output for any issue even when the number of dies used is known'.[30]

Roman imperial coinage traditionally denotes coinage produced in Rome or subsidiary imperial mints from the time that Octavian received the title Augustus (27 BCE) until

---

[20] Michael H. Crawford, *Coinage and Money under the Roman Republic: Italy and the Mediterranean Economy* (Berkeley: University of California Press, 1985).

[21] H. Mattingly, *Roman Coins from the Earliest Times to the Fall of the Western Empire*, 2nd ed. (London: Methuen, 1960).

[22] Kenneth W. Harl, *Coinage in the Roman Economy* (Baltimore, MD: Johns Hopkins University Press, 1996).

[23] Theodor Mommsen, *Geschichte des römischen Münzwesens* (Berlin: Weidmann, 1860).

[24] Andrew Burnett discusses Greek influence on the design of early Roman coinage, Andrew Burnett, 'The Iconography of Roman Coin Types in the Third Century BC', *Numismatic Chronicle* 146 (1986): 67–75.

[25] Ernest Babelon, *Description Historique et Chronologique de monnaies de la République Romaine* (Paris: Rollin et Feuardent, 1885).

[26] Edward Allen Sydenham, *Coinage of the Roman Republic* (London: Spink, 1952).

[27] Michael H. Crawford, *Roman Republican Coinage* (New York: Cambridge University Press, 1974).

[28] Françoise De Callataÿ, *L'histoire des Guerres Mithridatiques vue par les Monnaies* (Louvain-la-Neuve: Département d'archéologie et d'histoire de l'art, Séminaire de numismatique Marcel Hoc, 1997).

[29] T. Buttrey and S. Buttrey, 'Calculating Ancient Coin Production Again', *American Journal of Numismatics* 9 (1997): 113–135.

[30] Buttrey and Buttrey, 'Calculating', 114.

Anastasius I established the first Byzantine imperial coinage (498 CE). There is little value, in the present context, to detail the many historical attempts from the sixteenth century onwards, to categorize and classify the Roman imperial coinage en toto. Rather, it is sufficient for our purposes to bring to attention four works, three to embrace and one to avoid. First, Jean-Baptiste Giard's three-volume work in French[31] is a significant catalogue which includes commentary and presents the holdings of the Bibliothèque Nationale de France. To date only five volumes have appeared, covering the reigns of Augustus (volume 1), the period from Tiberius to Nero (volume 2), the period from the crisis of 68 CE to the reign of Nerva (volume 3), the period of Trajan (volume 4), and the period of Aurelian, Severina, Tacitus and Florian (volume 12). Second, C. H. V. Sutherland and C. M. Kraay document coins struck under Augustus in the Ashmolean Collection in their volume and combine imperial and provincial coinage, a helpful collation of numismatic primary source material for the Augustan period.[32] Third, Henry Cohen's French catalogue, *Description Historique des Monnaies Frappées sous l'Empire Romaine*,[33] is the source upon which most derivative corpora are based. It must be used with great discernment as it includes several errors, even in later works. Finally, by far the most successful, exhaustive and accurate published corpus of Roman imperial numismatic material is Harold Mattingly's ten-volume edited work *The Roman Imperial Coinage*,[34] commonly abbreviated as RIC in the literature. It is the golden standard corpus for Roman imperial coins from Augustus (27 BCE) to the Divided Empire (491 CE). In addition to the detailed history of the coinage, including a description of legend, type and other standard features, the authors provide notation on the rarity of known examples.[35] Several volumes have been revised, with updated material expected in the process of further revision.

Roman provincial coinage is commonly understood to refer to that which is produced by Greek cities under imperial rule. Traditionally these coins were catalogued as Greek imperial coinage, and are found in what is known as the 'sylloges' which deserve our attention before commenting on the latest developments in catalogues of provincial coinages. The *Sylloge Nummorum Graecorum* (SNG; trans. 'Collection of Greek Coins') was a project that was originally funded by the British Academy in 1930 for the publication of Greek coins in private and public collections in the UK. Since then the initiative has expanded to include over 200 published volumes in collections from 23 countries, tabulated below in alphabetical order with accompanying abbreviations[36] for ease of reference (see Tables 3–6).

---

[31] Jean-Baptiste Giard, *Bibliothèque Nationale: Catalogue des Monnaies de l'empire Romaine*, 3 vols. (Paris: Bibliothèque Nationale de France, 1976–2008).

[32] C. H. V. Sutherland, and C. M. Kraay, *Coins of the Roman Empire in the Ashmolean Museum. Vol. 1, Augustus, c. 31 B.C.–A.D. 14* (Oxford: Clarendon, 1975). See further Rodolfo Martini and N. Vismara, *Sylloge Nummorum Romanorum Italia: Milano; Civiche Raccolte Numismatiche* (Milan: Civiche Raccolte Numismatiche, 1990–1994), and Anne S. Robertson, *Roman Imperial Coins in the Hunter Coin Cabinet* (Oxford: Oxford University Press, 1962–1982).

[33] Henry Cohen, *Description Historique des Monnaies Frappées sous l'Empire Romaine*, 2nd ed. (Paris: Rollin and Feuardent, 1890–1892).

[34] H. Mattingly, *The Roman Imperial Coinage*, 10 vols. (London: Spink, 1923–2007).

[35] The notation is as follows: C: common; R1: rare, only twenty or so known; R2: between five and fifteen known; R3: four or five known; R4: two or three known; R5: only one known, unique.

[36] The nation abbreviation, for example SNG Österreich is an umbrella term for any of the SNG volumes listed below it, in this case any of SNG Dreer 1, SNG Dreer 2, SNG Dreer 3, SNG Leypold 1, and SNG Leypold 2.

48 Numismatics and Greek Lexicography

Table 3 Published volumes of the *Sylloge Nummorum Graecorum*

Australia	SNG Australia
Sheedy, K. A. *Sylloge Nummorum Graecorum: Australia 1. Australian Centre for Ancient Numismatic Studies: The Gale Collection of South Italian Coins*. Sydney: Numismatic Association of Australia, 2008.	SNG Gale
Austria	SNG Österreich
Springschitz, L. *Sylloge Nummorum Graecorum [:Österreich]. Sammlung Dreer, Klagenfurt, im Landesmuseum für Kärnten: Teil 1. Italien, Sizilien*. Klagenfurt: Geschichtsverein für Kärnten, 1967.	SNG Dreer 1
Springschitz, L. *Sylloge Nummorum Graecorum [:Österreich]. Sammlung Dreer, Klagenfurt, im Landesmuseum für Kärnten: 2. Spanien, Gallien, Keltenländer*. Klagenfurt: Geschichtsverein für Kärnten, 1984.	SNG Dreer 2
Springschitz, L. *Sylloge Nummorum Graecorum [:Österreich]. Sammlung Dreer, Klagenfurt, im Landesmuseum für Kärnten: Teil 3. Thracien – Macedonien, Päonien*. Klagenfurt: Geschichtsverein für Kärnten, 1999.	SNG Dreer 3
Szaivert W., and C. Daburon, *Sylloge Nummorum Graecorum: Österreich. Sammlung Leypold, Wiener Neustadt: Kleinasiatische Münzender Kaiserzeit. 1 Pontus – Lydien*. Vienna: Institutfür Numismatik und Geldgeschichte, 2000.	SNG Leypold 1
Szaivert, W., and C. Daburon, *Sylloge Nummorum Graecorum: Österreich. Sammlung Leypold, Wiener Neustadt: Kleinasiatische Münzen der Kaiserzeit. 2 Phrygien – Kommagene: mit Nachträgen, Korrekturen und Indizes zu beiden Bänden*. Wien: Institut für Numismatik und Geldgeschichte, 2004.	SNG Leypold 2
Belgium	SNG Belgium
Bar, M. *Sylloge Nummorum Graecorum: Belgique 1. Bibliothèque Royale de Belgique: La collection de bronzes grecs de Marc Bar*. Bruxelles: Bibliothèque Royale de Belgique, 2007.	SNG Bar
Brazil	SNG Brasil
Magalhães, M. M. *Sylloge Nummorum Graecorum: Brasil. Museu Histórico Nacional: Moedas gregas e provinciais romanas*. Rio de Janeiro: Museu Histórico Nacional, 2011.	SNG Brasil 1
Bulgaria	SNG Bulgaria
Draganov, D. *Sylloge Nummorum Graecorum: Bulgaria. Ruse. Bobokov Brothers Collection: Thrace & Moesia Inferior. Part 1. Deultum*. Ruse: Bobokov Brothers Foundation, 2005.	SNG Deultum 1
Croatia	SNG Croatia
Mirnik, I. *Sylloge Nummorum Graecorum: Croatia. Zagreb. The Archaeological Museum Numismatic Collection. Part 8. Aegyptus. Ptolemaei–Roman Provincial Coinage*. Zagreb: Archaeological Museum of Zagreb, 2017.	SNG Croatia 8

Czech Republic	SNG Czech Republic
Militký, J. *Sylloge Nummorum Graecorum: Czech Republic 1. The National Museum, Prague. Part 3. Macedonia and Paeonia.* Prague: The National Museum, 2016.	SNG Czech Republic 3
Denmark	SNG Denmark
Schwabacher, W., and C. Jørgenstein, *Sylloge Nummorum Graecorum: Denmark. The Royal Collection of Coins and Medals, Danish National Museum. Part 1. Italy 1: Etruria-Campania.* Copenhagen: Munksgaard, 1942.	SNG Cop. 1
Schwabacher, W. and C. Jørgenstein, *Sylloge Nummorum Graecorum: Denmark. The Royal Collection of Coins and Medals, Danish National Museum. Part 2. Italy 2: Apulia-Lucania (Metapontum).* Copenhagen: Munksgaard, 1942.	SNG Cop. 2
Schwabacher, W. and C. Jørgenstein, *Sylloge Nummorum Graecorum: Denmark. The Royal Collection of Coins and Medals, Danish National Museum. Part 3. Italy 3: Lucania (Poseidonia)-Bruttium.* Copenhagen: Munksgaard, 1942.	SNG Cop. 3
Breitenstein, N. *Sylloge Nummorum Graecorum: Denmark. The Royal Collection of Coins and Medals, Danish National Museum. Part 4. Sicily 1: Abacaenum-Petra.* Copenhagen: Munksgaard, 1942.	SNG Cop. 4
Breitenstein, N. *Sylloge Nummorum Graecorum: Denmark. The Royal Collection of Coins and Medals, Danish National Museum. Part 5. Sicily 2: Segesta-Sardinia.* Copenhagen: Munksgaard, 1942.	SNG Cop. 5
Schwabacher, W. *Sylloge Nummorum Graecorum: Denmark. The Royal Collection of Coins and Medals, Danish National Museum. Part 6. Thrace 1: The Tauric Chersonese-Thrace (Mesembria).* Copenhagen: Munksgaard, 1942.	SNG Cop. 6
Schwabacher, W. *Sylloge Nummorum Graecorum: Denmark. The Royal Collection of Coins and Medals, Danish National Museum. Part 7. Thrace 2: Odessus-Sestos. Islands. Kings and Dynasts.* Copenhagen: Munksgaard, 1943.	SNG Cop. 7
Breitenstein, N. *Sylloge Nummorum Graecorum: Denmark. The Royal Collection of Coins and Medals, Danish National Museum. Part 8. Macedonia 1: Acanthus-Uranopolis. Dynasts.* Copenhagen: Munksgaard, 1943.	SNG Cop. 8
Breitenstein, N. *Sylloge Nummorum Graecorum: Denmark. The Royal Collection of Coins and Medals, Danish National Museum. Part 9. Macedonia 2: Alexander I-Alexander III.* Copenhagen: Munksgaard, 1943.	SNG Cop. 9
Breitenstein, N. *Sylloge Nummorum Graecorum: Denmark. The Royal Collection of Coins and Medals, Danish National Museum. Part 10. Macedonia 3: Philip III-Philip VI. Macedonia under the Romans. Kings of Paeonia.* Copenhagen: Munksgaard, 1943.	SNG Cop. 10
Schwabacher, W. *Sylloge Nummorum Graecorum: Denmark. The Royal Collection of Coins and Medals, Danish National Museum. Part 11. Thessaly-Illyricum.* Copenhagen: Munksgaard, 1943.	SNG Cop. 11

(Continued)

Schwabacher, W. *Sylloge Nummorum Graecorum: Denmark. The Royal Collection of Coins and Medals, Danish National Museum. Part 12. Epirus-Acarnania.* Copenhagen: Munksgaard, 1943. SNG Cop. 12

Schwabacher, W., and N. Breitenstein, *Sylloge Nummorum Graecorum: Denmark. The Royal Collection of Coins and Medals, Danish National Museum. Part 13. Aetolia-Euboea.* Copenhagen: Munksgaard, 1944. SNG Cop. 13

Schwabacher W., and N. Breitenstein, *Sylloge Nummorum Graecorum: Denmark. The Royal Collection of Coins and Medals, Danish National Museum. Part 14. Attica-Aegina.* Copenhagen: Munksgaard, 1944. SNG Cop. 14

Schwabacher W., and N. Breitenstein, *Sylloge Nummorum Graecorum: Denmark. The Royal Collection of Coins and Medals, Danish National Museum. Part 15. Corinth.* Copenhagen: Munksgaard, 1944. SNG Cop. 15

Schwabacher W., and N. Breitenstein, *Sylloge Nummorum Graecorum: Denmark. The Royal Collection of Coins and Medals, Danish National Museum. Part 16. Phliasia-Laconia.* Copenhagen: Munksgaard, 1944. SNG Cop. 16

Breitenstein, N. *Sylloge Nummorum Graecorum: Denmark. The Royal Collection of Coins and Medals, Danish National Museum. Part 17. Argolis-Aegean Islands.* Copenhagen: Munksgaard, 1944. SNG Cop. 17

Breitenstein, N. *Sylloge Nummorum Graecorum: Denmark. The Royal Collection of Coins and Medals, Danish National Museum. Part 18. Bosporus-Bithynia.* Copenhagen: Munksgaard, 1944. SNG Cop. 18

Breitenstein, N. *Sylloge Nummorum Graecorum: Denmark. The Royal Collection of Coins and Medals, Danish National Museum. Part 19. Mysia.* Copenhagen: Munksgaard, 1945. SNG Cop. 19

Breitenstein, N. *Sylloge Nummorum Graecorum: Denmark. The Royal Collection of Coins and Medals, Danish National Museum. Part 20. Troas.* Copenhagen: Munksgaard, 1945. SNG Cop. 20

Breitenstein, N. *Sylloge Nummorum Graecorum: Denmark. The Royal Collection of Coins and Medals, Danish National Museum. Part 21. Aeolis-Lesbos.* Copenhagen: Munksgaard, 1945. SNG Cop. 21

Breitenstein, N. *Sylloge Nummorum Graecorum: Denmark. The Royal Collection of Coins and Medals, Danish National Museum. Part 22. Ionia 1: (Clazomenae-Ephesus).* Copenhagen: Munksgaard, 1946. SNG Cop. 22

Breitenstein, N. *Sylloge Nummorum Graecorum: Denmark. The Royal Collection of Coins and Medals, Danish National Museum. Part 23. Ionia 2: (Erythrae-Priene).* Copenhagen: Munksgaard, 1946. SNG Cop. 23

Breitenstein, N. *Sylloge Nummorum Graecorum: Denmark. The Royal Collection of Coins and Medals, Danish National Museum. Part 24. Ionia 3: (Smyrna-Teos. Islands).* Copenhagen: Munksgaard, 1946. SNG Cop. 24

Breitenstein, N. *Sylloge Nummorum Graecorum: Denmark. The Royal Collection of Coins and Medals, Danish National Museum. Part 25. Caria 1: (Alabanda-Orthosia).* Copenhagen: Munksgaard, 1947. SNG Cop. 25

Breitenstein, N. *Sylloge Nummorum Graecorum: Denmark. The Royal Collection of Coins and Medals, Danish National Museum. Part 26. Caria 2: (Sebastopolis-Trapezopolis). Satraps. Islands.* Copenhagen: Munksgaard, 1947. SNG Cop. 26

The Study of Coinage

Breitenstein, N. *Sylloge Nummorum Graecorum: Denmark. The Royal Collection of Coins and Medals, Danish National Museum. Part 27. Lydia 1: (Acrasus-Saïtta).* Copenhagen: Munksgaard, 1947.
SNG Cop. 27

Breitenstein, N. *Sylloge Nummorum Graecorum: Denmark. The Royal Collection of Coins and Medals, Danish National Museum. Part 28. Lydia2: (Sala-Tripolis).* Copenhagen: Munksgaard, 1947.
SNG Cop. 28

Breitenstein, N. *Sylloge Nummorum Graecorum: Denmark. The Royal Collection of Coins and Medals, Danish National Museum. Part 29. Phrygia 1: (Abbaïtis-Eumeneia).* Copenhagen: Munksgaard, 1948.
SNG Cop. 29

Breitenstein, N. *Sylloge Nummorum Graecorum: Denmark. The Royal Collection of Coins and Medals, Danish National Museum. Part 30. Phrygia 2: (Grimenothyrae-Trajanopolis).* Copenhagen: Munksgaard, 1948.
SNG Cop. 30

Breitenstein, N., and O. Mørkholm, *Sylloge Nummorum Graecorum: Denmark. The Royal Collection of Coins and Medals, Danish National Museum. Part 31. Lycia. Pamphylia.* Copenhagen: Munksgaard, 1955.
SNG Cop. 31

Breitenstein, N., and O. Mørkholm, *Sylloge Nummorum Graecorum: Denmark. The Royal Collection of Coins and Medals, Danish National Museum. Part 32. Pisidia.* Copenhagen: Munksgaard, 1956.
SNG Cop. 32

Breitenstein, N., and O. Mørkholm, *Sylloge Nummorum Graecorum: Denmark. The Royal Collection of Coins and Medals, Danish National Museum. Part 33. Lycaonia-Cilicia.* Copenhagen: Munksgaard, 1956.
SNG Cop. 33

Mørkholm, O. *Sylloge Nummorum Graecorum: Denmark. The Royal Collection of Coins and Medals, Danish National Museum. Part 34. Cyprus-Cappadocia. Uncertain Coins. Imperial Cistophori.* Copenhagen: Munksgaard, 1956.
SNG Cop. 34

Mørkholm, O. *Sylloge Nummorum Graecorum: Denmark. The Royal Collection of Coins and Medals, Danish National Museum. Part 35. Syria: Seleucid Kings.* Copenhagen: Munksgaard, 1959.
SNG Cop. 35

Mørkholm, O. *Sylloge Nummorum Graecorum: Denmark. The Royal Collection of Coins and Medals, Danish National Museum. Part 36. Syria: Cities.* Copenhagen: Munksgaard, 1959.
SNG Cop. 36

Mørkholm, O. *Sylloge Nummorum Graecorum: Denmark. The Royal Collection of Coins and Medals, Danish National Museum. Part 37. Phoenicia.* Copenhagen: Munksgaard, 1961.
SNG Cop. 37

Mørkholm, O. *Sylloge Nummorum Graecorum: Denmark. The Royal Collection of Coins and Medals, Danish National Museum. Part 38. Palestine-Characene.* Copenhagen: Munksgaard, 1961.
SNG Cop. 38

Jacobsen, A., and O. Mørkholm, *Sylloge Nummorum Graecorum: Denmark. The Royal Collection of Coins and Medals, Danish National Museum. Part 39. Parthia-India.* Copenhagen: Munksgaard, 1965.
SNG Cop. 39

Kromann, A., and O. Mørkholm, *Sylloge Nummorum Graecorum: Denmark. The Royal Collection of Coins and Medals, Danish National Museum. Part 40. Egypt: The Ptolemies.* Copenhagen: Munksgaard, 1977.
SNG Cop. 40

Christiansen, E., and A. Kromann, *Sylloge Nummorum Graecorum: Denmark. The Royal Collection of Coins and Medals, Danish National Museum. Part 41. Alexandria-Cyrenaica.* Copenhagen: Munksgaard, 1974.
SNG Cop. 41

(Continued)

Jenkins, G. K. *Sylloge Nummorum Graecorum: Denmark. The Royal Collection of Coins and Medals, Danish National Museum. Part 42. North Africa. Syrtica-Mauretania.* Copenhagen: Munksgaard, 1969.	SNG Cop. 42
Jenkins, G. K., and A. Kromann, *Sylloge Nummorum Graecorum: Denmark. The Royal Collection of Coins and Medals, Danish National Museum. Part 43. Spain-Gaul.* Copenhagen: Munksgaard, 1979.	SNG Cop. 43
Schultz, S., and J. Zahle, *Sylloge Nummorum Graecorum: Denmark. The Royal Collection of Coins and Medals, Danish National Museum. Supplement. Acquisitions 1942–1996.* Copenhagen: Munksgaard, 2002.	SNG Cop. Supp.
Mathiesen, H. E. *Sylloge Nummorum Graecorum: Denmark. Aarhus University Part 1. Aarhus University Collection.* Copenhagen: Munksgaard, 1986.	SNG Aarhus 1
Mathiesen, H. E. *Sylloge Nummorum Graecorum: Denmark. Aarhus University Part 2. The Fabricius Collection (Collections of Aarhus University and the Danish National Museum).* Copenhagen: Munksgaard, 1987.	SNG Aarhus 2

Finland	SNG Finland
Westermark, U., and R. H. J. Ashton. *Sylloge Nummorum Graecorum: Finland. The Erkki Keckman Collection in the Skopbank, Helsinki. Part 1. Karia.* Helsinki: Finnish Society of Sciences and Letters, 1994.	SNG Keckman 1
Ashton, R. H. J. *Sylloge Nummorum Graecorum: Finland. The Erkki Keckman Collection in the Skopbank, Helsinki. Part 2. Asia Minor Except Karia.* Helsinki: Finnish Society of Sciences and Letters, 1999.	SNG Keckman 2

France	SNG France
Nicolet-Pierre, H., J. Delepierre, M. Delepierre, and G. Le Rider, *Sylloge Nummorum Graecorum: France 1. Bibliothèque Nationale de France: Collection Jeanet Marie Delepierre.* Paris: Bibliothèque Nationale de France, 1983.	SNG Paris 1
Levante, E. *Sylloge Nummorum Graecorum: France 2. Bibliothèque Nationale de France: Cilicie.* Paris and Zurich: Bibliothèque Nationale de France and Numismatica Ars Classica, 1993.	SNG Paris 2
Levante, E. *Sylloge Nummorum Graecorum: France 3.* Bibliothèque Nationale de France: Pamphylie, Pisidie, Lycaonie, Galatie. Paris and Zurich: Bibliothèque Nationale de France and Numismatica Ars Classica, 1994.	SNG Paris 3
Bakhoum, S. *Sylloge Nummorum Graecorum: France 4. Bibliothèque Nationale de France: Alexandrie 1, Auguste-Trajan.* Paris and Zurich: Bibliothèque Nationale de France and Numismatica Ars Classica, 1998.	SNG Paris 4
Levante, E. *Sylloge Nummorum Graecorum: France 5. Bibliothèque Nationale de France: Mysie.* Paris and Zurich: Bibliothèque Nationale de France and Numismatica Ars Classica, 2001.	SNG Paris 5
Parente, A. R. *Sylloge Nummorum Graecorum: France 6. Bibliothèque Nationale de France: Italie 1, Étrurie, Calabre.* Paris and Zurich: Bibliothèque Nationale de France and Numismatica Ars Classica, 2003.	SNG Paris 6

Dalaison, J. *Sylloge Nummorum Graecorum, France 7, Bibliothèque Nationale de France: Paphlagonie, Pont, Arménie Mineure.* Bordeaux: Ausonius, 2015.	SNG Paris 7

Germany	SNG Deutschland
Kleiner, G. *Sylloge Nummorum Graecorum: Deutschland. Sammlung v. Aulock: Hefte 1.-3. Pontus, Paphlagonien, Bithynien.* Berlin: Gebrüder Mann, 1957.	SNG von Aulock 1–3
Kleiner, G. *Sylloge Nummorum Graecorum: Deutschland. Sammlung v. Aulock: Heft 4. Mysien.* Berlin: Gebrüder Mann, 1957.	SNG von Aulock 4
Kleiner, G. *Sylloge Nummorum Graecorum: Deutschland. Sammlung v. Aulock: Heft 5. 5. Troas, Aeolis, Lesbos.* Berlin: Gebrüder Mann, 1959.	SNG von Aulock 5
Küthmann, H., and K. Kraft. *Sylloge Nummorum Graecorum: Deutschland. Sammlung v. Aulock: Heft 6. Ionien.* Berlin: Gebrüder Mann, 1960.	SNG von Aulock 6
Kraft, K., and D. Kienast. *Sylloge Nummorum Graecorum: Deutschland. Sammlung v. Aulock: Heft 7. Karien.* Berlin: Gebrüder Mann, 1962.	SNG von Aulock 7
Von Aulock, H. *Sylloge Nummorum Graecorum: Deutschland. Sammlung v. Aulock: Heft 8. Lydien.* Berlin: Gebrüder Mann, 1963.	SNG von Aulock 8
Ritter, H.-W. *Sylloge Nummorum Graecorum: Deutschland. Sammlung v. Aulock: Heft 9. Phrygien.* Berlin: Gebrüder Mann, 1964.	SNG von Aulock 9
Mørkholm, O. *Sylloge Nummorum Graecorum: Deutschland. Sammlung v. Aulock: Heft 10. Lykien.* Berlin: Gebrüder Mann, 1964.	SNG von Aulock 10
Mørkholm, O. *Sylloge Nummorum Graecorum: Deutschland. Sammlung v. Aulock: Heft 11. Pamphylien.* Berlin: Gebrüder Mann, 1965.	SNG von Aulock 11
Von Aulock, H. *Sylloge Nummorum Graecorum: Deutschland. Sammlung v. Aulock: Heft 12. Pisidien, Lykaonien, Isaurien.* Berlin: Gebrüder Mann, 1964.	SNG von Aulock 12
Von Aulock, H. *Sylloge Nummorum Graecorum: Deutschland. Sammlung v. Aulock: Heft 13. Kilikien.* Berlin: Gebrüder Mann, 1966.	SNG von Aulock 13
Von Aulock, H., and P. R. Franke. *Sylloge Nummorum Graecorum: Deutschland. Sammlung v. Aulock: Heft 14. Galatien, Kappadokien, kaiserzeitliche Kistophoren, posthume Lysimachus- und Alexander-tetradrachmen, Incerti.* Berlin: Gebrüder Mann, 1967.	SNG von Aulock 14
Von Aulock, H., and P. R. Franke. *Sylloge Nummorum Graecorum: Deutschland. Sammlung v. Aulock: Heft 15. Nachträge 1. Pontus, Armenia Minor, Paphlagonien, Bithynien.* Berlin: Gebrüder Mann, 1967.	SNG von Aulock 15
Von Aulock, H., and P. R. Franke. *Sylloge Nummorum Graecorum: Deutschland. Sammlung v. Aulock: Heft 16. Nachträge 2. Mysien,Troas, Aeolis, Lesbos.* Berlin: Gebrüder Mann, 1967.	SNG von Aulock 16
Von Aulock, H., P. R. Franke. *Sylloge Nummorum Graecorum: Deutschland. Sammlung v. Aulock: Heft 17. Nachträge 3. Ionien, Karien, Lydien.* Berlin: Gebrüder Mann, 1968.	SNG von Aulock 17

(Continued)

Von Aulock, H., P. R. Franke. *Sylloge Nummorum Graecorum: Deutschland. Sammlung v. Aulock: Heft 18. Nachträge 4. Phrygien, Lykien, Pamphylien, Pisidien, Lykaonien, Isaurien, Kilikien, Galatien, Kappadokien, kaiserzeitl. Kistophoren, Incerti.* Berlin: Gebrüder Mann, 1968. — SNG von Aulock 18

Franke, P. R., W. Leschhorn, and A. U. Stylow. *Sylloge Nummorum Graecorum: Deutschland. Sammlung v. Aulock: Index.* Berlin: Gebrüder Mann, 1981. — SNG von Aulock Index

Franke, P. R., and H. Küthmann. *Sylloge Nummorum Graecorum: Deutschland. Staatliche Münzsammlung München: Heft 1. Hispania – Gallia Narbonensis.* Berlin: Gebrüder Mann, 1968. — SNG München 1

Franke, P. R., and H. Küthmann. *Sylloge Nummorum Graecorum: Deutschland. Staatliche Münzsammlung München: Heft 2. Etruria – Umbria – Picenum – Latium – Samnium – Frentani – Campania -Apulia.* Berlin: Gebrüder Mann, 1970. — SNG München 2

Franke, P. R., and H. Küthmann. *Sylloge Nummorum Graecorum: Deutschland. Staatliche Münzsammlung München: Heft 3. Kalabrien – Lukanien.* Berlin: Gebrüder Mann, 1973. — SNG München 3

Franke, P. R., and H. Küthmann. *Sylloge Nummorum Graecorum: Deutschland. Staatliche Münzsammlung München: Heft 4. Bruttium – Karthager in Italien.* Berlin: Gebrüder Mann, 1974. — SNG München 4

Franke, P. R., and S. Grunauer von Hoerschelmann. *Sylloge Nummorum Graecorum: Deutschland. Staatliche Münzsammlung München: Heft 5. Sikelia.* Berlin: Gebrüder Mann, 1977. — SNG München 5

Küthmann, H., U. Pause-Dreyer, *Sylloge Nummorum Graecorum: Deutschland. Staatliche Münzsammlung München: Heft 6. Sikelia – Punier in Sizilien – Lipara – Sardinia – Punier in Sardinien – Nachträge.* Berlin: Gebrüder Mann, 1980. — SNG München 6

Küthmann, H., U. Pause-Dreyer, *Sylloge Nummorum Graecorum: Deutschland. Staatliche Münzsammlung München: Heft 7. Taurische Chersones – Sarmatien – Dacia – Moesia superior – Moesia inferior.* Berlin: Gebrüder Mann, 1985. — SNG München 7

Liampi, K. *S ylloge Nummorum Graecorum: Deutschland. Staatliche Münzsammlung München: Heft 10/11. Makedonien: Könige.* Berlin: Gebrüder Mann, 2001. — SNG München 10/11

Liampi, K. *Sylloge Nummorum Graecorum: Deutschland. Staatliche Münzsammlung München: Heft 12. Thessalien – Illyrien – Epirus – Korkyra.* Berlin: Gebrüder Mann, 2007. — SNG München 12

Kroll, J. H. *Sylloge Nummorum Graecorum: Deutschland. Staatliche Münzsammlung München: Heft 14. Attika – Megaris – Ägina.* Berlin: Gebrüder Mann, 2002. — SNG München 14

Baldus, H. R. *Sylloge Nummorum Graecorum: Deutschland. Staatliche Münzsammlung München: Heft 19. Troas – Lesbos.* Berlin: Gebrüder Mann, 1991. — SNG München 19

Klose, D. O. A. *Sylloge Nummorum Graecorum: Deutschland. Staatliche Münzsammlung München: Heft 20. Ionien 1: Frühes Elektron–Priene.* Berlin: Gebrüder Mann, 1995. — SNG München 20

The Study of Coinage

Baldus, H. R. *Sylloge Nummorum Graecorum: Deutschland. Staatliche Münzsammlung München: Heft 22. Karien.* Berlin: Gebrüder Mann, 2006.
SNG München 22

Leschhorn, W. *Sylloge Nummorum Graecorum: Deutschland. Staatliche Münzsammlung München: Heft 23. Lydien.* Berlin: Gebrüder Mann, 1997.
SNG München 23

Leschhorn, W. *Sylloge Nummorum Graecorum: Deutschland. Staatliche Münzsammlung München: Heft 24. Phrygien.* Berlin: Gebrüder Mann, 1989.
SNG München 24

Baldus, H. R. *Sylloge Nummorum Graecorum: Deutschland. Staatliche Münzsammlung München: Heft 28. Syrien: Nicht-königliche Prägungen.* Berlin: Gebrüder Mann, 2001.
SNG München 28

Mannsperger, D. *Sylloge Nummorum Graecorum: Deutschland. Münzsammlung der Universität Tübingen: Heft 1. Hispania – Sikelia.* Berlin: Gebrüder Mann, 1981.
SNG Tübingen 1

Mannsperger, D. *Sylloge Nummorum Graecorum: Deutschland. Münzsammlung der Universität Tübingen: Heft 2. Taurische Chersones – Korkyra.* Berlin: Gebrüder Mann, 1982.
SNG Tübingen 2

Mannsperger, D., and G. Fischer-Heetfeld. *Sylloge Nummorum Graecorum: Deutschland. Münzsammlung der Universität Tübingen: Heft 3 Akarnanien – Bithynien.* Berlin: Gebrüder Mann, 1985.
SNG Tübingen 3

Mannsperger, D. *Sylloge Nummorum Graecorum: Deutschland. Münzsammlung der Universität Tübingen: Heft 4. Mysien – Ionien.* Berlin: Gebrüder Mann, 1989.
SNG Tübingen 4

Mannsperger, D. *Sylloge Nummorum Graecorum: Deutschland. Münzsammlung der Universität Tübingen: Heft 5. Karien und Lydien.* Berlin: Gebrüder Mann, 1994.
SNG Tübingen 5

Mannsperger, D., and M. Matzke. *Sylloge Nummorum Graecorum: Deutschland. Münzsammlungder Universität Tübingen: Heft 6. Phrygien – Kappadokien, Römische Provinzprägungen in Kleinasien.* Berlin: Gebrüder Mann, 1998.
SNG Tübingen 6

Schultz, S. *Sylloge Nummorum Graecorum: Deutschland. Sammlungder Universitätsbibliothek Leipzig: 1 Autonome griechische Münzen.* München: Hirmer, 1993.
SNG Leipzig 2

Hausmann, E. *Sylloge Nummorum Graecorum: Deutschland. Sammlung der Universitätsbibliothek Leipzig: 2 Römische Provinzialprägungen, Addenda und Corrigenda zum 1. Band.* München: Hirmer, 2008.
SNG Leipzig 2

Nollé, J. *Sylloge Nummorum Graecorum: Deutschland. Pfälzer Privatsammlungen: 4. Pamphylien.* München: Hirmer, 1993.
SNG Pfälz. 4

Nollé, J. *Sylloge Nummorum Graecorum: Deutschland. Pfälzer Privatsammlungen: 5. Pisidien und Lykaonien.* München: Hirmer, 1999.
SNG Pfälz. 5

Ziegler, R. *Sylloge Nummorum Graecorum: Deutschland. Pfälzer Privatsammlungen: 6. Isaurien und Kilikien.* München: Hirmer, 2001.
SNG Pfälz. 6

Leschhorn, W. *Sylloge Nummorum Graecorum: Deutschland. Herzog Anton Ulrich-Museum Braunschweig, Kunstmuseum des Landes Niedersachsen.* München: Hirmer, 1998.
SNG Braunschweig

(Continued)

Great Britain

Robinson, E. S. G. *Sylloge Nummorum Graecorum: Great Britain 1. Part 1: The Collection of Capt. E.G. Spencer-Churchill, M.C., of Northwick Park and The Salting Collection in the Victoria and Albert Museum.* London: Oxford University Press, 1931.
SNG UK 1

Robinson, E. S. G. *Sylloge Nummorum Graecorum: Great Britain 1. Part 2: The Newnham Davis Coins in the Wilson Collection of Classical and Eastern Antiquities. Marischal College, Aberdeen.* London: Oxford University Press, 1936.
SNG UK 2

Robinson, E. S. G. *Sylloge Nummorum Graecorum: Great Britain 2. The Lloyd Collection: Part 1. Etruria to Lucania (Thurium).* London: Oxford University Press, 1933.
SNG Lloyd 1

Robinson, E. S. G. *Sylloge Nummorum Graecorum: Great Britain 2. The Lloyd Collection: Part 2. Bruttium (Caulonia)-Sicily (Eryx).* London: Oxford University Press, 1934.
SNG Lloyd 2

Robinson, E. S. G. *Sylloge Nummorum Graecorum: Great Britain 2. The Lloyd Collection: Part 3. Sicily (Galaria-Selinus).* London: Oxford University Press, 1935.
SNG Lloyd 3

Robinson, E. S. G. *Sylloge Nummorum Graecorum: Great Britain 2. The Lloyd Collection: Part 4. Sicily (Syracuse-Lipara).* London: Oxford University Press, 1937.
SNG Lloyd 4

Robinson, E. S. G. *Sylloge Nummorum Graecorum: Great Britain 3. The Lockett Collection: Part 1. Spain-Italy (gold and silver).* London: Oxford University Press, 1938.
SNG Lockett 1

Robinson, E. S. G. *Sylloge Nummorum Graecorum: Great Britain 3. The Lockett Collection: Part 2. Sicily-Thrace (gold and silver).* London: Oxford University Press, 1939.
SNG Lockett 2

Robinson, E. S. G. *Sylloge Nummorum Graecorum: Great Britain 3. The Lockett Collection: Part 3. Macedonia-Aegina (gold and silver).* London: Oxford University Press, 1942.
SNG Lockett 3

Robinson, E. S. G. *Sylloge Nummorum Graecorum: Great Britain 3. The Lockett Collection: Part 4. Peloponnese-Aeolis (gold and silver).* London: Oxford University Press, 1945.
SNG Lockett 4

Robinson, E. S. G. *Sylloge Nummorum Graecorum: Great Britain 3. The Lockett Collection: Part 5. Lesbos-Cyrenaica. Addenda (gold and silver).* London: Oxford University Press, 1949.
SNG Lockett 5

Heichelheim, F. M. *Sylloge Nummorum Graecorum: Great Britain 4. Fitzwilliam Museum: Leake and General Collections: Part 1. Spain (Emporiae, Rhoda)-Italy.* London: Oxford University Press, 1940.
SNG Fitzwilliam 1

Heichelheim, F. M. *Sylloge Nummorum Graecorum: Great Britain 4. Fitzwilliam Museum: Leake and General Collections: Part 2. Sicily-Thrace.* London: Oxford University Press, 1947.
SNG Fitzwilliam 2

Heichelheim, F. M. *Sylloge Nummorum Graecorum: Great Britain 4. Fitzwilliam Museum: Leake and General Collections: Part 3. Macedonia-Acarnania (Anactorium).* London: Oxford University Press, 1951.
SNG Fitzwilliam 3

Heichelheim, F. M., and E. S. G. Robinson. *Sylloge Nummorum Graecorum: Great Britain 4. Fitzwilliam Museum: Leake and General Collections: Part 4. Acarnania (Argos Amphilochicum)- Phliasia.* London: Oxford University Press, 1956.	SNG Fitzwilliam 4
Heichelheim, F. M., and E. S. G. Robinson, *Sylloge Nummorum Graecorum: Great Britain 4. Fitzwilliam Museum: Leake and General Collections: Part 5. Sicyon-Thera.* London: Oxford University Press, 1958.	SNG Fitzwilliam 5
Heichelheim, F. M., E. S. G. Robinson, *Sylloge Nummorum Graecorum: Great Britain 4. Fitzwilliam Museum: Leake and General Collections: Part 6. Asia Minor: Pontus-Phrygia.* London: Oxford University Press, 1965.	SNG Fitzwilliam 6
Price, M. J. *Sylloge Nummorum Graecorum: Great Britain 4. Fitzwilliam Museum: Leake and General Collections: Part 7. Asia Minor: Lycia-Cappadocia.* London: Oxford University Press, 1967.	SNG Fitzwilliam 7
Price, M. J. *Sylloge Nummorum Graecorum: Great Britain 4. Fitzwilliam Museum: Leake and General Collections: Part 8. Syria-Nabathaea.* London: Oxford University Press, 1971.	SNG Fitzwilliam 8
Milne, J. G. *Sylloge Nummorum Graecorum: Great Britain 5. Ashmolean Museum (Oxford): Pt. 1, Evans Collection. Italy.* London: Oxford University Press, 1951.	SNG Ashmolean 1
Kraay, C. M. *Sylloge Nummorum Graecorum: Great Britain 5. Ashmolean Museum (Oxford): Pt. 1A, Etruria-Lucania (Thurium).* London: Oxford University Press, 1962.	SNG Ashmolean 1A
Kraay, C. M. *Sylloge Nummorum Graecorum: Great Britain 5. Ashmolean Museum (Oxford): Pt. 2, Italy: Lucania (Thurium) – Bruttium, Sicily, Carthage.* London: Oxford University Press, 1969.	SNG Ashmolean 2
Kraay, C. M. *Sylloge Nummorum Graecorum: Great Britain 5. Ashmolean Museum (Oxford): Pt. 3, Macedonia.* London: Oxford University Press, 1976.	SNG Ashmolean 3
King, C. E., and C. M. Kraay. *Sylloge Nummorum Graecorum: Great Britain 5. Ashmolean Museum (Oxford): Pt. 4, Paeonia-Thessaly.* London: Oxford University Press, 1981.	SNG Ashmolean 4
Ashton, R., and S. Ireland. *Sylloge Nummorum Graecorum: Great Britain 5. Ashmolean Museum (Oxford): Pt. 9, Bosporus-Aeolis.* London: Oxford University Press, 2007.	SNG Ashmolean 9
Ashton, R., and S. Ireland. *Sylloge Nummorum Graecorum: Great Britain 5. Ashmolean Museum (Oxford): Pt. 11, Caria to Commagene.* London: Oxford University Press, 2013.	SNG Ashmolean 11
Price, M. J. *Sylloge Nummorum Graecorum: Great Britain 6. The Lewis Collection in Corpus Christi College, Cambridge. Pt 1, The Greek and Hellenistic Coins (with Britain and Parthia).* London: Oxford University Press, 1972.	SNG Lewis 1
Carradice, I. A. *Sylloge Nummorum Graecorum: Great Britain 6. The Lewis Collection in Corpus Christi College, Cambridge. Pt 2, The Greek Imperial Coins.* London: Oxford University Press, 1992.	SNG Lewis 2
Healy, J. F. *Sylloge Nummorum Graecorum: Great Britain 7. Manchester University Museum. The Raby and Güterbock Collections.* London: Oxford University Press, 1986.	SNG Manchester

(Continued)

58 Numismatics and Greek Lexicography

Sugden, K. F. *Sylloge Nummorum Graecorum: Great Britain 8. The Hart Collection, Blackburn Museum.* London: Oxford University Press, 1989. — SNG Hart

Price, M. J. *Sylloge Nummorum Graecorum: Great Britain 9. The British Museum: Part 1. The Black Sea.* London: The British Museum, 1993. — SNG BM 1

Bagwell-Purefoy, P., and A. R. Meadows, *Sylloge Nummorum Graecorum: Great Britain 9. The British Museum: Part 2. Spain.* London: The British Museum, 2001. — SNG BM 2

Morcom, J., and M. J. Price. *Sylloge Nummorum Graecorum: Great Britain 10. The John Morcom Collection of Western Greek Bronze Coins.* London: Oxford University Press, 1995. — SNG Morcom

Stancomb, W., A. M. Burnett,, A. R. Meadows, K. Sheedy, U. Wartenberg. *Sylloge Nummorum Graecorum: Great Britain 11. The William Stancomb Collection of Coins of the Black Sea Region.* London: Oxford University Press, 2000. — SNG Stancomb

Goddard, J., and I. A. Carradice. *Sylloge Nummorum Graecorum: Great Britain 12. The Hunterian Museum University of Glasgow: Part 1. Roman Provincial Coins, Spain – Kingdoms of Asia Minor.* London: Oxford University Press, 2004. — SNG Hunterian 1

Goddard, J., and I. A. Carradice. *Sylloge Nummorum Graecorum: Great Britain 12. The Hunterian Museum University of Glasgow: Part 2. Roman Provincial Coins, Cyprus- Egypt.* London: Oxford University Press, 2007. — SNG Hunterian 2

Williams, R. T., and A. R. Meadows. *Sylloge Nummorum Graecorum: Great Britain 13. The Collection of the Society of Antiquaries, Newcastle upon Tyne.* London: Oxford University Press, 2005. — SNG Newcastle

---

Greece — SNG Greece

Hackens, T. Sylloge Nummorum Graecorum: Grèce 1.1. Collection Réna H. Evelpidis, Athènes: Italie, Sicilie, Thrace. Louvain: Institut supérieur d'archéologie et d'histoire de l'art, 1970. — SNG Evelpidis 1

Hackens, T. *Sylloge Nummorum Graecorum: Grèce 1.2. Collection Réna H. Evelpidis, Athènes: 12 Macédoine, Thessalie, Illyrie, Epire, Corcyre.* Louvain: Institut supérieur d'archéologie et d'histoire de l'art, 1975. — SNG Evelpidis 2

Kremydi-Sicilianou, S. *Sylloge Nummorum Graecorum: Greece 2. The Alpha Bank Collection: Macedonia I, Alexander I – Perseus.* Athens: Alpha Bank, 2000. — SNG Alpha Bank 1

Oikonomídou-Karamesíni, M. *Sylloge Nummorum Graecorum: Grèce. 3, Musée numismatique d'Athènes: Collection Antoine Christomanos. Première partie, Italie-Eubée.* Athens: Academy of Athens, 2004. — SNG Chistomanos

Psoma, S., and G. Touratsoglou. *Sylloge Nummorum Graecorum: Greece 4. National Numismatic Museum: the Petros Z. Saroglos Collection, Use-Loan by the Club of the Officers of the Armed Forces. Part 1. Macedonia.* Athens: KERA, Academy of Athens, 2005. — SNG Saroglos

Tsourti, E., and M. D. Trifiró. *Sylloge Nummorum Graecorum: Greece 5. National Numismatic Museum: the A.G. Soutzos Collection.* Athens: Academy of Athens, 2007. — SNG Soutzos

The Study of Coinage

Tsangari, D. I. *Sylloge Nummorum Graecorum: Greece 6. The Alpha Bank Collection: From Thessaly to Euboea*. Athens: Academy of Athens, 2011. — SNG Alpha Bank 2

Penna, V., and Y. Stoyas. *Sylloge Nummorum Graecorum: Greece 7, Volume 1. The KIKPE Collection of Bronze Coins*. Athens: Academy of Athens, 2012. — SNG KIKPE 1

Hungary — SNG Hungary

Torbágyi, M. *Sylloge Nummorum Graecorum: Hungary. Budapest, Magyar Nemzeti Múzeum: Part 1 Hispania – Sicilia: fasc. 1 Hispania – Apulia*. Milan: Ed. Ennerre, 1992. — SNG Budapest 1

Torbágyi, M. *Sylloge Nummorum Graecorum: Hungary. Budapest, Magyar Nemzeti Múzeum: Part 1 Hispania – Sicilia: fasc. 2 Calabria-Bruttium*. Milan: Ed. Ennerre, 1992. — SNG Budapest 2

Torbágyi, M. *Sylloge Nummorum Graecorum: Hungary. Budapest, Magyar Nemzeti Múzeum: Part 1 Hispania – Sicilia: fasc. 3 Sicilia*. Milan: Ed. Ennerre, 1993. — SNG Budapest 3

Bakos, M. *Sylloge Nummorum Graecorum: Hungary. Budapest, Magyar Nemzeti Múzeum: Part 2. Dacia – Moesia Superior*. Milan: Ed. Ennerre, 1994. — SNG Budapest 4

Vida, I. *Sylloge Nummorum Graecorum: Hungary. Budapest, Magyar Nemzeti Múzeum: Part 3. Moesia Inferior: Callatis, Dionysopolis, Istrus, Marcianopolis, Nicopolis ad Istrum, Odessus, Tomis*. Milan: Ed. Ennerre, 2000. — SNG Budapest 5

Israel — SNG Israel

Houghton, A., A. Spaer, and C. Lorber, C. *Sylloge Nummorum Graecorum: Israel 1. The Arnold Spaer Collection of Seleucid Coins*. London: I. Vecchi Ltd., 1998. — SNG Spaer

Italy — SNG Italia

Martini, R., B. Fischer, N. Vismara. *Sylloge Nummorum Graecorum: Italia. Milano. Civiche Raccolte Numismatiche: Part 1. Hispania-Gallia anellenica*. Milano: Ed. Ennerre, 1988. — SNG Milano 1

Vismara, N. *Sylloge Nummorum Graecorum: Italia. Milano. Civiche Raccolte Numismatiche: Part 2. Gallia ellenica-Guerra Sociale*. Milano: Ed. Ennerre, 1990. — SNG Milano 2

Vismara, N. *Sylloge Nummorum Graecorum: Italia. Milano. Civiche Raccolte Numismatiche: Part 3. Campania-Calabria*. Milano: Ed. Ennerre, 1989. — SNG Milano 3

Vismara, N. *Sylloge Nummorum Graecorum: Italia. Milano. Civiche Raccolte Numismatiche: Part 4. Lucania-Bruttium. Fasc. 1: Lucania*. Milano: Ed. Ennerre, 1997. — SNG Milano 4.1

Vismara, N. *Sylloge Nummorum Graecorum: Italia. Milano. Civiche Raccolte Numismatiche: Part 4. Lucania-Bruttium. Fasc. 2: Bruttium*. Milano: Ed. Ennerre, 1998. — SNG Milano 4.2

Vismara, N. *Sylloge Nummorum Graecorum: Italia. Milano. Civiche Raccolte Numismatiche: Part 6. Macedonia – Thracia. Fasc. 1: Macedonia greca, Paeonia, Emisssioni di area celtica*. Milano: Ed. Ennerre, 1999. — SNG Milano 6.1

(Continued)

60   *Numismatics and Greek Lexicography*

Vismara, N. *Sylloge Nummorum Graecorum: Italia. Milano. Civiche Raccolte Numismatiche: Part 6. Macedonia – Thracia. Fasc. 3: Chersonesus Tauricus – Sarmatia – Thracia – Chersonesus Thraciae – Isole della Thracia*. Milano: Ed. Ennerre, 2000.   SNG Milano 6.3

Vismara, N. *Sylloge Nummorum Graecorum: Italia. Milano. Civiche Raccolte Numismatiche: Part 12. Syria-Bactria et India. Fasc. 1. Seleucides (reges) – Chalcidice*. Milano: Ed. Ennerre, 1992.   SNG Milano 12.1

Vismara, N. *Sylloge Nummorum Graecorum: Italia. Milano. Civiche Raccolte Numismatiche: Part 12. Syria-Bactria et India. Fasc. 4. Iudaea-Bactria et India*. Milano: Ed. Ennerre, 1991.   SNG Milano 12.4

Martini, R. *Sylloge Nummorum Graecorum: Italia. Milano. Civiche Raccolte Numismatiche: Part 13. Aegyptus. Fasc. 1. Ptolemaei*. Milano: Ed. Ennerre, 1989.   SNG Milano 13.1

Martini, R. *Sylloge Nummorum Graecorum: Italia. Milano. Civiche Raccolte Numismatiche: Part 13. Aegyptus. Fasc. 2. Octavianus Augustus-Lucius Verus*. Milano: Ed. Ennerre, 1991.   SNG Milano 13.2

Martini, R. *Sylloge Nummorum Graecorum: Italia. Milano. Civiche Raccolte Numismatiche: Part 13. Aegyptus. Fasc. 3. Commodus-Galerius Caesar*. Milano: Ed. Ennerre, 1992.   SNG Milano 13.3

Martini, R. *Sylloge Nummorum Graecorum: Italia. Milano. Civiche Raccolte Numismatiche: Part 14. Cyrenaica-Mauretania*. Milano: Ed. Ennerre, 1989.   SNG Milano 14

Guido, F. *Sylloge Nummorum Graecorum: Italia. Sassari. Museo Archeologico 'G.A. Sanna': Part 14 1. Sicilia – Numidia*. Milano: Ed. Ennerre Catanzaro, 1994.   SNG Sassari 1

Arslan, E. A. *Sylloge Nummorum Graecorum: Italia. Catanzaro, Museo Provinciale: Part II. Bruttium*. Catanzaro: Amministrazione provinciale di Catanzaro, Ufficio cultura.Agrigento, 1999.   SNG Catanzaro

Caccamo-Caltabiano, M. *Sylloge Nummorum Graecorum: Italia. Agrigento, Museo archeologico regionale: fondo dell'ex Museo civico e altre raccolte del Medagliere*. Palermo: Regione siciliana assessorato regionale dei beni culturali e ambientali e della P.I.Cremona, 1999.   SNG Agrigento

Barello, F. *Sylloge Nummorum Graecorum: Italia. Cremona, Museo civico Ala Ponzone*. Cremona: Museo civico Ala Ponzone, 2006.   SNG Cremona

Catalli, F. *Sylloge Nummorum Graecorum: Italia. Firenze, Museo Archeologico Nazionale: Part 2, Etruria*. Rome, Florence and Zurich: Istituto central per il catalogo e la documentazione, Ministero per i Beni e le Attività Culturali, Soprintendenza per i Beni Archeologici della Toscana, Numismatica Ars Classica, 2007.   SNG Firenze

Poland

Mielczarek, M. *Sylloge Nummorum graecorum: Poland 1. The Archaeological and Ethnographical Museum in Łódź: Part 4. Galatia – Zeugitana*. Kraków: The Polish Academy of Arts and Sciences, 1998.   SNG Poland 1

Walczak, E. *Sylloge Nummorum Graecorum, Poland, Vol. 2. The National Museum in Warsaw, Part 1 – The Northern Black Sea Coast Chersonesus – Bosporus*. Kraków: The Polish Academy of Arts and Sciences, 2015.   SNG Poland 2

The Study of Coinage

Bodzek, J. *Sylloge Nummorum Graecorum: Poland 3. The National Museum in Cracow: Part 4. Sarmatia – Bosporus.* Kraków: The Polish Academy of Arts and Sciences, 2006.

SNG Poland 3

| **Russia** | SNG Russia |

Kovalenko, S. *Sylloge Nummorum Graecorum: Russia. State Pushkin Museum of Fine Arts, Volume I. Coins of the Black Sea Region: Part 1 Ancient Coins from the Northern Black Sea Littoral.* Leuven: Peeters, 2011.

SNG Pushkin 1

Kovalenko, S. *Sylloge Nummorum Graecorum: Russia. State Pushkin Museum of Fine Arts, Volume I. Coins of the Black Sea Region: Part 2 Ancient Coins of the Black Sea Littoral.* Leuven: Peeters, 2014.

SNG Pushkin 2

Kovalenko, S. *Sylloge Nummorum Graecorum: Russia. State Pushkin Museum of Fine Arts: Volume II. Greek Coins of Italy and Sicily.* Rome, L'Erma di Bretschneider, 2017.

SNG Pushkin 3

| **Slovenia** | SNG Slovenia |

Kos, P., and A. Šemrov. *Sylloge Nummorum Graecorum: Slovenia. Ljubljana, Narodni Muzej. Volume 3. Moesia Superior. Part 1. Viminacium.* Milano: Ed. Ennerre, 1996.

SNG Kecskés 3.1

| **Spain** | SNG Spain |

Alfaro, A. C. *Sylloge Nummorum Graecorum: España. Museo Arqueológico Nacional, Madrid: Volumen I. Hispania; Ciudades Feno-púnicas. Parte 1: Gadir y Ebusus.* Madrid: Museo Arqueológico Nacional, 1994.

SNG Madrid 1.1

Alfaro, A. C. *Sylloge Nummorum Graecorum: España. Museo Arqueológico Nacional, Madrid: Volumen I. Hispania; Ciudades Feno-púnicas. Parte 2: Acuñaciones cartaginesas en Iberia y emisiones ciudadanas.* Madrid: Museo Arqueológico Nacional, 2004.

SNG Madrid 1.2

Alfaro, A. C., and G. A. Arévalo, *Sylloge Nummorum Graecorum: España. Museo Arqueológico Nacional, Madrid: Volumen 2. Hispania; ciudades del área meridional. Acuñaciones con escritura indígena.* Madrid: Artegraf, 2005.

SNG Madrid 2

| **Sweden** | SNG Sweeden |

Westermark, U. *Sylloge Nummorum Graecorum: Sweden: 1.1 The Collection of His Late Majesty King Gustav VI Adolf. The Fred Forbat Collection.* Stockholm: The Royal Academy of Letters, History and Antiquities, 1974.

SNG Sweden 1.1

Boehringer, C., W. Schwabacher, W, and E. von Post. *Sylloge Nummorum Graecorum: Sweden: 1.2. Sammlung Eric von Post.* Stockholm: The Royal Academy of Letters, History and Antiquities, 1995.

SNG Sweden 1.2

Westermark, U. *Sylloge Nummorum Graecorum: Sweden 2. The Collection of the Royal Coin Cabinet National Museum of Monetary History: Part 1. Gallia – Sicily.* Stockholm: The Royal Academy of Letters, History and Antiquities, 1976.

SNG Sweden 2.1

Westermark, U. *Sylloge Nummorum Graecorum: Sweden 2. The Collection of the Royal Coin Cabinet National Museum of Monetary History: Part 2. Thrace – Euboia.* Stockholm: The Royal Academy of Letters, History and Antiquities, 1980.

SNG Sweden 2.2

(Continued)

Westermark, U., and H. Nilsson. *Sylloge Nummorum Graecorum: Sweden 2. The Collection of the Royal Coin Cabinet National Museum of Monetary History: Part 3. Attica – Lesbos.* Stockholm: The Royal Academy of Letters, History and Antiquities, 1991. — SNG Sweden 2.3

Ripollès, P. P., and H. Nilsson. *Sylloge Nummorum Graecorum: Sweden 2. The Collection of the Royal Coin Cabinet National Museum of Monetary History: Part 6. The G. D. Lorichs Collection.* Stockholm: The Royal Academy of Letters, History and Antiquities, 2003. — SNG Sweden 2.6

Switzerland — SNG Switzerland

Levante, E. *Sylloge Nummorum Graecorum: Switzerland 1. Levante – Cilicia.* Berne: Credit Suisse, 1986. — SNG Levante 1

Levante, E. *Sylloge Nummorum Graecorum: Switzerland 1. Levante – Cilicia. Supplement 1.* Zurich: Numismatica Ars Classica, 1993. — SNG Levante 1 Supp.

Kapossy, B. *Sylloge Nummorum Graecorum: Switzerland 2. Katalog der Sammlung Jean-Pierre Righetti im Bernischen Historischen Museum.* Bern: P. Haupt, 1993. — SNG Righetti

Turkey — SNG Turkey

Konuk, K. *Sylloge Nummorum Graecorum: Turkey 1. The Muharrem Kayhan Collection.* Istanbul and Bordeaux: Ausonius Publications, 2002. — SNG Turkey 1.1

Konuk, K., O. Tekin, A. E. Özdizbay. *Sylloge Nummorum Graecorum. Turkey 1, The Muharrem Kayhan Collection Part 2.* Istanbul: Turkish Institute of Archaeology, 2015. — SNG Turkey 1.2

Tekin, O., and S. Altinoluk. *Sylloge Nummorum Graecorum: Turkey 2. Anamur Museum. 1. Roman Provincial Coins.* Istanbul: Turkish Institute of Archaeology, 2007. — SNG Turkey 2

Tekin, O., S. Altınoluk, and F. Körpe. *Sylloge Nummorum Graecorum: Turkey 3. Çanakkale Museum. 1. Roman Provincial Coins of Mysia, Troas etc.* Istanbul: Turkish Institute of Archaeology, 2009. — SNG Turkey 3

Tekin, O., and A. E. Özdizbay, *Sylloge Nummorum Graecorum: Turkey 4. Ancient Coins from Mysia, Troad and Aeolis in the Collection of Selçuk Tanrikulu.* Istanbul: Turkish Institute of Archaeology, 2010. — SNG Turkey 4

Tekin, O., S. Altınoluk, and E. Sağır. *Sylloge Nummorum Graecorum: Turkey 5. Tire Museum. 1. Roman Provincial Coins from Ionia, Lydia, Phrygia and, etc.* Istanbul: Turkish Institute of Archaeology, 2011. — SNG Turkey 5

Köker, H. *Sylloge Nummorum Graecorum: Turkey 6. Burdur Museum.* Istanbul: Turkish Institute of Archaeology, 2012. — SNG Turkey 6

Tekin, O., and S. Altınoluk. *Sylloge Nummorum Graecorum: Turkey 7. Ödemiş Museum.* Istanbul: Turkish Institute of Archaeology, 2012. — SNG Turkey 7

Özdizbay, A.E., and O. Tekin. *Sylloge Nummorum Graecorum: Turkey 8. Muğla Museum 1. Caria.* Istanbul: Turkish Institute of Archaeology, 2013. — SNG Turkey 8

Tekin, O., and A. E. Özdizbay. *Sylloge Nummorum Graecorum Turkey 9.1 The Ozkan Arikanturk Collection Volume 1 Troas.* Istanbul: Turkish Institute of Archaeology, 2015. — SNG Turkey 9.1

Tekin, O., and A. E. Özdizbay. *Sylloge Nummorum Graecorum Turkey 9.2 The Ozkan Arikanturk Collection Volume 1 Aeolis*. Istanbul: Turkish Institute of Archaeology, 2017.

SNG Turkey 9.2

Tekin, O. *Sylloge Nummorum Graecorum Turkey 10. The Yavuz Tatis Collection Part 1. Ionia and Lydia*. Istanbul: Turkish Institute of Archaeology, 2016.

SNG Turkey 10

United States

SNG USA

Thompson M., and R. R. Holloway. *Sylloge Nummorum Graecorum, the Burton Y. Berry Collection: Part 1. Macedonia to Attica*. New York: The American Numismatic Society, 1961.

SNG Berry 1

Thompson, M., and I. L. Merker. *Sylloge Nummorum Graecorum, the Burton Y. Berry Collection: Part 2. Megaris to Egypt*. New York: The American Numismatic Society, 1962.

SNG Berry 2

Fischer, J. E. *Sylloge Nummorum Graecorum: The Collection of the American Numismatic Society. Part 1. Etruria-Calabria*. New York: The American Numismatic Society, 1969.

SNG ANS 1

Troxell, H. A. *Sylloge Nummorum Graecorum: The Collection of the American Numismatic Society. Part 2. Lucania*. New York: The American Numismatic Society, 1972.

SNG ANS 2

Troxell, H. A. *Sylloge Nummorum Graecorum: The Collection of the American Numismatic Society. Part 3. Bruttium-Sicily 1 (Abacaenum-Eryx)*. New York: The American Numismatic Society, 1975.

SNG ANS 3

Jaunzems, E. *Sylloge Nummorum Graecorum: The Collection of the American Numismatic Society. Part 4. Sicily 2 (Galaria-Styella)*. New York: The American Numismatic Society, 1977.

SNG ANS 4

Bérend, D. *Sylloge Nummorum Graecorum: The Collection of the American Numismatic Society. Part 5. Sicily 3 (Syracuse-Siceliotes)*. New York: The American Numismatic Society, 1988.

SNG ANS 5

Meshorer, Y. *Sylloge Nummorum Graecorum: The Collection of the American Numismatic Society. Part 6. Palestine-South Arabia*. New York: The American Numismatic Society, 1981.

SNG ANS 6

Waggoner, N. *Sylloge Nummorum Graecorum: The Collection of the American Numismatic Society. Part 7. Macedonia 1 (Cities, Thraco-Macedonian Tribes, Paeonian Kings)*. New York: The American Numismatic Society, 1987.

SNG ANS 7

Troxell, H. A. *Sylloge Nummorum Graecorum: The Collection of the American Numismatic Society. Part 8. Macedonia 2 (Alexander I-Philip II)*. New York: The American Numismatic Society, 1994.

SNG ANS 7

Bopearachchi, O. *Sylloge Nummorum Graecorum: The Collection of the American Numismatic Society. Part 9. Graeco-Bactrian and Indo-Greek Coins*. New York: The American Numismatic Society, 1998.

SNG ANS 7

Numismatics and Greek Lexicography

Table 4 Numismatic basis for RPC series

Abbreviation	Collection
B	Berlin, Staatliche Museen
C	Cambridge, Fitzwilliam Museum
Cop	Copenhagen, Nationalmuseet
G	Glasgow, Hunterian Museum
L	London, British Museum
Mu	Munich, Staatliche Münzsammlung
NY	New York, American Numismatic Society
O	Oxford, Ashmolean Museum
P	Paris, Bibliothèque Nationale de France
V	Vienna, Kunsthistorisches Museum

Positively, the SNG volumes provide an objective description of the Greek coins (attribution, direction of axis, weight) with very minimal commentary, conveying only necessary details. The volumes are laid out in a consistent and clear format with full and detailed photographic plates of all objects in the particular collection under consideration. This is especially helpful for documenting and making known (with photographs) those coins that would have otherwise, potentially, been overlooked for publication. The published photographic plates also facilitate a range of other numismatic investigations, including die-comparisons and countermark series. However, the strength of the SNG endeavour is also its weakness. Given the nature of the publication, by individual collection, it necessarily only provides a small fraction of the full numismatic picture of a particular geographical location or people. Furthermore, the prospect of a modern-day researcher being able to sift through over 200 SNG volumes to distil the relevant iconographic, inscriptional or other information renders much of the material inaccessible, or at least very difficult to obtain, if one requires a full picture of a theme, topic or location.

In recent decades, in part to address the desideratum for a synthesis of so-called 'Greek imperial' numismatic material, but also due to an increased interest in Roman social history, the monumental project entitled *Roman Provincial Coinage* (RPC), which seeks to produce a standard typology of the provincial coinage of the Roman Empire from 44 BCE to 296 CE. The undertaking was initiated as an international collaborative project with support from various institutions and sources, including the American Numismatic Society, British Academy, Heberden Coin Room, Ashmolean Museum and the Generalitat Valenciana. The directors of the project are Christopher Howgego (Keeper of the Heberden Coin Room in the Ashmolean Museum, Professor of Greek and Roman Numismatics in the University of Oxford) and Jerome Mairat (curator of the Heberden Coin Room in the Ashmolean Museum, Oxford), both of whom, with Andrew Burnett (Deputy Director, British Museum) and Michel Amandry (former director of the Cabinet des Médailles, the Department of Coins, Medals

The Study of Coinage

Table 5 Roman provincial coinage volumes: Status and contributors

Volume	Name and period	Contributors	Status
1	Julio-Claudian period (BC 44–AD 69)	A. Burnett (London) M. Amandry (Paris) P. P. Ripollès (Valencia)	Printed: 1992; reprinted 1998 and 2006
2	The Flavians (AD 69–96)	A. Burnett (London) M. Amandry (Paris) I. Carradice (St Andrews)	Printed: 1999 Online: 2019
3	Nerva–Hadrian (AD 96–138)	M. Amandry (Paris) A. Burnett (London) J. Mairat (Oxford) W. Metcalf (New Haven) L. Bricault (Toulouse) M. Blet-Lemarquand (Orléans)	Printed: 2015 Online: 2015
4	The Antonines (AD 138–192)	V. Heuchert (Oxford) C. Howgego (Oxford)	Online: 2006 (with temporary numbers)
5	The Severan period (AD 193–218)	M. Amandry (Paris) S. Kremydi (Athens) E. Papaefthymiou (Athens) F. Delrieux (Chambéry) L. Bricault (Toulouse) A. Hostein (Paris) J. Dalaison (Lyon) B. Rémy (Grenoble) S. Matthies (Berlin)	Undefined
6	Elagabalus–Maximinus (AD 218–238)	D. Calomino (London) A. Burnett (London) S. Matthies (Berlin)	Online: 2017 (Asia Minor and Egypt only; with temporary numbers)
7.1	Gordian I–Gordian III (AD 238–244): Province of Asia	M. Spoerri (Warwick)	Printed: 2006; Online: 2016
7.2	Gordian I–Gordian III (AD 238–244): Moesia Superior–Egypt (except Asia)	J. Mairat (Oxford) (ed.) M. Spoerri (Warwick) (ed.) M. Amandry (Paris) R. Bland (Cambridge) K. Butcher (Warwick) J. Nollé (Munich) J. Nurpetlian (Beirut) U. Peter (Berlin)	Undefined
8	Philip I (AD 244–249)	J. Mairat (Oxford) (ed.) M. Spoerri (Warwick) (ed.) M. Amandry (Paris) R. Bland (Cambridge) K. Butcher (Warwick) J. Nollé (Munich) J. Nurpetlian (Beirut) U. Peter (Berlin)	Undefined

(Continued)

Volume	Name and period	Contributors	Status
9	Trajan Decius–Uranius Antoninus (AD 249–254)	A. Hostein (Paris) J. Mairat (Oxford)	Online: 2014 (with temporary numbers); 2016 (with final numbers) Printed: 2016
10	Valerian–Diocletian (AD 253–297)	W. E. Metcalf (New Haven)	Pending

Table 6 Electronic resources for numismatics

Name and description	URL
Sylloge Nummorum Graecorum Database A relational database which contains 25,000 coins from the SNG British volumes is online in a searchable form. Most items are accompanied by a digital image. Search parameters include collection, state, ruler, period, denomination, hoard, obverse description, reverse description, weight, width, mint, material, weight standard, site, die axis and the ability to limit results to those records that include images.	http://www.sylloge-nummorum-graecorum.org
British Museum Collection Database Currently has 456,338 online entries for numismatic items; 153,091 have high-resolution images available. There are 30,220 items listed under provincial coinage.	https://www.britishmuseum.org/research/collection_online/search.aspx
American Numismatic Society Collections Database (MANTIS – A Numismatic Technologies Integration Service) Online searchable database of over 600,000 items in the collection divided into 11 departments which allow customizable search pages (Greek, Roman, Byzantine, Islamic, East Asian, South Asian, Medieval, Modern, United States, Latin American and Medals/Decorations). Roman coinage includes approximately 6,000 coins of the Republic, 56,000 of the mainstream imperial coinage, 3,000 provincial silver and 13,000 Alexandrian pieces. Greek coinage includes approximately 100,000 items classified according to region and mints of the ancient world, which includes the bronze coinage of the Greek and other cities under Roman administration until the third century CE.	http://numismatics.org/search/department/Roman http://numismatics.org/search/department/Greek
American Numismatic Society Library Catalogue (DONUM – Database of Numismatic Materials) Originally a 31-page printed index, the online catalogue of the American Numismatic Society library now contains over 100,000 items including books, periodicals, manuscripts, photographs, pamphlets, auction catalogues and microforms.	https://donum.numismatics.org
The Münzkabinett Online Database of the Staatliche Museen zu Berlin Includes basic descriptions of over 500,000 items from the seventh century BCE through to the modern period. The collection also has sealings, dies and historical minting tools.	http://www.smb.museum/ikmk/https://ikmk.smb.museum/home?lang=en

(Continued)

Name and description	URL
Online Coins of the Roman Empire (OCRE) A collaborative project of the American Numismatic Society and the Institute for the Study of the Ancient World at New York University. It is a tool designed to assist in the identification and classification of coinage of the Roman Empire. It covers Roman imperial coinage from Augustus in 31 BCE until the death of Zeno in AD 491, recording over 43,000 types.	http://numismatics.org/ocre/
Digital Library Numis An open access depository of numismatic books, journals and papers available online. All entries have detailed metadata, often with an accompanying synopsis.	https://sites.google.com/site/digitallibrarynumis/
Roman Provincial Coinage Project Online A support site to the print publications noted above.	http://rpc.ashmus.ox.ac.uk/project/
Coins & Medals Department, Fitzwilliam Museum, University of Cambridge Contains over 200,000 numismatic objects, most with images and basic descriptions.	https://www.fitzmuseum.cam.ac.uk/aboutus/coins

and Antiquities of the Bibliothèque Nationale de France) serve as general editors of the project. The numismatic basis for the work is eleven of the most important and accessible public collections in the world, together with the extensive body of published material in one form or another.

Thus far the project has produced five printed volumes in hardcopy and, in addition, some progress towards other volumes online.[37] The first two volumes are edited by Andrew Burnett, Michel Amandry and Ian Carradice,[38] and cover all coinages struck in the Roman provinces in the period from the reign of Augustus to the death of Domitian. These volumes are the first instalments of a projected ten-volume series (see Table 5) which aim, and thus far succeed, in producing a provincial equivalent to Mattingly's *Roman Imperial Coinage* (noted above). The publication of these volumes was hailed an immediate success and monumental advance in the study of Roman coinage. It is hard to overestimate the significance of these volumes for the study of Greek inscriptions on Roman coins, which have been so carefully defined and catalogued, both geographically and chronologically. Volume 7.1 was published by Marguerite Spoerri Butcher in 2006[39] and covers the issues struck in the province of Asia in the period from Gordian I to Gordian III (238–244 CE). Volume 3 was published by Michel Amandry, Andrew Burnett, Jerome Mairat, William E Metcalf and Laurent Bricaul in 2015[40] and covers Nerva, Trajan and Hadrian in the period of 96–138 CE. Volume 9 was published by Antony Hostein and Jerome Mairat in 2016[41] and covers Trajan Decius to Uranius Antoninus in the period of 249–254 CE.

[37] http://rpc.ashmus.ox.ac.uk/project/.
[38] Andrew Burnett, Michel Amandry, and Ian Carradice, *Roman Provincial Coinage: Volumes 1–2* (London: British Museum, 1992–1999).
[39] Marguerite Spoerri Butcher, *Roman Provincial Coinage*, vol. 7 (London: British Museum, 2006).
[40] Michel Amandry, Andrew Burnett, Jerome Mairat, William E Metcalf, and Laurent Bricaul, *Roman Provincial Coinage*, vol. 3 (London: British Museum Press, 2015).
[41] Antony Hostein and Jerome Mairat, *Roman Provincial Coinage*, vol. 9 (London: British Museum Press, 2016).

Given the significance of the RPC volumes and the foundational contribution it will provide to our current endeavour of the numismatic contribution to Greek lexicography, it will serve our purposes, given the target audience of this volume, to demonstrate a worked example of reading an entry from the volume. An example, selected for its simplicity and illustrative value will suffice to introduce the main features of an entry. In volume one of RPC, page 405 has the following entry:

2379   AE. 17mm, 3.04g (2). Axis:12.   [5]
        BMC 8, Cop 572
        Head of Heracles, r.
        ΘΥΑΤΕΙΡΗΝΩΝ; double axe
        1. **L** = **BMC 8**, 3.19; 2. Cop 572, 2.89; 3. V 30589; 4-5. B (Fox, I-B)

The number 2379 is the entry number in the volume, and thus would commonly be referred to, and referenced as RPC 1.2379. The catalogue takes a standard format but the arrangement of cities is atypical. The coinage of the cities is arranged on a geographical and political basis (Roman provinces) from west to east. A full listing of cities in catalogue order is provided on pages 58–62, or alphabetically on pages 729–731. This particular example, RPC 1.2379 is classified under Asia and chronologically listed (early first century CE) below a short introduction on critical issues of coinage in the city of Thyatira, highlighting and interacting with any relevant secondary literature. The RPC numbers for volume one run from 1 to 5467 (gaps exist because the province or regions was numbered separately). 'AE' refers to metrological information, in this case bronze. 17 mm refers to the maximum diameter, followed by the mean weight in grams. The number of specimens whose weight is known is given in round brackets, here (2). The axis figure refers to die alignment or coin rotation, that is, how the obverse and reverse aligned to each other when the coin was struck. Die alignment is expressed as a clock face hour. In other contexts, die alignment can be expressed in degrees or with arrows.[42] Aligned to the right of the entry on the first line is the number 5 in square brackets. This number indicates the number of extant examples in the base collections noted above. The second line provides representative standard references, here BMC = *British Museum Coinage*, and Cop = Copenhagen, Danish National Museum, published in SNG 1942–79. The third and fourth lines provide a basic description of the inscription and design. The obverse is treated first, here 'Head of Heracles', followed by a description of the r. (reverse) 'ΘΥΑΤΕΙΡΗΝΩΝ; double axe'. Within the inscriptions themselves rounded brackets indicate minor variants, and square brackets indicate restorations of the legend due to poor preservation of the extant examples. A superlinear line indicates ligatures (two or more letters joined as a single glyph) in the inscription. The fourth line (and below) is the apparatus which provides the collection, reference numbers, publication details and weights if known. The specimen in bold indicates the item illustrated in the plates. Sometimes further information is provided regarding die links, metal analysis, or countermarks.

---

[42] It may be of interest to note that most Roman coins have a consistent die alignment of either 0 or 180 degrees. Athenian tetradrachms almost always have a die alignment of 270 degrees. Other types do not show consistent patterns, and are often described as struck with loose dies. Aberrations in die alignment for a type set may indicate modern forgery.

Abbreviations for collections and published works in the catalogue entries are provided in ix-xi. With this introduction to the entries in RPC and the general background of the endeavour, the reader is now equipped to assess and analyse the primary sources for themselves. The numismatic journey formally begins.

In addition to the in-progress multi-volume work of RPC, there are also a variety of mint- or region-specific catalogues that could benefit for further investigation. Kevin Butcher,[43] for example, offers a detailed commentary of the coinages struck at the mints in northern Syria (Seleucis and Commagene). David MacDonald[44] provides an overview of the provincial coinage struck by Aphrodisias and includes discussion of the coinage in relation to the 1972 Kraft thesis of centralized workshops serving the coining needs of multiple cities in a region. Konrad Kraft's classic (German) study[45] of die sharing among cities of Roman Asia Minor led to the widely supported conclusion that central workshops provided dies and sometimes even struck the coinage at the order of other individual cities. C. J. Howgego's extensive catalogue of countermarks found on Roman provincial coinage from the first century BCE to the third century CE provides detailed commentary on their political and economic use.[46] The political use of coinage is taken up by Kenneth W. Harl[47] who offers a general discussion of the rivalries between the cities of the Greek East under Roman rule and how coins were used polemically in this process. C. Howgego, Volker Heuchert and Andrew Burnett edit a collection of sixteen conference papers discussing provincial coinage as a tool for establishing local identities through the use of iconography, dating systems and inscriptions.[48] Ann Johnston contributes to this discussion by assessing the nature of value marks and inflation in the provinces.[49] Her work is a groundbreaking synthesis of the use of value marks and value countermarks on Roman provincial coins, and discussion of their implications for charting the advance of inflation and ultimate collapse of the provincial coinages. One recent but underused source is Adriano Savio's catalogue (in Italian) of over seven thousand coins struck in Roman Alexandria, including illustration and description.[50] The identification and interpretation of Greco-Roman provincial coinage is also aided by a range of other sources.[51]

---

[43] Kevin Butcher, *Coinage in Roman Syria: Northern Syria, 64 BC–AD 253* (London: Royal Numismatic Society, 2004).

[44] David MacDonald, *The Coinage of Aphrodisias* (London: Royal Numismatic Society, 1992).

[45] K. Kraft, *Das System der kaiserzeitlichen Münzprägung in Kleinasien* (Berlin: Mann, 1972).

[46] C. J. Howgego, *Greek Imperial Countermarks: Studies in the Provincial Coinage of the Roman Empire* (London: Royal Numismatic Society, 1985).

[47] Kenneth W. Harl, *Civic Coins and Civic Politics in the Roman East* (Berkeley: University of California Press, 1987).

[48] C. Howgego, Volker Heuchert, and Andrew Burnett, *Coinage and Identity in the Roman Provinces* (Oxford: Oxford University Press, 2005).

[49] Ann Johnston, *Greek Imperial Denominations, ca. 200–275: A Study of the Roman Provincial Coinages of Asia Minor* (London: Royal Numismatic Society, 2007).

[50] Adriano Savio, *Catalogo Completo Della Collezione Dattari: Numi augg. Alexandrini* (Trieste: G. Bernardi, 1999).

[51] For extensive multilingual bibliography on Roman provincial coinage during the period 1990–2013, see H.-D. Schultz, 'Römische Provinzialprägung', in *A Survey of Numismatic Research 1990–1995*, ed. C. Morrison and B. Kluge (Berlin: International Numismatic Commission and International Association of Professional Numismatists, 1997), 219–39; V. Heuchert, 'Roman Provincial Coinage', in *A Survey of Numismatic Research 1996–2001*, ed. C. Alfaro and A. Burnett (Madrid: International

One final note on the emergence of electronic databases and their value for the study of ancient coinage sketches new possibilities for the dissemination of material. Both the cost of production and difficulty of updating pose a significant hurdle for the traditional large format multi-volume works. The electronic medium allows new flexible possibilities with virtually unlimited storage, retrieval and review capabilities. There are several online open-access databases that would complement the other physical resources discussed above. These are provided as a table for ease of reference. There is, of course, the possibility that some of the website URLs or projects may be relocated, discontinued or modified, but I am confident that the projects listed below will remain in effect and available for the foreseeable future and will benefit the reader of this volume.

Conclusion

This chapter has sought to introduce the many and varied resources available for the study of ancient numismatics, with a particular emphasis on the project under discussion, namely the contribution of numismatic inscriptions to Greek lexicography. No survey can do justice to the breadth of relevant research, nor the detail that will satisfy every enquiry. However, those works surveyed and introduced above will provide at least the first critical point of departure for investigation of the numismatic material. Further and more specific resources will be engaged with through this volume, and especially in the case studies. It is hoped that both this chapter and the case studies will provide cogent examples of the manner in which the material can be engaged in a robust and linguistically beneficial manner.

Numismatic Commission and International Association of Professional Numismatists, 2003), 313–43; S. Kremydi, 'Roman Provincial Coinage', in *A Survey of Numismatic Research 2002-2007*, ed. D. Bateson and M. Amandry (Glasgow: International Numismatic Commission and International Association of Professional Numismatists, 2009), 182–95; M. Spoerri Butcher and D. Calomino, 'Provincial Coinages: Eastern Provinces', in *A Survey of Numismatic Research 2008-2013*, ed C. Arnold-Biucchi and M. Caccamo-Caltabiano (Taormina: International Numismatic Commission and International Association of Professional Numismatists, 2015), 228–243.

4

Critical Issues in the Appeal to Coinage

Introduction

The incorporation of a new and distinct form of literary or documentary evidence for Greek lexicography necessarily raises a range of methodological and linguistic questions. This chapter seeks to address some of the most important questions arising, but is, by no means, an exhaustive analysis of the full range of issues that may be relevant to our enquiry. We will not, for example, examine the methodological issues of applying visual phenomena in hermeneutics,[1] although it is readily acknowledged that image and inscription are to be mutually interpreted.[2] Our focus in this chapter will be on the specific issues relating to the use of coinage for lexicographic purposes.

Coins as propaganda: Can we trust them?

One frequently encounters reference to the term 'propaganda' in discussions of ancient coinage.[3] In typical English parlance, the word is derogatively used in reference to information publicized that is biased and intended to promote a particular political

---

[1] For a discussion of this issue, see Annette Weissenrieder and Friederike Wendt, 'Images as Communication: The Methods of Iconography', in *Picturing the New Testament: Studies in Ancient Visual Images*, ed. Annette Weissenrieder, Friederike Wendt, and P. von Gemünden (Tübingen: Mohr Siebeck, 2005), 3–49.

[2] Erika Manders notes, 'on many coins the image either presents a visualization of the legend or the legend forms a textual rendering of the image. This cooperation between text and image facilitated not only illiterates' understanding of the messages present on coins, it also reduced the various possibilities of how Romans could interpret a message'; Erika Manders, *Coining Images of Power: Patterns in the Representation of Roman Emperors on Imperial Coinage, AD 193–284* (Leiden: Brill, 2012), 30. The *Lexicon Iconographicum Numismatica* is an effort to categorize visual types into a systematized catalogue, including the 'creation of a coin iconographic lexicon'. See related DIANA project website here: http://ww2.unime.it/diana/, and further M. Caccamo-Caltabiano, L. Campagna, and A. Pinzone, eds., *Nuove prospsettive della ricerca sulla Sicilia del III sec. a.C.: archeologia, numismatica, storia* (Messina: Dipartimento di Scienze dell' Antichita dell'Università degli Studi di Messina, 2004); Marianna Spinelli, 'The "Soma" of the God: Subtypes as Qualification of the Corporal Gestures of the Main Subject on the Kaulonia Coins', in *Identity and Connectivity: Proceedings of the 16th Symposium on Mediterranean Archaeology*, ed. Luca Bombardieri, Anacleto D'Agostino, Guido Guarducci, Valentina Orsi, and Stefano Valentini (Oxford: Aracheopress, 2013), 793.

[3] On the use of coins in Roman propaganda, see C. Howgego, *Ancient History from Coins* (London: Routledge, 1995), 62–87; A. H. M. Jones, 'Numismatics and History', in *The Roman Economy: Studies in Ancient Economic and Administrative History*, ed. P. Brunt (Oxford: Blackwell, 1974),

point of view,[4] typified in George Orwell's maxim, 'all propaganda is lies, even when one is telling the truth.'[5] Jane DeRose Evans, however, suggests that within the Roman Empire the concept was subtler and had a more neutral definition: 'the educational efforts or information used by an organized group that is made available to a selected audience, for the specific purpose of making the audience take a particular course of action or conform to a certain attitude desired by the organized group.'[6] J. Ellul argues that propaganda is any effort to change the audience's opinion or indeed any form of communication.[7] While this broader definition may well be difficult to fully substantiate, its essence resonates with modern notions of communication theory.[8] L. Doob thus notes that if this is the case, propaganda and education would be extremely difficult to separate.[9]

The eminent numismatist H. Mattingly has noted the relationship of coins and forms of propaganda in the Roman world: 'coin types are constantly changing, and constantly emphasising definite events and policies, and, as they change move in close agreement with the political changes of the time.'[10] He continues by stating, 'the possible influence

---

61–81; Michael H. Crawford, 'Roman Imperial Coin Types and the Formation of Public Opinion', in *Studies in Numismatic Method Presented to Philip Grierson*, ed. C. Brooke, B. Steward, J. Pollard, and T. Volk (Cambridge: Cambridge University Press, 1983), 47–64; B. Levick, 'Propaganda and the Imperial Coinage', *Antichthon* 16 (1982): 104–116; C. Ehrhardt, 'Roman Coin Types and the Roman Public', *JNG* 34 (1984): 41–54; A. Meadows and J. Williams, 'Moneta and the Monuments: Coinage and Politics in Republican Rome', *JRS* 91 (2001): 27–49. For earlier Republic coins, see Andrew Burnett, 'The Iconography of Roman Coin Types in the Third Century BC', *Numismatic Chronicle* 146 (1986): 67–75; A. Alföldi, 'The Main Aspects of Political Propaganda on the Coinage of the Roman Republic', in *Essays in Roman Coinage Presented to Harold Mattingly*, ed. R. A. G. Carson and C. H. V. Sutherland (Oxford: Oxford University Press, 1956), 63–95. H. Flower, *Ancestor Marks and Aristocratic Power in Roman Culture* (Oxford: Clarendon Press, 1996); P. V. Hill, 'Coin Symbolism and Propaganda during the Wars of Vengeance (44–36 B.C.)', *Quaderni Ticinese* 4 (1975): 157–207. For discussion of propaganda and coins of the Imperial period, see T. Hölscher, *Staatsdenkmal und Publikum: vom Untergang der Republik bis zur Festigung des Kaisertums in Rom* 9 (Konstanz: Konstanzer althistorische Vorträge und Forschungen, 1984); Pierre Bastien, *Le buste monétaire des empereurs romains* (Wetteren: Editions numismatiques romaines, 1992); N. Hannestad, *Roman Art and Imperial Policy* (Arhus: University Press, 1986); C. H. V. Sutherland, *Coinage in Roman Imperial Policy 31 B.C–A.D. 68* (London: Methuen, 1951); A. Wallace-Hadrill, 'The Emperor and His Virtues', *Historia* 30 (1981): 298–323; C. F. Noreña, 'The Communication of the Emperor's Virtues', *JRS* 91 (2001): 146–168; Paul Zanker, *The Power of Images in the Age of Augustus*, trans. Alan Shapiro (Ann Arbor: University of Michigan Press, 1988); A. Wallace-Hadrill, 'Image and Authority in the Coinage of Augustus', *JRS* 76 (1986): 66–87.

4   First appearing with this meaning on 7 December 1822 in a letter of the Scottish philosopher Thomas Carlyle, see 'propaganda, n.' OED Online. December 2016. Oxford University Press. http://www.oed.com/view/Entry/152605?rskey=JegCgh&result=1 (accessed 20 December 2016).

5   Diary entry 14 March 1942, George Orwell, *All Propaganda Is Lies, 1941–1942*, ed. P. Davison (London: Secker and Warburg, 1998), 229.

6   Jane DeRose Evans, *The Art of Persuasion: Political Propaganda from Aeneas to Brutus* (Ann Arbor: University of Michigan Press, 1992), 1.

7   J. Ellul, *Propaganda: The Formation of Men's Attitudes* (New York: Vintage Books, 1973), xi–xiii, 61.

8   James Price Dillard, 'Persuasion', in *Handbook of Communication and Science*, ed. C. R. Berger, M. E. Roloff, and D. R. Roskos-Ewoldsen (London: Sage Publishers, 1987), 203–218.

9   L. Doob, *Public Opinion and Propaganda*, 2nd ed. (Hambden: Archon Books, 1966), 240.

10   H. Mattingly, *Coins of the Roman Empire in the British Museum, vol. 3* (London: British Museum, 1936), xlv.

of such coinage on public opinion could not possibly be overlooked or minimized by the Emperor. He must ... have censored, if not inspired it'.[11] In similar regard, W. Carter states that 'coins demonstrated Roman sovereignty ... [and] symbolized Roman accomplishments and the blessings of the gods which the emperor mediated to the people. There was no escaping Roman presence even in daily transactions'.[12] K. Dyer suggests that, in first-century Mediterranean village life, the circulation of coinage operated as one of the most efficient and concrete forms of communication.[13]

The various media available in this effort of persuasion in the ancient Roman world reinforced Roman ideals. Everything from architecture and inscriptions to the provision of 'conveniences' (*commoda*), such as public leisure (baths), mass entertainment (chariot racing, gladiatorial games) and processions (*triumphus*), contributed to a well-defined Roman cultural narrative. Coins distinctly contribute to our understanding of this phenomenon due to their ubiquity, distribution and continuous use. J. R. Fears suggests that the numismatic material is preferable to any other evidence in the discernment of imperial ideology:

> The literary sources are secondary sources; at their best, they are idiosyncratic, and at their worst they consciously distort the deeds and intentions of individual emperors. Thus we will never know much of what 'really' transpired under Trajan, and nothing at all of his actual intentions. Through the coinage, however, we know an inordinate amount about what the Roman government wanted its citizens and subjects to believe happened and how it wished the person and deeds of Trajan to be perceived by those citizens and subjects. The coinage was a medium of propaganda. Its purpose was the creation and propagation of a belief. It is the medium by which we can best approach the ideology of the imperial system.[14]

Although literary sources may never reveal the historical intentions of the ruling elite, be they in Rome or in the provinces, coinage reveals, at a minimum, an objective

---

[11] Mattingly, *Coins of the Roman Empire*, 3.xlv.

[12] W. Carter, *Matthew and the Margins* (Sheffield: Sheffield Academic Press, 2000), 38.

[13] K. D. Dyer, '"But Concerning That Day..." (Mark 13:32). "Prophetic" and "Apocalyptic" Eschatology in Mark 13', *Society of Biblical Literature 1999 Seminar Papers* (Atlanta, GA: Society of Biblical Literature, 1999), 112. Richard Oster, 'Numismatic Windows into the Social World of Early Christianity', *JBL* 101 (1982): 195–223 has also argued at length that coinage was one of the main methods of disseminated ideas and information in antiquity. See further C. Howgego, 'The Supply and Use of Money in the Roman World 200 B.C. to A.D. 300', *JRS* 82 (1992): 1–31; Michael H. Crawford, 'Money and Exchange in the Roman World', *JRS* 60 (1970): 40–46; J. Andreau, *Banking and Business in the Roman World* (Cambridge: Cambridge University Press, 1999). Attention to the numismatic record also helps define the circulation and models of the monetary economy, see C. Howgego, 'Coin Circulation and the Integration of the Roman Economy', *JRA* 7 (1994): 5–21; K. Hopkins, 'Taxes and Trade in the Roman Empire (200 B.C–A.D. 400)', *JRS* 70 (1980): 101–125; R. Duncan-Jones, *Structure and Scale in the Roman Economy* (Cambridge: Cambridge University Press, 1990); R. Duncan-Jones, 'Mobility and Immobility of Coin in the Roman Empire', *Annali* 36 (1989), 121–137.

[14] J. Rufus Fears, 'The Cult of Virtues and Roman Imperial Ideology', *ANRW* 17 2 (1981): 945. It is what Andrew Meadows refers to as 'a privileged place in the discourse between king and subjects', A. Meadows, 'The Spread of Coins in the Hellenistic World', in *Explaining Money and Financial Innovation: A Historical Analysis*, ed. P. Bernholz and R. Vaubel (New York: Springer, 2014), 173.

perspective of how rulers wanted their subjects to perceive their political activity. E. A. Judge alludes to a similar phenomenon of the treatment of history by ancient writers: 'in the case of Roman history, we typically mean by "documents" the coins, inscriptions, and papyri that survive directly from the time, as distinct from the treatment of the history by ancient writers'.[15] While the ancient coin was certainly not ideologically neutral, they do accurately depict the accurate content of how the emperor wanted to be perceived.[16] In this respect, the image, and text in particular (given its specificity) can be used to accurately record how the language was being used and in what ways it was being employed.[17]

The serious, scientific and academic incorporation of numismatic material into historical analysis was significantly impeded by the disparaging comments by A.H.M. Jones:

> If a modern analogy is to be sought for the varying types and legends of Roman imperial coins it is perhaps to be found in the similar variations in the postage stamps of modern countries other than our own (England). These often show a certain propagandistic tendency, its artistic monuments, or its principal industries. They are also sometimes topical, or commemorative of great events in national history. They throw a sidelight on the history of the period, but they mainly reflect the mentality of the post-office officials. No serious historian would use them as a clue which revealed changes of government policy, even if other evidence were totally lacking. It would be better if numismatists took the coin types and legends less seriously, and if historians of the empire, instead of building fantastic history upon them, frankly admitted that the political history of periods when coins are the sole evidence is irrecoverable, apart from the bare bones of chronology of the reigns, the areas which the various emperors effectively controlled, and any salient events which the coins directly celebrate.[18]

---

[15] E. A. Judge, 'Setting the Record Straight: Alternative Documents of a Protest in the Roman Army of Egypt', in *The First Christians in the Roman World: Augustan and New Testament Essays*, ed. James R. Harrison (Tübingen: Mohr Siebeck, 2008), 378.

[16] Catherine M. Murphy notes that 'coins are government-sponsored art, and coin iconography therefore usually reflects the official ideology by means of recognizable symbols. The wide circulation of these coins thus affords an opportunity for political propaganda', Catherine M. Murphy, *Wealth in the Dead Sea Scrolls and in the Qumran Community* (Leiden: Brill, 2001), 316. Andrew Burnett is in agreement when he observes that 'self-representation in this way was never as systematically developed as the products of modern propaganda machines, but, as with the study of portraiture, it can be very revealing about the aspirations and claims of any regime, matters which are as interesting to the historian as the reality of what actually happened', Andrew Burnett, *Coins: Interpreting the Past* (Berkeley: University of California Press, 1991), 37. Similarly Mark A. Chancey, 'coins provide a clear example of government-sponsored inscriptions, their designs chosen by and expressing the values of social elites'. Mark A. Chancey, 'The Epigraphic Habit of Hellenistic and Roman Galilee', in *Religion, Ethnicity, and Identity in Ancient Galilee: A Region in Transition*, ed. J. Zangenberg, H. W. Attridge and D. B. Martin (Tübingen: Mohr Siebeck, 2007), 86.

[17] Brennan, Turner and Wright are accurate in stating, 'they [coins] are a true reflection of their time – of a "face of power's" perception of what he had done, what he was going to do, what he was going to get others to do, or what others were going to get him or her to do', P. Brennan, M. Turner, and N. L. Wright, *Faces of Power: Imperial Portraiture on Roman Coins* (Sydney: Nicholson Museum, 2007), 5.

[18] Jones, 'Numismatics and History', 15–16 cited in Oster, 'Numismatic', 196.

A swift and satisfying rebuttal of Jones was forthcoming in the work of C. H. V. Sutherland:

Analogy is of course always tempting, but very often dangerous, especially when the precise degree of parallelism – upon which the efficacy of analogy depends most powerfully – is open to serious question. At best it can serve as a stimulating suggestion – that is, where no direct causal connection exists: at worst it may be fallacious. Thus when the function and behaviour of Roman imperial coin types is likened to that of modern postage-stamps the analogy is to be regarded with the utmost skepticism. It is true that both authenticate a government product, and that both, without question, reflect the activity of government officials, and that both, again, incorporate the principle of variety, but there the likeness ends. The modern postage stamp has always existed in an age when official propaganda of news has depended on organs of information far more ample than mere stamp-design, which is therefore devoted, apart from its essential symbolism of authority, to often quite formal aspects of general national interest. In imperial coinage, however, not only is there seen to be an overwhelming desire to vary types, but those types play so constantly and (even to modern eyes) so skillfully with different concepts of imperial government that, in an age when news could not be propagated by newspaper and radio, their intention cannot be doubted. They were, in essence, organs of information.[19]

The question of the 'author' of an inscription on a coin can be answered from at least two perspectives. At one level, Jonathan Williams is correct in identifying the emperor as the author; he states, 'the emperor came to be regarded as the effective author of the Roman public coinage and the regulator of its system of production at the imperial mint at Rome'.[20] The second view is that the Senate and people of Rome were the authors as they apparently issued the power to mint the coin, under the auspices of the emperor nonetheless. Either position adopted implies intentionality as a human-made object, and that the minting of a coin was an act of intentional communication. In support of the general conclusion above, Christopher Howgego notes that 'in periods of autocracy ... whether coin types were dictated from above to present an official image, or chosen by lower officials to flatter, the result will have been the same. The coins showed what was desirable to the regime. That is what matters'.[21] But the question which naturally arises is, did the population that used the coins notice any details on the coin such as inscription or image?

---

[19] C. H. V. Sutherland, 'The Intelligibility of Roman Imperial Coin Types', *JRS* 49 (1959): 54 cited in Oster, 'Numismatic', 197.

[20] Jonathan Williams, 'Religion and Roman Coins', in *A Companion to Roman Religion*, ed. J. Rüpke (Oxford: Blackwell, 2007), 157.

[21] Howgego, *Ancient History,* 70.

Coins as currency: Did people notice them?

Limited literary evidence suggests that people did pay attention to and were aware of the images, symbols and inscriptions on the coinage that was handled on a daily basis. The Stoic philosopher Epictetus, writing towards the end of the first century or beginning of the second century CE, notes that 'τοὺς χαρακτῆρας, οὓς ἔχων ἐν τῇ διανοίᾳ ἐλήλυθεν, οἵους καὶ ἐπὶ τῶν νομισμάτων ζητοῦντες, ἂν μὲν εὕρωμεν, δοκιμάζομεν, ἂν δὲ μὴ εὕρωμεν, ῥιπτοῦμεν. τίνος ἔχει τὸν χαρακτῆρα τοῦτο τὸ τετράσσαρον; Τραιανοῦ; φέρε. Νέρωνος; ῥῖψον ἔξω, ἀδόκιμόν ἐστιν, σαπρόν' (trans. 'the imprints which he brought with him in his mind, such as we look for also upon coins, and, if we find them, we accept the coins, but if we do not find them, we throw the coins away. "Whose imprint does this sestertius bear? Trajan's? Give it to me. Nero's? Throw it out, it will not pass, it is rotten"').[22] While the images and symbols on the coins were the most noticeable and prominent features,[23] coin inscriptions were used to explain and clarify the imagery which was often complex was further extended for a particular purpose.[24] On another occasion, the people of Antioch 'broke out against the emperor [Julian, 331–363 CE) and shouted ... that his coinage had a bull, and the world was subverted' (Socrates, *Hist. Eccl.* III, 17; PG LXVII, 424–425). Despite Socrates' inaccurate description which follows, including reference to a non-existent altar on the coinage of Julian, the incident is indicative of the attention to the imagery and inscriptions on coinage by a populace.[25] The famous incident concerning Jesus in the temple when asked about paying taxes to Caesar also appeals to the hearer's knowledge of the imagery on a denarius, 'Is it lawful to pay taxes to the emperor, or not?' [18] But Jesus, aware of their malice, said, 'Why are you putting me to the test, you hypocrites? [19] Show me the coin used for the tax'. And they brought him a denarius. [20] Then he said to them, 'Whose head is this, and whose title?' [21] They answered, 'The emperor's'. Then he said to them, 'Give therefore to the emperor the things that are the emperor's, and to God the things that are God's' (Mt 22:17b–21; cf. Mt 22:15–22; Mk 12:13–17; Lk 20:20–26). These and other incidents provide some literary evidence that the images and inscriptions on coinage were noticed and often elicited a vivid response.

---

[22] Epictetus, *Discourses of Epictetus*, 4.5.16–17. W. A. Oldfather, trans. *Epictetus. Discourses, Books 3–4. Fragments. The Encheiridion* (LCL 218; Cambridge, MA: Harvard University Press, 1928), 336–337. An important distinction is to be acknowledged between Roman coins and their Greek predecessors. Although 'designs on Greek coins typically remained unchanged for decades or even centuries, varying only in style or detail over time' (Williams, 'Religion', 143), Roman coinage exhibited both continuity and discontinuity in its iconography stamped on coinage. It is true that 'it was the usual practice in the ancient world to imitate existing types that were current locally, in order to secure greater confidence in and prestige for a new coin minted by a recently established authority' (Y. Meshorer, *Jewish Coins of the Second Temple Period* (Tel-Aviv: Am Hassefer, 1967), 58), but it is also apparent that Roman coinage was much more dynamic and adaptable to new images and environments.

[23] Crawford, 'Coin Types', 54–57.

[24] Howgego, *Ancient History*, 75.

[25] For further evidence that imagery on coins was noticed, especially in the east Roman Empire, see L. M. Hans, 'Der Kaiser mit dem Schwert', *JNG* 33 (1983): 57–66, especially 63–64 and n. 21.

In addition to the literary evidence, T. Hölscher and P. Zanker have developed a theory by which imperial imagery became embedded in private context from Augustus onward.[26] Zanker notes that numismatic imagery appears on 'jewelry and utensils, furniture, textiles, walls and stuccoed ceilings, door jambs, clay facings, roof tiles, and even on tomb monuments and marble ash urns'.[27] It is thus evident that numismatic imagery was one way in which imperial symbols and ideas came to be present in private Roman life. Thus we may conclude that not only did people notice what was on coinage, but they were demonstrably influenced by them explicitly through active response and implicitly through culture adaptation.

Coins as witnesses: A truncated view?

A specific area of concern for the use of coinage is the social origin of the coins and the way in which this influences our historical or linguistic reconstruction. Historians have frequently noted that coins are issued by the narrow upper stratum of society, and thus forming a historical picture based only on numismatic evidence is not only methodological suspicious, but may in many circumstances be seriously misleading. This admission of a limitation seems obvious. However, rather than one's response to be dismissal of numismatic evidence en toto, a more plausible solution is to simply acknowledge that the distillation of historical, social and philological reconstruction on coinage does not represent the full spectrum of the contemporary social world. However, this does not discount the potential for valid contribution of the evidence, albeit of a relatively narrow section of elite social life. This being said, there are several significant contributions that do pertain to the larger social milieu, as will be discussed in the various case studies below.

A second domain of potential limitation is whether the extant numismatic record is representative, by ratio, of numbers of ancient coinage minted and circulated in antiquity. An illuminating study by C. Howgego found that the absolute number of coins retrieved from an archaeological site was heavily dependent on local factors.[28] Elsewhere he notes that 'the hoards left in the ground are the ones that were not recovered in antiquity. Concentrations of coin hoards tend to reflect not prosperity or heavily monetized contexts, but rather the insecurity (particularly warfare) which resulted in owners not recovering their treasure'.[29] Hoards, which mainly consist of the more precious metals, may then give a skewed picture of the circulation of coinage, excluding bronze coinage and lower denominations.[30] It is also a relatively crude and

---

[26] Zanker, *Power of Images*, 265–295; Hölscher, *Staatsdenkmal und Publikum*, 20–32.

[27] Zanker, *Power of Images*, 266.

[28] Howgego, 'Supply and Use', 1–31.

[29] Howgego, *Ancient History*, 88. Cf. R. Duncan-Jones, *Money and Government in the Roman Empire* (Cambridge: Cambridge University Press, 1994), 85.

[30] For example, Galba's silver and gold coinage focused on garnering provincial support while bronze coins focused on rallying the urban citizens and featured urban symbols, see Olivier Hekster, 'Coins and Messages: Audience Targeting on Coins of Different Denominations?' in *Representation and Perception of Roman Imperial Power*, ed. Paul Erdkamp, O. Hekster, G. de Kleijn, Stephan T.A.M. Mols, and Lukas de Blois (Leiden: Brill, 2003), 26.

obvious fact that we possess only a fraction of a fraction of a fraction of numismatic material which originally circulated in antiquity. Edwin Yamauchi astutely notes the severely limited view which archaeological excavation affords in this regard: only a fraction of what is made or what is written survives, only a fraction of that material is preserved in archaeological sites that have been surveyed, only a fraction of the surveyed sites have been excavated, only a fraction of any excavated site is actually examined and only a fraction of materials are actually published.[31] Numismatic material which is published generally consists of the large and prestigious museum collections, which naturally marginalizes poor-quality or illegible coins which do not find their way into those collections. There is also the problem of unprovenanced coins which appear in private collections and auction catalogues. As will be demonstrated in the present discussion, problems abound with inaccurate attribution or failure to recognize inauthentic examples, especially so in the older collections.[32] These can and have misled scholars in the recent past on the very topic of consideration. We, therefore, will limit our discussion to those numismatic examples which have appeared in bona fide peer-reviewed publication outlets, and carefully weigh, where necessary, questions of authenticity.

Strengths of coinage as evidence

Despite these limitations, there are also several methodological strengths of numismatic evidence. First is the relative ubiquity of coinage in archaeological sites and throughout the Mediterranean. The broad geographic distribution of evidence is particularly helpful for lexicography of the NT. The composition, dissemination and reception of the NT are not confined to the Levant. Indeed, early Christian missionary interactions span the entire scope of the Mediterranean world. The extant record of contemporaneous coinage which circulated in the geographical areas inhabited by the recipients of Paul's epistles, for example, provides ideal linguistic evidence for comparison. Coinage in these provincial areas of the Roman Empire varied in value, shape and size as much as they did in type, depiction and linguistic value. Paul's movement 'from city to city and region to region from the years spanning the mid 30s to the mid 50s, exposed him to an extraordinary maze of small change',[33] examples of which are mostly accessible and the main museum collections mentioned in the previous chapter. This geographical specificity is invaluable for consideration of localized communication in the provinces or cities, particularly in relation to civic rivalries.

---

[31] Edwin Yamauchi, *The Stones and the Scriptures* (New York: Holman, 1972), 146–154.

[32] See, for example, J. Eckhel, *Doctrina numorum veterum*, 8 vols. (Vienna: Sumptibus J.V. Degen, 1792–1839), 4.288–306, who catalogues a list of misreadings in T. Mionnet, *Description des médailles antiques* (Paris: Toulouse, 1806–1808), 105. Cited in B. Burrell, *Neokoroi: Greek Cities and Roman Emperors* (Leiden: Brill, 2004), 12.

[33] P. Lewis and Ron Bolden, *The Pocket Guide to Saint Paul: Coins Encountered by the Apostle on His Travels* (Kent Town: Wakefield Press, 2002), vii.

Second, unlike literary texts, coins can often be precisely dated, or at the very least limited ranges which allow a clear demarcation for their introduction and circulation. Dating imperial issues is usually based on inscribed names and titles on coinage. Roman names were tripartite. The *praenomen* was the personal name conferred upon the child by parents, and on coinage was regularly abbreviated.[34] The *nomen* was the name which belonged to all members of the same family, initially on the basis of geographical location, but later was indicative of members of the same gens or clan.[35] The *cognomen* as the family name within a particular gens or clan. For example, in the gens of Cornelius there were, among others, the Cethegi, Lentuli and the Scipiones. One of the difficulties of Roman numismatics is that epigraphers typically engraved the entire inscription around the perimeter of the obverse without word divisions. Thus, on the obverse of RIC *Nero* 181 (Figure 27) we find NERO CLAUD CAESAR AUG GER PM TR P IMP PP.

NERO refers to the praenomen Nero in unabbreviated form; CLAUD is the nomen and abbreviates Claudius as the name of the gens to which the family belonged; CAESAR is the inherited name of the Julian family and adopted by the Claudians as well as later emperors used by heirs to the throne; AUG stands for Augustus and is the most distinctive title of the emperor; GER abbreviates Germanicus and is both

Figure 27 RIC *Nero* 181 (used with permission).

---

[34] AULUS (A, AU, AUL); DECIMUS (D, DEC); CAIUS/GAIUS (C); GNAEUS (CN, GN); LUCIUS (L, LU); MARCUS (M); PUBLIUS (P, PUP); QUINTUS (Q); SERVIUS (SER); SERGIUS (S); SEXTUS (SEX, SX); SPURIUS (S, SP); TIBERIUS (TI); TITUS (T); APPIUS (AP, APP); NUMERICUS (N); VIBIUS (V).

[35] The nomen usually ended in 'ius', 'aius', 'eius' or 'eus'. Aemilius, Cornelius, Furius, Manlius and Pompeius are examples.

80   *Numismatics and Greek Lexicography*

a hereditary title as well as a title of honour originally given to acclaim victory in campaigns in Germania; PM abbreviates Pontifex Maximus which acknowledges the emperor's title as the supreme head of the Roman religion (literally 'head priest'), a title which was held by the emperor Augustus and all subsequent emperors; TR P (also commonly TRIB P, TRIB POT) refers to Tribunicia Potestas (trans. 'Tribunition Power') for the civil head of state, and is a key inscription to determine a particular year a coin was struck. When TR P was renewed annually a number would be added afterward, so that TR P would indicate that the coin was struck during the first year the emperor held the title, and TR P III would indicate the third year. Thus, a coin of Nero with TR P indicates that it was minted between October 54 CE and September 55 CE. Table 7 below provides further detail on the specific dates attributed by the Tribunicia Potestae in regard to each emperor.

Table 7 First-century Tribunicia Potestae dates

AUGUSTUS	TR P, June 27, 23 BCE. TR P II, same day and month, 22 BCE, and renewed annually on the same date. Thus at his death in 14 CE he was in the course of his TR P XXXVII.
TIBERIUS	TR P, June 27, 6 BCE. Renewed annually until TR P V in 2 BCE, TR P VI not until June 27 4 CE. In order to find the year Anno Domini, deduct 2 from the TR P (thus, TR P XXX would be in the year 28 CE, or really 28–29 CE because it is renewed in June of each year and ran to June of the next year).
CALIGULA	TR P, March 18, 37 CE. Renewed annually on the same date in the years 38, 39 and 40 CE.
CLAUDIUS	TR P, January 25, 41 CE. Renewed annually on that date. At his death in 54 he was in the course of his TR P XIIII.
NERO	TR P, October 13, 54 CE. Renewed annually on that date until 59 CE, when apparently he started a new system by shortening his TR P VI and counting, thereafter, from December 4 (or 10), when he took TR P VII and renewed annually on that date. At his death in June, 68 CE, he was in the course of TR P XIIII.
GALBA	TR P, April 3, 68 CE–January 15, 69 CE.
OTHO	TR P, January 15, 69 CE–April 17, 69 CE.
VITELLIUS	TR P, 69 CE.
VESPASIAN	TR P, July 1, 69 CE. Renewed annually on the same date. At his death in June, 79 CE, he was in the course of TR P X.
TITUS	TR P, July 1, 71 CE. Renewed annually on the same date. At his death in September 81 CE, he was in the course of his TR P XII.
DOMITIAN	TR P, September 13, 81 CE. Renewed annually on the same date. At his death in September 96 CE, he was in the course of his TR P XVI.
NERVA	TR P, September 18, 96 CE. TR P II from the same date in the year 97 CE. Apparently started TR P III in December of the same year (97 CE), however some inscriptions fail to recognize TR P III and carry the TR P II to his death on January 25, 98 CE.

Another inscribed title regularly found on imperial (and some Latin provincial coins, e.g. RPC 77, 78, 185, 278, 300, 301, 303) although not present on the current example is COS referring to consul, one of the two chief magistrates of the Roman state. The emperor himself was quite frequently one of the consuls. When he was not, he usually appointed someone to serve in his place. The consulship also lasted for a year and is a possible means to determine date, but not to be used in the same way as TR P, even though numerals were placed after COS as per TR P. The difficulty in using COS by itself is that frequently a period of years would pass between each time the emperor held the consulship. An example of this is difficulty is Augustus who served as COS XI in 23 BCE and COS XII in the year 5 BCE.

The abbreviation IMP refers to *imperator*, Commander-in-Chief of the armed forces. It usually appears at the beginning of the legend. It is to be distinguished from IMP IMP.II, IMP.III etc. at the end of the legend, signifying a victorious army's acclamation of its commander. From Tiberius onward it was a title used by no one except the emperor himself, who also added numbers after this title to designate extraordinary events or victories in the field by his commanders or subordinates. Finally, PP designated the phrase *Pater Patriae* (trans. 'father of his country') and refers to a title originally bestowed upon the emperor by the senate. The title was refused by some of the emperors, Tiberius famously so (in Suetonius, *Tib.* 26; Dio Cassius *Historia Romana* 57.8.1 and Tacitus, *Ann.* 1.72; 2.87), even though he issued coins with the words Divus Augustus Pater, which many commentators understand as implying a positive view towards Augustus as father of the country. Nero at first refused the title, apparently due to his youthful age of seventeen, however within two years was using the title (Seneca, *Clem.* 1.14.2; Suetonius, *Nero* 8), and Vespasian adopted it later in life (Suetonius, *Vesp.* 12) (see the summary of evidence in Table 8).

Table 8 Collated first-century dates for abbreviated titulature

Augustus		Tiberius
COS XI	23 BCE	
IMP VIIII	20 BCE	
IMP X	15 BCE	
	13 BCE	COS
IMP XI	12 BCE	
P M		
IMP XII	11 BCE	
IMP XIII	9 BCE	
IMP XIIII	8 BCE	
	7 BCE	COS II
COS XII	5 BCE	
COS XIII	2 BCE	
PP		

(Continued)

IMP XV	2 CE	
IMP XVI(?)	6 CE	
IMP XVII	6 CE	IMP III
IMP XVIII		IMP IIII
IMP XIX	9 CE	IMP V
IMP XX	11 CE	IMP VI
	12 CE	IMP VII
IMP XXI	14 CE	PRINCEPS
	15 CE	P M
	18 CE	COS III
		IMP VIII
	21 CE	COS IIII
	31 CE	COS V
CALIGULA		**CLAUDIUS**
IMP	37 CE	
P M		
COS		
P P	38 CE	
COS II	39 CE	
COS III	40 CE	
COS IIII	41 CE	IMP
		IMP II
		IMP III
		IMP IIII
		P M
	42 CE	COS II
		P P
	43 CE	COS III
	44 CE	IMP V
		IMP VI
		IMP VII
	45 CE	IMP VIII
	46 CE	IMP VIIII
		IMP X
		IMP XI
	47 CE	COS IIII
		IMP XII
		IMP XIII

(Continued)

	48 CE	IMP XIIII
	49 CE	IMP XVI
	50 CE	IMP XVII
		IMP XVIII
	51 CE	COS V
		IMP XXI
	52 CE	IMP XXIIII
	53 CE	IMP XXVII
NERO		**GALBA, OTHO**
IMP	54 CE	
P M		
COS	55 CE	
P P		
COS II	57 CE	
IMP III		
COS III	58 CE	
IMP IIII		
IMP V		
IMP VI	59 CE	
COS IIII	60 CE	
IMP VII		
IMP VIII	61 CE	
IMP VIIII		
IMP XI	66 CE	
IMP XII	67 CE	
COS V	68 CE	IMP; PM (Galba)
	69 CE	COS II (Galba)
	69 CE	IMP; COS; P M (Otho)
VESPASIAN		**VITELLIUS**
	69 CE	IMP; GERM; COS
IMP	69 CE	
IMP II		
COS	69 CE	
P M		
P P		
COS II	70 CE	
IMP III		

(Continued)

IMP IIII		
IMP V		
COS III	71 CE	
IMP VI		
IMP VII		
IMP VIII		
COS IIII	72 CE	
IMP X	73 CE	
COS V	74 CE	
IMP XI		
IMP XII		
COS VI	75 CE	
IMP XIII		
IMP XIIII		
COS VII	76 CE	
IMP XV		
IMP XVI		
IMP XVII		
IMP XVIII		
COS VIII	77 CE	
IMP XIX	78 CE	
COS VIIII	79 CE	
IMP XX		
AUG		
P M		

TITUS		**DOMITIAN**
COS	70 CE	
IMP	71 CE	COS
IMP II		
P M		
COS II	72 CE	
IMP III		
CENSOR	73 CE	COS II
IMP IIII		
COS III	74 CE	COS III
IMP VI		

(Continued)

IMP VII		
COS IIII	75 CE	
IMP VII		
IMP VIII		
COS V	76 CE	COS IIII
IMP VIIII(?)		
IMP X(?)		
IMP XI		
IMP XII		
COS VI	77 CE	COS V
IMP XIII	78 CE	
COS VII	79 CE	COS VI
IMP XIIII		
IMP V		
AUG		
P M		
P P		
COS VIII	80 CE	COS VII
IMP XVI	81 CE	IMP
		AUG
		P M
		P P
	82 CE	COS VIII
		IMP II
	83 CE	COS VIIII
		IMP III
		IMP IIII(?)
	84 CE	COS X
		IMP V
		IMP VI

DOMITIAN		**NERVA**
IMP VII	84 CE	
GERM		
COS XI	85 CE	
IMP VIII		
IMP VIIII		
IMP X		

(Continued)

IMP XI		
CENS		
PERPET		
COS XII	86 CE	
IMP XII		
IMP XIII		
IMP XIIII		
COS XIII	87 CE	
COS XIIII	88 CE	
IMP V		
IMP VI		
IMP VII		
IMP VIII		
IMP XIX		
IMP XX		
IMP XXI		
COS XV	90 CE	
COS XVI	92 CE	
COS XVII	95 CE	
	96 CE	COS II
		IMP
		CAES
		AUG
	97 CE	COS III
		IMP II
		GERM
	98 CE	COS IIII

Dating Greek provincial issues also follows a relatively simple but not always straightforward formula. The most obvious is, of course, the obverse portrait and titles, at least for a broad demarcation of date to ruling years of a particular emperor. But frequently the coins have a year mark in addition which allows greater specificity. The three types of Jerusalem-minted small denomination coinage of the procurator Pontius Pilate (Judea) are distinguished, among other iconographic features, by a regnal year of Tiberius. The obverse of RPC 1.4967 (Figure 28) depicts a simpulum (ladle used by pagan priests for libation offering) surrounded by the legend ΤΙΒΕΡΙΟΥ ΚΑΙΣΑΡΟΣ L ΙϹ, which gives the name and title of the reigning emperor (trans. '[coin] of Tiberius

Figure 28 RPC 1.4967 (used with permission).

Table 9 Ancient Greek numerals

	Units	Tens	Hundreds
1	A Alpha	I Iota	P Rho
2	B Beta	K Kappa	Σ Sigma
3	Γ Gamma	Λ Lambda	T Tau
4	Δ Delta	M Mu	Υ Upsilon
5	E Epsilon	N Nu	Φ Phi
6	F/Ϛ Digamma	Ξ Xi	X Chi
7	Z Zeta	O Omicron	Ψ Psi
8	H Eta	Π Pi	Ω Omega
9	Θ Theta	Ϙ Koppa	ϡ Sampi

Caesar'), followed by the abbreviation for year 'L'[36] and the Greek numeral IϚ (=16, cf. Table 9) which equates to the year 29 CE. The reverse has ΙΟΥΛΙΑ ΚΑΙΣΑΡΟΣ with three ears of corn. RPC 1.4968 (Figure 29) has on the obverse ΤΙΒΕΡΙΟΥ ΚΑΙΣΑΡΟΣ around the depiction of a lituus, a wooden staff used by an augur to make predictions while examining the animal's entrails for portents. The reverse has the date L IZ (year 17 = 30 CE) within a wreath. RPC 1.4969 (Figure 30) is similar to RPC 1.4968 except it has the date L IH (year 18 = 31 CE).

[36] This abbreviation symbol had been used since the Ptolemaic period on coinage to indicate year, and was borrowed from conventions in the papyri.

Figure 29 RPC 1.4968 (used with permission).

Figure 30 RPC 1.4969 (used with permission).

If a specific regnal year is not inscribed on a coin, the date of issue can sometimes be inferred on the basis of other factors, even if these are somewhat debated. For example, RPC 1.76 is a coin of Colonia Romula (Seville), and despite lacking a specific date it has specific features which lend support to a date during Augustus's reign. M. Grant[37]

---

[37] M. Grant, *From Imperium to Auctoritas: A Historical Study of Aes Coinage in the Roman Empire, 49 B.C.–A.D. 14* (Cambridge: Cambridge University Press, 1946), 220.

argues that it was an issue of Augustus on the occasion of his visit in 15–14 BCE. This is argued on the basis that the reverse iconography in depicting cornucopia, rudder and globe was an allegory to Fortuna, and hence is to be dated to Augustus's reign. On the other hand, A. Burnett, M. Amandry and P. Ripollès attribute the same coin to the reign of Tiberius, not on the basis of a proposed imperial visit, but on the basis of metallurgical analysis and stylistic grounds. Burnett and colleagues highlight the type of bronze, which is consistent with Tiberius's other issues and portraiture style which again is similar to his asses and semis.[38]

A third broad area of methodological consideration is the time frame that coins continued to circulate and be used. From the available evidence, it appears that coins potentially had a much longer period of circulation than the issuing emperor. The implication of this observation, which will be elaborated below, is that both the legends and symbols of coinage would have had exposure and circulation beyond the immediate period of issue. J. Magness comments that 'coins in antiquity often remained in circulation for long periods-up to hundreds of years after they were minted'.[39] This is not only accurate as far as the famous Greek tetradrachms of Athens, a phenomenon regularly noted,[40] but also their Roman imperial and provincial decedents. It is this phenomenon that caused Stefan Krmnicek to note that coins have a biography of their own.[41] This phenomenon can explicitly be seen in the countermarking of coinage. Close to 10,000 countermarked Roman coins, mostly from the east and on copper, were analysed and catalogued by C. J. Howgego's landmark study into approximately 900 varieties.[42] Richard Baker notes that there were three primary reasons that a coin was countermarked:[43] first, to extend the geographical area in which the coin would be accepted as legal tender, such as (i) countermarking by imperial authority a coin of the mint of Rome so it could be used as legal tender in a province by the Roman legions stationed there, (ii) countermarking done in the name of the Roman governor, Legate, proconsul or prefect in charge of a particular province, (iii) countermarking local 'provincial imitations' of Roman coinage to give official sanction to them by Rome; second, to continue in use a coin which had been in circulation for a considerable period of time, such as a coin in a worn condition (DVP = Dupondius, struck on worn specimens of sestertii and downgrading their value by half; AS = As, struck on worn specimens of dupondii and downgrading value by half); and third, to designate a new authority usurping the coins of another for their own use, such as in times of revolution where the names, monograms or mottos of revolting generals and legions

---

[38] Burnett, Amandry, and Carradice, *Roman Provincial Coinage 1*, 50.

[39] Jodi Magness, *The Archaeology of Qumran and the Dead Sea Scrolls* (Grand Rapids, MI: Eerdmans, 2002), 10.

[40] B. V. Head, *Catalogue of Greek Coins in the British Museum: Attica, Megaris, Aegina* (London: British Museum, 1888), xxii.

[41] Stefan Krmnicek, 'Das Konzept der Objektbiographie in der antiken Numismatik', in *Coins in Context 1: New Perspectives for the Interpretation of Coin Finds*, ed. H. V. Kaenel and F. Kemmers (Mainz: Philipp Von Zabern, 2009), 51.

[42] Only 13 of ~900 types in Howgego's catalogue (nos. 838–850) are attested as countermarks on silver coins, Howgego, *Countermarks*, 293–295.

[43] Richard Baker, 'The Countermarks Found on Ancient Roman Coins: A Brief Introduction', *Journal for the Society of Ancient Numismatics* 15, no. 3 (1984): 52–58.

were countermarked by their adherents upon the available coinage.[44] Countermarking the coins of their predecessors not only served political purposes, but also saved great time and expense of minting new coins while still conveying an important message affirming the power and control to the inhabitants of the region. Howgego rightly concludes that the only overarching explanation of countermarking is that the process help regulate and bring order to a complex coinage which was issued independently and irregularly by more than 500 authorities over three centuries.[45]

One of the implications of this well-established countermarking practice is that coinage could circulate for much longer and more broadly than the initial time or place of minting would suggest. For example, T. O. Mabbott notes that the evidence of finds 'indicates that Nero's money circulated after his death in most parts of the Empire'.[46] This common phenomenon enhances the prospect of visibility and impact of coinage, which in the context of our current discussion could potentially enhance exposure to the relevant numismatic inscriptions. The specific manner in which a countermarked series aids our knowledge of the broad circulation is that the countermarked series effectively acts as a dispersed hoard, and as a corollary, countermarks applied to coins that had originally been minted elsewhere demonstrate the movement and longevity of those coins. Howgego demonstrates the usefulness of legionary countermarks for this purpose and provides a discussion of Roman army units on regional economics, and summarizes his analysis in maps illustrating various countermarked groups, demonstrating what is effectively a skeleton of local economic networks.[47]

Further evidence in broad dissemination of coinage beyond the original mint is evident in the distribution of provincial coinage in archaeological finds. For example, Howgego analyses the patterns of civic bronzes in Asia Minor and the implications for the aggregate movements of people, especially as it pertains to trade, soldiers and tourists, but also in regard to private rents, loans and other movements of coins.[48] The connection between the circulation of bronze coinage and movement of ancient peoples has had a profitable application in various historical contexts within scholarly discussion, including the period of Alexander,[49] the Hellenistic

---

[44] See further R. Martini, *The Pangerl Collection Catalog and Commentary on the Countermarked Roman Imperial Coins* (Milan: Ennerre, 2003); David M. May, 'The Empire Strikes Back: The Mark of the Beast in Revelation', *Review and Expositor* 106 (2009): 83–97; D. Barag and S. Qedar, 'A Countermark of the Legio Quinta Scytica from the Jewish War', *Israel Numismatic Journal* 13 (1994): 66–69; D. Barag, 'The Countermarks of the Legio Decima Fretensis' in *Proceedings of the International Numismatic Convention (Jerusalem, 26–31 December, 1963)* ed. A. Kindler (Tel Aviv: Schocken, 1967), 117–125; M. Rosenberger, *The Coinage of Eastern Palestine, and Legionary Countermarks, Bar-Kochba Overstrucks* (Jerusalem: Rosenberger 1978); S. Topalov, *Novi prinosi kŭm prouchvane kontramarkiraneto na moneti v raĭona na zapadnopontiĭskite gradove prez III - I v. pr. n. e.: = New Contributions to the Study of the Countermarking of the Coins in the Area of the West Pontic Cities 3rd-1st c. B.C.* (Sofia: Nasko, 2002).

[45] Howgego, *Countermarks*, 1–16.

[46] T. O. Mabbott, 'Epictetus and Nero's Coinage', *Classical Philology* 36.4 (1941): 398–399.

[47] Howgego, *Countermarks*, 17–31.

[48] Howgego, *Countermarks*, 32–51.

[49] M. J. Price, *The Coinage in the Name of Alexander the Great and Philip Arrhidaeus: A British Museum Catalogue* (London: British Museum Press, 1991), 65–66.

descendants,[50] the Republic[51] and under the Empire.[52] The application of these findings to the distribution of coinage, including the symbols and inscriptions is particularly relevant in strengthening the broad spread and documented dissemination of provincial issues beyond their original borders.

Conclusion

This chapter has sought to engage with various dimensions of the critical issues in the appeal to coinage as it pertains to both historical studies and application to lexicography. In particular three questions were posed of our numismatic sources. First it was asked whether we could trust coinage as a source due to its propagandistic tendencies. Our above discussion sought to clarify that despite the numismatic issues having considerable 'bias' in representation of the issuing authority, this did not detract from their value in demonstrating the linguistic capabilities of the lexeme or phrase under discussion. Rather it was seen that rather than detracting from the usefulness of coinage as a source, the propagandistic feature of numismatic evidence was not subject to the same weaknesses of typical literary sources, and was in fact preferable to these sources in discerning imperial or civic ideology. Second, it was asked whether inhabitants of the ancient world noticed the imagery and legends on the coinage. The ancient literature surveyed certainly indicated that people were regularly aware of the inscribed surface of a coin and it often elicited a response or demonstrated cultural influence whereby the imagery became embedded in the private life of the population. Third, it was questioned whether coinage could provide, necessarily, only a truncated and overtly limited view of the circumstances in which it was produced. This limitation was readily conceded and it was acknowledged that despite their limited reflection of the narrow upper stratum of society, numismatic evidence could nonetheless be profitably employed, albeit in a more nuanced and limited fashion. In no way did the forgoing discussion, or broader aim of this volume, seek to give preferential treatment to numismatic evidence, but rather suggest that its omission is detrimental to the full picture of the linguistic and historical landscape. Notwithstanding these methodological hurdles, the final portion of our discussion above addressed the particular strengths of numismatic evidence. These included the ubiquitous and specific geographic attestation of provincial coinage throughout the Mediterranean, which is particularly suited to NT studies given the breadth of material and specificity of location. The tangible nature of the possibility of accurate numismatic dating was also seen to have potential benefit for engagement with NT documents. Finally, we discussed the implications of how attention to countermarking could historically not only trace the skeletal network of economic local trade patterns,

[50] M. Crawford, 'Trade and Movement of Coinage across the Adriatic in the Hellenistic Period', in *Scripta Nummaria Romana: Essays Presented to Humphrey Sutherland*, ed. R. A. G. Carson and C. M. Kraay (London: Spink, 1978), 1–11.

[51] Michael H. Crawford, *Coinage and Money under the Roman Republic: Italy and the Mediterranean Economy* (Berkeley: University of California Press, 1985), 178–179, 319–320.

[52] Howgego, *Ancient History*, 92, 101.

92   *Numismatics and Greek Lexicography*

but also establish documented circulation patterns beyond the time and place of issue. The question that arises at this juncture of our discussion is: why has so much written text in the form of legends on coinage been ignored by lexicographers? In part the following chapters partially fulfil Elkins's observation that 'to produce a more complete picture of the past, coins must be studied in multiple contexts and in conjunction with other disciplines'.[53] Part Two in particular, with extensive case studies, will hopefully demonstrate that numismatic evidence should be included as one piece of the literary source evidence, and that this should be reflected in lexicons moving forward.

Excursus: The buying power of coinage in antiquity

It is commonly recognized that the function of money is a medium of exchange as a standard unit with a store of value in which prices and debts can be expressed.[54] Keith Hopkins famously argued that the chief purpose of Roman coinage was the payment of taxes,[55] to which Richard Duncan-Jones added payment of the army.[56] The function of common money and its adoption more broadly can be seen to encourage the growth of trade.[57] The study of numismatics naturally raises economic questions pertaining to the buying power of coinage in antiquity.[58] There have been various attempts to compile and tabulate monetary prices in antiquity by historians, economists and analysts of the Roman Empire.[59] The following discussion seeks to provide a general framework (or more plausibly reference points) for estimating the value of coinage in terms of buying power across the Mediterranean in various locations and in various time periods, as far as can be determined by the limited sources available. Clearly this

---

[53] Nathan T. Elkins, 'The Trade in Fresh Supplies of Ancient Coins: Scale, Organisation, and Politics', in *All the King's Horses: Essays on the Impact of Looting and the Illicit Trade on Our Knowledge of the Past*, ed. P. K. Lazarus and A. W. Baker (Washington, DC: Society for American Archaeology Press, 2012), 95.

[54] Kevin Greene, *The Archaeology of the Roman Economy* (Berkeley: University of California Press, 1986), 50–51.

[55] Hopkins, 'Taxes and Trade', 101–125.

[56] R. Duncan-Jones, 'The Denarii of Septimus Severus and the Mobility of Roman Coin', *Numismatic Chronicle* 161 (2001): 75–89.

[57] D. Schaps, *The Invention of Coinage and the Monetization of Ancient Greece* (Ann Arbor: University of Michigan Press, 2004).

[58] No attempt will be made to equate modern monetary value to the coinage as any estimation will be out of date in the few months between completing this chapter and the time the volume goes to press. Modern comparisons might be more profitably based on base salary or minimum wage occupations; however, even a cursory survey of 193 United Nation member states indicate a vast disparity. Even if one limits the analysis to major developed economies (G7) the maximum range is greater by a factor of two.

[59] R. Duncan-Jones, *The Economy of the Roman Empire: Quantitative Studies* (Cambridge: Cambridge University Press, 1982); Hans-Joachim Drexhage, *Preise, Mieten/Pachten, Kosten und Lohne im romischen Agypten bis zum Regierungsantritt Diokletians* (St. Katharinen: Scripta Mercaturae, 1991); Dominic Rathbone, 'Prices and Price Formation in Roman Egypt', in *Economic antique. Prix et formation des prix dans les economies antiques*, ed. Jean Andreau, Pierre Briant, and Raymond Descat (Saint-Bertrand-de-Comminges: Musee archeologique departmental, 1997), 183–244.

Critical Issues in the Appeal to Coinage

Table 10 Augustan values 27 BCE–301 CE

1 unit ↓ equals →	Aureus	Quinarius Aureus	Denarius	Quinarius
Aureus	1	2	25	50
Quinarius Aureus	0.5	1	12.5	25
Denarius	0.04	0.08	1	2
Quinarius Argenteus	0.02	0.04	0.5	1
Sestertius	0.01	0.02	0.25	0.5
Dupondius	0.005	0.01	0.125	0.25
As	0.0025	0.005	0.0625	0.125
Semis	0.00125	0.0025	0.03125	0.0625
Quadrans	0.000625	0.00125	0.015625	0.03125

1 unit ↓ equals →	Sestertius	Dupondius	As	Semis	Quadrans
Aureus	100	200	400	800	1600
Quinarius Aureus	50	100	200	400	800
Denarius	4	8	16	32	64
Quinarius Argenteus	2	4	8	16	32
Sestertius	1	2	4	8	16
Dupondius	0.5	1	2	4	8
As	0.25	0.5	1	2	4
Semis	0.125	0.25	0.5	1	2
Quadrans	0.0625	0.125	0.25	0.5	1

sketch will be fragmentary and by no means do I assume that the discussion exhausts the relevant questions or responses that are generated by such an examination. The relevance of this issue for the broader topic under discussion, numismatics and Greek lexicography, is that the influence, circulation or exposure of various coins is clarified if the buying power of the coin is known. For instance, the regularity with which the physical coin may have changed hands and in what context directly contributes to the cogency of the questions pertaining to circulation and who would have been exposed to the iconography and inscription on the coinage. If a coin's value is so high or low to exclude it from some or other context of ancient life, this too needs to be taken into consideration.

The coinage reforms of Augustus between 23 and 19 BCE not only saw Augustus emerge as the sole minting authority but also involved a comprehensive reform of denominations below the denarius.[60] Augustus set fixed standards for the sestertius (minted from orichalcum rather than silver and worth one quarter of a denarius) and dupondius (minted from orichalcum and worth one half of a sestertius). Augustus also reintroduced pure copper coins (previously 84 BCE) in the form of an as (half a dupondius), semis (half an as) and quadrans (half a semis).[61] The Augustan values of denominations of coinage are listed in Table 10.

When Octavian took possession of Egypt in 30 BCE, he found an established currency system with traditions going back nearly 300 years. From this time Egypt maintained a separate currency until Diocletian's monetary reform. Table 11 indicates the relative value of the Egyptian denominations. Hoard evidence also indicates that when crossing into Egypt all imperial coinage had to be exchanged for Egyptian and when leaving all Egyptian coinage had to be exchanged for imperial coinage. The drachm was officially valued at one denarius, and a drachm equivalent to that of a sestertius. Constantina Katsari notes that while 'these denominations may have been used, initially, for state payments; eventually … they facilitated minor commercial

Table 11 Egyptian denominations

1 unit ↓ equals →	Tetradrachm (staters)	Drachm	Diobol	Obol	Hemiobol
Tetradrachm (staters)	1	4	12	24	48
Drachm	0.25	1	3	6	12
Diobol	0.125	0.5	1	2	4
Obol	0.042	0.167	0.5	1	2
Hemiobol	0.020	0.083	0.25	0.5	1

Table 12 Conversion rate between Egypt and the provincial denominations

1 unit ↓ equals →	Tetradrachm (staters)	Drachm	Diobol	Obol	Hemiobol
Denarius	0.25	1	3	6	12
Sestertius	0.0625	0.25	1	1.5	3
As	0.03125	0.125	0.5	0.75	1.5
Semis	0.015625	0.0625	0.25	0.375	0.75
Quadrans	0.0078125	0.03125	0.125	0.1875	0.375

[60] Crawford, *Coinage and Money*, 258.
[61] Crawford, *Coinage and Money*, 257–260.

transactions in the markets'.[62] Table 12 indicates the denominational conversion between Egypt and other Roman provinces.

First and foremost, it must be acknowledged that the investigation of the buying power of coinage in the ancient Roman Empire is fraught with complexity and difficulties on every side. In an unpublished working paper within the Department of Economics at the Massachusetts Institute of Technology,[63] David Kessler and Peter Temin examine the monetization in the early Roman Empire through consideration of the prices of wheat across the empire, noting variables such as proximity of location to Rome and distance discount,[64] and governmental interventions of which there were at least nineteen during the first century BCE and first century CE.[65] They conclude that 'monetary measures … [were] virtually universal'[66] in the Roman Empire, which few would dispute. However, the problem for historians is that the many hundreds of references to specific prices for goods and services in ancient sources, although listed with specific and known terminology, frequently pertain to distinctive or ad hoc services or goods, which are not easily comparable due to the implicit uniqueness of the transaction.[67] As Kessler and Temin note, 'The accounts reveal that people thought in terms of prices, but they do not provide a data set with which to examine prices.' [68]

A corollary of this complexity is the lack of widespread evidence for prices in different locations around the Mediterranean. There are some fixed points which aid in this process, such as Geoffrey Rickman's account of the supply of wheat for Rome and some outlying areas,[69] or the papyri which give some indication of prices for other goods and services in Egypt,[70] but reliable literary evidence is relatively

---

[62] Constantina Katsari, *The Roman Monetary System: Eastern Provinces from the First to Third Century AD* (Cambridge: Cambridge University Press, 2011), 209.

[63] David Kessler and Peter Temin, *Money and Prices in the Early Roman Empire* (Massachusetts Institute of Technology, Department of Economics, Working Paper Series, 2005), 1–32.

[64] Kessler and Temin, *Money*, 25–26, 28–29.

[65] Kessler and Temin, *Money*, 27.

[66] Kessler and Temin, *Money*, 1.

[67] Texts often specify amount paid, when it was paid and who paid, but it is regularly not clear why these payments were made. For example, P. Wisc 2.38 is a list of payments of money for the months Choiah, Tybi, Mecheir and Phamenoth of an unknown year between 54 and 67 in the first century CE, but it is not clear why these payments were made. Alternatively, O. Ber 2.210 from the provenance Berenike is a single ostrakon composed of seven fragment measuring 13.5cm x 15.0cm and has 11 lines of text. It is an account for the 22nd to 27th of an unknown month (the 24th is missing and the 25th and 26th are reversed), listing amounts received for various items sometime during the period between 50 CE and 75 CE. It provides several specific transaction reference points and deserves more attention than it has generally received, 'Account: 22nd: of bunch of cabbage, []; of bunch of parsley, (1 obol). 23rd: of salt fish (or meat), []; of salt fish (or meat), (two obols); of revenue, (three obols); of cabbage, (4 obols); of bread, (2 obols). 26th: of salt fish (or meat), (2 obols). 25th: of bread, (2 obols). 27th: of bread, (2 obols?); of artabas (of wheat), (2 obols)'.

[68] Kessler and Temin, *Money*, 1. Wheat is one commodity which Dominic Rathbone exploits to measures inflation. Rathbone, 'Prices', 191–192.

[69] Geoffrey Rickman, *The Corn Supply of Ancient Rome* (Oxford: Oxford University Press, 1980), 143–155.

[70] See below for further discussion.

96   *Numismatics and Greek Lexicography*

sparse on specifics of time and place. Literary references are often general rather than recording specific transactions, and therefore only approximations.[71]

Both the proximity to Rome and the method of transport affected the price of certain commodities such as wheat.[72] Polybius *Histories* 2.15.1 discusses wheat prices in the Po Valley: 'its fertility is not easy to describe. It produces such an abundance of grain, that often in my time the price of wheat was four obols per Sicilian medimnus and that of barley two obols, a metretes of wine costing the same as the medimnus of barley'.[73] Diocletian's *Price Edict* fixed river transport prices at five times the amount of sea transport, but despite it being later chronologically, the additional expense for transport via river seems to have remained constant in the first centuries of the first millennium.

Despite all these limitations, presented below in Table 13 is a sample of documented transactions from circa first century CE provided as a representative sample of costs associated with ancient life. Each item is presented in general chronological order with as much available information as possible including date, entity, location, amount (including conversion to equivalent Augustan denarii) and source.[74]

Table 13 Documented price transactions[75]

Date	Item	Location	Expense/ wage	Equivalent	Source
8 BC	300 cotylae (85 litres) of wine	Egypt	18 dr.	18 d	PBM 1171
2 BC	1,000 bundles of reeds	Egypt	15 dr.	15 d	P. Oxy 742
1 CE	Wax tablet and stylus	Egypt	1 ob.	0.167 d	P. Oxy 736
1 CE	1 jar of wine	Egypt	6 dr	6 d	P. Oxy 745
1 CE	1 chus (1.1 litres) of oil.	Egypt	4 dr., 4ob.	4.67 d	P. Oxy 736
1 CE	1 chus (1.1 litres) of oil.	Egypt	4 dr., 2ob.	4.33 d	P. Oxy 739
1 CE	1 chus (1.1 litres) of oil.	Egypt	5 dr.	5 d	P. Oxy 819
1 CE	Employment of weaver for 1 day	Egypt	3.5 asses	0.21875 d	P. Oxy 737
1 CE	Hired man 1 day	Egypt	4 asses	0.25 d	P. Oxy 737

---

[71] See, for example, Cicero in *Verrine Orations* 2.3.189, 'the attack I do make is this: that whereas a peck of wheat was then locally worth 2 sesterces according to Verres' own letter to you, or 3 sesterces at the most, as has been demonstrated alike by the evidence of all our witnesses and by the farmers' accounts, Verres nevertheless exacted from the farmers 12 sesterces for every peck of wheat', L. H. G. Greenwood, trans. *Cicero. The Verrine Orations, Volume II: Against Verres, Part 2, Books 3–5* (LCL 293; Cambridge, MA: Harvard University Press, 1935), 232–235.

[72] Greene, *Archaeology*, 40; Kessler and Temin, *Money*, 1–31.

[73] W. R. Paton, trans. *Polybius. The Histories, Volume I: Books 1–2* (LCL 128; Cambridge, MA: Harvard University Press, 2010), 303.

[74] Several of the following entries are based on the work of Louis C. West, 'The Cost of Living in Roman Egypt', *Classical Philology* 11.3 (1916): 293–314.

[75] PBM = British Museum Papyri; P. Oxy = Oxyrhynchus Papyri; CIL = Corpus Inscriptiones Latinae.

Date	Item	Location	Expense/wage	Equivalent	Source
1 CE	Foremen of weavers	Egypt	6 asses	0.375 d	P. Oxy 737
1 CE	Bread	Egypt	0.5 ob.	0.083 d	P. Oxy 736
1 CE	Cake	Egypt	0.5 ob.	0.083 d	P. Oxy 736
1 CE	Cabbage	Egypt	0.5 ob.	0.5 d	P. Oxy 736
1 CE	1 artaba of Coriander	Egypt	6 dr., 3 ob.	6.5 d	P. Oxy 819
1 CE	Pigeon	Egypt	1 ob.	0.167	P. Oxy 736
1 CE	Breakfast	Egypt	1 ob.	0.167	P. Oxy 736
1 CE	1 artaba of grinding wheat	Egypt	3–4 ob.	3–4 d	P. Oxy 736
1 CE	Paenula cloak	Egypt	10 dr.	10 d	P. Oxy 736
1 CE	Weaving a paenula	Egypt	1 dr., 2 ob.	2.33 d	P. Oxy 736
1 CE	Needle and thread	Egypt	1 ob.	0.167 d	P.Oxy 736
1 CE	Basket	Egypt	1.5 ob.	0.25 d	P.Oxy 739
8–9 CE	Performing artist contract for 30 days	Egypt	1 dr., 2 ob. Per day, plus 13 dr. 2 ob.	1.78 d/day	P. Oxy 731
13 CE	Acacia tree (2 fallen)	Egypt	8 dr	8 d	P. Oxy 1188
13 CE	Persea tree (dried or living branch)	Egypt	1 dr	1 d	P. Oxy 1188
15 CE	Wheat per modius	Palestine	2 HS	0.5 d	T. Frank[76]
21 CE	Linen clothes	Egypt	3 dr	3 d	P. Oxy 1281
30 CE	Maintenance of injured man (parable)	Palestine	2 d	2 d	Lk 10:35
30 CE	Hired worker (parable)	Palestine	1 d	1 d	Mt 20:2
30 CE	2 sparrows	Palestine	1 as		Mt 10:29
30 CE	5 sparrows	Palestine	2 asses		Lk 12:6
36 CE	White robe	Egypt	12 dr	12 d	P. Oxy 267
36 CE	Gold earrings	Egypt	20 dr	20 d	P. Oxy 267
45–47 CE	Wheat per modius	Egypt			
50 CE	Linen chiton	Egypt	8 dr.	8 d	P. Oxy 285
54 CE	Weaving loom	Egypt	30 dr.	20 d	P. Oxy 264
56 CE	Wheat per modius	Egypt (Region of the Fayum)	4 HS	1 d	P. Mich 2 1271.1.8–38

(Continued)

[76] Tenney Frank, *An Economic Survey of Ancient Rome*, 6 vols. (Paterson, NJ: Pageant Books, 1933–1940), 4.181–183.

Date	Item	Location	Expense/ wage	Equivalent	Source
64 CE	Wheat per modius	Rome	3 HS	0.75 d	Tacitus, *Ann.* 2.87
70 CE	Donkey	Pompeii	520 sesterces	130 d	CIL 4.3340
77 CE	Girl, 8 years old	Egypt	640 dr.	640 d	P. Oxy 263
77 CE	Wheat per modius				
78–79 CE	Farm labourers	Egypt	3–5 ob.	0.5–0.83 d	PBM 131
78–79 CE	Donkey boys	Egypt	2.5 ob.	0.42 d	PBM 131
78–79 CE	1 jar of wine	Egypt	10 dr.	10 d	PBM 131
78–79 CE	1 measure of beer	Egypt	1.5 ob.	0.25 d	PBM 131
78–79 CE	1 artaba of wheat	Egypt	11 dr	11 d	PBM 131
78–79 CE	1 artaba of vegetables	Egypt	20–21 dr	20–21 d	PBM 131
78–79 CE	1 artaba of lentils	Egypt	2.5 dr	2.5 d	PBM 131
79 CE	Woman with 2 children	Egypt	1,800 dr	1,000 d	P. Oxy 375
80 CE	Wheat per modius	Pisidian Antioch (Asia Minor	2 HS	0.5 d	AEpigr. (1925), 126b[77]
92 CE	Guard	Egypt	1.33 dr	1.33 d	PBM 701
1st c. CE	Guard	Egypt	1.83 dr	1.83 d	P. Oxy 390
1st c. CE	Labours	Egypt	4 ob.	0.667 d	P. Oxy 985
101 CE	Donkey	Egypt	208 dr	208 d	P. Teb 474
113	100 water jars	Egypt	6 dr.	6 d	PBM 1177
143 CE	50 wicks	Egypt	1 ob.	0.167 d	P. Oxy 520

One brief corrective note seems necessary given the current state of NT secondary literature on the buying power of the denarius in the first century. Most discussions of the buying power of specific coinage (e.g. denarius) by NT commentators assume on the basis of Matthew 20:2, συμφωνήσας δὲ μετὰ τῶν ἐργατῶν ἐκ δηναρίου τὴν ἡμέραν ἀπέστειλεν αὐτοὺς εἰς τὸν ἀμπελῶνα αὐτοῦ, that a denarius was the typical wage for a day's work in antiquity. But several translations are misleading here. The NRSV has 'after agreeing with the laborers for the *usual* daily wage, he sent them into

---

[77] *AEpigr.* (1925), 126b documents the price of wheat during governmental intervention at a time of scarcity. The inscription reveals that the normal price of wheat was 8–9 asses per modius, but a maximum of one denarius per modius was in force until after the shortage. Limiting the price to double during the famine. See William Mitchell Ramsay, 'Studies in the "Roman Province Galatia" VI – Some Inscriptions of Colonial Caesarea Antiochea', *JRS* 14 (1924): 180.

his vineyard' (italics mine). But there is no justification in the Greek text for including the word 'usual'. All we are told is that the landowner 'agrees to pay them a denarius for the day', not that this was necessarily normative for the type of work undertaken. In fact, from the comparison of labour wages in the above table it is evident that the landowner in Matthew 20 was already being overly generous in offering what would be at least 100 per cent more than the expected norm for this type of manual labour performed. The closest parallels are 0.25 denarii per day for fieldwork in P. Oxy 737 dated to 1 CE, and 0.5–0.83 denarii for farm labourers in PBM 131 dated to 78–79 CE, although it must be admitted that the precise nature of the work is not known. Given the earlier date of P. Oxy 737 and the later (inflated rate) of PBM 131, an amount during the 30s CE might be approximately calculated as follows: take the daily labour wages in PBM 131 (0.665) and P. Oxy 737 (0.25) and average them for an approximate 0.4575 denarii per working day during the life of Jesus. This, of course, is only a very broad approximate, but it goes some way to nuance the typical 1 denarius per day for an unskilled worker. BAGD is very misleading at this point, and although BDAG was updated to eliminate the reference to eighteen cents, it still perpetuates the idea that a denarius was the standard for any day's work rather than a highly skilled labourer.

BAG (1957)

δηνάριον, ου, τό (Lat. denarius as δηνάριον first in two inscr. fr. Acraephiae of the time of Sulla [Inscr. Gr. Sept. 4147f]. Exx. fr. later times in Hahn 271 word-index; Dit., Or. Ind. VIII; loanw. in rabb.) *denarius*, **a Roman silver coin worth normally about 18 cents; the debasement of the coinage under Nero reduced it in value to about 8 cents; it was a worker's average daily wage** Mt 18:28; 20:2, 9f, 13; 22:19; Mk 6:37; 12:15; 14:5; Lk 7:41; 10:35; 20:24; J 6:7; 12:5; Rv 6:6. τὸ ἀνὰ δηνάριον *a denarius each*, like the others before them Mt 20:10 (Bl-D. §266, 2). – Hultsch, Pauly-W. V 202ff.; Other ref. s.v ἀργύριον end. – M-M.

BAGD (1979)

δηνάριον, ου, τό (Lat. denarius as δηνάριον first in two inscr. fr. Acraephiae of the time of Sulla [Inscr. Gr. Sept. 4147f]. Exx. fr. later times in Hahn 271 word-index; Dit., Or. Ind. VIII; loanw. in rabb.) *denarius*, **a Roman silver coin worth normally about 18 cents; the debasement of the coinage under Nero reduced it in value to about 8 cents; it was a worker's average daily wage** Mt 18:28; 20:2, 9f, 13; 22:19; Mk 6:37; 12:15; 14:5; Lk 7:41; 10:35; 20:24; J 6:7; 12:5; Rv 6:6. τὸ ἀνὰ δηνάριον *a denarius each*, like the others before them Mt 20:10 (Bl-D. §266, 2). – Hultsch, Pauly-W. V 202ff.; Other ref. s.v ἀργύριον end. – M-M.

BDAG (2000)

δηνάριον, ου, τό (Lat. denarius as δηνάριον first in two ins fr. Acraephiae of the time of Sulla [IG IX/2, 415 b, 89]. Exx. fr. later times in Hahn 271 word-index; OGI ind. VIII; cp. Preis. III 346; loanw. in rabb.) denarius, a Roman silver coin orig. c. 4.55 g; **the debasement of coinage under Nero reduced it in value; it was a worker's average daily wage** (cp. Tob 5:15; Talmud Babli: Aboda Zara 62a; SBastomsky,

Greece and Rome, ser. 2, 37, '90, 37) Mt 18:28; 20:2, 9f, 13; 22:19; Mk 6:37; 12:15; 14:5; Lk 7:41; 10:35; 20:24; J 6:7; 12:5; Rv 6:6. τὸ ἀνὰ δηνάριον a denarius each, like the others before them Mt 20:10 (B-D-F §266, 2). – Hultsch, Pauly-W. V 202ff; KRegling, Wörterbuch der Münzkunde, ed. FSchrötter, 1930, 126ff; Kl. Pauly I, 1488–1490; IDB III 428, illustr. 29 p. 433; Schürer II 65. – Other reff. s. ἀργύριον end. – M-M.

Much more thorough work and nuanced conclusions are necessary so as not to mislead lexicon readers that a δηνάριον is the average daily pay rate within the empire during the lifetime of Jesus. In reality there was a far broader range, regularly on the lower end of the spectrum of the range attested in the examples above. A final and exhaustive summary chart has been provided of coins mentioned in the NT (Table 14).

Table 14 Coinage and related terminology in the New Testament

Terminology	Definition	References	Notes
Specific terminology			
δηνάριον	Roman silver coin	Mt 18:28; 20:2, 9–10, 13; 22:19; Mk 6:37; 12:15; 14:5; Lk 7:41; 10:35; 20:24; Jn 6:7; 12:5; Rev 6:6	KJV misleadingly renders this coin 'penny' or 'pence'
δραχμή	Greek silver coin	Lk 15:8	
ἀσσάριον	Assarion, Roman copper coin worth 1/16 of Denarius	Mt 10:29; Lk 12:6	
κοδράντης	Quadrans, Roman copper coin worth 1/4 of an assarion or 1/64 of a denarius	Mt 10:29; Mk 12:42; Lk 12:6	KJV misleadingly renders this coin 'farthing'
λεπτόν	Lepton, copper (or bronze) coin worth 1/2 of a quadrans or 1/128 of a denarius	Mk 12:42; Lk 12:59; 21:2	
στατήρ	Stater, a silver coin worth two didrachma or approximately four denarii	Mt 17:27	
μνᾶ	Mina, Greek monetary unit worth one hundred denarii	Lk 19:13, 16, 18, 20, 24–25	
τάλαντον	Talent, originally a unit of weight (26–36 kgs); then a Greek monetary unit with a value which fluctuated considerably, depending on the particular monetary system which prevailed at a particular period of time and place	Mt 18:24; 25:15–16, 20, 22, 24–25, 28	

Terminology	Definition	References	Notes
Non-specific but related terminology			
ἄργυρος (masc.) ἀργύριον (neut.)	silver, money, a generic expression for currency or material	ἄργυρος: Mt 10:9; Acts 17:29; 1 Cor 3:12; Jas 5:3; Rev 18:12; ἀργύριον: Mt 25:18, 27; 26:15; 27:3, 5–6, 9; 28:12, 15; Mk 14:11; Lk 9:3; 19:15, 23; 22:5; Acts 3:6; 7:16; 8:20; 19:19; 20:33; 1 Pet 1:18	
κέρμα	coins of lesser value, coins, change	Jn 2:15	
νόμισμα	common and official currency, coin	Mt 22:19	
χαλκός	coins of bronze or copper, bronze	Mt 10:9, Mk 6:8; Mk 12:41	The term also occurs in 1 Corinthians 13:1 and Revelation 18:12, but there it refers to bronze metal in general rather than currency.
χρῆμα	possessions, wealth, generic term for currency, normally used in reference to actual coins	Lk 18:24; Acts 4:37; 8:18, 20; 24:26	The term also occurs in Mark 10:23 in reference to generic economic resources, implying an abundance of assets.
χρυσός	gold, money, a generic expression for money or material	Mt 2:11; 10:9; 23:16–17; Acts 17:29; 1 Cor 3:12; Jas 5:3; Rev 9:7; 18:12	It is possible that each of these instances should be understood as the material rather than currency.

Part Two

5

ΦΙΛΟΣ

Introduction

This chapter employs numismatic inscriptional evidence to explore the ΦΙΛ– lexeme and more carefully denote the semantic domains of related terminology. Commentators regularly note the alleged tension in John 15 between 'friendship' and 'obedience'. John 15 consists of what is commonly referred to as the 'vine metaphor discourse',[1] wherein Jesus encourages his followers to 'remain in him' (vv. 4, 7), as well as warning them of the world's hatred of them, and consequent future suffering (vv. 18-26). In verse 14, Jesus declares to those in his hearing that ὑμεῖς φίλοι μού ἐστε ἐὰν ποιῆτε ἃ ἐγὼ ἐντέλλομαι ὑμῖν. The reference to φίλος is variously understood by commentators, the majority of whom equate the reference to the basic semantic domain provided in BDAG; that is, (1) pertaining to having a special interest in someone, loving, kindly disposed, devoted or (2) one who is on intimate terms or in close association with another, that is, a friend.[2] There is, however, a fundamental tension in the secondary literature as to whether φίλος is intended to highlight the emotional dimension of intimacy or a sense of obligation within the context of John 15. The following analysis explores this apparent tension within the socio-political context in which the gospel was written. The inclusion of specific political terminology on Roman coins (e.g. ΦΙΛΙΑ; ΦΙΛΟΚΑΙΣΑΡ; ΦΙΛΟΚΛΑΥΔΙΟΣ; ΦΙΛΟΡΩΜΑΙΟΣ; ΦΙΛΟΣΕΒΑΣΤΩΝ) is explored as one way in which elite concepts of political friendship, evidenced in Cicero and Seneca, were communicated to the masses.

ΦΙΛ–lexeme

Robert Kysar is representative of this interpretive tradition when he states, the 'declaration that the disciples are friends involves a transformation of the usual servant/ master pattern ... Friendship implies ... relationship [and] intimacy, as opposed to the singular quality of the obedience demanded of a slave'.[3] Although in no way dependent,

---

[1] B. Lindars, *The Gospel of John* (Grand Rapids, MI: Eerdmans, 1982), 281.
[2] BDAG, 1058–1059.
[3] R. Kysar, *John* (Minneapolis, MN: Augsburg Publishing House, 1986), 240.

this echoes Ambrose of Milan (333–397 CE), who also defines friendship in terms of close companionship and intimacy: 'God himself made us friends instead of servants ... He gave us a pattern of friendship to follow. We are to fulfill the wish of a friend, to unfold to him our secrets that we hold in our own hearts, and are not to disregard his confidences. Let us show him our heart, and he will open his to us ... A friend, then, if he is a true one, hides nothing' (*Duties of the Clergy* 3.135).

One of the first modern commentators to recognize a tension between the emotional connotations and the element of obligation was Rudolf Bultmann, who noted that 'the reciprocity of the relationship created by his [i.e. Jesus's] choosing them is of a different sort from that of a purely human friendship'.[4] Raymond Brown argued in a similar manner that φίλος 'does not capture sufficiently this relationship of love'.[5] Bultmann, however, contended that v. 14, ὑμεῖς φίλοι μού ἐστε ἐὰν ποιῆτε ἃ ἐγὼ ἐντέλλομαι ὑμῖν, was 'not a question of their still having to *become* his friends by fulfilling his commands; they *are* his friends already'.[6] Bultmann maintained this interpretation through appeal to v. 15 which he states 'specifies the condition whereby what they already are can be fully realised in them'.[7]

In contrast to this view, however, Urban C. von Wahlde notes that 'the language of contingency here strikes the modern reader as peculiar'.[8] Similarly, Ernst Haenchen observes that 'with respect to his friends Jesus is the one who gives commands, who assigns tasks'.[9] C. K. Barrett highlights the tension in v. 14 by noting that 'it is clear that the status of a friend is not one which precludes obedient service; this is rather demanded'.[10] Barrett, however, draws back from affirming A. Deissmann's observation that φίλος is attested in reference to a highly placed official in the Ptolemaic court,[11] simply stating that 'there is no need to suppose ... that this usage strongly influenced John'.[12]

D. Carson does not permit an interpretation of friendship 'of the modern variety',[13] yet he seems to do so out of a concern for 'demeaning God'[14] rather than

---

[4] Rudolf Bultmann, *The Gospel of John: A Commentary*, trans. G. R. Beasley Murray (Philadelphia, PA: Westminster Press, 1971), 545.

[5] Raymond E. Brown, *The Gospel According to John xiii–xxi* (New York: Doubleday & Company Inc., 1970), 664.

[6] Bultmann, *John*, 543.

[7] Bultmann, *John*, 543.

[8] Urban C. von Wahlde, *The Gospel and Letters of John: Volume 2* (Grand Rapids, MI: Eerdmans, 2010), 682.

[9] Ernst Haenchen, *John: Volume 2*, trans. R. W. Funk and U. Busse (Philadelphia, PA: Fortress Press, 1984), 132.

[10] C. K. Barrett, *The Gospel According to St. John*, 2nd ed. (Cambridge: SPCK, 1978), 477.

[11] Adolf Deissmann, *Light from the Ancient East: The New Testament Illustrated by Recently Discovered Texts of the Greco-Roman World*, trans. Lionel R. M. Strachan (New York: Harper & Brothers, 1922), 249. Several commentators in the late nineteenth-century trace the friendship idea to Abraham; see, for example, B. F. Westcott, *The Gospel According to St. John* (London: Buttler and Tanner, 1882), 220; cf. Rudolf Schnackenburg, *The Gospel According to Saint John: Volume Three*, trans. David Smith and G.A. Kon (New York: Crossroad, 1982), 109–110 who traces the theme of friendship in Jewish sapiential literature citing examples such as Ecclus 6:5–17.

[12] Barrett, *John*, 477.

[13] D. A. Carson, *The Gospel According to John* (Grand Rapids, MI: Inter-Varsity Press, 1991), 533.

[14] Carson, *John*, 533.

on any lexicographic or contextual grounds. Carson focuses on the 'revealed plan' as foundational to the definition of friendship, even though he confesses that such a definition was not a component of the friendship of Moses (Exod 33:11) or Abraham (Isa 41:8; 2 Chron 20:7): 'In times past God's covenant people were not informed of God's saving plan in the full measure now accorded to Jesus' disciples'.[15] In tacit agreement with Bultmann, Carson argues that 'obedience is not what makes them friends; it is what characterizes his friends'.[16] As noted above, this view is untenable in light of the subsequent conditional phrase 'if you do what I command you' (Jn 15:14b).

J. Ramsey Michaels attempt to avert the conditional nature of v. 14 by suggesting 'if it were a true conditional we would have expected "If you do the things I command you, you *will be* my friends," making friendship dependent on performance'.[17] Yet such an explanation is not sustainable in light of the many examples, even within John's Gospel, of conditional statements consisting of a verb in the present tense followed by the conjunction ἐάν (see, for example, John 3:2; 5:19; 7:51). So it remains that the friendship of which Jesus speaks in 15:14 entails and presupposes obedience as a condition, an aspect that would presumably be difficult to reconcile if φίλος, in this context, was referring solely to intimacy and/or emotional companionship.

The Greco-Roman context

A revealing aspect of the semantic domain of φίλος (and related terminology) is evident in Roman friendships of 'unequals'. W. Carter defines this phenomenon as 'involving people of different socioeconomic levels, where inequalities of wealth, power, and status were common in patron–client relations, with their attendant repertoire of duties and obligations'.[18] Φίλος τοῦ Καίσαρος (friend of the emperor) or the related Φίλος τοῦ Σέβαστοῦ (friend of Augustus) were official titles which A. Deissmann traced back to the 'language of the court under the successors of Alexander'.[19]

In a compelling monograph, David Braund explores the representation of imperial period provincial rulers and the portrayal of their relationship with Rome to their subjects.[20] In providing a study of the institution of client kings as a whole, the study helpfully highlights the extent to which a ruler 'might advertise his friendship with Rome in his very titulature'.[21] As will become evident in our analysis below, not only did this titulature take the form of the φιλ-stem, but this terminology occurs

---

[15] Carson, *John*, 533.
[16] Carson, *John*, 522.
[17] J. R. Michaels, *The Gospel of John* (Grand Rapids, MI: Eerdmans, 2010), 813.
[18] W. Carter, *Empire and John* (London: T&T Clark, 2008), 278.
[19] Deissmann, *Light*, 383.
[20] David Braund, *Rome and the Friendly King: The Character of Client Kingship* (New York: St. Martin's Press, 1984), esp. 105–108.
[21] Braund, *Rome*, 105.

108   *Numismatics and Greek Lexicography*

most regularly on the provincial coinage of Rome.[22] Braund concludes that 'a king with a special debt to Rome and emperor might be particularly expected to use these epithets',[23] and provides, among other examples, that of Mannus VIII of Osrhoene who, after he was restored to his throne by Rome, issued coins with φιλορώμαιος.

John Crook traces the evolution of the *amici principis* from the Hellenistic kingdoms through the Republic and into the imperial period.[24] He suggests that ultimate catalyst for the designation φίλοι seems to have been that of legitimation,[25] initially as advisors and then later 'an honourific institution'.[26] Crook argues that 'the concept of *amicus* was an integral part of the complicated political pattern of the Republic. Political *amicitia* was bound up with *clientela, hospitium, patronatus,* and *patrocinium* as one of the innumerable ways in which a man could win support by lending it – the nearest thing, in fact, that Rome ever had to a party system'.[27] Relevant to our discussion is Crook's conclusion that 'it was not necessary, in order to be an *amicus principis*, to be a personal friend of the emperor in any emotional sense'[28] and that this friendship 'is often shown not as a passive, but an active and arduous honour, which may take a man's whole time and attention'.[29]

Further literary evidence for the pervasive phenomenon of the φίλον Καίσαρος comes from the Jewish philosopher Philo of Alexandria's 'historical' treatise *In Flaccum.* In sections 36–40, there is a mocking ceremony, of sorts, against Agrippa, where the antagonists of the Jewish people parade a lunatic named Karabas as a king, paying him royal honours. Philo condemns Flaccus, the governor of Egypt, appointed by Tiberius, for not 'interfering in this insult ... [and] thus giving the Alexandrians immunity and free play in their actions against the Jews'.[30] Philo suggests that it would have been more prudent if Flaccus 'had apprehended the maniac and put him in prison, that he might not give to those who reviled him any opportunity or excuse for insulting their superiors, and if he had chastised those who dressed him up for having dared both openly and disguisedly, both with words and actions, to insult a king and a friend of Caesar (φίλον Καίσαρος), and one who had been honoured by the Roman senate with

---

[22] The earliest attested use of φιλορώμαιος is that of Ariobarzanes I, king of Cappadocia from 95 to 63 BCE (R. D. Sullivan, 'The Dynasty of Cappadocia', *ANRW* 7, no. 2 [1980]: 1125–1168). After the advent of the Principate both φιλόκαισαρ and φιλοσέβαστος were common titles adopted by client kings. The more specific designations of φιλογερμάνικος (Gaius) [Polemo II of Pontus, IGR iv 145] and φιλοκλαύδιος (Claudius) [Herod of Chalcis], see A. Reifenberg, *Ancient Jewish Coins* (Jerusalem: R. Mass, 1947), 23–24. E. Schürer suggests that this action would be 'a natural act of homage to the emperor to whom he owed all his splendor' (E. Schürer, *The History of the Jewish People in the Age of Jesus* Christ *(175 BCE–AD135)* revised G. Vermes and F. Millar, vol. 1 (Edinburgh: T&T Clark, 1973), 572).

[23] Braund, *Rome,* 107.

[24] John Crook, *Consilium Principis: Imperial Councils and Counsellors from Augustus to Diocletian* (Cambridge: Cambridge University Press, 1955), 21–30.

[25] Crook, *Consilium Principis,* 21.

[26] Crook, *Consilium Principis,* 21.

[27] Crook, *Consilium Principis,* 22.

[28] Crook, *Consilium Principis,* 22.

[29] Crook, *Consilium Principis,* 26.

[30] Peter W. Van der Horst, *Philo's Flaccus: The First Pogrom* (Leiden: Brill, 2003), 128.

imperial authority; but he not only did not punish them, but he did not think fit even to check them, but gave complete license and impunity to all those who designed ill'.

Similarly, in Tacitus's discussion of the otherwise unknown Marcus Terentius (*Annals* 6.8), he records the deep entrenchment of the patron–client relationship in which Terentius was involved. Tacitus has these words on the lips of Terentius: 'I confess that not only was I the friend of Sejanus [commander of the Praetorian Guard from 14–31 CE], but that I strove for his friendship, and that when I attained it, I rejoiced … The closer a man's intimacy with Sejanus, the stronger his claim to the emperor's friendship.' Among other references to advisors and colleagues, the political relationship is described in terms of friendship (*amicitia*) with the emperor.

Furthermore, the geographer Strabo (*Geogr.* 8.5.5), writing of the political turmoil of the Laconians, refers favourably to their φιλιαὶ λειτουργίαι (friendly services) to the Romans after the overthrow of the Macedonians. In description, Strabo refers specifically to a certain man named Eurycles who 'stirred up some disturbances among them, having apparently abused the friendship of Caesar (τῇ Καίσαρος φιλίᾳ) unduly to maintain his authority of his subjects.'[31] In doing so, Strabo correlates 'the exercise of his authority' with his τῇ Καίσαρος φιλίᾳ (friendship of Caesar).[32]

The cumulative weight of this evidence, together with that which follows, suggests that the semantic domain of φίλοι included clients who were the recipients of political favours or privilege from their patron. This political matrix indebted the client to a relationship of obligation, responsibility and commitment to their patron, in what could only be described as fidelity and allegiance.[33]

The numismatic evidence

Turning to the numismatic record, a sample of the relevant material that contributes to this debate can be summarized in Table 15.

Table 15 Sample of relevant material for ΦΙΛ–lexeme

ΦΙΛΙΑ	Iudaea	42–44 CE	RPC 1.4982
ΦΙΛΟΚΑΙΣΑΡ	Iudaea	40–95 CE	RPC 1.4979
	Iudaea	40–95 CE	RPC 1.4983
	Iudaea	40–95 CE	RPC 1.4985
	Philadelphia/Lyd.	37–41 CE	RPC 1.3027

(Continued)

---

[31] For a disparaging ancient perspective on Eurycles, see Josephus, *Ant.* 16:301, 306, 309–310; *War* 1:513, 518, 526, 530, 532.

[32] For further discussion on 'friend of Caesar', see Fergus Millar, *The Emperor in the Roman World* (London: Duckworth, 1992), 110–122; G. H. R. Horsley, *New Documents Illustrating Early Christianity, Volume 1: A Review of the Greek Inscriptions and Papyri Published in 1976* (North Ryde: Ancient History Documentary Research Centre, 1981), 87–89.

[33] Bruce J. Malina and Ricard L. Rohrbaugh, *Social Science Commentary on the Gospel of John* (Minneapolis, MN: Fortress, 1998), 236.

	Philadelphia/Lyd.	37–41 CE	RPC 1.3028
	Philadelphia/Lyd.	37–41 CE	RPC 1.3029
	Philadelphia/Lyd.	37–41 CE	RPC 1.3030
	Philadelphia/Lyd.	37–41 CE	RPC 1.3031
	Tripolis/Lyd.	14–37 CE	RPC 1.3054
	Tripolis/Lyd.	14–37 CE	RPC 1.3055
	Tripolis/Lyd.	14–37 CE	RPC 1.3056
	Tripolis/Lyd.	14–37 CE	RPC 1.3057
ΦΙΛΟΚΛΑΥΔΙΟΣ	Chalkis	43–44 CE	RPC 1.4778
ΦΙΛΟΡΩΜΑΙΟΣ	Galatien	58 CE	SNG France 233
	Kappadokien	96–63 BCE	Alram 166
	Kommagene	36–20 BCE	Alram 248
ΦΙΛΟΣΕΒΑΣΤΩΝ	Stratonikeia/Kar.	79–81 CE	RPC 2.1196

Of particular interest is the occurrence of ΦΙΛΙΑ in Roman Provincial Coinage volume 1[34] (RPC 1) 4982 (Figure 31), a coin of Agrippa I. The obverse has three figures, and the inscription reads (reconstructed on the basis of several specimens), ΒΑΣ ΑΓΡΙΠΠΑΣ ΣΕΒ ΚΑΙΣΑΡ ΒΑΣ ΗΡΩΔΗΣ ('King Agrippa, Augustus [i.e. Claudius] Caesar, King Herod), LH [year 8]'). Agrippa is to the left, Claudius in the centre and Herod of Chalcis (i.e. Agrippa's brother) to the right. Agrippa and Herod have an arm extended and crown the central figure with a wreath. On the basis of Josephus *Ant.* 19.274–279,[35] Ya'akov Meshorer concludes that this scene is a reference 'to a ceremony held in the forum of Rome on the occasion of the signing of a treaty of friendship between Claudius

---

[34] Burnett, Amandry, and Carradice, *Roman Provincial Coinage 1*, 50.

[35] [274] 'Now, when Claudius had taken out of the way all those soldiers whom he suspected, which he did immediately, he published an edict, and therein confirmed that kingdom to Agrippa which Caius had given him, and therein commended the king highly. He also made an addition to it of all that country over which Herod, who was his grandfather, had reigned, that is, Judea and Samaria; [275] (19.5.1) and this he restored to him as due to his family. But for Abila of Lysanias, and all that lay at Mount Libanus, he bestowed them upon him, as out of his own territories. He also made a league with this Agrippa, confirmed by oaths, in the middle of the forum, in the city of Rome: [276] he also took away from Antiochus that kingdom which he was possessed of, but gave him a certain part of Cilicia and Commagena: he also set Alexander Lysimachus, the alabarch, at liberty, who had been his old friend, and steward to his mother Antonia, but had been imprisoned by Caius, whose son [Marcus] married Bernice, the daughter of Agrippa. [277] But when Marcus, Alexander's son, was dead, who had married her when she was a virgin, Agrippa gave her in marriage to his brother Herod, and begged for him of Claudius the kingdom of Chalcis. [278] Now, about this time there was a sedition between the Jews and the Greeks, at the city of Alexandria; for, when Caius was dead, the nation of the Jews, which had been very much mortified under the reign of Caius, and reduced to very great distress by the people of Alexandria recovered itself, and immediately took up their arms to fight for themselves. [279] So Claudius sent an order to the president of Egypt, to quiet that tumult; he also sent an edict, at the request of king Agrippa and king Herod, both to Alexandria and to Syria, whose contents were as follows...'

ΦΙΛΟΣ

Figure 31 RPC 1.4982 (used with permission).

and the Jewish kings'.[36] And indeed the image of clasped hands (a symbol of agreement) and inscription on the reverse confirms this interpretation, ΟΡΚΙΑ ΒΑΣ(ΙΛΕΩΣ) ΜΕ(ΓΑΛΟΥ) ΑΓΡΙΠΠΑ ΠΡ(ΟΣ) ΣΕΒ(ΑΣΤΟΝ) ΚΑΙΣΑΡΑ Κ(ΑΙ) ΣΥΝΚΛΗΤΟΝ Κ(ΑΙ) ΔΗΜΟ(Ν) ΡΩΜ(ΑΙΩΝ) ΦΙΛΙ(Α) Κ(ΑΙ) ΣΥΝΜΑΧΙ(Α) ΑΥΤΟΥ ('sworn treaty of Great King Agrippa to Augustus Caesar [i.e. Claudius] and to the Senate and to the People of the Romans, his friendship and alliance'). Perhaps a result of Claudius's willingness to grant Agrippa rule of the Judea and Sameria, in addition to consular rank, in effect, restoring the extent of territory 'governed by his grandfather Herod the Great'.[37] Josephus Ant. 19.339 demonstrates the extent of Agrippa's diplomatic participation in the patron–client matrix when, at a meeting with other Roman client kings in Tiberius (Antiochus, king of Commagene, Sampsigeramus, king of Emesa, Cotys king of the Lesser Armenia, Polemo king of Pontus, and Herod of Chalcis), 'His converse with all of them when he entertained and showed them courtesies was such as to demonstrate an elevation of sentiment that justified the honour done him by a visit of royalty'. Other coins similarly celebrate the political 'friendship' of Agrippa I with the Caesar. RPC I 4983 translates as 'Great King Agrippa, friend of Caesar'. The reverse depicts a temple with two columns.

Among the coins from Stratonicea is RPC 2.1196, a coin bearing the inscription ΤΙΤΟΣ ΚΑΙΣΑΡ ΣΕΒΑΣΤΟΣ with the laureate head of Titus on the obverse, and ΣΤΡΑΤΟΝΙΚΕΩΝ ΦΙΛΟΣΕΒΑΣΤΩΝ with a goddess standing facing holding the patera (libation bowl) and torch. In view, perhaps is that the city herself is indebted to Titus.

The coins of Philadelphia fall into three categories, the second of which have a Capricorn on the reverse and the title ΦΙΛΟΚΑΙΣΑΡ. Interestingly all coins from

---

[36] Y. Meshorer, A Treasury of Jewish Coins (Jerusalem: Amphora Books, 2001), 101.
[37] D. Hendin, Guide to Biblical Coins, 5th ed. (Jerusalem: Amphora, 2010), 265.

Attalikos, Moschion, Kleandros and Antiochus seem to be from the same obverse die. Under Caligula, no fewer than seven ΦΙΛΟΚΑΙΣΑΡ types are in circulation. RPC 1.3031 (Figure 32) has the bare head of Caligula looking right, with the standard inscription ΓΑΙΟΣ ΚΑΙΣΑΡ. On the reverse there is a Capricorn leaping to the left, and cornucopia with the inscription ΦΙΛΟΚΑΙΣΑΡ ΦΙΛΑΔΕΛΦΕΩΝ ΜΑΚΕΔΩΝ.

The coinage of Tripolis is renowned for illustrating the difficulty in sorting issues by Augustus or Tiberius. However, RPC 1.3056 (Figure 33) is certainly for Tiberius, despite some curious features of the portrait on the obverse. The reverse has the inscription ΜΕΝΑΝΔΡΟΣ ΦΙΛΟΚΑΙΣΑΡ ΤΟ Δ.

The title 'friend of the emperor' (or equivalent) on provincial coinage was certainly not empty titulature but served to 'indicate to the inhabitants of the Empire the importance of those sent to govern them … [that] they are representative of the *auctoritas* [authority] of the emperor'.[38] This relationship was one defined by obligation and responsibility rather than affection or an emotional connection. This aspect of obligation is plainly seen in a later episode within the Gospel of John where the Jewish crowds taunt Pilate, in what could be mistaken as political blackmail, οἱ δὲ Ἰουδαῖοι ἐκραύγασαν λέγοντες· ἐὰν τοῦτον ἀπολύσῃς, οὐκ εἶ φίλος τοῦ Καίσαρος· πᾶς ὁ βασιλέα ἑαυτὸν ποιῶν ἀντιλέγει τῷ Καίσαρι (Jn 19:12).[39] This is precisely the force of the word in the context in John 15:14, that is, being Jesus's friend (φίλοι μού) comes with responsibilities and obligations (nota bene verse14b, ἐὰν ποιῆτε ἃ ἐγὼ ἐντέλλομαι

Figure 32 RPC 1.3031 (used with permission).

---

[38] Crook, *Consilium Principis*, 24.
[39] Cf. Philo *Leg. ad Gai.* 302 where Jewish leaders threatened to refer a matter to Tiberius, whereupon Pilate 'feared that if they actually sent an embassy they would also expose the rest of his conduct as a governor by stating in full the briberies, the insults, the outrages and wonton injuries, the executions without trial constantly repeated, the ceaseless and repeated cruelty'.

Figure 33 RPC 1.3056 (used with permission).

ὑμῖν). Just as being a 'friend of Caesar' entailed responsibility, duty and obedience, so too does 'friendship with Jesus' in which his followers are to 'do as I say' or else risk their standing as friends of Jesus.

Warren Carter and others have demonstrated that there is a porous interchange of Roman imperial ideology and the NT, at the level of literary structure, thematic elements and lexicographic detail. Carter's most recent extended work on the subject, *John and Empire*,[40] although controversial, has raised the vivid possibility of a thorough connection between John and imperial ideology as a viable and attractive contributing feature to the narrative interpretive horizon. The foregrounding of the Roman political context avoids the dichotomy of either the too narrow identification of sectarian disputes or, conversely, the historical de-contextualization of the Gospel. The reading of John 15:14 presented here, confirmed and illuminated through the numismatic record, not only does justice to the semantic range of φίλος, but also coheres with the political and literary context of the Johannine pericope.

Conclusion

Scholarly attention to the numismatic record, as it pertains to the study of the NT, is in its infancy. Studies on the shared symbolic iconography of Roman coins and the NT are increasingly more common,[41] but only a paucity of attention has been devoted

---

[40] Carter, *John*.
[41] Some pertinent examples are Oster, 'Numismatic', 195–223; Oster, '"Show me a denarius"', 107–115; Larry J. Kreitzer, *Striking New Images: Roman Imperial Coinage and the New Testament World*, JSNTSup 134 (Sheffield: Sheffield Academic, 1996); Marius Reiser, 'Numismatik und Neues Testament', *Biblica* 81 (2000): 457; Annette Weissenrieder and Friederike Wendt, 'He is a god! Acts

to the question as it relates to lexicography.[42] I have argued in this chapter that when one takes into consideration the numismatic material in conjunction with the literary evidence, a substantial case can be made that the ΦΙΛ-lexeme includes not merely an emotional or personal dimension of friendship, but also the dimension of obligation. This is not to say that the emotional dimension is lacking in John's Gospel, or elsewhere in the NT (see, for example, Jesus's friendship with Mary, Martha and Lazarus in John 11:5),[43] but the term can also be used to highlight the responsibilities and obligation of two parties, and it is this force that seems to be highlighted in John 15. The attestation of the ΦΙΛ-lexeme and associated symbolism in the numismatic record is particularly significant because of the widespread geographic distribution of the coins across the Mediterranean world and their ability to clearly communicate an ideological message to a semi-literate or illiterate audience.

28: 1-9 in the Light of Iconographical and Textual Sources Related to Medicine', in *Picturing the New Testament: Studies in Ancient Visual Images*, ed. A. Weissenrieder, F. Wendt, and P. von Gemünden (Tübingen: Mohr Siebeck, 2005), 127–156; David M. May, 'The Empire Strikes Back: The Mark of the Beast in Revelation', *Review and Expositor* 106 (2009): 83–98; David May, 'Interpreting Revelation with Roman Coins: A Test Case, Revelation 6:9–11', *Review & Expositor* 106 (2009): 445–465.

[42] Some exceptions are Frank Thielman, 'God's Righteousness as God's Fairness in Romans 1:17: An Ancient Perspective on a Significant Phrase', *JETS* 54 (2011): 35–48.

[43] Cf. Aristotle's description of happiness, 'good birth, plenty of friends, good friends, wealth, good children, plenty of children......' (*Rhet.* 1.5.4).

6

ΚΑΡΠΟΦΟΡΟΣ

Introduction

'καρποφόρος' (trans. 'fruitful') is a *hapax legomenon* which occurs in Acts 14:17 as a masculine accusative plural adjective modifying the preceding noun in the phrase 'καιροὺς καρποφόρους' (trans. 'fruitful seasons'). The literary context is that of Paul's first missionary journey and relates to Paul and Barnabas's encounter with the inhabitants of Lystra (Acts 14:8–18), who sought to venerate them upon seeing the miraculous healing of a certain individual 'who could not use his feet' (Acts 14:8). Paul and Barnabas respond in an attempt to quell the inhabitants' desire to sacrifice to them as representatives of Zeus and Hermes (Acts 14:12), noting in particular that they (Paul and Barnabas) were mere mortals (Acts 14:15) and that God 'made the heaven and the earth and the sea and all that is in them' (Acts 14:15), and by implication God alone is worthy to receive such devotion. Verses 16–17 glimpses a theme that re-emerges more fully in Paul's speech at the Areopagus (cf. Acts 17:22–33, esp. v. 30), namely that 'until the full revelation of God came to the Gentiles, he overlooked their errors insofar as these arose from ignorance of his will'.[1] The testimony of God's presence is identified as 'οὐρανόθεν ὑμῖν ὑετοὺς διδοὺς καὶ καιροὺς καρποφόρους' (trans. 'giving you rains from heaven and fruitful seasons'). While the adjective occurs only once, in the verbal form καρποφορέω occurs eight times in the NT. This paper will explore the contribution of contemporaneous numismatic material (see Table 16) for nuancing and further clarifying this rare term.

Table 16 Attestations of the adjective καρποφόρος and verb καρποφορέω in the New Testament

καρποφόρος (fruitful)	
Acts 14:17	καίτοι οὐκ ἀμάρτυρον αὐτὸν ἀφῆκεν ἀγαθουργῶν, οὐρανόθεν ὑμῖν ὑετοὺς διδοὺς καὶ καιροὺς **καρποφόρους,** ἐμπιπλῶν τροφῆς καὶ εὐφροσύνης τὰς καρδίας ὑμῶν yet he has not left himself without a witness in doing good – giving you rains from heaven and **fruitful** seasons, and filling you with food and your hearts with joy

---

[1] F. F. Bruce, *The Acts of the Apostles: Greek Text with Introduction and Commentary* (Grand Rapids, MI: Eerdmans, 1990), 324.

116 Numismatics and Greek Lexicography

	καρποφορέω (to bring forth fruit)
Matt 13:23	ὁ δὲ ἐπὶ τὴν καλὴν γῆν σπαρείς, οὗτός ἐστιν ὁ τὸν λόγον ἀκούων καὶ συνιείς, ὃς δὴ **καρποφορεῖ** καὶ ποιεῖ ὃ μὲν ἑκατόν, ὃ δὲ ἑξήκοντα, ὃ δὲ τριάκοντα But as for what was sown on good soil, this is the one who hears the word and understands it, who indeed **bears fruit** and yields, in one case a hundredfold, in another sixty, and in another thirty.
Mark 4:20	καὶ ἐκεῖνοί εἰσιν οἱ ἐπὶ τὴν γῆν τὴν καλὴν σπαρέντες, οἵτινες ἀκούουσιν τὸν λόγον καὶ παραδέχονται καὶ **καρποφοροῦσιν** ἐν τριάκοντα καὶ ἐν ἑξήκοντα καὶ ἐν ἑκατόν And these are the ones sown on the good soil: they hear the word and accept it and bear fruit, thirty and sixty and a hundredfold.
Mark 4:28	αὐτομάτη ἡ γῆ **καρποφορεῖ**, πρῶτον χόρτον εἶτα στάχυν εἶτα πλήρη[ς] σῖτον ἐν τῷ στάχυϊ The earth **produces** of itself, first the stalk, then the head, then the full grain in the head.
Luke 8:15	τὸ δὲ ἐν τῇ καλῇ γῇ, οὗτοί εἰσιν οἵτινες ἐν καρδίᾳ καλῇ καὶ ἀγαθῇ ἀκούσαντες τὸν λόγον κατέχουσιν καὶ **καρποφοροῦσιν** ἐν ὑπομονῇ But as for that in the good soil, these are the ones who, when they hear the word, hold it fast in an honest and good heart, and **bear fruit** with patient endurance
Rom 7:4	ὥστε, ἀδελφοί μου, καὶ ὑμεῖς ἐθανατώθητε τῷ νόμῳ διὰ τοῦ σώματος τοῦ Χριστοῦ, εἰς τὸ γενέσθαι ὑμᾶς ἑτέρῳ, τῷ ἐκ νεκρῶν ἐγερθέντι, ἵνα **καρποφορήσωμεν** τῷ θεῷ In the same way, my friends, you have died to the law through the body of Christ, so that you may belong to another, to him who has been raised from the dead in order that we may **bear fruit** for God
Rom 7:5	ὅτε γὰρ ἦμεν ἐν τῇ σαρκί, τὰ παθήματα τῶν ἁμαρτιῶν τὰ διὰ τοῦ νόμου ἐνηργεῖτο ἐν τοῖς μέλεσιν ἡμῶν, εἰς τὸ **καρποφορῆσαι** τῷ θανάτῳ While we were living in the flesh, our sinful passions, aroused by the law, were at work in our members to **bear fruit** for death
Col 1:6	τοῦ παρόντος εἰς ὑμᾶς, καθὼς καὶ ἐν παντὶ τῷ κόσμῳ ἐστὶν **καρποφορούμενον** καὶ αὐξανόμενον καθὼς καὶ ἐν ὑμῖν, ἀφ᾽ ἧς ἡμέρας ἠκούσατε καὶ ἐπέγνωτε τὴν χάριν τοῦ θεοῦ ἐν ἀληθείᾳ that has come to you. Just as it is **bearing fruit** and growing in the whole world, so it has been doing among yourselves from the day you heard it and truly comprehended the grace of God
Col 1:10	περιπατῆσαι ἀξίως τοῦ κυρίου εἰς πᾶσαν ἀρεσκείαν, ἐν παντὶ ἔργῳ ἀγαθῷ **καρποφοροῦντες** καὶ αὐξανόμενοι τῇ ἐπιγνώσει τοῦ θεοῦ so that you may lead lives worthy of the Lord, fully pleasing to him, as you **bear fruit** in every good work and as you grow in the knowledge of God

Definition of καρποφόρος in the literature and lexicons

Louw and Nida's *Greek-English Lexicon of the New Testament Based on Semantic Domains* classifies καρποφόρος in Domain 23: Physiological Processes and States, which includes a number of physiological processes particularly characteristic of plants.[2] The term is further classified as belonging to subsection L: Ripen, Produce Fruit, Bear Seed (23.197–

---

[2] Johannes P. Louw and Eugene A. Nida, eds., *Greek-English Lexicon of the New Testament: Based on Semantic Domains*, 2nd edn., 2 vols. (New York: United Bible Societies, 1988–1989), 276.

ΚΑΡΠΟΦΟΡΟΣ

23.204), and is said to pertain to producing seed or harvest,[3] although the authors suggest that the term can also refer to 'fruitful seasons … seasons when crops become ripe or … the time of the year when there is always plenty to eat'.[4] However, the use in Acts 14:17, which Louw and Nida cite, also has the adjacent complement noun καιρός, which may have influenced this conclusion. C. K. Barrett comments nonetheless, that the term καρποφόρος is 'used more frequently of trees and lands … [and] points to harvest time'.[5]

The related verb καρποφορέω is classified as belonging in Doman 13: Be, Become, Exist, Happen,[6] which as noted by Louw and Nida, is a broad and generic category 'indicating various aspects of states, existence, and events',[7] which are often associated with Doman 68: Aspect, and Domain 71: Mode. Within Domain 13, καρποφορέω is classified with subsection C: exist. Etymologically the verbal form consists of ποιέω and καρπόν which effectively becomes an idiom for 'fruitfulness' although the expanded form (verb + noun) is also variously attested in the NT, and deserves further investigation (albeit elsewhere).[8] Olga Tribulato argues that the compound καρποφόρος 'reflects the frequency of the phrase in the technical register of botany and medicine … ',[9] a phenomenon which D. R. Langslow identifies as a frequent phenomenon in relation to technical languages.[10] Other related compound forms such as φερέκαρπος and φερεστάφυλος are common in the poetic register.

The term καρποφόρος has a fairly wide semantic usage. Herodotus had previously noted in 1.193 that the paucity of rain in Assyria nourishes only the roots of the grain, but it is irrigation from the river that ripens the crop and brings the grain to fullness. In 2.193.4 he notes, εἰσὶ δέ σφι φοίνικες πεφυκότες ἀνὰ πᾶν τὸ πεδίον, οἱ πλεῦνες αὐτῶν καρποφόροι, ἐκ τῶν καὶ σιτία καὶ οἶνον καὶ μέλι ποιεῦνται (trans. 'there are palm trees there growing all over the plain, most of them yielding fruit, from which food is made and wine and honey').[11] The term is again used in a description of trees near a temple of Apollo in Buto, Egypt, ἐν δὲ ὦν ταύτῃ νηός τε Ἀπόλλωνος μέγας ἔνι καὶ βωμοὶ τριφάσιοι ἐνιδρύαται, ἐμπεφύκασι δ᾽ ἐν αὐτῇ φοίνικες συχνοὶ καὶ ἄλλα δένδρεα καὶ καρποφόρα καὶ ἄφορα πολλά (trans. 'however that be, there is a great shrine of Apollo thereon, and three altars stand there; many palm trees grow in the island, and other trees too, some yielding fruit and some not').[12] Theophrastus uses

---

[3] Louw and Nida, *Greek-English Lexicon*, 276.

[4] Louw and Nida, *Greek-English Lexicon*, 276. English translations generally translate καρποφόρος in Acts 14:17 as 'fruitful' (NASB, RSV, NRSV, ESV, NKJV, ASV, HCSB, YLT), or 'crops' (NIV, CJB, GW, GNB, NCV, NLT; cf. 'bumper crops' [MES]).

[5] C. K. Barrett, *A Critical and Exegetical Commentary on the Acts of the Apostles* (Edinburgh: T&T Clark, 2002), 682.

[6] Louw and Nida, *Greek-English Lexicon*, 159.

[7] Louw and Nida, *Greek-English Lexicon*, 166.

[8] Mt 3:8, 10; 7:17–19; 12:33; 13:26; 21:43; Lk 3:8–9; 6:43; 8:8; 12:17; 13:9; Jn 15:5; Rev 22:2.

[9] Olga Tribulato, *Ancient Greek Verb-Initial Compounds: Their Diachronic Development within the Greek Compound System* (Berlin: de Gruyter, 2015), 112.

[10] D. R. Langslow, *Medical Latin in the Roman Empire* (Oxford: Oxford University Press, 2000), 206.

[11] A. D. Godley, trans. *Herodotus. The Persian Wars, Volume I: Books 1–2* (LCL 117; Cambridge, MA: Harvard University Press, 1920), 468–469.

[12] Herodotus, 4.172.1; Godley, *Herodotus*, 244–245. For similar usage, see Herodotus 4.183.1; Xenophon, *Ways and Means*, 1.3.

118 *Numismatics and Greek Lexicography*

the lexeme in a literal description of trees thirty times in his writings, the first of which is his discussion on the viability of the classification of plants based upon their fruit-bearing capacity or not: Διὰ δὴ ταῦτα ὥσπερ λέγομεν οὐκ ἀκριβολογητέον τῷ ὅρῳ ἀλλὰ τῷ τύπῳ ληπτέον τοὺς ἀφορισμούς· ἐπεὶ καὶ τὰς διαιρέσεις ὁμοίως, οἶον ἡμέρων ἀγρίων, καρποφόρων ἀκάρπων, ἀνθοφόρων ἀνανθῶν, ἀειφύλλων φυλλοβόλων (trans. 'For these reasons then, as we are saying, one must not make a too precise definition; we should make our definitions typical. For we must make our distinctions too on the same principle, as those between wild and cultivated plants, fruit-bearing and fruitless, flowering and flowerless, evergreen and deciduous').[13] In a Greek parchment from 88 BCE καρποφόρος occurs in the context of the description of vineyard which is provided μετὰ ὕδατος καὶ ἀκρρδρύοις καρποφόροις τε καὶ ἀκάρποις (trans. 'with water and vine-stocks, both those fruit bearing and those not').[14]

Other texts use the term in description, not of individual trees, but of entire lands. Pindar's *Pythian Odes* 4.6 records, οἰκιστῆρα Βάττον καρποφόρου Λιβύας, ἱερὰν νᾶσον ὡς ἤδη λιπὼν (trans. 'that Battus would be the colonizer of fruit-bearing Libya, and that he should at once leave the holy island [Thera]').[15] Euripides, also in a description of Libya, in *Helen* 1485 says (referring to a leader of birds): ὃς ἄβροχα πεδία καρποφόρα τε γᾶς ἐπιπετόμενος ἰαχεῖ (trans. 'who flies to the rainless and fruitful lands and shrills as he goes').[16] Diodorus Siculus, the Greek historian of Agyrium in Sicily (80–20 BCE), comments in his *Library of History* 5.10, ἔστι δὲ καὶ ἡ νῆσος τῶν Λιπαραίων μικρὰ μὲν τὸ μέγεθος, καρποφόρος δὲ ἱκανῶς καὶ τὰ πρὸς ἀνθρώπων τρυφὴν ἔχουσα διαφερόντως·καὶ γὰρ ἰχθύων παντοδαπῶν παρέχεται πλῆθος τοῖς κατοικοῦσι καὶ τῶν ἀκροδρύων τὰ μάλιστα δυνάμενα παρέχεσθαι τὴν ἐκ τῆς ἀπολαύσεως ἡδονήν (trans. 'The island of the Liparians is also small in extent but sufficiently fruitful and, so far as the wants of men are concerned, it supports even a high degree of luxury; for it supplies the inhabitants with a multitude of fish of every kind and contains those fruit trees which can offer the most pleasure when one enjoys them').[17] This is precisely the sense of the term in Psalm 107[106 LXX]:34 where Yahweh is said to turn γῆν καρποφόρον εἰς ἅλμην (trans. 'a fruitful land into saltness') in description of the punishment of the wicked.[18]

As one might expect, the term is also regularly associated with and used in relation to Demeter. Pausanius, *Description of Greece*, 8.53.7 states the following:Ἔστι δὲ καὶ

---

[13] Theophrastus, *Enquiry*, 1.3.5; Arthur F. Hort, trans. *Theophrastus: Enquiry into Plants, Volume I: Books 1–5* (LCL 70; Cambridge, MA: Harvard University Press, 1916), 26–27, cf. similar use in Psalm 148:9; Jer 2:21;

[14] Parchment 1.A.14. Ellis H. Minns, 'Parchments of the Parthian Period from Avroman in Kurdistan', *JHS* 35 (1915): 28.

[15] William H. Race, trans. *Pindar. Olympian Odes* (LCL 56; Cambridge, MA: Harvard University Press, 1997), 266–267.

[16] David Kovacs, *Euripides. Helen. Phoenician Women. Orestes* (LCL 11; Cambridge, MA: Harvard University Press, 2002), 178–179.

[17] C. H. Oldfather, trans. *Diodorus Siculus. Library of History, Volume III: Books 4.59–58* (LCL 340; Cambridge, MA: Harvard University Press, 1939), 124–125.

[18] S. T. Bloomfield, *A Greek and English Lexicon to the New Testament* (London: Longman, Orme, Brown, Green, & Longmans, 1840), 201; Robert G. Bratcher and William David Reyburn, *A Translator's Handbook on the Book of Psalms* (New York: United Bible Societies, 1991), 929.

Δήμητρος ἐν Τεγέᾳ καὶ Κόρης ναός, ἃς ἐπονομάζουσι Καρποφόρους (trans. 'There is also at Tegea a temple of Demeter and the Maid, whom they surname the Fruit-bringers').[19] Similarly, the chorus leader responds to the chorus in Aristophanes, *Frogs* 383–384, ἄγε νυν ἑτέραν ὕμνων ἰδέαν τὴν καρποφόρον βασίλειαν, Δήμητρα θεάν, ἐπικοσμοῦντες ζαθέοις μολπαῖς κελαδεῖτε (trans. 'come now, celebrate in another form of song the queen of bounteous harvests, the goddess Demeter, adorning her with holy hymns').[20] In addition, LSJ lists a second first-century BCE inscription (SEG 30.1341.5) from Miletus which makes a similar connection between Demeter and καρποφόρος.[21] As an epithet of Demeter, Moulton and Milligan note the Ephesian inscription Syll 6555 from 83 CE, Δήμητρι Καρποφόρῳ καὶ Θεσμοφόρῳ.[22]

The Roman context

Upon the division of Herod the Great's kingdom by Augustus between his three surviving sons, one conspicuous numismatic feature when compared with their father's coinage is the absence of the titular 'βασιλεύς' (trans. 'king'). Philip became tetrarch ('τετράρχης') over Gaulanitis, Trachonitis, Auranitis, Batanea and Paneas, mostly consisting of a non-Jewish population. Given the distance from Jerusalem and the make-up of the population, it is no surprise that Philip's numismatic issues were inconsistent with the worldview of the population, that is, he paid little attention to Jewish sensitivities. Thus, human images of both Caesar's household and Philip are attested on his coinage. The depiction of Philip himself is quite remarkable as this is the very first time a Jewish ruler depicted their own image on a coin. One honorary issue depicted the Augusteum (temple built by Herod the Great in Paneus during his visit there in 10 BCE [Jos. *Ant.* 15.363] and was possibly renovated by Philip).[23] Philip built a mint in Caesarea Philippi in the fifth year of his reign (1 CE) and produced coins frequently after that point. The introduction of a new numismatic issue, roughly at the time of the installation of a new ruler of Judea, is suggestive of a desire to emphasize his own tetrarchy.

The obverse of RPC 1.4949 (Figure 34) has the draped bust of Livia facing right, with the inscription 'ΙΟΥΛΙΑ ΣΕΒΑΣΤΗ' (trans. 'Julia Augusta' [Livia]).[24] The reverse depicts a hand holding three ears of grain, with the inscription 'ΚΑΡΠΟΦΟΡΟΣ' (trans. 'fruit-bearing') with an accompanying date 'ΛΛΔ' (abbreviation for, 'year thirty-four') which equates to 30/31 CE.[25]

---

[19] W. H. S. Jones, trans. *Pausanias. Description of Greece, Volume IV: Books 8.22–10* (LCL 297; Cambridge, MA: Harvard University Press, 1935), 162–163.

[20] Jeffrey Henderson, trans. *Aristophanes. Frogs. Assemblywomen. Wealth* (LCL 180; Cambridge, MA: Harvard University Press, 2002), 76–79.

[21] LSJ, 880.

[22] MM 321–22.

[23] Y. Meshorer, *A Treasury of Jewish Coins* (Jerusalem: Amphora Books, 2001), 85.

[24] Frederick M. Strickert, 'The First Woman to Be Portrayed on a Jewish Coin: Julia Sebaste', *JSJ* 33, no. 1 (2002): 65–91.

[25] Jacob Maltiel-Gerstenfeld, *New Catalogue of Ancient Jewish Coins* (Tel Aviv: Minerva, 1987), 132 reads another piece as year 37 but the identification is uncertain, cf. Jacob Maltiel-Gerstenfeld, *260 Years of Ancient Jewish Coins: A Catalogue* (Tel Aviv: Kol Print Service, 1982).

Figure 34 RPC 1.4949 (used with permission).

The significance of this coin inscription for the lexeme in general and Acts 14:17 in particular is that Paul in Lystra uses a well-known reference to Demeter/Ceres to subvert Roman views regarding the source of human sustenance. This argument can be consolidated through four lines of enquiry. First, several have argued that the depiction of Livia on the obverse of 4949 is evidence of an effort to deify Livia[26] on the basis of both the inscription (καρποφόρος) and iconography (ears of grain). In this case Livia is depicted as Demeter/Ceres, a coinage issue that sought to uphold and highlight Philip's own commitment to the Roman imperial cult.[27] The depiction of Livia as Demeter/Ceres is consistent with other inscriptions and sources during the

---

[26] C. S. Evans, '"On This Rock I Will Build My Church" (Matthew 16.18): Was the Promise to Peter a Response to Tetrarch Philip's Proclamation?' in *The Earliest Perceptions of Jesus in Context: Essays in Honor of John Nolland*, ed. Aaron White, David Wenham, and Craig A. Evans (London: Bloomsbury, 2018), 26; Gertrude Grether, 'Livia and the Roman Imperial Cult', *AJP* 67 (1946): 222–252; Frederick M. Strickert, 'The Dying Grain Which Bears Much Fruit: John 12:24, the Livia Cult, and Bethsaida', in *Bethsaida: A City by the North Shore of the Sea of Galilee*, 4 vols. ed. Rami Arav and Richard A. Freund (Kirksville, MO: Truman State University Press, 1995–2009), 3.155–170.

[27] There were three issues of coinage by Philp in 30/31 CE. First, RPC 1.4949, as noted above. Second, RPC 1.4948 which on the obverse has a bare head of Tiberius facing right, with the inscription, ΤΙΒΕΡΙΟΣ ΣΕΒΑΣΤΟΣ ΚΑΙΣΑΡ (trans. 'Tiberius Augustus Caesar'). The reverse has a temple with four columns, with the inscription, ΕΠΙ ΦΙΛΙΠΠΟΥ ΤΕΤΡΑΡΧΟΥ ΚΤΙΣ L ΛΔ (trans. 'In the time of the founder Philip the tetrarch, year 34') and commemorates the founding of Bethsaida, see Frederick M. Strickert, 'The Coins of Philip', in *Bethsaida: A City by the North Shore of the Sea of Galilee*, 4 vols, ed. Rami Arav and Richard A. Freund (Kirksville, MO: Truman State University Press, 1995–2009), 1.181–189. Strickert argues that RPC 1.4948 was minted in honour of the founding of Julias (Bethsaida) in 30/31 CE because she had died in 29 CE and this city was in honour of her, although the coin was struck in Paneas. Third, RPC 1.4950 has a bare head of Philp facing right on the obverse with accompanying inscription ΦΙΛΙΠΠΟΥ (of Philp). The reverse has only the date in a wreath, L ΛΔ (year 34). Each coin (RPC 1.4948–4950) in their own way gives support for commitment to the imperial agenda, as one might naturally expect.

ΚΑΡΠΟΦΟΡΟΣ

period.[28] Demeter was primarily the goddess of agriculture and cultivated soil.[29] As one of the first-generation Olympian gods (daughter of Rhea and Kronos, and wife [and sister] of Zeus, who gave birth to Kore/Persephone),[30] she held panhellenic popularity. Although she rarely held the status of a city's main deity, her cults were spread throughout the entire Mediterranean, a phenomenon of the importance of agriculture to the inhabitants.[31] One of the most important and well-known stories of Demeter involves Hades abducting Demeter's daughter Persephone to make her his bride (Callimachus, *Hom. Hymn. Cer.*). When Demeter is informed by Hermes of Persephone's fate, Demeter's grief is so severe that she prevents the earth from bearing fruit which results in a famine for humanity and a complete absence of sacrifices for the gods. This threatening of world order for the gods is only resolved when Persephone is reunited with Demeter; a reunion which resulted in the sending of Prince Triptolemos to teach the cultivation of grain to humanity after the joyful reunion of mother and daughter.[32] In the Roman world, Demeter was known as Ceres, part of the Aventine Triad (Dion. Hal. *Ant. Rom.* 6.94.2), and enjoyed wide and early popularity.[33] She was worshipped in a variety of agrarian rites including the Feriae Sementivae in which grain and a pregnant sow were offered (Ovid, *Fast.* 1.659–74).[34] During the third century BCE Ceres underwent further Hellenization with the incorporation of the Greek festival of the Thesmophoria dedicated to Demeter and Persephone, in which only women could participate. For the Romans, the Ceres cult emphasized chastity and motherhood, which were characteristics of the ideal Roman woman. During the imperial period, women of the imperial household were associated with Ceres as emblematic of these ideals and were given Ceres' attributes as attested by inscriptions, coins and sculpture.[35] This is precisely the reason the association is made on RPC 1.4949 as noted above.

Second, local Roman provincial coinage of Lystra portrays the same fertility iconography (ears of grain grasped by a hand) and the same specific identification of the deity, albeit in Latinized form. For the following discussion I accept the catalogue of coinage and dating from Lystra compiled by H. von Aulock.[36] Barbara Levick dates the

---

[28] B. S. Spaeth, 'The Goddess Ceres in the Ara Pacis Augustae and the Carthage Relief', *AJA* 98, no. 1 (1994): 88–89.

[29] Jenny Wallensten, 'Demeter', *EAH* 4 (2013): 1992.

[30] Hesiod, *Theogony* 912–914, αὐτὰρ ὁ Δήμητρος πολυφόρβης ἐς λέχος ἦλθεν· ἣ τέκε Περσεφόνην λευκώλενον, ἣν Ἀϊδωνεὺς ἥρπασεν ἧς παρὰ μητρός, ἔδωκε δὲ μητίετα Ζεύς (trans. 'Then bounteous Demeter came to his bed; she bore white-armed Persephone, whom Aïdoneus snatched away from her mother – but the counsellor Zeus gave her to him'), Glenn W. Most, trans. *Hesiod. Theogony. Works and Days. Testimonia* (LCL 57; Cambridge, MA: Harvard University Press, 2007), 76–77.

[31] There is also evidence that she was worshipped for fertility of fields and fecundity in the Greek world, see A. C. Brumfield, *The Attic Festivals of Demeter and Their Relation to the Agricultural Year* (New York: Arno Press, 1981); S. G. Cole, 'Demeter in the Greek City and Its Countryside', in *Oxford Readings in Greek Religion*, ed. R. Buxton (Oxford: Oxford University Press, 2000), 133–154.

[32] Isoc. *Paneg.* 28; Xen. *Hell.* 6.3.6; *Hom. Hymn. Cer.* See H. Foley, *The Homeric Hymn to Demeter: Translation, Commentary and Interpretive Essays* (Princeton, NJ: Princeton University Press, 1994); N. J. Richardson, *The Homeric Hymn to Demeter* (Oxford: Clarendon Press, 1974).

[33] Cf. the Faliscan inscription from 600 BCE which states 'Let Ceres give grain', E. Simon, *Die Götter der Römer* (Munich: Hirmer, 1990), 43.

[34] B. S. Spaeth, 'Ceres', *EAH* 3 (2013): 1418.

[35] B. S. Spaeth, *The Roman Goddess Ceres* (Austin: University of Texas Press, 1996), 113–23, 169–81.

[36] H. von Aulock, 'Die römische Kolonie Lystra und ihre Münzen', *Chiron* 2 (1972): 509–18.

122   *Numismatics and Greek Lexicography*

Lystran coins issued by Augustus to 25 BCE, and interprets them as foundation issues of that year.[37] She goes on to argue that the similar coins of Aurelius were bicentennial pieces.[38] However, as Burnett has noted, 'it would be surprising to find a portrait of Augustus looking so mature at so early a date,'[39] and suggests the last two decades of his reign. Von Aulock is surely more accurate in dating the Lystran Augustan coinage to 6 BCE. There are two denominations of Roman provincial coinage in Lystra, a larger copper 25 mm/9.19 g and a medium copper 19 mm/6.91 g issue. RPC 1.3540 (Figure 35) depicts on the obverse a laureate head of Augustus with the inscription IMP AUG. The obverse depicts Ceres seated facing left on backless throne holding ears of grain and poppies in right hand over altar and torch in left hand with CERERIS (trans. 'of Ceres') legend in upper left perimeter. Also of interest are the other two issues from the city RPC 1.3538 and 1.3539. RPC 1.3538 (Figure 36) is a bronze issue depicting the laureate head of Augustus facing left on the obverse with cornucopia behind (symbol of prosperity and fertility) with IMPE AUGUSTI (trans. 'of the emperor Augustus'). The reverse depicts a colonist ploughing with two hump-backed oxen, with inscription COL IVL FEI GEM LVSTRA (trans. 'The Colonia Julia Felix Gemina Lystra').[40] RPC 1.3539 consists of the medium denomination (AE 25 mm) and is identical to RPC 1.3538 with the exception of the absence of the cornucopia and FEI for FEL on the obverse.

Third, Paul uses the word (καρποφόρος) in Lystra Acts 14:17 to describe God's activity of providing seasonal food for humanity. In Horace's *Odes* 2.12.22, the fertility of the region as *pinguis* (fertile),[41] but Strabo's *Geography* 12.6.1 notes the general inhospitable nature of the region for agricultural development, καὶ τὰ τῶν Λυκαόνων ὀροπέδια ψυχρὰ καὶ ψιλὰ καὶ ὀναγρόβοτα, ὑδάτων δὲ σπάνις πολλή· ὅπου δὲ καὶ εὑρεῖν δυνατόν, βαθύτατα φρέατα τῶν πάντων (trans. 'also the plateaus of the Lycaonians, are cold, bare of trees, and grazed by wild asses, though there is a great scarcity of water; and even where it is possible to find water, the wells are the deepest in the world').[42] W. Ramsey questions whether Lystra was on the original itinerary for the Pauline mission, 'one must wonder how Lystra came to be one of the list. How did the cosmopolitan Paul drift like a piece of timber into this quite backwater?'[43] But the city's status as a Roman colony, Paul's own citizenship, and the geographical proximity to his location in Asia Minor provide more than sufficient justification.

---

[37] B. Levick, *Roman Colonies in Southern Asia Minor* (Oxford: Clarendon Press, 1967), 37.

[38] Levick, *Roman Colonies*, xx.

[39] Andrew Burnett, Michel Amandry, and Ian Carradice, *Roman Provincial Coinage: Volumes 1–2* (London: British Museum, 1992–1999).

[40] On this issue further, see below.

[41] Niall Rudd, trans. *Horace. Odes and Epodes* (LCL 33; Cambridge, MA: Harvard University Press, 2004), 120–121.

[42] Horace Leonard Jones, trans. *Strabo. Geography, Volume V: Books 10–12* (LCL 211; Cambridge, MA: Harvard University Press, 1928), 472–475. Strabo does acknowledge that ὅμως δὲ καίπερ ἄνυδρος οὖσα ἡ χώρα πρόβατα ἐκτρέφει θαυμαστῶς, τραχείας δὲ ἐρέας, καί τινες ἐξ αὐτῶν τούτων μεγίστους πλούτους ἐκτήσαντο (trans. 'But still, although the country is unwatered, it is remarkably productive of sheep; but the wool is coarse, and yet some persons have acquired very great wealth from this alone'), pages 474–475.

[43] William Mitchell Ramsay, *The Cities of St Paul: Their Influence on His Life and Thought* (New York: Armstrong and Son, 1908), 408.

ΚΑΡΠΟΦΟΡΟΣ 123

Figure 35 RPC 1.3540 (used with permission).

Figure 36 RPC 1.3538 (used with permission).

Lystra was founded by Augustus in approximately 6 BCE. A Latin inscription discovered by J. R. S. Sterrett on a large carved stone confirmed both the location and status of the city as a Roman colony.[44] It reads, DIVVM AVG COL IVL FELIX

---

[44] Kirsopp Lake and Henry J. Cadbury, *English Translation and Commentary. Vol. 4 of The Beginnings of Christianity: The Acts of the Apostles*, ed. F. J. Foakes-Jackson and Kirsopp Lake (London: Macmillan, 1933), 162; Hans Conzelmann, *A Commentary on the Acts of the Apostles*, trans. James Limburg, A. Thomas Kraabel, and Donald H. Juel (Philadelphia, PA: Fortress, 1987), 108; Levick, *Roman Colonies*, 29–41.

GEMINA LUSTRA CONSEGRAVIT DD (trans. 'The Colonia Julia Felix Gemina Lystra consecrates the divine Augustus by order of the decurions'). The inscription presumably referred to a temple of statue or altar of Augustus. The desirability of a colony here was to provide a defensive outpost against mountain tribes to south and west.[45] Gemina refers to Augustus designating both Lystra and her sister city Pisidian Antioch as Roman colonies. As noted above, the earliest Roman provincial coins of the city also celebrate its status as a colony and depict a togate male ploughing with two oxen tracing the limits of the city (RPC 1.3538).[46]

When Paul and Barnabas are identified as Hermes and Zeus respectively (Acts 14:12) with accompanying garlanded oxen to be sacrificed to the two gods in human form (Acts 14:13), they refuse the honour and attempt to persuade the Lystran crowd that they are mere mortals (Acts 14:15). Commentators have readily attempted to find relevant mythological background for the episode. Greek traditions often have gods disguise themselves and appear in human form, as Athena famously does to Telemachus in an episode of the *Odyssey* (*Od.* 1.96–324, 405–419). The conventional view of commentators is that the story is an allusion to the Baucis and Philemon myth of Zeus and Hermes coming to the inhabitants of Phrygia (Ovid, *Metam.* 8.612–727),[47] but the story could well have multiple points of local reference.

Paul declares God as the source of all life, ὃς ἐποίησεν τὸν οὐρανὸν καὶ τὴν γῆν καὶ τὴν θάλασσαν καὶ πάντα τὰ ἐν αὐτοῖς (trans. 'who made the heaven and the earth and the sea and all that is in them'). The declaration could be a citation from any number of Old Testament texts (Exod 20:11; Neh 9:6; Ps 146:6 [145:6 LXX]; Amos 9:6; cf. Acts 4:24). The threefold combination of heaven, earth and sea is also popular with Roman poets for describing Jupiter's activity. Ovid (*Metam.* 1.177–180) notes that 'when the gods had taken their seats within the marble council chamber, the king himself, seated high above the rest and leaning on his ivory sceptre, shook thrice and again his awful locks, wherewith he moved the land and sea and sky'.[48] At nearby Phrygia, inhabitants, as was typical in the broader milieu, treated heaven, earth and sea as separate deities. Literary evidence suggests Phrygians worshipped the earth mother,[49] and a similar

---

[45] P. Lewis and Ron Bolden, *The Pocket Guide to Saint Paul: Coins Encountered by the Apostle on His Travels* (Kent Town: Wakefield Press, 2002), 84.

[46] In addition an inscription at Pisidian Antioch on a statue of Concord put up in honour of Antioch by the 'colonia Lystra', see J. R. S. Sterrett, *The Wolfe Expedition to Asia Minor* (Boston, MA: Damrell and Upham, 1888) and William Mitchell Ramsay, *The Church in the Roman Empire before A.D. 170* (London: Hodder, 1903), 47.

[47] See Craig S. Keener, *Acts. Volume 2, 3: 1–14:28:An Exegetical Commentary* (Grand Rapids, MI: Baker Academic, 2013), 2146 n.1554 and 2148 n.1573 for many examples. W. M. Calder's discovery of inscriptions in the vicinity of Lystra referring to 'priests of Zeus' and a statue of Hermes dedicated to Zeus which are often appealed to by commentators for historical confirmation of the episode (cf. D. A. Hagner, 'Lystra', *ISBE* 3 [1988]: 193) are anachronistic as they postdate the episode by at least 200 years.

[48] Frank Justus Miller, trans. *Ovid. Metamorphoses, Volume I: Books 1–8* (LCL 42; Cambridge, MA: Harvard University Press, 1916), 14–15. Cf. Hor. *Odes* 1.12.13–18;

[49] Mother Rhea (mother of Zeus) is also frequently associated with Phrygia (Eurip. *Bacch.* 58–59; Diog. *Laert.* 6.1.1).

phenomenon could be possible in Lystra.[50] An expression of this was the veneration of Ceres/Demeter on the coinage of Lystra as seen above on RPC 3540. In essence Ceres/Demeter was a manifestation of the earth mother. Paul and Barnabas, as males, were identified with two of the male deities associated with Ceres/Demeter both in regard to fertility and the mythological background to Ceres/Demeter. In this sense, Peter Lewis and Ron Bolden note, 'Ceres can be seen as a Roman veneer for these male agricultural deities … [and] was a "stand in" for the Lycaonian agricultural gods on the coin of Lystra.'[51] It is therefore no accident that Paul and Barnabas, having been identified as the fertility gods by the Lystrans, specifically redirect their audience to the legitimate source of fruitfulness using the specific terminology (καρποφόρος) found on numismatic inscriptional evidence in reference to Ceres/Demeter (RPC 1.4949) and associated with their own goddess on local Lystran coinage (RPC 1.3540) which circulated before and during Paul's visit in the mid-first century CE.

An additional element which strengthens this reading is the sociological demographic of the city. There seems to be considerable discontinuity between those residing in the countryside of the town and Lystra proper. Barbara Levick notes that 35 of Lystra's 107 inscriptions are in Latin,[52] and almost all the Latin inscriptions were found on the site of the town itself. The surrounding countryside produces epigraphic evidence of only Greek and local names. This suggests that there was minimal overlap between the two and very likely a significant gulf between them. Indeed, Peter Garnsey and Richard Saller note the regular occurrence of Roman cities exploiting the production of the neighbouring countryside.[53] It was a frequent phenomenon that the countryside immediately surrounding a city would be insufficient even medium cities within the empire.[54] In this light, Paul and Barnabas 'respond with a speech that was designed to appeal to people whose culture and religious beliefs had little urban sophistication'.[55] Acts 14:17 is designed to both indicate the legitimate source of the earth's production and demonstrate God's benevolence by his care for the rural population.[56]

---

[50] Eurip. *Bacch.* 79; Lucret. *Nat.* 2.611; Cciero (attrib.) Rhet. Her. 4.59.62. Although Lystra is Lycaonian, it is geographically and culturally aligned to Phrygian culture to allow this widespread emphasis to be applicable here. Ferguson notes that the Earth-Mother and Ceres/Demeter received sacrifice for the dead, 'Ceres, the power of growth (creare), is thus seen to transcend her position as power of the harvest and appear as another aspect of the Mother,' J. Ferguson, *The Religions of the Roman Empire* (London: Thames and Hudson,1970), 25.

[51] Lewis and Bolden, *Saint Paul*, 86. Barbara Levick notes that RPC 1.3540 'probably does honour to a native or Hellenized cult adopted by the colony', Levick, *Roman Colonies*, 154.

[52] Levick, *Roman Colonies*, 154.

[53] Peter Garnsey and Richard Saller, *The Roman Empire: Economy, Society and Culture* (London: Bloomsbury, 2014), 119.

[54] P. Erdkamp, 'Agriculture, Underemployment, and the Cost of Rural Labour in the Roman World', *CQ* 49, no. 2 (1999): 556–572.

[55] Stephen Mitchell, *Anatolia: Land, Men, and Gods in Asia Minor*, 2 vols. (Oxford: Clarendon, 1993), 2.11.

[56] See further Mitchell, *Anatolia*, 2.11.

Conclusion

This paper has sought to locate and geographically contextualise καρποφόρος, a *hapax legomenon*, which occurs in Acts 14:17 within Paul and Barnabas's speech to the local population of Lystra. In so doing it was evident that on a fresh reading of the epigraphic and literary sources cited in the lexica, that the term καρποφόρος displayed a wide semantic domain including fruitfulness of trees, fertility of land, and as a regular label and epithet for Demeter/Ceres, including the coinage of tetrarch Philip in 30/31 CE. Further analysis of the coinage of Lystra revealed the interest in the depiction of Ceres/Demeter on local coinage. Paul's motivation in Acts 14:17 in employing the relatively rare term καρποφόρος was to identify the true source of seasonal provision in a manner in which the inhabitants of Lystra would readily recognize. Joseph Fitzmeyer observes that 'such gifts from heaven should make humans aware of the source of them, or at least should make them inquire into whence such blessings of nature come'.[57] But is this something local that inhabitants would recognize, and how does our above discussion relate to Acts 14:11, that the inhabitants spoke in τὴν φωνὴν αὐτῶν Λυκαονιστὶ (trans. 'their Lycaonian language')? As noted, funerary inscriptions indicate that the inhabitants of Lystra likely spoke Greek[58] and that their native religious expression coupled with their interest in Ceres/Demeter makes recognition highly probable. In sum, our above discussion (a) provides new, and hitherto uncited, numismatic inscriptional evidence for a lexicon entry on the term καρποφόρος, (b) enhances and provides a concrete localized reference to the use of this term in the NT and (c) confirms that in no other city that Paul visited according to Acts and the epistles, with the exception of Thessalonica,[59] does Ceres/Demeter play any role in the iconography of the local coinage of the city.

---

[57] Joseph A. Fitzmeyer *The Acts of the Apostles: A New Translation with Introduction and Commentary* (New Haven, CT: Yale University Press, 2008), 532.

[58] The mountainous interior of Anatolia also provided a degree of isolation which aided in sustaining and preserving the native speech. Commentators are divided on whether the reference to λυκαονιστί in Acts 14:11 refers to a Greek dialect of Asia minor (Carlo Consani, 'La koiné et les dialectes grecs dans la documentation linguistique et la réflexion métalinguistique des premiers siècles de notre ère', in *La koiné grecque antique*, ed. Claude Brixhe (Nancy: Presses universitaires de Nancy, 1993), 32–33; S. E. Porter, *Paul in Acts* (Peabody, MA: Hendrickson, 2001), 137; Lyman Abbott, *The Acts of the Apostles: With Notes, Comments, Maps, and Illustrations* [New York: A. S. Barnes, 1876], 160) or a more distinct language which would indicate that Paul and Barnabas could only address the Greek speakers directly (William Mitchell Ramsay, *The Bearing of Recent Discovery on the Trustworthiness of the New Testament* [London: Hodder & Stoughton, 1915], 67 n. 2). The possibility remains that Paul and Barnabas made use of an interpreter.

[59] See Chapter 8 below for discussion of coinage at Thessalonica.

7

ΝΕΩΚΟΡΟΣ

Introduction

The term 'νεωκόρος' is a New Testament *hapax legomenon*, which occurs in the speech of the unnamed Ephesian town clerk (γραμματεύς) in Acts 19:35. The context of his speech is that of the ensuing riot instigated by Demetrius the silversmith (Acts 19:21–41), who was concerned for the economic viability of his trade-guild in light of Paul's message, 'οὐκ εἰσὶν θεοὶ οἱ διὰ χειρῶν γινόμενοι' (trans. '[gods] made with hands are not gods' [v.26]). Demetrius subsequently protests that 'τὸ τῆς μεγάλης θεᾶς Ἀρτέμιδος ἱερὸν εἰς οὐθὲν λογισθῆναι, μέλλειν τε καὶ καθαιρεῖσθαι τῆς μεγαλειότητος αὐτῆς ἣν ὅλη ἡ Ἀσία καὶ ἡ οἰκουμένη σέβεται' (trans. 'the temple of the great goddess Artemis will be regarded as worthless and she whom all of Asia and the world worship will even be dethroned from her magnificence' [v.27]). This, in turn, generated a series of ideological objections by the inhabitants of the city who had assembled in the theatre to engage in a verbal demonstration of support for Artemis, 'μεγάλη ἡ Ἄρτεμις Ἐφεσίων' (trans. 'great is Artemis of the Ephesians' [v.28]). In response, the town clerk (γραμματεύς), seeking to placate the crowds, reassured the inhabitants that the great reputation of Ephesus as the 'νεωκόρον' was not at risk ('νεωκόρον οὖσαν τῆς μεγάλης Ἀρτέμιδος καὶ τοῦ διοπετοῦς', trans. 'guardian of the temple of the great Artemis and of the image which fell down from heaven' [v.35]). Citing the decrees of Ephesus, A. N. Sherwin-White notes that the '[γραμματεύς] appears in conjunction with the *strategoi* as a senior partner, acting as the director of affairs in council or assembly',[1] providing evidence that his role was akin to a magistrate, rather than an administrative assistant. P. Trebilco notes that the position was of such significance that 'inscriptions were often dated by the clerk's year in office'.[2] The 'γραμματεύς' is thus well placed to 'take control of the assembly'.[3]

One of the pertinent questions which arises within this pericope is the precise meaning of Ephesian town clerk's reference to the city as the 'νεωκόρον'. The term is variously translated in English versions as 'guardian of the temple' (NASB, NIV),

---

[1] A. N. Sherwin-White, *Roman Society and Roman Law in the New Testament* (Oxford: Clarendon Press, 1963), 86.

[2] Paul R. Trebilco, 'Asia', in *The Book of Acts in Its Graeco-Roman Setting*, ed. D. W. J. Gill and C. Gempf (Grand Rapids, MI: Eerdmans, 1994), 351.

[3] I. H. Marshall, *Acts* (Grand Rapids, MI: Eerdmans, 1980), 360.

'temple guardian' (HCSB), 'official guardian of the temple' (NLT), 'keeper of the temple' (NET, GW), 'temple keeper' (ASV, ESV), 'worshipper' (KJV, DR) and 'devotee' (YLT). This paper brings to bear the relevant numismatic material, and the manner in which it can be employed to illuminate this designation.

Context and background

Ephesus was the leading city in the Roman province of Asia. It could boast a rich and complex history of occupation dating back, at the very least, to the Mycenaean period (*c.* 1400 BCE).[4] Its coastal location offered the ideal conditions for developing into a large seaport, which in turn generated considerable wealth for the city and created a prosperous commercial entity. So much so that Strabo states, 'ὁ μὲν οὖν λιμὴν τοιοῦτος· ἡ δὲ πόλις τῇ πρὸς τὰ ἄλλα εὐκαιρίᾳ τῶν τόπων αὔξεται καθ' ἑκάστην ἡμέραν, ἐμπόριον οὖσα μέγιστον τῶν κατὰ τὴν Ἀσίαν τὴν ἐντὸς τοῦ Ταύρου' (trans. 'Such, then, is the harbour; and the city, because of its advantageous situation in other respects, grows daily, and is the largest emporium in Asia this side [of] the Taurus').[5]

It is estimated that in the first century CE the population of Ephesus exceeded 200,000.[6] Amid the cosmopolitan population of Ionians, Lydians, Phrygians and Mysians, there was a substantial Jewish population. Josephus notes that Dolabella, the governor of Asia, exempted Ephesian Jewish Roman citizens from military service, 'διὰ τὸ μήτε ὅπλα βαστάζειν δύνασθαι μήτε ὁδοιπορεῖν ἐν ταῖς ἡμέραις τῶν σαββάτων, μήτε τροφῶν τῶν πατρίων καὶ συνήθων κατὰ τούτους εὐπορεῖν' (trans. 'because they are not allowed to bear arms, or to travel on the Sabbath days, nor there to procure themselves those sorts of food which they have been used to eat from the times of their forefathers').[7] It would thus appear that the Ephesian Jewish community had a 'cordial relationship with the civic officials and the local populace.'[8]

One of the ways the local inhabitants chose to bestow acclamation upon the emperor was to build a temple in his honour, and thus to provide a central location for the cities of the province to sacrifice to the emperor. It was in the first century CE that a transition of terminology occurred. As will be discussed below, before the first century

---

[4] See further E. Akurgal, *Ancient Civilizations and Ruins of Turkey* (Ankara: Haşet Kitabevi, 1985); M. J. Mellink, 'Archaeology in Asia Minor', *AJA* 63 (1959): 73–85; Veronika Mitsopoulos-Leon, 'Ephesus', in *The Princeton Encyclopedia of Classical Sites*, ed. Richard Stillwell, William L. MacDonald, and Marian Holland McAllister (Princeton, NJ: Princeton University Press, 1976), 306–310.

[5] Strabo, *Geography* 14.1.24. Translation from Jones, trans. *Strabo*, 231.

[6] O. F. A. Meinardus, *St. Paul in Ephesus and the Cities of Galatia and Cyprus* (New Rochelle: Caratzas Brothers, 1979), 54 estimates 200,000; T. R. S. Broughton, 'Roman Asia', in *An Economic Survey of Ancient Rome*, vol. 4, ed. T. Frank (Baltimore, MD: Johns Hopkins Press, 1938), 813 estimates >225,000; and R. Oster, 'Ephesus, Ephesians', *EEC* (1990): 301 estimates 250,000. It is notable that only Rome and Alexandria were more populous during this period.

[7] Josephus, *Ant.* 14.226; Cf. 223–227, 262–264.

[8] C. E. Arnold, 'Ephesians', in *Zondervan Illustrated Bible Backgrounds* Commentary, *Vol. 3: Romans to Philemon*, ed. Clinton E. Arnold and Steven M. Baugh (Grand Rapids, MI: Zondervan, 2002), 301–302.

CE, the term 'νεωκόρος' referred to a temple official (or the like) whose duties ranged from priestly to economic and administrative support for a temple; later, however, this term underwent a significant evolution.

Etymologically, the derivation of the compound 'νεωκόρος' comes from two Greek words. The first part, 'ναός,' denotes a 'place or structure specifically associated with or set apart for a deity',[9] in which the 'deity is worshipped'.[10] B. Burrell, however,[11] cites P. Chantraine who distinguishes 'ναός' as a built structure, from a sacred unroofed enclosure.[12] M. Silva further distinguishes the term from 'τέμενος' which he defines as 'a space fenced in, or at least clearly marked as an area a theophany has once occurred and is expected again on the ground of tradition'[13] as distinct to 'ναός' which is 'a dwelling for the gods; used for sacrifice, worship and the reception of oracles',[14] and a place which 'required a local priesthood'.[15] Nonetheless, a definition of the term 'νάος', which at its core has linkage with a sacred place and associated deity, is readily evident.

The second part of the compound, '-κόρος', is more ambiguous. Burrell notes that Hesychius of Alexandria identifies the derivation of the term as 'keep in order' and specifically 'sweep'.[16] This indeed is the definition that W. Buechner attributes the term on the basis of Euripides' *Ion* (lines 54–55), in which one of his tasks was to sweep the temple of Apollo.[17] Burrell accurately counters, however, that Ion is never specifically referred to as a 'νεωκόρος' by Euripides, but only as a 'χρυσοφύλαξ' (guard for gold) and 'ταμίας' (steward).[18] Furthermore, the *Suda* primarily identifies the derivation as 'maintain',[19] with the meaning 'sweeper' as only a secondary derivation.[20]

The role and function of the human 'νεωκόρος' as documented in later literary sources includes an impressive variety of duties. A papyrus from the early third century BCE, *P.Magd* 35, preserves 'νακόρος' (the Doric form of νεωκόρος) in reference to Nicomachus, apparently an official of a Jewish synagogue in a local Egyptian village.[21] The 'νεωκόρος' as a temple functionary could include a variety of tasks, including (1) priestly duties, (2) being involved in sacrificial procedures, (3) performing and

---

[9] BDAG, 665. νεώς is Attic, whereas most of Greek has the -αο- form, this is due to phonological changes. I am grateful to A.A. Thompson for bringing attention to this.

[10] L&N, 83 §7.15.

[11] B. Burrell, *Neokoroi: Greek Cities and Roman Emperors* (Leiden: Brill, 2004), 4.

[12] P. Chantraine, *Dictionnaire étymologique de la langue grecque* (Paris: Klincksieck, 1968–1980), ad loc.

[13] *NIDNTTE* 'ναός, νεωκόρος' 3:370.

[14] *NIDNTTE* 'ναός, νεωκόρος' 3:370.

[15] *NIDNTTE* 'ναός, νεωκόρος' 3:370.

[16] Burrell, *Neokoroi*, 4.

[17] W. Buechner, *De Neocoria* (Gissae: Typis Guilelmi Keller, 1888), 2–21.

[18] Burrell, *Neokoroi*, 4.

[19] Burrell, *Neokoroi*, 4.

[20] *Suda* κόρη, κόρος, νεωκόρος, ζάκορος, νεωκορήσει. See further κορέω in Chantraine, *Dictionnaire*, 2:565–66. Linear B tablets from the Mycenean period include references to a 'da-ko-ro' and 'da-mo-ko-ro' without reference to any kind of 'sweeper' but rather 'a high official'. See C. Ruijgh, 'Observations sur κορέσαι, κορέω, myc. da-ko-ro δακόρος, etc.', in *O-o-pe-ro-si: Festschrift für Ernst Risch zum 75 Geburtstag*, ed. A. Etter (Berlin: de Gruyter, 1986), 376–392; M. Petrusevki, 'Aukewa damokoro', *Ziva Antika* 15 (1965): 12, cited by Burrell, *Neokoroi*, 4.

[21] J. Lesquier, *Papyrus de Magdola being Papyrus Grecs de Lille II* (Paris: Leroux, 1912). See further MM, 425. An even earlier occurrence of 'νεωκόρος' is attested in *I.Priene* 231, see further below.

130   *Numismatics and Greek Lexicography*

receiving sacrifices on behalf of the god, (4) acting as key-holder for the temple, (5) being responsible for other valuables in the temple, (6) collecting pilgrim fees, (7) issuing tickets and (8) listing names and cities on wooden tablets. These composite duties incline Burrell to conclude that 'it is possible that "neokoros" was the title that the chief priest used in his practical or financial functions'.[22] In this light, the term encompasses a diverse and wide-ranging set of referents.

The term occurs twice in Josephus. In *Jewish War* 1.153, Josephus refers to certain individuals who were responsible for the cleansing of the Jerusalem temple, 'οὔτε δὲ τούτων οὔτε ἄλλου τινὸς τῶν ἱερῶν κειμηλίων ἥψατο, ἀλλὰ καὶ μετὰ μίαν τῆς ἁλώσεως ἡμέραν καθᾶραι τὸ ἱερὸν τοῖς νεωκόροις προσέταξεν καὶ τὰς ἐξ ἔθους ἐπιτελεῖν θυσίας' (trans. 'Yet did not he touch the money, nor any thing else that was there reposited; but he commanded the ministers about the temple, the very next day after he had taken it, to cleanse it, and to perform their accustomed sacrifices'). The second reference to the term occurs in Josephus's own account of his speech to those who had yet to surrender during the siege of Jerusalem (*War* 9.4), 'τίς οὐκ οἶδεν τὴν παντὸς θηρίου καταπλησθεῖσαν Αἴγυπτον καὶ πάσῃ φθαρεῖσαν νόσῳ, τὴν ἄκαρπον [γῆν], τὸν ἐπιλείποντα Νεῖλον, τὰς ἐπαλλήλους δέκα πληγάς, τοὺς διὰ ταῦτα μετὰ φρουρᾶς προπεμπομένους πατέρας ἡμῶν ἀναιμάκτους ἀκινδύνους, οὓς ὁ θεὸς αὑτῷ νεωκόρους ἦγεν' (trans. 'Who is there that does not know that Egypt was overrun with all sorts of wild beasts, and consumed by all sorts of distempers? How their land did not bring forth its fruits? Now the Nile failed of water; how the ten plagues of Egypt followed one upon another? And how, by those means, our fathers were sent away, under a guard, because God conducted them as his peculiar servants?'). Herein, the title is used with reference to an entire people – that is, all Jews – as 'νεωκόροι'.[23] The element of particular interest here is that Josephus is referring to a historical time period during which the people were in exile and no temple, per se, stood in Jerusalem. Burrell thus concludes that this indicates 'that the Jews' ward over their temple … was a spiritual one'.[24]

The term 'νεωκόρος' occurs even more frequently in Philo, most often in reference to the tribe of Levi. *On Flight and Finding* 1.90 is typical when it states, 'ἆρ' οὖν διὰ τοῦτο μόνον ἢ καὶ δι' ἐκεῖνο, ὅτι ἡ τῶν νεωκόρων Λευιτικὴ φυλὴ τοὺς θεοπλαστήσαντας τὸν χρυσοῦν μόσχον, τὸν Αἰγυπτιακὸν τῦφον, ἡβηδὸν ἐξ ἐπιδρομῆς κατέκτειναν, ὀργῇ δικαίᾳ σὺν ἐνθουσιασμῷ καί τινι κατοκωχῇ θεοφορήτῳ χρησάμενοι' (trans. 'Either, therefore, it is for this reason alone, or perhaps for this other also, that the Levitical tribe of the persons set apart for the service of the temple ran up, and at one onset slew those who had made a god of the golden calf, the pride of Egypt, killing all who had arrived at the age of puberty, being inflamed with righteous danger, combined with enthusiasm, and a certain heaven-sent inspiration'). Although several other passages could be cited and discussed,[25] it is sufficient for our purposes to note that Philo consistently uses the term 'νεωκόρος' in reference to the tribe of Levi 'especially in their function as priests … guardians, gatekeepers, purifiers, and general caretakers

---

[22] Burrell, *Neokoroi*, 4–5.
[23] Burrell, *Neokoroi*, 5.
[24] Burrell, *Neokoroi*, 5.
[25] Flight 1.93–94; Moses 1.316, 318; 2.72, 159, 174, 276; Spec. Laws 2.120; Rewards 1.74; QG 2.17.

of the temple at Jerusalem'.[26] Philo does, however, distinguish between an 'ἱερεύς' and a 'νεωκόρος', as per *On the Life of Moses* 2.276 where he states, 'τῶν περὶ τὸν νεὼν λειτουργῶν δύο τάξεις εἰσίν, ἡ μὲν κρείσσων ἱερέων, ἡ δ᾽ ἐλάττων νεωκόρων· ἦσαν δὲ κατ᾽ ἐκεῖνον τὸν χρόνον τρεῖς μὲν ἱερεῖς, νεωκόρων δὲ πολλαὶ χιλιάδες' (trans. 'there were two classes of ministrations concerning the temple; the higher one belonging to the priests, and the lower one to the keepers of the temple; and there were at this time three priests, but many thousand keepers of the temple').[27]

Commentators have thus detected a diachronic development of 'νεωκόρος', shifting from a reference to human individuals initially, to a term that officially designated a particular type of temple, 'a provincial temple for the cult of the emperor'.[28] F. F. Bruce acknowledges this shift in stating that the term 'was applied as a title of honor, first to individuals and later to cities'.[29] G. H. R. Horsely similarly concludes that 'the claim of a city to be the neokoros of a temple and its deity was an important feature of its political self-promotion in the context of inter-city rivalry, especially (from the end of the first century) in relation to temples of the Imperial cult'.[30]

On the basis of the voluminous material culture of the period, it can thus be stated with some confidence that during the first century the term 'νεωκόρος' became a special title bestowed upon cities that dedicated a temple to the current emperor. In addition to imperial favour, Burrell identifies two further criteria essential for a city's securing of the title, namely the 'koinon's backing … and the Senate's approval'.[31] Ephesus wanted to have such an honour with regard to Augustus, but this distinction was first given to Pergamon in Mysia, primarily on the basis that Ephesus was perceived to be wholly devoted to Artemis (Tacitus, *Annals* 4.55). The significance of Ephesian devotion to Artemis, within the context of both the numismatic evidence (see below) and the context of 'νεωκόρος' in Acts 19 (see above) justifies the full citation of the passage in Tacitus:

> Sed Caesar quo famam averteret, adesse frequens senatui legatosque Asiae, ambigentis quanam in civitate templum statueretur pluris per dies audivit. Undecim urbes certabant, pari ambitione, viribus diversae. Neque multum distantia inter se memorabant de vetustate generis, studio in populum Romanum per bella Persi et Aristonici aliorumque regum. Verum Hypaepeni Trallianique Laodicenis ac Magnetibus simul tramissi ut parum validi; ne Ilienses quidem, cum parentem urbis Romae Troiam referrent, nisi antiquitatis gloria pollebant. Paulum addubitatum, quod Halicarnasii mille et ducentos per annos nullo motu terrae nutavisse sedes suas vivoque in saxo fundamenta templi adseveraverant. Pergamenos (eo ipso nitebantur) aede Augusto ibi sita satis adeptos creditum. **Ephesii Milesiique, hi**

---

[26] Burrell, *Neokoroi*, 5.

[27] For 'νεωκόρος' as the 'ἐν τῇ δευτέρᾳ τάξει', see *Spec. Laws* 1:156.

[28] Burrell, *Neokoroi*, 5.

[29] F. F. Bruce, *The Acts of the Apostles: Greek Text with Introduction and Commentary* (Grand Rapids, MI: Eerdmans, 1990), 420.

[30] G. H. R. Horsley 'The Inscriptions of Ephesos and the New Testament', *Novum Testamentum* 34 (1992): 136–137.

[31] B. Burrell, 'Neokoros', *EAH* 9 (2013): 4743.

132 *Numismatics and Greek Lexicography*

Apollinis, illi Dianae caerimonia occupavisse civitates visi. Ita Sardianos inter Zmyrnaeosque deliberatum. Sardiani decretum Etruriae recitavere ut consanguinei: nam Tyrrhenum Lydumque Atye rege genitos ob multitudinem divisisse gentem; Lydum patriis in terris resedisse, Tyrrheno datum novas ut conderet sedes; et ducum e nominibus indita vocabula illis per Asiam, his in Italia; auctamque adhuc Lydorum opulentiam missis in insulam1 populis, cui mox a Pelope nomen. Simul litteras imperatorum et icta nobiscum foedera bello Macedonum ubertatemque fluminum suorum, temperiem caeli ac ditis circum terras memorabant.

To divert criticism, the Caesar attended the senate with frequency, and for several days listened to the deputies from Asia debating which of their communities was to erect his temple. Eleven cities competed, with equal ambition but disparate resources. With no great variety each pleaded national antiquity, and zeal for the Roman cause in the wars with Perseus, Aristonicus and other kings. But Hypaepa and Tralles, together with Laodicea and Magnesia, were passed over as inadequate to the task: even Ilium, though it appealed to Troy as the parent of Rome, had no significance apart from the glory of its past. Some little hesitation was caused by the statement of the Halicarnassians that for twelve hundred years no tremors of earthquake had disturbed their town, and the temple foundations would rest on the living rock. The Pergamenes were refuted by their main argument: they had already a sanctuary of Augustus, and the distinction was thought ample. **The state-worship in Ephesus and Miletus was considered to be already centred on the cults of Diana and Apollo respectively**: the deliberations turned, therefore, on Sardis and Smyrna. The Sardians read a decree of their 'kindred country' of Etruria. 'Owing to its numbers,' they explained, 'Tyrrhenus and Lydus, sons of King Atys, had divided the nation. Lydus had remained in the territory of his fathers, Tyrrhenus had been allotted the task of creating a new settlement; and the Asiatic and Italian branches of the people had received distinctive titles from the names of the two leaders; while a further advance in the Lydian power had come with the despatch of colonists to the peninsula which afterwards took its name from Pelops.' At the same time, they recalled the letters from Roman commanders, the treaties concluded with us in the Macedonian war, their ample rivers, tempered climate, and the richness of the surrounding country.[32]

After Pergamon was bestowed this honour under Augustus, Smyrna in Ionia was next to receive it under Tiberius, then Miletos in Ionia under Gaius, and then finally to Ephesus in Ionia under Nero.[33] Pergamon also had the prestigious honour of being the first city to become twice neokoros (under Trajan). In sum, 'thirty-seven cities in fifteen koina called themselves neokoroi on inscriptions and coins up to the Christianization

---

[32] Text and translation from John Jackson, trans. *Tacitus, Annals: Books 4–6, 11–12* (LCL 312; Cambridge, MA: Harvard University Press, 1937), 96–101.

[33] Moving forward chronologically in the koinon of Asia: Kyzikos in Mysia under Hadrian; Sardis in Lydia under Antoninus Pius; Aizanoi and Laodikeia in Phrygia under Commodus; Philadelphia and Tralles in Lydia, and Antandros in the Troad under Caracalla; Hierapolis in Phrygia under Elagabalus; Magnesia in Ionia under Severus Alexander; Synnada in Phrygia under the Tetrarchy.

ΝΕΩΚΟΡΟΣ 133

of the empire'.[34] Of significance for our own discussion is that Ephesus was only one of three cities (together with Aizanoi and Magnesia) who was permitted to extend the title to their patron god's temple,[35] a subject to which we will return below.[36]

Numismatic evidence

The earliest scholarly attempt to explore the manner in which the term 'νεωκόρος' was adopted as a title for cities, was that of Wilhelm Buechner in 1888.[37] Other monographs and technical studies since, have significantly supplemented this earlier work with more recent literary, numismatic, epigraphic and archaeological evidence.[38] The present study will focus on the contribution of numismatic material, in so far as it might elucidate the term's usage in reference to Ephesus and Acts 19:35.

Our introductory comments have already noted the paucity of attention generally afforded to numismatic material. We will here attempt to present an exhaustive account of the relevant numismatic material, noting not merely the economic function of the coinage, but also its political and symbolic value. Appropriate caution must be employed when interpreting depictions of temples and their associated symbols, so that one does not fail to distinguish between ancient reality and the medium of the symbolic representation.[39] Our analysis in the present chapter will focus solely on

[34] Burrell, 'Neokoros', 4743.

[35] Burrell, 'Neokoros', 4743.

[36] It is worth noting that the apparent decline of the Artemis cult in Ephesus based on E. L. Hicks reconstruction of inscription 482.B.l9 in *The Collection of Ancient Greek Inscriptions in the British Museum: Ephesos* (Oxford: Clarendon, 1890), 142–145, '[Ἐπειδὴ ἡ π]ροεστῶσα τῆς πόλεως ἡμων θεὸς Ἄρτε[μις οὐ μόνον] ἐν τῇ ἑαυτῆς πατρίδι ἀτιμᾶται' (trans. '[Since the] guardian of our city, the goddess Artemis, is dishonored [not only] in her own native city...') is a misreading which has produced erroneous conclusions. For example, F. J. Foakes-Jackson and Kirsopp Lake, eds., *The Beginnings o' Christianity: The Acts of the Apostles*, 5 vols. (London: Macmillan, 1933), 5.255, state 'About a century later [mid. 2nd C.E.] the cult of the goddess was again on the wane, and we find the Ephesian senate taking active measures to restore the goddess to her former prominence. Again, it was probably the growing power of Christianity which caused the decline of Ephesian Artemis.' R. Oster restores the corrected reading as '[Ἐπειδὴ ἡ π]ροεστῶσα τῆς πόλεως ἡμων θεὸς Ἄρτε[μις οὐ μόνον] ἐν τῇ ἑαυτῆς πατρίδι τειμᾶται' (trans. '[Since the] guardian of our city, the goddess Artemis, is honored [not only] in her own native city...'). See further R. Oster, 'Acts 19: 23-41and an Ephesian Inscription', *HTR* 77, no. 2 (1984): 233–237. This reconstruction is in accordance with Pausanius writing in the late second century CE, 'But all cities worship Artemis of Ephesus and individuals hold her in honour above the gods... three other points have contributed to her renown, the size of the temple, surpassing all buildings among men, the eminence of the city of the Ephesians, and the renown of the goddess who dwells there' (4.31.8).

[37] Buechner, *De Neocoria*, 2–21.

[38] S. R. F. Price, *Rituals and Power: The Roman Imperial Cult in Asia Minor* (Cambridge: Cambridge University Press, 1984), 64–65; S. J. Friesen, *Twice Neokoros: Ephesus, Asia, and the Cult of the Falvian Imperial Family* (Leiden: Brill, 1993); Burrell, *Neokoroi*.

[39] The spectrum is, as expected, broad ranging. On the points of connection with history M. Price, B. Trell and C. Vermeule are optimistic (M. Price and B. Trell, *Coins and Their Cities* [London: Vecchi, 1977]; C. Vermeule, *The Cult Images of Imperial Rome* [Rome: Bretschneider, 1987]). T. Drew-Bear and J. Nollé are highly sceptical (T. Drew-Bear, 'Representations of Temples on the Greek Imperial Coinage', *American Numismatic Society Museum Notes* 19 [1974]: 27–63; J. Nollé, 'Zur neueren Forschungsgeschichte der kaiser- zeitliche Stadtprägungen Kleinasiens', in

134   *Numismatics and Greek Lexicography*

those coins with a clear and unambiguous unobscured legend, 'νεωκόρος' and/or its abbreviations and derivatives. The first step of our analysis is to list out in tabular form the relevant numismatic evidence for discussion. Table 17 draws on the work of B. Burrell,[40] the inventory of W. Leschhorn,[41] and the location list catalogue of the Heberden Coin Room, Ashmolean Museum, Oxford.

Table 17 Numismatic evidence for ΝΕΩΚΟΡΟΣ

Entry	Ruler	Legend/title	Publication[42]	Collection(s)[43]
1	Nero	Neokoros	*SNGvA* 7863	Berlin (3 exx.), London (2 exx.), Oxford, Paris, Vienna.
2	Trajan	Neokoros	*BMC* 223; *SNGvA* 1884	Berlin (2 exx.), New York, Oxford.
3	Hadrian	Twice Neokoros	*BMC* 227, 228; *SNGMün* 127	Berlin, New York, Paris (3 exx.), Vienna (2 exx.).
4	Hadrian and Aelius Verus	Twice Neokoros		Paris.
5	Antoninus Pius	Twice Neokoros	*BMC* 233–236; *SNGCop* 397; *SNGvA* 1888; *SNGMün* 132, 133	Berlin (7 exx.), London (2 exx.), New York (2 exx.), Oxford (5 exx.), Paris (7 exx.), Vienna (5 exx.), Warsaw.

(Continued)

Internationales Kolloquium zur kaiserzeitlichen Münzprägung Kleinasiens, ed. J. Nollé, B. Overbeck, and P. Weiss [Milan: Ennerre, 1997], 11–26). For a nuanced discussion, see A. Burnett, 'Buildings and Monuments on Roman Coins', in *Roman Coins and Public Life under the Empire*, ed. G. Paul (Ann Arbor: University of Michigan Press, 1999), 137–164.

[40] Burrell, *Neokoroi*, 59–85. Burrell lists a number of coins which are in collections but not yet published in corpora which are taken up and adapted for our listing here. See below for relevant abbreviations.

[41] W. Leschhorn, *Lexikon der Aufschriften auf griechischen Münzen* (Wien: Verlag der Österreichischen Akademie der Wissenschaften, 2002), 210–214.

[42] Abbreviations are as follows: SNGvA (Hans von Aulock and Gerhard Kleiner, *Sylloge nummorum Graecorum Deutschland. Sammlung von Aulock* [Berlin: Mann, 1957–1968]); *BMC* (British Museum, Department of Coins and Medals. *Catalogue of Greek Coins*); *SNGMün* (D. Klose, ed. *Sylloge nummorum Graecorum, 20.1. Ionia* [Deutschland: Staatliche Munzsammlung München, 1995]); *SNGCop* (*Sylloge nummorum Graecorum. The Royal Collection of Coins and Medals. Danish National Museum* [Copenhagen: E. Munksgaard, 1942–]); *SNGLewis* (*Sylloge nummorum Graecorum 6. Lewis Collection in Corpus Christi College. Cambridge 2. Greek Imperial Coins* (London: Oxford University Press, 1972–)); *SNGRighetti* (*Sylloge nummorum Graecorum Schweiz 2. Katalog der Sammlung Jean-Pierre Righetti im Bernischen Historischen Museum* (Bern: P. Haupt, 1993)); *SNGParis* (*Sylloge nummorum Graecorum France. Bibliothèque nationale. Cabinet des médailles 2: Cilicie. 3: Pamphylie, Pisidie Lycaonie, Galatie. 5: Mysie* (Paris: La Bibliothèque, 1983–)).

[43] Adapted from Burrell, Neokoroi, 84–85; Abbreviations for locations of extant examples are as follows: Berlin (Münzkabinett, Staatliche Museen), Boston (Classical Department, Museum of Fine Arts), London (British Museum, Department of Coins and Medals), New York (American Numismatic Society), Oxford (Heberden Coin Room, Ashmolean Museum), Paris (Cabinet des Médailles, Bibliothèque Nationale), Vienna (Münzkabinett, Kunsthistorisches Museum) and Warsaw (Narodowe Museum).

ΝΕΩΚΟΡΟΣ

Entry	Ruler	Legend/title	Publication	Collection(s)
6	Marcus Aurelius Caesar	Twice Neokoros	*BMC* 242	Berlin (2 exx.), Oxford, Paris (2 exx.).
7	Marcus Aurelius Augustus	Twice Neokoros	*BMC* 243; *SNGCop* 400; *SNGvA* 1890, 1891; *SNGMün* 141–145; *SNGLewis* 1448	Berlin (10 exx.), London, New York (2 exx.), Oxford (4 exx.), Paris (4 exx.), Vienna (9 exx.), Warsaw.
8	Faustina the Younger	Twice Neokoros	*BMC* 235; *SNGCop* 402	Berlin (4 exx.), Oxford, Paris, Vienna (2 exx.).
9	Lucius Verus	Twice Neokoros	*BMC* 247	Berlin (3 exx.), Oxford, Paris.
10	Commodus Caesar	Twice Neokoros	*BMC* 254	Berlin, Boston, New York, Paris.
11	Commodus Augustus	Twice Neokoros	*BMC* 255; *SNGCop* 409	Berlin (2 exx.), London, New York, Paris (5 exx.), Vienna (2 exx.).
12	Septimius Severus	Twice Neokoros	*BMC* 259, 260; *SNGCop* 411; *SNGvA* 1893, 7869; *SNGMün* 152–155; *SNGRighetti* 853	Berlin (7 exx.), London (3 exx.), New York (3 exx.), Oxford (10 exx.), Paris (12 exx.), Vienna (7 exx.).
13	Julia Domna	Twice Neokoros	*BMC* 263, 265; *SNGCop* 415, 416; *SNGvA* 1895; *SNGMün* 158; *SNGLewis* 1449	Berlin (2 exx.), Oxford (2 exx.), Paris (3 exx.), Vienna (4 exx.).
14	Caracalla	Twice Neokoros	*BMC* 271–275; *SNGCop* 419–423; *SNGvA* 1896–1898; *SNGMün* 160, 161, 163, 164	Berlin (9 exx.), London, New York (2 exx.), Oxford (7 exx.), Paris (6 exx.), Vienna (10 exx.).
15	Geta Caesar	Twice Neokoros	*SNGCop* 425; *SNGvA* 7874; *SNGMün* 168	Oxford, Paris (2 exx.), Vienna (2 exx.).
16	Geta Augustus	Twice Neokoros	*BMC* 281, 282; *SNGCop* 431; *SNGvA* 1902, 1903, 7877; *SNGMün* 173	Berlin (4 exx.), Boston, London, New York, Oxford (3 exx.), Paris (5 exx.), Vienna (4 exx.).
17	Geta Augustus	Three times Neokoros		Gotha (genuine?)
18	Julia Domna	Three times Neokoros and of Artemis		Berlin, London, Paris.
19	Caracalla	Three times Neokoros and of Artemis	*SNGvA* 7871	Berlin.
20	Caracalla and Geta	Three times Neokoros and of Artemis	*BMC* 292; *SNGCop* 436;	Berlin (2 exx.), Paris.

(Continued)

Numismatics and Greek Lexicography

Entry	Ruler	Legend/title	Publication	Collection(s)
21	Geta Augustus	Three times Neokoros and of Artemis	*SNGvA* 1904	Berlin, London.
22	Caracalla	Twice Neokoros and of Artemis	*BMC* 269	
23	Julia Domna	Three times Neokoros	*BMC* 266, 267; *SNGCop* 417	Berlin (4 exx.), New York, Oxford (2 exx.), Paris (3 exx.), Vienna (5 exx.).
24	Caracalla	Three times Neokoros	*BMC* 276–279, Adramyttium 24, 25; *SNGvA* 1899, 1900, 7872, 7873; *SNGMün* 162, 165, 166; *SNGLewis* 1450; *SNGParis* Adramyttium 59	Berlin (17 exx.), London (2 exx.), New York (6 exx.), Oxford (6 exx.), Paris (11 exx.), Vienna (13 exx.), Warsaw.
25	Elagabalus	Four times Neokoros	*BMC* 300, 302–305, 307; *SNGCop* 442–448; *SNGvA* 1905, 1906; *SNGMün* 184; *SNGRighetti* 854	Berlin (21 exx.), London (7 exx.), New York (4 exx.), Oxford (8 exx.), Paris (19 exx.), Vienna (13 exx.).[44]
26	Julia Paula	Four times Neokoros	*BMC* 308; *SNGCop* 453, 454; *SNGvA* 1907; *SNGRighetti* 856	Berlin (4 exx.), London, Oxford (2 exx.), Paris (3 exx.), Vienna (2 exx.).
27	Annia Faustina	Four times Neokoros	*BMC* 309; *SNGvA* 1908; *SNGMün* 187[45]	Berlin (2 exx.), London, Paris (4 exx.), Vienna.
28	Julia Soaemias	Four times Neokoros		New York, Paris (2 exx.).
29	Julia Maesa	Four times Neokoros	*BMC* 310	Paris (3 exx.)
30	Severus Alexander Caesar	Four times Neokoros	*BMC* 312; *SNGMün* 189	Berlin (2 exx.), Oxford, Paris (4 exx.), Vienna.
31	Severus Alexander Augustus	Four times Neokoros	*BMC* 311, 314, 318; *SNGCop* 460–462; *SNGvA* 7880; *SNGMün* 190, 193, 196; *SNGLewis* 1453; *SNGRighetti* 857	Berlin (4 exx.), London, New York, Oxford (3 exx.), Paris (8 exx.), Vienna (5 exx.).
32	Julia Mamaea	Four times Neokoros	*BMC* 328	Berlin.

---

[44] H.-D. Schultz, 'Falschungen ephesischer Münzen', *Mitteilungen der Österreichischen Numismatischen Gesellschaft* 35, no. 1 (1995): 7–14, notes that *SNGCop* 444 and several of the Berlin examples appear to be cast copies. Cited in Burrell, *Neokoroi*, 84.

[45] D. Klose, 'Münz – oder Gruselkabinett?' in *Internationales Kolloquium zur kaiserzeitlichen Münzprägung Kleinasiens*, ed. J. Nollé, B. Overbeck, and P. Weiss (Milan: Ennerre, 1997), 253–264, argues that this coin is inauthentic.

ΝΕΩΚΟΡΟΣ

Entry	Ruler	Legend/title	Publication	Collection(s)
33	Maximinus	Three times Neokoros	*BMC* 329, 330; *SNGCop* 472, 473; *SNGvA* 1912; *SNGMün* 208, 209	Berlin (5 exx.), Boston, London (3 exx.), New York, Oxford (4 exx.), Paris (8 exx.), Vienna (6 exx.).
34	Maximus Caesar	Three times Neokoros	*SNGMün* 212	London, Paris.
35	Gordian III	Three times Neokoros	*BMC* 331; *SNGvA* 1913; *SNGMün* 213–215; *SNGLewis* 1454; *SNGRighetti* 860	Berlin (2 exx.), New York, Oxford (2 exx.), Paris (5 exx.), Vienna (4 exx.).
36	Otacilia	Three times Neokoros	*BMC* 342, 343; *SNGCop* 486	Berlin, New York (2 exx.), Oxford, Paris, Vienna.
37	Philip Caesar	Three times Neokoros	*SNGCop* 488, 489; *SNGvA* 1914; *SNGMün* 224	New York, Oxford, Paris, Vienna (2 exx.).
38	Trajan Decius	Three times Neokoros	*SNGvA* 1916	Berlin, London, Oxford, Paris (2 exx.), Vienna.
39	Valerian	Three times Neokoros	*BMC* 350–358; *SNGCop* 496–500; *SNGvA* 1921–1923; *SNGMün* 234–238, 240, 241, 243; *SNGLewis* 1457; *SNGRighetti* 861–863	Berlin (23 exx.), Boston (2 exx.), London (8 exx.), New York (12 exx.), Oxford (12 exx.), Paris (19 exx.), Vienna (12 exx.), Warsaw.
40	Gallienus	Three times Neokoros	*BMC* 370–376; *SNGCop* 510–512; *SNGvA* 1928–1930, 7887; *SNGMün* 249–254, 263; *SNGLewis* 1459	Berlin (20 exx.), Boston, London (5 exx.), New York (3 exx.), Oxford (10 exx.), Paris (12 exx.), Vienna (7 exx.).
41	Salonina	Three times Neokoros	*BMC* 390–391, 393–394; *SNGCop* 532–534; *SNGvA* 1933, 1934; *SNGMün* 266–268, 270; *SNGLewis* 1461	Berlin (6 exx.), London (3 exx.), New York (4 exx.), Oxford (7 exx.), Paris (8 exx.), Vienna (6 exx.), Warsaw (2 exx.).
42	Valerianus	Three times Neokoros	*SNGMün* 276; *SNGLewis* 1463	Berlin, New York, Oxford, Paris (2 exx.).
43	Saloninus	Three times Neokoros	*SNGCop* 541	Berlin, London, Paris.
44	Valerian	Four times Neokoros	*BMC* 359–363; *SNGCop* 501–503; *SNGvA* 1924, 1925;	Berlin (4 exx.), London, New York (2 exx.), Oxford (5 exx.), Paris (3 exx.), Vienna (3 exx.).
45	Gallienus	Four times Neokoros	*BMC* 377–379, 381–384; *SNGCop* 513–520; *SNGvA* 1931, 7888, 7889; *SNGMün* 257–260; *SNGRighetti* 864, 868	Berlin (12 exx.), London (6 exx.), New York (6 exx.), Oxford (9 exx.), Paris (13 exx.), Vienna (10 exx.).

(Continued)

Entry	Ruler	Legend/title	Publication	Collection(s)
46	Salonina	Four times Neokoros	*BMC* 395; *SNGCop* 535, 536; *SNGMün* 275; *SNGRighetti* 869	Berlin (4 exx.), New York (3 exx.), Oxford (2 exx.), Paris (4 exx.), Vienna (2 exx.).
47	Valerianus	Four times Neokoros	*SNGCop* 538	Berlin, Vienna. Saloninus: Paris.

Modern scholarship on the coinage of Ephesus has suffered considerably from issues related to the (in)authenticity of some material. Typically, problems range from naive misattribution, such as the Ephesian coin in the Saarbrucken Archiv attributed to Julia and Agrippa,[46] to the complete fabrication or tooling of inscriptions, such as the more than a dozen examples cited by Burnett and colleagues in *Roman Provincial Coinage 1*.[47] Misattribution and forgery are not, of course, unique problems to the numismatic material of Ephesus,[48] yet the problem is felt in a unique manner when considering the history and function of the 'νεωκόρος'.

The identification of coins as modern forgeries involves a range of observational and analytic approaches, including comparison of coin die typology, observation of the characteristics of the metal and the coin surface, diagnosing additional coercions and identifying artificial patination. There are multiple cases where the 'νεωκόρος' coins are demonstrably Renaissance casts of genuine ancient coins. Particularly notable examples are *BMC* 380, 384, 392; *SNGCop* 444, 521; *SNGRighetti* 867.[49] As M. Crawford notes, however, these cast copies of genuine ancient coins 'do not ... falsify the picture totally, [but] they can ... give a wrong impression of how common a particular coin is'.[50] More problematic, of course, are those coins which are complete fabrications or that have been recut or tooled to alter the inscription or iconography. Such is the case with two important coins listed in RPC 2 which 'seem to attest to a second neocorate temple for Domitian at Ephesus'.[51] RPC 2.F1064 is a bronze coin (30 mm, 19.83 g),

---

[46] Zeno catalogue III (1957), no. 3969 (M S6.126.322 Sestini), a specimen that Burnett and colleagues attribute to a worn example of RPC 1.2620 (Burnett, Amandry, and Carradice, *Roman Provincial Coinage 1*, 424).

[47] Burnett, Amandry and Carradice, *Roman Provincial Coinage 1*, 433–434.

[48] D. Dimitrov, I. Prokopov and B. Kolev, *Modern Forgeries of Greek and Roman Coins* (Sofia: K&K Publishers, 1997); D. Hendin, *Not Kosher: Forgeries of Ancient Jewish and Biblical Coins* (New York: Amphora, 2005); S. Hurter, 'The Black Sea Hoard: The Cache of an Ancient Counterfeit Mint', *Bulletin on Counterfeits* 15, no. 1 (1990): 2–4; C. A. Marinescu, 'Modem Imitations of Ancient Coins from Bulgaria', *Minerva* 9, no. 5 (1998): 46–48; W. G. Sayles, *Classical Deception. Counterfeits, Forgeries and Reproductions of Ancient Coins* (Iola: Krause Publications, 2001), 61–65, 87–89; I. Prokopov, K. Kissyov, and E. Paunov, *Modem Counterfeits of Ancient Greek and Roman Coins from Bulgaria* (Sofia: K&K Publishers, 2003); I. Prokopov, *Contemporary Coin Engravers and Coin Masters from Bulgaria* (Sofia: K&K Publishers, 2004); I. Prokopov and E. Paunov, *Cast Forgeries of Classical Coins from Bulgaria* (Sofia: K&K Publishers, 2004).

[49] See further Schultz, 'Falschungen ephesischer Münzen', 7–14.

[50] Michael H. Crawford, 'Numismatics', in *Sources for Ancient History*, ed. M. Crawford (Cambridge: Cambridge University Press, 1983), 188.

[51] Burnett, Amandry and Carradice, *Roman Provincial Coinage 2*, 165.

which on the obverse depicts the laureate head of Domitian, facing to the right, with aegis. The inscription reads, 'ΔΟΜΙΤΙΑΝΟΣ ΚΑΙΣΑΡ ΣΕΒΑΣ-ΓΕΡΜ ΑΥΤΟΚΡΑΤ' (trans. 'Domitian Caesar Augustus Germanicus Emperor'). The reverse has a temple with four columns enclosing a cult statue of Artemis with the inscription, 'ΕΦΕΣΙΟ-Ν Β ΝΕΟΚΟΡΩΝ' (trans. 'Ephesus twice neokoros'). RPC 2.F1065 is a bronze coin (30 mm, 22.10 g) which on the obverse portrays the draped bust of Domitia, facing right, with the inscription 'ΔΟΜΙΤΙΑ ΣΕΒΑΣΤΗ' (trans. 'Domitia Augusta'). The reverse has a temple with eight columns enclosing a statue of Artemis, with the inscription '[ΝΕΩ] ΚΟΡΟΝ ΕΦΕΣΙΟΩΝ' (trans. 'Ephesus Neocorate').[52] Both RPC 2.F1064 and 2.F1065 were accepted as genuine by S. Friesen and utilized to reconstruct the developments in cultic traditions within the city.[53] Friesen states that on the basis of 'at least two coins of the Domitianic period [2.F1064; 2.F1065], the Ephesians called themselves "twice neokoros," i.e., of Artemis and of the Sebastoi'[54] and that 'these two coins present a vivid visual image of the city's new religious situation'.[55] Friesen concludes that the city thus had 'two dominant cults of equivalent significance: that of Ephesian Artemis, and that of the Emperors'.[56] M. Dräger similarly accepts these coins as genuine and comes to comparable conclusions.[57]

Unfortunately, however, both Friesen and Dräger have uncritically followed the error of J. Keil in accepting the coins as genuine.[58] As Burnett notes, both coins display obvious signs of having been altered (RPC 2.F1064), or completely reworked by tooling (RPC 2.F1065). That the coins were re-cut or altered from existing types, for example RPC 2.F1064 from RPC 2.1070, has been subsequently confirmed in more recent analysis.[59] Burnett's conclusion, that the possibility of a second neocorate at Ephesus under Domitian, or for that matter a temple of Domitian, 'seems extremely doubtful',[60] is entirely justifiable.

The earliest attestation of the titular 'νεωκόρος' occurs on an Ephesian coin under Nero. SNGvA 7863 (cf. RPC 2.2626) is a bronze issue (26 mm, 11.72 g), which on the obverse has the laureate head of Nero facing right with the accompanying inscription, 'ΝΕΡΩΝ ΚΑΙΣΑΡ' (trans. 'Nero Caesar'). The reverse has a three-quarter view of a temple on a three-step podium and an inscription reading, 'ΑΟΥΙΟΛΑ ΑΝΘΥΠΑΤΩ ΑΙΧΜΟΚΛΗΣ, ΝΕΟΚΟΡΩΝ, ΕΦΕ' (trans. 'Aviola Aichmokles proconsul, neokoros Ephesus').[61] By virtue of the preservation of the name of the proconsul, M. Acilius

---

[52]   See B. Pick, 'Die Neokorien von Ephesos', in *Corolla Numismatica: Numismatic Essays in Honour of Barclay V. Head*, ed. G. F. Hill (Oxford: Oxford University Press, 1906), 234–244.

[53]   Friesen, *Twice Neokoros*.

[54]   Friesen, *Twice Neokoros*, 56.

[55]   Friesen, *Twice Neokoros*, 56–57.

[56]   Friesen, *Twice Neokoros*, 57.

[57]   M. Dräger, *Die Stiidte der Provinz Asia in der Flavierzeit. Studien zur kleinasiatischen Stadt- und Regionalgeschichte* (Frankfurt: Peter Lang, 1993), 118, 123 n.2, 292–93.

[58]   Josef Keil, 'Die erste Kaiserneokorie von Ephesos', *Numismatische Zeitschrift N.F.* 12 (1919): 118–120; Trebilco, 'Asia', 329–330 also accepts uncritically the assumptions of the Friesen and colleagues which are adopted without further consideration.

[59]   Klose, 'Münz', 253–264; Burrell, *Neokoroi*, 65.

[60]   Burnett, Amandry, and Carradice, *Roman Provincial Coinage 2*, 165.

[61]   RPC 2.2627 is of the same type but with laureate head facing left on the obverse.

Aviola, the coin can be dated to 65/66 CE.[62] A second type during the same period, RPC 2.2626, has the head of Nero facing right on the obverse, with the inscription 'ΝΕΡΩΝ ΚΑΙΣΑΡ' (trans. 'Nero Caesar'). The reverse depicts a six-column temple on a three-step podium, disc in pediment and a bee on either side with the accompanying inscription, 'ΕΦΕΣΙΟΝ ΝΕΟΚΟΡΟΝ' (trans. 'Ephesus Neokoros').

Implications for the 'νεωκόρος' of Acts 19:35

We now turn to the question of how our discussion above might illuminate a reading of Acts 19:35. Within the speech of the town clerk (γραμματεύς) in Acts 19:35–40, Ephesus is directly identified as the 'νεωκόρον οὖσαν τῆς μεγάλης Ἀρτέμιδος' (trans. 'guardian of the temple of the great Artemis' [v.35]). Critically weighing evidence from the Pauline letters, and Acts of the Apostles (particularly with reference to the Edict of Claudius, the Delphi inscription and the Proconsulship of Gallio) scholars typically are inclined to date Paul's reported stay in Ephesus to August 52 CE–October 54 CE.[63] If this is so, then an acute historical problem arises for the text of Acts, for the term 'νεωκόρος' is applied to Ephesus under Claudius (nephew of Tiberius), rather than a decade later under Nero (great-great-nephew of Tiberius). As per numismatic evidence surveyed above, Ephesus seems to be claiming the title, according to the book of Acts, before our earliest evidence for the use of the term in a titular sense.

In light of this apparent tension Stephan Witetschek asks, 'Does the narrative of Acts 19 report what really happened in the mid-50s of the 1st C.E., when Paul was in Ephesos?'[64] He concludes in the negative stating that the passage 'addresses the concerns of Luke's readers in the late 1st century, when Christianity in Asia Minor would already have become a factor that made some impact on the economy',[65] and that 'Acts is a source not so much for the narrated time of Paul, but rather for Luke's own time, and as such of interest for both exegetes and historians'.[66] Michael L. White similarly concludes that 'at best it [i.e. νεωκόρος] would seem to have been a new accolade for the city in Paul's day; at worst, if one posits a date later in Nero's reign, the phrase would not yet have been operative'[67] and that 'the setting in Acts seems anachronistic, even if it does suggest direct knowledge of Ephesos at a later date'.[68]

---

[62] *Prosopographia Imperii Romani Saeculorum*[2] A.49; Crook, *Consilium Principis*, 148; G. W. Houston, 'Roman Imperial Administrative Personnel during the Principates of Vespasian and Titus' (Ph.D. diss., University of North Carolina, Chapel Hill, 1971).

[63] J. Murphy-O'Connor, *Paul: A Critical Life* (Oxford: Oxford University Press, 1996), 1–31.

[64] Stephan Witetschek, 'Artemis and Asiarchs: Some Remarks on Ephesian Local Colour in Acts 19', *Biblica* 90, no. 3 (2009): 334.

[65] Witetschek, 'Artemis', 352.

[66] Witetschek, 'Artemis', 355.

[67] Michael L. White, 'Urban Development and Social Change', in *Ephesos, Metropolis of Asia: An Interdisciplinary Approach to Its Archaeology, Religion, and Culture*, ed. Helmut Koester (Valley Forge, PA: Trinity Press International, 1995), 37.

[68] White, 'Development', 37. Similarly, Richard I. Pervo states that '[νεωκόρος] may be a bit of an anachronism here', see Richard I. Pervo, *Acts: A Commentary* (Minneapolis, MN: Fortress, 2009), 498 n.117.

ΝΕΩΚΟΡΟΣ

There is, however, an alternative, more nuanced historical approach that seems to account for the reference in Acts, the numismatic evidence, as well as the inscriptional data. First, it is important to note that Acts 19 does not explicitly use the title with reference to the imperial cult, but rather applies the title to the Ἐφεσίων πόλιν' (v. 35). The references surveyed above from Josephus and Philo indicate that the term 'νεωκόρος' underwent a significant shift in the first century CE, the end point of which was commonly used with reference to a representative people or city rather than a particular individual(s) necessarily.[69] Second, of interest is *I. Eph.* III647 which consists of a statue base of white marble with an inscription which documents that by 211–212 CE Ephesus was 'μητροπόλεως τῆς Ἀσίας καὶ νεωκόρου τῆς Ἀρτέμιδος καὶ τρὶς νεωκόρου τῶν Σεβαστῶν' (trans. 'metropolis of Asia and temple-warden of Artemis and three times temple-warden of the emperors'). In R. A. Kearsley's discussion of this inscription she notes the manner in which the inscription sheds further light on the 'importance of Artemis to Ephesus and therefore also assists understanding of the incident in Acts 19'.[70] It is noteworthy that the titulature is used in later inscriptions with reference to both the name of the city (*I. Eph.* VII3005) as well as the citizens themselves (*I. Eph.* III857). A. N. Sherwin-White cautions, however, that 'the late inscriptions do not illustrate the usage in Acts'.[71] Although this may be technically accurate, both the inscriptional and numismatic evidence demonstrate a trajectory which is consistent with the later material. Sherwin-White does, however, note an honorary base inscription from Priene (*I.Priene* 231) dated to 333 BCE which records the following, 'Μεγάβυζος Μεγαβύζου νεωκόρος τῆς Ἀρτέμιδος τῆς ἐν Ἐφέσωι' (trans. 'Megabyzos, son of Megabyzos, temple-warden in Ephesus').[72] As such Luke could hardly be charged with anachronism if he was using the term metaphorically, contra Witetschek, White and Pervo.[73] When the term 'νεωκόρος' was uttered by the town clerk in Acts 19:35 (52–54 CE) it was presumably a metaphor drawing on the long and illustrious association of Artemis with Ephesus, and indicative of the city's civic pride. It was thus no coincidence that approximately a decade later, the word would appear so prominently on the coinage of the city under Nero. Burrell notes that 'it is possible that at this point it meant what it came to mean later, that Ephesos possessed a koinon temple for the cult of the Emperor, in this case for Nero'.[74]

---

[69] I. H. Marshall notes simply that 'when applied to Ephesus as temple keeper of Artemis in the third century, the usage is an extension of the imperial use', Marshall, I. H. *Acts*, 360.

[70] R. A. Kearsley, 'Ephesus: Neokoros of Artemis', in *New Documents Illustrating Early Christianity: A Review of the Greek Inscriptions and Papyri Published in 1980–1981*, vol. 6, ed. S. R. Llewelyn (Sydney: Macquarie University, 1992), 203.

[71] Sherwin-White, *Roman Society*, 89.

[72] Sherwin-White, *Roman Society*, 89. Further to this, Craig S. Keener comment is intuitively satisfying, '[a] term's first appearance in our surviving, fragmentary sources is rarely its first actual occurrence', Craig S. Keener, *Acts. Volume 3, 15: 1–23:35:An Exegetical Commentary* (Grand Rapids, MI: Baker Academic, 2013), 2930.

[73] Witetschek, 'Artemis', 355; White, 'Development', 37; Pervo, *Acts*, 498 n.117.

[74] Burrell, *Neokoroi*, 4. Strangely however, no mention of this historical conundrum is made in the otherwise excellent treatment of the historical issues in the passage in Paul R. Trebilco, *The Early Christians in Ephesus from Paul to Ignatius* (Tübingen: Mohr Siebeck, 2004), 155–196.

142   *Numismatics and Greek Lexicography*

Several commentators have noted the religious, social and political knowledge displayed in Acts 19:21–40. So much so that Helmut Koester has suggested that the entire volume was, in fact, composed in Ephesus.[75] One need not, however, accept Koester's conclusions regarding the provenance of Acts to validly identify the obvious local features, such as the reference to 'νεωκόρος', the sale of silver shrines, Asiarchs as political figures and the mention of 'the scribe of the Demos'.[76]

Conclusion

Throughout this study we have sought to identify a distinctive contribution of the numismatic material for our understanding of the history of Ephesus, particularly as it pertains to Acts 19:35 and the use of the term 'νεωκόρος'. The arguments put forward in our discussion allowed a fruitful comparison of both the continuity and discontinuity of motifs across several historical periods. There are principally five outcomes of our investigation. First, scholarly endeavours to incorporate numismatic material into NT studies generally, and Greek lexicography in particular, are in their infancy. Much work remains to be developed in this area, in regard to methodology as well as disseminating numismatic collections in published, well-illustrated, catalogues. Second, there continues to be a lack of discernment of relevant authentic numismatic material. In the present study, this expresses itself as (a) the uncritical acceptance of the inauthentic 'νεωκόρος' coinage, and (b) attempting to apply the numismatic material too generally which necessarily leads to inaccuracies. Both these issues persist in the literature, but are especially pronounced in NT commentaries.[77] Third, there is a clear diachronic development of 'νεωκόρος' from a reference to human individuals, to a term which officially designated a particular type of temple in service of the cult of the emperor. Fourth, the allegiance of the Ephesians to Artemis is readily appreciated through the extended quotation and discussion of Tacitus's account of inter-city rivalry and Ephesus's apparent complete devotion to Artemis (*Annals* 4.55). Finally, rather than posing a genuine historical conundrum, the reference to the 'νεωκόρος' in Acts 19:35 should be situated within the larger trajectory of the city's devotion to Artemis.

---

[75] Helmut Koester, 'Ephesos in Early Christian Literature', in *Ephesos, Metropolis of Asia: An Interdisciplinary Approach to Its Archaeology, Religion, and Culture*, ed. Helmut Koester (Valley Forge, PA: Trinity Press International, 1995), 130–131.

[76] Koester, 'Ephesos', 130 n.42; Ben Witherington, *The Acts of the Apostles: A Socio-Rhetorical Commentary* (Grand Rapids, MI: Eerdmans, 1998), 585; Colin J. Hemer, *The Book of Acts in the Setting of Hellenistic History*, ed. Conrad H. Gempf (Tübingen: Mohr Siebeck, 1989), 121–122.

[77] For example, L. T. Johnson notes, 'for Ephesus, the title ["νεωκόρος"] appears on coins of the period', see L. T. Johnson, *The Acts of the Apostles* (Collegeville, PA: Liturgical Press, 1992), 350.

8

ΘΕΟΣ, ΕΛΕΥΘΕΡΙΑ, ΕΙΡΗΝΗ ΚΑΙ ΑΣΦΑΛΕΙΑ, ΚΑΒΕΙΡΟΣ

Introduction

It has long been noted that our Roman literary sources 'at their best ... are idiosyncratic, and at their worst ... consciously distort the deeds and intentions of individual emperors'.[1] Although literary sources may never reveal the historical intentions of the ruling elite, be they in Rome or in the provinces, coinage reveals, at a minimum, an objective perspective of how rulers wanted their subjects to perceive their political activity. This chapter seeks to demonstrate that Roman provincial coinage significantly aides in contextualizing Paul at Thessalonica within the matrix of the Roman political world. Issues to be addressed in this study include Thessalonica's (1) divine honours for Caesar and Octavian (including the language and iconography of crowning), (2) favoured political relationship with Rome and (3) religious identity shaped by the city's past.

Thessalonian coinage

The first autonomous coins to be struck at Thessalonica occurred approximately a decade after the defeat of Perseus at the battle of Pydna (168 BCE). Livy and other ancient authors inform us that Macedonia was divided into four administrative regions,[2] presumably to increase dependence on Rome, who prohibited trade between the regions and controlled the profitable mines and forests (cf. Livy). Thessalonica was capital of the second region. Almost all the coinage of this period is struck in the name of the first region. SNG Ashmolean 3300[3] (Figure 37) is a silver tetradrachm from the first region minted in Amphipolis during the period 167–149 BCE. The obverse

---

[1] J. Rufus Fears, 'The Cult of Virtues and Roman Imperial Ideology', *ANRW* 17, no. 2 (1981): 945.

[2] Livy 45.18.3–7, 29.5–11; Diod. 31.8.7–8; Strabo, *Geography* 7.47. The first was east of the Strymon with its capital at Amphipolis, the second was between the Strymon and Axios with its capital at Thessalonica, the third between the Axios and Peneos with its capital at Pella and the fourth included most of Upper Macedonia with its capital at Heraclea Lynci.

[3] C. E. King and C. M. Kraay, *Sylloge Nummorum Graecorum: Great Britain 5. Ashmolean Museum (Oxford): Pt. 4, Paeonia-Thessaly* (London: Oxford University Press, 1981).

Figure 37 SNG Ashmolean 3300 (used with permission).

depicts a diademed draped bust of Artemis facing right with a bow and quiver on her shoulder at the base of a Macedonian shield. The reverse depicts a club separating the inscription ΜΑΚΕΔΟΝΩΝ ΠΡΩΤΗΣ with monogram above and Ν below, all within an oak wreath. In the outer field is a thunderbolt. Only very limited numbers of tetradrachms are attested from the second region, and no known coinage during the period from the third and fourth regions. AMNG III/2, 41 (Figure 38) is a silver tetradrachm from the second region minted in Thessalonica during the period 167–149 BCE. The obverse and reverse is similar to that of the first region example previously stated, except that the inscription reads ΜΑΚΕΔΟΝΩΝ ΔΕΥΤΕΡΑΣ, has a different monogram and excludes the Ν mintmark below.

The region divisions were dissolved in 148 BCE when the territory became a Roman province. Although silver coinage was not minted for another half-century, governors issued a variety of bronze coinage. Silver coinage resumed again in 93 BCE, and the most widespread issue was by the quaestor Aesillas. SNG Ashmolean 3301 (Figure 39) is a silver tetradrachm of Aesillas Quaestor (c. 95–65 BCE) with, on the obverse, the diademed head of Alexander the Great facing right with the horn of Ammon, with inscription below ΜΑΚΕΔΟΝΩΝ below and Θ behind. The reverse inscribes AESILLAS Q in two lines above a money chest, club and chair; all within a wreath.

Recent studies of Thessalonian coinage have resolved several key problems associated with their interpretation, although some residual ambiguities still persist. The Roman coinage of Thessalonica can be divided into three broad periods: Republic, Triumviral and Imperial. The influence of Rome is clearly visible on the Republic coinage of Thessalonica. SNG Copenhagen 369 (Figure 40) is an assarius of Thessalonica from 187 to 168/7 BCE. On the obverse is depicted the laureate head of Janus, with a value mark of I above. The reverse has ΘΕΣΣΑΛΟΝΙΚΗΣ below the Dioscuri on

Figure 38 AMNG III/2, 41 (used with permission).

Figure 39 SNG Ashmolean 3301 (used with permission).

Figure 40 SNG Copenhagen 369 (used with permission).

horses rearing left and right with a grain ear in exergue.[4] In relation to the Triumviral period, M. Grant introduced a curious identification of the bronzes of Q HORTENSI PROCOS, PRAEF COLON DEDVC to Macedonia,[5] but later studies, including the monumental *Roman Provincial Coinage* project, confirm that this series was minted for Dium or Cassandrea.[6] Ioannis Touratsoglou[7] has produced an erudite and extensive catalogue and discussion of Macedonian coins in the Imperial period, and reattributes several coins which had previously been dated to an earlier period by Hugo Gaebler.[8] It is hoped that the current discussion will aid in nuancing the often uncritical use of numismatic evidence in relation to the Pauline circumstances at Thessalonica.

Case studies

Divine honours for Caesar

The accusation by the Thessalonian mob against Paul, Silas and their host Jason to the city's authorities in Acts 17:6 was that they were τὴν οἰκουμένην ἀναστατώσαντες (trans. 'turning the world upside down' [NRSV]), and had now come to Thessalonica to do the same. In particular they are accused of acting 'contrary to the δογμάτων Καίσαρος (decrees of Caesar), saying that there is another βασιλέα (king), Jesus' (Acts 17:7). Similar themes are found throughout the Thessalonian correspondence, in particular through the usage of key terminology such as παρουσία (1 Thess. 4:15), ἐπιφάνεια (2 Thess. 2:8), ἀπάντησις (1 Thess. 4:17), εἰρήνη καὶ ἀσφάλεια (1 Thess. 5:3), and ἐλπίδα σωτηρίας (1 Thess. 5:8). Jeffrey A. D. Weima highlights the significance of these matters for the Thessalonians by noting that the inhabitants would be especially concerned about these charges due to the 'memory still fresh in their mind of the loss of their senatorial status under Tiberius and its recovery just six years earlier under Claudius'.[9]

As has been explored by several commentators, the imperial cult at Thessalonica shaped the city.[10] One avenue to further explore this imperial emphasis is through the

---

[4] Cf. Semis of Thessalonica (half an as) which depict on the obverse the laureate head of Zeus right, and on the reverse have ΘΕΣΣΑΛΟΝΙΚΗΣ (top and bottom) with a bull charging right, with monograms, below (Moushmov 6594), H. Moushmov, *Ancient Coins of the Balkan Peninsula*, trans. Denista Genkova, Dave Surber, and Slavei Theodore Slaveev (Sofia: K&K Publishers, 1912).

[5] M. Grant, *From Imperium to Auctoritas* (Cambridge: Cambridge University Press, 1946), 33.

[6] Andrew Burnett, Michel Amandry, and Ian Carradice, *Roman Provincial Coinage: Volumes 1–2* (London: British Museum, 1992–1999), 297.

[7] Ioannis Touratsoglou, *Die Münzstätte von Thessaloniki in der römischen Kaiserzeit: 32/31 v. Chr. bis 268 n. Chr.* (Berlin: De Gruyter, 1988).

[8] H. Gaebler, *Die antiken Münzen von Makedonia und Paionia, Die antiken Münzen Nord-Griechenlands Vol. III* (Berlin: De Gruyter, 1935), 26.

[9] Jeffrey A. D. Weima, *1–2 Thessalonians* (Grand Rapids, MI: Baker Academic, 2014), 7.

[10] James R. Harrison, *Paul and the Imperial Authorities at Thessalonica and Rome: A Study in the Conflict of Ideology* (Tübingen: Mohr Siebeck, 2011), 55–56; James R. Harrison, 'Paul and the Imperial Gospel at Thessaloniki', *JSNT* 25.1 (2002): 71–96; James R. Harrison, '"The Fading Crown": Divine Honour and the Early Christians', *JTS* 54.2 (2003): 493–529; James R. Harrison, 'Paul and Empire II: Negotiating the Seduction of Imperial "Peace and Security" in Galatians, Thessalonians and Philippians', in *New Testament and Empire*, ed. A. Winn (Atlanta, GA: SBL Press, 2015), 165–184; Christoph Heilig, *Hidden Criticism?: The Methodology and Plausibility of the Search for a Counter-Imperial Subtext in Paul* (Tübingen: Mohr Siebeck, 2015), 91.

numismatic record. RPC 1.1554 (Figure 41) is a leaded bronze minted in Thessalonica and is often appealed to in regard to divine honours worn by deified Caesar. However, the provincial coinage of Augustus at Thessalonica poses a number of problems. RPC 1.1554 has the letter Δ under the head of Augustus, which Hugo Gaebler claims stands for the number 4 (asses).[11] The weakness of this proposal is that the E on the Triumvir coinage such as the leaded bronze RPC 1.1552 (Figure 42) refers to year 5 (which is

Figure 41 RPC 1.1554 (used with permission).

Figure 42 RPC 1.1552 (used with permission).

[11] Hugo Gaebler, *Die antiken Münzen Nord-Griechenlands*, vol. 3, part 2 (Berlin: G. Reimer, 1935), 125.

accepted by Gaebler). The obverse has ΑΓΩΝΟΘΕΣΙΑ with the personified head of Agonothesia facing right and the alphabetic numeral Ε referring to year 5 which corresponds to 37 BCE. The reverse has ΑΝΤ ΚΑΙ in a wreath. A strong case can then be made by analogy that the Δ on RPC 1.1554 should also refer to a date.[12]

RPC 1.1555 (Figure 43) omits several features including the date and wreath on Caesar's head on the obverse. On the reverse the inscription has the lunate sigma rather than the four-bar sigma (contra RPC 1554), and is 30 per cent lighter (7.33 g vs. 10.34 g). Touratsoglou argues on the basis of style, epigraphy and weight that RPC 1.1555 was issued during the reign of Domitian.[13] C. J. Howgego, however, notes that several of the countermarks on these coins 'are otherwise found on only Augustan coins of Amphipolis, and has questioned so late a date'.[14] Despite the fact that the lunate sigma is found on the coinage of Tiberius, a more telling critique against Touratsoglou's later date is that a portrait of Julius Caesar would be highly unusual on provincial coinage after the Julio-Claudian period.

RPC 1.5421 (Figure 44) is a 7.65 g bronze issue with the bare head of Caesar facing right on the obverse with ΘΕΟΣ in the left field. The reverse depicts the bare head of Augustus facing right with ΣΕΒΑΣΤΟΣ in right field and ΘΕ in left field. This was assigned to Thessalonica by B. V. Head in *BMC* 5.61,[15] presumably on the basis of the general similarity with RPC 1.1554 and RPC 1.1555. This was disputed

Figure 43 RPC 1.1555 (used with permission).

---

[12] Touratsoglou, *Thessaloniki*, 25.
[13] Touratsoglou, *Thessaloniki*, 42–43.
[14] C. J. Howgego, *Greek Imperial Countermarks: Studies in the Provincial Coinage of the Roman Empire* (London: Royal Numismatic Society, 1985), 702, 705.
[15] B. V. Head, *Catalogue of Greek Coins in the British Museum: Attica, Megaris, Aegina* (London: British Museum, 1888), xxii.

ΘΕΟΣ, ΕΛΕΥΘΕΡΙΑ, ΕΙΡΗΝΗ ΚΑΙ ΑΣΦΑΛΕΙΑ, ΚΑΒΕΙΡΟΣ 149

Figure 44 RPC 1.5421 (used with permission).

by Touratsoglou on the basis of style and axis orientation (6 o'clock).[16] The authors of RPC followed Touratsoglou, listing this type as 'Uncertain Mint'. However, the appearance CNG 75.2007.798[17] (Figure 45), which is die-linked to a coin bearing the ethnic of Thessalonica and minted by that city, thus establishes RPC 1.5421 as having been issued by that city, and contemporary with RPC 1.1555. The coinage of Thessalonica canonically includes the ethnic, and a closer examination of the coin suggests that the original ethnic may have been altered to accommodate the new legend. One possible explanation could be that the dies were reused shortly after the deification of Augustus in 14 CE, with the reverse ethnic removed and the new legend put in its place, with coins commemorating the new divus being struck. ΘΕ is an otherwise unknown abbreviation for ΘΕΟΥ, and an otherwise unnecessary one, given the plentiful amount of space on the die. It is possible, although not certain, that the dies were re-worked to accommodate the deification of Augustus, although questions still remain over the peculiar use of the abbreviation ΘΕ for ΘΕΟΥ.

RPC 1.1563 (Figure 46) is also relevant for the imperial cult at Thessalonica. It depicts a bust of Livia facing right with the inscription ΘΕΑ/ΘΕΟΥ ΛΙΒΙΑ. The reverse has a horse galloping right and ΘΕΣΣΑΛΟΝΙΚ. This seems to be a lifetime issue of Augustus, despite the honorific ΘΕΑ/ΘΕΟΥ because it uses Livia rather than Sebaste which is normal after 14 CE. The use of ΘΕΟΥ on one die, apparently

---

[16] Touratsoglou, *Thessaloniki*, 43 n.69. Touratsoglou further argues that RPC 1.5421 should be associated with RPC 1.5420 based on similar obverse inscription; however, the style is not similar and hence doubt remains.

[17] CNG [Classical Numismatics Group] Auction 75, 23 May 2007, lot 798.

Figure 45 CNG 75.2007.798 (used with permission).

Figure 46 RPC 1.1563 (used with permission).

referring to Augustus, is surprising (possibly a mistake for ΘEA as most examples).[18] Although no other coins minted in Thessalonica ascribe divinity to Augustus during his lifetime, a parallel issue from Larissa, RPC 1.1427 (Figure 47) does exist under the Thessalian League (a loose confederacy of city states in Northern Greece) where Augustus is referred to as ΘEOΣ and Livia is referred to as ΛIBIA rather than

---

[18] Touratsoglou, *Thessaloniki*, 28 n.12.

Figure 47 RPC 1.1427 (used with permission).

ΣΕΒΑΣΤΕ.[19] RPC 1.1427 has, on the obverse, ΘΕΟΣ ΚΑΙΣΑΡ ΘΕΣΣΑΛ ΙΤΑ with bare head facing right. The reverse has ΗΡΑ ΛΕΙΟΥΛΙΑ ΠΕΤ (monogram) with the head of Livia. The ΙΤΑ and ΠΕΤ refer to the magistrates Italos and Petraios. The Thessalian League produced silver and bronze coinage in the second and first centuries BCE.[20] E. Rogers dates the coinage mentioning Petraios to 48–27 BCE,[21] and this is affirmed by Burnett and Crawford.[22] Enhancing this divine portrayal of Augustus is a marble statue discovered in the Serapium of Thessalonica which depicts the emperor in a divine posture.[23] H. Hendrix concludes that Thessalonica displayed a 'distinctive sensitivity to propaganda about Roman rule'.[24]

The manner in which the above numismatic evidence informs our reading of Paul at Thessalonica is primarily twofold. First, the prominence of the imperial cult in Thessalonica and the way in which the visual culture and ideology of the city was shaped by the iconography on coinage. This, of course, is corroborated by many other forms of evidence such as an inscription (IG [X] II/I 31) attesting to a Thessalonian temple to Caesar during the time of Augustus. As far as the numismatic contribution

---

[19] Burnett, Amandry and Carradice, *Roman Provincial Coinage 1*, 298.
[20] Bruno Helly, 'Le groupe des monnaies fédérales thessaliennes avec Athéna "aux pompons"', *Revue Numismatique* 6 (1966): 7–32; E. Rogers, *The Copper Coinage of Thessaly* (London: Spink & Son Ltd., 1932).
[21] Rogers, *Copper Coinage*, 20.
[22] Burnett, Amandry, and Carradice, *Roman Provincial Coinage 1*, 280.
[23] Holand Lee Hendrix, 'Archaeology and Eschatology at Thessalonica', in *The Future of Early Christianity: Essays in Honor of Helmut Koester*, ed. Birger A. Pearson (Minneapolis, MN: Fortress Press, 1991), 116–117. There is no consensus on whether the marble statue was an import into Thessalonica or a local production. Hendrix and others have generally dated the statue to the time of Claudius and have noted that the Thessalonians had great interest in supporting and strengthening imperial propaganda.
[24] Hendrix, 'Archaeology and Eschatology', 117–118.

152   *Numismatics and Greek Lexicography*

goes, we have at least three examples and several subtypes that attest to the prominence of the imperial cult at Thessalonica.[25]

Second, specific mention of the στέφανος (1 Thess. 2:19) is illuminated by our above discussion. In Paul's defence of his present absence from Thessalonica (1 Thess. 2:17–3:10) he assures his readers of his genuine desire to see τὸ πρόσωπον ὑμῶν ('your face', 1 Thess. 2:17). In verse 19 he refers to a στέφανος (crown) καυχήσεως (of boasting) directly in relation to the Thessalonian community themselves, ἢ οὐχὶ καὶ ὑμεῖς; (Is it not you?). We are told that this crown consists of the recipients themselves 'in the presence of our Lord Jesus at His coming' (1 Thess. 2:19b). The symbolic στέφανος could seek to recall (i) the civic crown (*corona civica*) which consisted of a wreath of oak leaves grated by the Senate in recognition of saving the life of a fellow Roman citizen in battle[26] or (ii) a laurel wreath awarded to a victor in an athletic contest.[27] In J. R. Harrison's definitive study 'The Fading Crown: Divine Honour and the Early Christians',[28] he argues that 'the postponement of crowning would have been puzzling in a culture that prized the prompt reciprocation of honour'.[29] This is reinforced by the clear evidence on the coins.[30]

Thessalonica's favoured political relationship with Rome

Three coins attest to Thessalonica's favoured political relationship with Rome. First, as a reward for lending its support to the Second Triumvirate after the death of Julius Caesar, the city was granted 'free status' in 42 BCE by Marcus Antoninus (Mark Antony).[31] This is evidenced in RPC 1.1551 (Figure 48), an issue of coinage under Antony in 37 BCE which on the obverse has ΘΕΣΣΑΛΟΝΙΚΕΩΝ ΕΛΕΥΘΕΡΙΑΣ with a bust of Eleutheria facing to the right. The reverse depicts Nike advancing left with a wreath and palm, accompanied by the standard catalogue of names and titles, Μ ΑΝΤ ΑΥΤ Γ ΚΑΙ ΑΥΤ. This series elevates Antony and Octavian and celebrates the defeat of Brutus and the subsequent freedom it afforded. Pliny, in *Naturalis Historia* 4.17, states that 'on the Macedonian coast of the gulf are the town of Chalastra and, farther in, Pylorus, Lete, and at the centre of the curve of the coast the *free* city of Saloniki'.[32] Further attestation

---

[25] On the prominence of the cult of Caesar in the provinces, see S. Weinstock, *Divus Julius* (Oxford: Oxford University Press, 1971), 401–410.

[26] *Res Gestae* 34 states, 'In my sixth and seventh consulships, after I had extinguished civil wars... For this service of mine I was named Augustus by decree of the senate, and the door-posts of my house were publicly wreathed with bay leaves and a civic crown was fixed over my door and a golden shield was set in the Curia Julia, which, as attested by the inscription thereon, was given me by the senate and people of Rome on account of my courage, clemency, justice and piety.' Translation from P. A. Brunt and J. M. Moore, *Res Gestae Divi Augusti: The Achievements of Divine Augustus* (Oxford: Oxford University Press, 1983), 35–37. Cf. Dio 53.16.4.

[27] W. E. Raffety, 'Crown', *ISBE* 1 (1979): 831–32.

[28] Harrison, 'The Fading Crown', 493–529.

[29] Harrison, 'The Fading Crown', 527.

[30] K. Kraft, 'Der goldene Kranz Caesars und der Kampf um die Entlarvung des "Tyrannen"', *JRS* 3/4 (1952–53): 7–97.

[31] C. A. Wanamaker, *The Epistles to the Thessalonians: A Commentary on the Greek Text* (Grand Rapids, MI: Eerdmans, 1990), 3.

[32] H. Rackham, trans. *Pliny. The Natural History, Volume II: Books 3–7* (LCL 352; Cambridge, MA: Harvard University Press, 1942), 144–45, italics mine.

Figure 48 RPC 1.1551 (used with permission).

of Thessalonica's free status is evidenced in IG X2 1.6. Holland Hendrix notes that this freedom was 'granted only to people and cities which had displayed remarkable loyalty to the interests of the Roman people'.[33] Benefits of this free status included (1) the right to mint both local and imperial coinage (although the latter did not occur until 298 CE under Diocletian;[34] (2) freedom from military occupation;[35] (3) tax concessions; and (4) exemption from being a Roman colony and therefore not subject to the *Ius Italicum* (legal institution), nor was the city responsible for the resettlement of discharged Roman soldiers as was the case in Philippi and elsewhere. 'This naturally left the local ruling elite in control of the city with its traditional institutions intact.'[36]

Second, numismatic evidence also supports the concept of an eager embrace of the imperial cult. Antony's defeat of Brutus in 42 BCE was commemorated as the dawn of a new age, including celebratory games.[37] RPC 1.1552 (Figure 49) is a bronze issue under M. Antony and Octavian in 37 BCE. The obverse reads ΑΓΩΝΟΘΕΣΙΑ with the personified head of Agonothesia facing right (with E denoting year 5). The reverse has ANT KAI in a wreath. The *agonothete* was the judge of the public games and RPC 1.1552 suggests 'the Thessalonians were actively cultivating the patronage of the emperor and imperial figures in seeking political leverage'.[38]

---

[33] Holland Lee Hendrix, 'Thessalonicans Honor Romans' (ThD diss., Harvard University, 1984), 245.
[34] See R. Jewett, *The Thessalonian Correspondence: Pauline Rhetoric and Millenarian Piety* (Philadelphia, PA: Fortress, 1986), 123.
[35] Frank Frost Abbott, *A History and Description of Roman Political Institutions* (Boston, MA: Ginn & Co., 1911), 90–91; Gene L. Green, *The Letters to the Thessalonians* (Grand Rapids, MI: Eerdmans, 2002), 18–20.
[36] Wanamaker, *Thessalonians*, 3. Green, *Thessalonians*, 19; on the politarchs, see G. H. R. Horsley, 'The Politarchs', in *The Book of Acts in Its First Century Setting, Volume 2, Greco-Roman Setting*, ed. David W. J. Gill and Conrad Gempf (Grand Rapids, MI: Eerdmans, 1994), 419–431.
[37] Richard A. Horsley, *Paul and the Roman Imperial Order* (New York: Trinity Press International, 2004), 57.
[38] Horsley, *Paul and the Roman Imperial Order*, 57.

Figure 49 RPC 1.1552 (used with permission).

Towards the end of the first century BCE, a temple was built in Thessalonica in honour of Caesar and a priesthood was established to service the temple. An important collection of inscriptions from Thessalonica includes IT 31,[39] which refers to 'the temple of Caesar', the 'priest and agōnothetēs of Imperator Caesar Augustus son [of god]' and the 'priest of the gods ... and priest of Roma and the Roman benefactors'.[40] Holland Hendrix's analysis of this and other inscriptions from Thessalonica (namely IT 32, 132, 133) suggests that officials, such as the *agonothete*, who were connected with the imperial cult were generally superior over other priesthoods, 'in every extant instance in which the "priest and agonothete of the Imperator" is mentioned, he is listed first in what appears to be a strict observance of protocol. The Imperator's priest and agonothete assumes priority, the priest of "the gods" is cited next, followed by the priest of Roma and Roman benefactors'.[41] Especially significant is IT 133, a dedication to a renovation to the gymnasium where priest and agonothete are listed first.[42]

Third, Thessalonica's favoured relationship with Rome is celebrated in the Homonoia between Thessalonica and Rome. The Homonoia established between Thessalonica and the Triumvirs is 'one of the earliest attested instances of such Homonoia between two cities'.[43] RPC 1.1553 (Figure 50) is an issue in 37 BCE by M. Antony and Octavian. The obverse reads OMONOIA with a bust of Homonoia facing right, while the reverse

---

[39] C. Edson, *IG X, 2 1 Inscriptiones Graecae, X: Inscriptiones Epiri, Macedoniae, Thraciae, Scythiae Pars II, fasc. 1: Inscriptiones Thessalonicae et viciniae* (Berlin: de Gruyter, 1972).
[40] Cited in Weima, *1–2 Thessalonians*, 35.
[41] Hendrix, 'Thessalonicans', 312.
[42] Hendrix, 'Thessalonicans', 312 n.1.
[43] Burnett, Amandry, and Carradice, *Roman Provincial Coinage 1*, 297.

Figure 50 RPC 1.1553 (used with permission).

has ΘΕΣΣΑΛΟΝ ΡΩΜ with a horse galloping, right. P. R. Franke and D. A. O. Klose[44] convincingly argue that there is no 'overall explanation for all the "alliance" coinages, but that they are a single manifestation of many different sets of circumstances (rivalry between cities, political or religious links, boundary disputes)'.[45] Examples in the Julio-Claudian period (such as RPC 1.1553 [Thessalonica and Rome], RPC 1.2143 [Amisus and Rome stand facing], RPC 1.2988 [Pergamum and Sardis under Augustus], RPC 1.5445 [Hypaepa and Sardis under Tiberius], RPC 1.5446 [Hypaepa and Sardis], RPC 1.2912 [Laodicea and Smyrna under Claudius] and RPC 1.2928 [Laodicea and Smyrna under Nero]) indicate that alliance coinages had not yet been standardized. For instance, the word OMONOIA does not always occur; rather two cities can simply be listed (RPC 1.1553, RPC 1.2143), joined by καί (RPC 1.2912) or even have a variant of OMONOIA, cf. ΟΜΗΡΟΣ (RPC 1.2928) – which may refer to the person responsible for the issue rather than the relationship per se, but still the phraseology is not standardized. Nonetheless, in regard to the coinage of Thessalonica, the composite picture is one of the aristocracy's imperial indebtedness, political commitment and ideological allegiance to Rome.

Other avenues for applying numismatic data to NT Thessalonica and Thessalonian correspondence have been suggested by commentators. A wide range of scholars over the last half-century, including E. Bammel,[46] K. P. Donfried,[47] K. Wengst,[48]

---

[44] P. R. Franke, 'Zu den Homonoia-Münzen Kleinasiens', in *Stuttgarter Kolloquium zur Historische Geographie des Altertums I, 1980*, ed. Eckart Olshausen (Bonn: Habelt, 1987), 81–102; D. O. A. Klose, *Die Münzprägung von Smyrna in der römischen Kaiserzeit* (Berlin: de Gruyter, 1987), 44–63.

[45] Burnett, Amandry, and Carradice, *Roman Provincial Coinage 1*, 48.

[46] E. Bammel, 'Ein Beitrag zur paulinishen Staatsanschauung', *TLZ* 85 (1960): 837–840. See also T. D. Still, *Conflict at Thessalonica: A Pauline Church and Its Neighbours* [Sheffield: Sheffield Academic, 1999], 260–267) who summarizes recent scholarship on the 'peace and security' phrase.

[47] Karl P. Donfried, 'The Cults of Thessalonica and the Thessalonian Correspondence', *NTS* 31 (1985): 341.

[48] K. Wengst, *Pax Romana and the Peace of Jesus Christ* (Philadelphia, PA: Fortress, 1987), 19–21, 77–79.

H. Koester[49] and H. L. Hendrix[50] have argued that the phrase εἰρήνη καὶ ἀσφάλεια (trans. 'peace and security', 1 Thess. 5:3) offers a critique of a Roman imperial slogan of the *Pax Roman*. The relevant terminology occurs frequently, not only on the coinage of the period,[51] but is also reflected in epigraphic materials. T. D. Still highlights, among other inscriptions, IT 32 (noted above) and IT 33, which consist of a selection of decrees of the city issued in conjunction with a specific Roman group, and IT 4, where Roma and Roman benefactors become part of the city cult of the gods.[52] An inscription at Ilium (SEG 46 1565; 62 BCE) honours Pompey for liberating the inhabitants of Alexandria Troas, ἀπό τε τῶν βαρβαρικῶν πολέμων [καῖ τῶν π] ιρατικῶν κινδύνων ἀποκαθεστάκοτα δὲ [τὴν εἰρ]ήνην καὶ τὴν ἀσφάλειαν καὶ κατὰ γῆν καὶ κατὰ θάλασσαν (trans. 'from wars with the Barbarians and the dangers from pirates, having restored peace and security on the land and the sea').[53] Furthermore, as IT 31 evidences, a temple was built at some point between 26 BCE and 14 CE in honour of Augustus. This evidence strongly suggests that the political overtones in the phrase εἰρήνη καὶ ἀσφάλεια are clearly in the foreground in 1 Thessalonians 5:3 J. R. Harrison[54] strengthens this proposal by drawing attention to the Jewish *Psalms of Solomon* 8:8 which refers to Rome's occupation by Pompey as follows: 'He entered in peace (μετ' εἰρήνης) as a father enters his son's house; he set his feet securely (μετὰ ἀσφαλείας).' In light of this, Hendrix's conclusion is certainly justified when he states, 'Thessalonica's interests increasingly were influenced by Romans and by regard for the Roman emperor.'[55]

More recently the debate has been reignited with the robust interchange between J. Weima[56] and J. R. White.[57] Weima presents a fresh articulation of the argument in support of the phrase εἰρήνη καὶ ἀσφάλεια (1 Thess. 5:3) as deriving from a critique of a Roman imperial slogan. White takes issue with the identification of the Thessalonian phrase with a slogan per se, and questions the role of *securitas* in the imperial equation. It is not that White denies Roman imperial political ideology, but contends there is only limited evidence that the two terms circulated as a slogan. The contribution of numismatics at this point would be to simply point out the frequency with which both terms are used on the imperial coinage of the first century. Harrison sums up the numismatic evidence perfectly in stating that 'both Latin words [*pax* and *securitas*] appear individually on the imperial coinage with monotonous regularity'.[58]

---

[49] Helmut Koester, 'From Paul's Eschatology to the Apocalyptic Schemata of 2 Thessalonians', in *The Thessalonian Correspondence*, ed. R. F. Collins (Leuven: Leuven University Press, 1990), 449–450.

[50] Hendrix, 'Archaeology and Eschatology', 107–118.

[51] Hendrix, 'Archaeology and Eschatology', 115.

[52] Still, *Conflict*, 263.

[53] P. Oakes, 'Re-Mapping the Universe: Paul and the Emperor in 1 Thessalonians and Philippians', *JSNT* 27 (2005): 317–318.

[54] Harrison, *Paul and the Imperial Authorities*, 61 n.64.

[55] Hendrix, 'Archaeology and Eschatology', 115.

[56] Jeffrey A. D. Weima, '"Peace and Security" (1 Thess. 5.3): Prophetic Warning or Political Propaganda?' *NTS* 58 (2012): 331–359.

[57] J. R. White, '"Peace and Security" (1 Thessalonians 5.3): Is It Really a Slogan?' *NTS* 59 (2013): 382–385; J. R. White, '"Peace" and "Security" (1 Thess. 5.3): Roman Ideology and Greek Aspiration', *NTS* 60 (2014): 499–510.

[58] Harrison, *Paul and the Imperial Authorities*, 61.

ΘΕΟΣ, ΕΛΕΥΘΕΡΙΑ, ΕΙΡΗΝΗ ΚΑΙ ΑΣΦΑΛΕΙΑ, ΚΑΒΕΙΡΟΣ

Particularly compelling examples include RIC *Claud.* 61 (Aureus) and RIC *Claud.* 62 (Denarius), newly issued by Claudius in 51–52 CE, the probable year of Paul's arrival to Thessalonica.[59] The obverse depicts the laureate head of Claudius facing right with the inscription TI CLAUD CAESAR AUG P M TR P XI IMP PP COS V. The reverse has PACI AUGUSTAE with a depiction of a winged Pax-Nemesis advancing right, with left hand holding a caduceus pointing down at a snake, and with the right hand holding out a fold of drapery below chin. Slightly less common but strongly attested is the legend SECURITAS, although more common on the coins from Nero onward. What is particularly striking on the coins of Claudius however, and which has thus far not been alluded to or drawn upon in this discussion, are the coinage issues with a conceptually related term to *securitas*, namely *servator*.

The OLD gives three senses for *servator*, (1) a saviour, preserver, (2) an observer, one who keeps watch or guard, and (3) one who observes or maintains (a rule of conduct),[60] and five main senses for *securitas*, (1) freedom from anxiety or care, (2) complacent negligence, (3) freedom from danger, safety, security, (4) the personification of public and political security, and (5) security for payment of a debt.[61] There has been a long-established scholarly tradition of interest in Latin synonyms, and especially nuances between related lexemes. From Marcus Terentius Varro's (116–27 BCE) nascent attempts, to Isidore of Seville's (560–636 CE) encyclopaedic projects,[62] to the sophisticated discipline in modern lexicography, scholarly interest in Latin lexicology in this area has not waned.[63] J. B. Gardin Dumesnil's *Synonymes Latins et Leurs Significations* (1777) contains over 7,000 words in 2,541 domains of synonyms.[64] Domain 2230 consists of *servator, conservator, liberator* and *soter*.[65] Although Dumesnil does not list *securitas*, the more comprehensive work of Ludwig Döderlein does list the term under domain 77, together with *tutus* and *incuriosus*[66] Franz Wagner's *Lexicon Latinum*

---

[59] This was the eighth time the reverse type was issued by Claudius during his reign (previously as RIC *Claud.* 9, 10 in 41–41 CE, RIC *Claud.* 21, 22 in 43–44 CE, RIC *Claud.* 27, 28 in 44 CE, RIC *Claud.* 38, 39 in 46–47 CE, RIC *Claud.* 46, 47 in 49–50 CE, RIC *Claud.* 51, 52, 57, 58 in 50–51 CE).

[60] OLD, 1745.

[61] OLD, 1722.

[62] The standard Latin text of Isidore's *Etymologiae* is W. M. Lindsay, *Isidori Hispalensis episcope etymologiarum sive originum libri XX*, 2 vols. (Oxford: Clarendon, 1911). For an English translation, see Stephen A. Barney, W. J. Lewis, J. A. Beach, and Oliver Berghof, *The 'Etymologies' of Isidore of Seville* (Cambridge: Cambridge University Press, 2006).

[63] Georg Goetz, 'Differentiae scriptores', in *Real-encyclopädie der classischen Altertumswissenschaft, volume 5*, ed. Georg Wissowa (Stuttgart: Metzler, 1903), 481–484; Georg Goetz, 'Glossographie', in *Real-encyclopädie der classischen Altertumswissenschaft, volume 7*, ed. Georg Wissowa and Wilhelm Kroll (Stuttgart: Metzler, 1910), 1433–1466. For a summary of the field of Latin glossaries, see Peter Schmidt, 'Differentiarum Scriptores', in *Der neue Pauly, volume 3*, ed. Hubert Cancik and Helmuth Schneider (Munich: Druckenmüller, 1997), 558–559. For a modern survey of the field of Latin lexicography, see Alfred Breitenbach, 'Lexikon II (lateinisch)', in *Reallexikon für Antike und Christentum, volume 23*, ed. Georg Schölgen, Heinzgerd Brakmann, Sible de Blaauw, Therese Fuhrer, Karl Hoheisel, Winrich Löhr, Wolfgang Speyer, and Klaus Thraede (Stuttgart: Anton Hiersemann, 2008), 1–29.

[64] M. J. B. Gardin Dumesnil, *Latin Synonyms with Their Different Significations: And Examples Taken from the Best Latin Authors*, trans. J. M. Gosset (London: Richard Taylor, 1888).

[65] Dumesnil, *Latin Synonyms*, 511.

[66] Ludwig Döderlein, *Lateinische Synonyme und Etymologieen: Dritter Theil*, 6 vols. (Leipzig: F. C. W. Vogel, 1829), 3.120.

Universae Phraseologiae Corpus Congestum (1878) implicitly associates both terms via function when he notes of *servator*: '*usus: Urbis, capitis mei servator et custos*'.[67]

When considering related lexemes or synonyms, several of the above lexicographers (Dumesnil, Döderlein Pompa) can, at times, be accused of drawing too fine a distinction between certain terminology. The difference in words is not always related to morphology but often more strongly correlate to register, style, genre and author. It is this with a more porous exchange in *meaning* that certain terminology on the record of Latin coinage of Claudius could illuminate a further dimension of the Greek phrase.

RIC *Claud*. 5 (aureus), and 6 (denarius) were issued in 41–42 CE and had inscribed on the obverse TI CLAUD CAESAR AUG P M TR P (Tiberius Claudius Caesar Augustus Pontifex Maximus Tribunicia Potestas [Tiberius Claudius Caesar, August, Greatest Pontiff invested with the Tribunician Power]). The reverse has lettering over four lines within an oak-wreath, EX S C OB CIVES SERVATOS (Ex Senatus Consulto Ob Cives Servatos [by Decree of the Senate on account of the citizens who have been saved]). As Duncan Fishwick notes, 'the concept of the *princeps* as *servator* is central in Augustan ideology'[68] and is replicated by Claudius on his coinage during his reign for the purposes of typological association. RIC *Claud*. 15 (aureus), and 16 (denarius) (Figure 51) were also issued in 41–42 CE with similar obverse (TI CLAUD CAESAR AUG GERM P M) and reverse (EX S C OB CIVES SERVATOS in three lines within an oak wreath) inscriptions. The obverse of RIC *Claud*. 96 (Sestertius) (Figure 52) depicts the laureate head of Claudius facing right with the inscription TI CLAVDIVS CAESAR AVG P M TR P IMP. The reverse has lettering over four lines within an oak-wreath,

Figure 51 RIC *Claud*. 16 (used with permission).

---

[67] Franz Wagner, *Lexicon Latinum Universae Phraseologiae Corpus Congestum*, trans. Augustin Borgnet (Ridgewood: Gregg Press: 1878), 642.
[68] Duncan Fishwick, *The Imperial Cult in the Latin West* (Leiden: Brill, 1993), 108.

Figure 52 RIC *Claud.* 96 (used with permission).

EX S C OB CIVES SERVATOS (Ex Senatus Consulto Ob Cives Servatos [by Decree of the Senate on account of the citizens who have been saved]). This is not to suggest that the meanings of *securitas* and *servatos* are synonymous, but that they share significant semantic overlap in their linguistic senses. This could potentially be one dimension of the phrase εἰρήνη καὶ ἀσφάλεια (trans. 'peace and security') in 1 Thessalonians 5:3 hitherto neglected. The chronological timeframe in regard to Paul's visit to Thessalonica, during the reign of Claudius, enhances the probability.

Thessalonica's religious identity shaped by the city's past

There were a number of co-existing and competing cults at Thessalonica, including Dionysus, Egyptian cults primarily focused on Serapis and Isis but also with interest in Osiris and Anubis, and of course the above discussed Imperial cult. The cult of Kabeiros, however, was perhaps the most prominent[69] and was regularly represented on coinage. It was not indigenous to the Macedonian area but imported from Samothrace.[70] Macedonians were interested in Samothracian gods from at least the time of Phillip II onward as Plutarch (*Alexander* 2) indicates: 'and we are told that Philip, after being initiated into the mysteries of Samothrace at the same time with Olympias, he himself being still a youth.'[71] Other early evidence is cited by Edson,[72] which includes reference

---

[69] *Contra* Colin R. Nicholl who claims that 'the significance of the cult of Cabirus has been greatly overstated', Colin R. Nicholl, *From Hope to Despair in Thessalonica* (Cambridge: Cambridge University Press, 2004), 78 n.110. Nicholl's conclusions are difficult to justify given the voluminous numismatic, inscriptional, monumental, and literary evidence for the cult at Thessalonica.

[70] C. Edson, 'Cults of Thessalonica', *HTR* 41 (1948): 188–204.

[71] Bernadotte Perrin, trans. *Plutarch. Lives, Volume VII: Demosthenes and Cicero. Alexander and Caesar* (LCL 99; Cambridge, MA: Harvard University Press, 1919), 225–227.

[72] Edson, 'Cults', 189 n.3.

to Antigona of Pella, who was captured by the Persian fleet in 333 BCE, en route from Macedonia to Samothrace to partake in mysteries, further strengthening the cultic association between the two locations. IG XII.8.195 connects the Macedonians with Samothracian gods by providing a list of visitors from Macedonia who participated in ΜΥΣΤΑΙ ΕΥΣΕΒΕΙΣ (trans. 'pious mysteries') dated securely to Augustus's reign. These and other factors suggest that, at the latest, by the time of Augustus, there was considerable interest in Samothracian gods in Thessalonica. Edson concludes that by Augustus 'members of the city's upper classes were showing interest in the cult of the Samothracian gods'.[73]

H. Koester has rightly noted the limitation of our knowledge of the Kabeiros cult at Thessalonika, as opposed to the specificity elsewhere in the empire, such as the single god in Thessalonica rather than twin gods in Samothrace who were conflated with the Dioscuri twins Castor and Polydeuces. Clement of Alexandria refers to the cult as pertaining to two brothers murdering and burying a third, to whom they set up a cult.[74] Jewett claims this is 'structurally similar'[75] to Paul's proclamation. But we must not assume that an imposition of our knowledge from other locations is assumed for Kabeiros at Thessalonica. The date of arrival of the Kabeiros cult to Thessalonica is ambiguous, but it clearly has an established history even before the first century.[76] Weima notes that the cult was also well known in Larisa, the capital of nearby Thessaly by 200 BCE,[77] but it is difficult to infer specific details about Thessalonica without further literary or archaeological evidence.

Karl P. Donfried notes a series of pre-imperial Thessalonian coins with the helmeted head of Roma and suggests that they can be used to shed light on texts such as, καὶ περικεφαλαίαν ἐλπίδα σωτηρίας (trans. 'and the hope of salvation as a helmet'; 1 Thess 5:8).[78] Donfried suggests that the laurel crown of Kabeiros or the rose crowns used in the commemoratory sacrifice of the cult of Dionysus would be the natural association for the recipients of the letter. But there are other possibilities and associations which may prove more viable avenues for accounting for the armour language in Thessalonians or other Pauline texts from the perspective of the writer, including Qumran literature,[79] Isaiah,[80] Jewish wisdom traditions[81] or indeed the broader cultural milieu of the presence of Roman military throughout the Mediterranean world.

Kabeiros at Thesslonica primarily evidences itself in the coinage of the Flavian period (69 CE–96 CE). RPC 2.327 (Figure 53) is a medium (20–23 mm) bronze coin which, on

---

[73] Edson, 'Cults', 190.
[74] Clement of Alexandria, *The Absurdity and Impiety of the Heathen Mysteries and Fables about the Birth and Death of Their Gods* (ANF 2.177).
[75] Jewett, *Thessalonian Correspondence*, 128.
[76] B. Hemberg, *Die Kabiren* (Uppsala: Almquist & Wiksells, 1950), 9.
[77] Weima, *1–2 Thessalonians*, 16.
[78] See discussion in Donfried, 'Cults', 341.
[79] David Luckensmeyer, *The Eschatology of First Thessalonians* (Göttingen: Vandenhoeck & Ruprecht, 2009), 303.
[80] Jeffrey A. D. Weima, '1–2 Thessalonians', in *Commentary on the New Testament Use of the Old Testament*, ed. G. K. Beale and D. A. Carson (Grand Rapids, MI: Baker Academic, 2007), 882.
[81] Wisdom 5:17–18, 'The Lord will take his zeal as his whole armor, and will arm all creation to repel his enemies; he will put on righteousness as a breastplate, and wear impartial justice as a helmet.'

Figure 53 RPC 2.327 (used with permission).

the obverse, depicts Kabeiros standing facing left, holding a rhyton (conical container for drinking or libation) and hammer, with an accompanying inscription ΚΑΒΕΙΡΟΣ. The reverse has ΘΕΣΣΑ/ΛΟΝΙΚΕ/ΩΝ in three lines, with a small eagle above, all of which is within an oak wreath. RPC 2.328 (Figure 54) has a draped bust of Kabeiros facing right on the obverse. The reverse, like RPC 2.327 has ΘΕΣΣΑ/ΛΟΝΙΚΕ/ΩΝ in three lines, eagle above, all within an oak wreath. RPC 2.329 has on the obverse the draped bust of the city-goddess facing right, with the inscription ΘΕΣΣΑΛΟΝΙΚΗ. The obverse depicts Kabeiros standing left, holding rhyton and hammer, with the inscription ΚΑΒΕΙΡΟΣ. RPC 2.330 (Figure 55) has on the obverse the draped and turreted bust of the city-goddess facing right, with the inscription ΘΕΣΣΑΛΟΝΙΚΕΩΝ. The obverse, similar to 329, depicts Kabeiros standing left, holding rhyton and hammer, with the inscription ΚΑΒΕΙΡΟΣ.

The regular depiction of Kabeiros carrying a hammer is significant. The hammer could refer to the city's pride in industry in general, that is, a celebration of hard work and labour built into the identity of the inhabitants. If so, then Paul's imperatives to work in 1 Thessalonians 4:9–12 (esp. v. 11) builds rapport and rhetorically appeals to their shared common values (cf. 1 Thess. 2:9, 'You remember our labor (κόπον) and toil (μόχθον), brothers and sisters; we worked (ἐργαζόμενοι) night and day, so that we might not burden any of you while we proclaimed to you the gospel of God').

The image of the hammer might also refer more specifically to the industry of blacksmiths which, as Acts 19 notes, was affected by the diminishing demand for idols, at least in Ephesus. Perhaps a similar dynamic arose in Thessalonica. J. Hardin's argument which takes the charges and judicial episode in Acts 17:1–10 as pertaining to Roman regulations of voluntary associations,[82] would more broadly allow this

---

[82] J. Hardin, 'Decrees and Drachmas at Thessalonica: An Illegal Assembly in Jason's House (Acts 17.1–10a)', NTS 52 (2006): 29–49.

Figure 54 RPC 2.328 (used with permission).

Figure 55 RPC 2.330.

possibility. But the word ἐργαζόμενοι in 2:9 would certainly include manual labour, even if it was physical challenging κόπος (labour) and μόχθος (toil). Nonetheless, Paul maintains a positive association despite the generally negative attitude towards labour by Roman elites in antiquity,[83] which perhaps implies the lower than elite social

---

[83] R. F. Hock, *The Social Context of Paul's Ministry: Tentmaking and Apostleship* (Philadelphia, PA: Fortress, 1980), 36; S. R. Joshel, *Work, Identity, and Legal Status at Rome: A Study of the Occupational Inscriptions* (Norman: University of Oklahoma Press, 1992), 63–69; R. MacMullen, *Roman Social Relations 50 B.C. to A.D. 284* (New Haven, CT and London: Yale University Press, 1974), 114–116, 138–141; R. Ascough, 'The Thessalonian Christian Community as a Professional Voluntary Association', *JBL* 52 (2006): 311–328.

status of Paul and his recipients. Either way, challenging the god of a city threatened the stability of the city both politically and ideologically. Paul's motivation for this emphasis on the continuance of normal working life is borne out of an apparent misunderstanding of the imminent return of Christ (1 Thess. 4:15–17; 5:1–9; 2 Thess. 2:1–3), which they appear to have interpreted as the suspension of their working lives. In light of the imagery on the numismatic record, this message would have certainly appealed to the inhabitants of the city.

Conclusion

Our analysis has sought to illuminate aspects of the Thessalonian correspondence in light of the numismatic record. The above numismatic analysis sought to demonstrate (1) that the imperial cult at Thessalonica shaped the city (evidenced through, among other mediums, divine honours for Caesar on coins); (2) that Thessalonica enjoyed favoured political relationship with Rome, and this subsequently brought appealing benefits for the inhabitants; and (3) that religious identity was shaped by the city's past, primarily through the embrace of the cult of Kabeiros. Taken together, the numismatic evidence supports the reconstruction of the Thessalonian aristocracy's 'active cultivation of Roman power',[84] and simultaneously supports the view of Thessalonians functioning as resistance literature. This study also reminds us that 'it is critical for us to realize how visible the Roman imperial ideology (as attested on the provincial coinage) would have been as a part of the everyday world of the Thessalonians when we read 1 Thessalonians'.[85]

---

[84] Horsley, *Paul and the Roman Imperial Order*, 58.
[85] Horsley, *Paul and the Roman Imperial Order*, 58.

9

ΧΑΡΑΚΤΗΡ

Introduction

Χαρακτήρ is a New Testament *hapax legomenon* (Heb 1:3), and is translated in the English versions with significant variation: 'express image' [KJV, NKJV, AV, JUB]; 'exact imprint' [ESV, NRSV]; 'very image' [ASV]; 'representation' [NET, LEB]; 'exact representation' [NIV, NASB]; 'exact likeness' [GW, GNT, ISV]; 'expression' [DARBY]; 'exact expression' [HCSB]; 'flawless; expression' [PHILLIPS]; 'very expression' [CJB]; 'very stamp' [RSV]; 'engraved form' [GNV] and 'impress' [YLT]. Attention to the numismatic record, which is conspicuously lacking in scholarly treatments, significantly enhances and refines the definition of the relevant semantic domain of this word, especially in regard to diachronic developments.

Historical context of Hebrews

The book of Hebrews has a long history of complicated historical–critical issues. Debates surrounding issues of authorship and the place of Hebrews within the canon overwhelmingly and unfortunately dominate most introductory discussions of this 'τοῦ λόγου τῆς παρακλήσεως' (trans. 'word of exhortation' [Heb 13:22]).[1] The identity of the recipients has received similar attention with scholarly opinion ranging from Wescott's 'Jewish Christians in Palestine' hypothesis to Kosmala's 'unconverted Jew' hypothesis.[2] The superscription 'ΠΡΟΣ ΕΒΡΑΙΟΥΣ' amply attested in extant Greek manuscripts, however, is likely derived from the overt Hebraic/Jewish tone of the letter. In recent

---

[1] Eusebius seems to make the most insightful comment in stating, 'only God truly knows who actually wrote this epistle!' Eusebius, Historia ecclesiastica VI, 25.14

[2] Wescott maintained that Hebrews was written prior to the war of 70 CE, when there was pressure for Christians to side with Jews (B. F. Westcott, *The Epistle to the Hebrews: The Greek Text with Notes and Essays* (New York: Macmillan, 1903). However, one problem with this is that the context is Hellenistic Judaism not Palestinian. While Wescott's scenario is congruous it does not seem adequately plausible. Moffatt asserts that the recipients were 'Gentile Christians', drawing support from 6:1 and 9:14 (James Moffatt, *A Critical and Exegetical Commentary on the Epistle to the Hebrews* [Edinburgh: T&T Clark International, 1924], xxiii). T. W. Manson suggested that 'Christians in the Lychus Valley', that is, those who were victims of the Colossian heresy (early Gnosticism, e.g. angels as intermediaries [Col 2:18 cf. Heb 13:9]) (T. W. Manson, 'The Problem of the Epistle to the Hebrews', *BJRL* 32 [1949–50], 1). However the parallels do not seem strong enough to validate this conclusion.

166   *Numismatics and Greek Lexicography*

times there has emerged somewhat of a consensus that the primary recipients were Hellenistic Jewish Christians, which in itself is a rather broad delineation. It would appear that the recipients were under some kind of threat (cf. Heb 10:23) and were tempted to abandon their Christian faith and revert to traditional systems of Judaism. This scenario would plausibly account for the familiarity with the LXX and the detailed background knowledge the author presupposes of his audience in presenting his treatise. It also plausibly explains the distinctive theological emphases. Jesus is presented as comprehensively superior to previous religious patterns. In this light, it is no surprise that the book of Hebrews contains thirteen of the nineteen NT usages of the term 'κρείττων' (trans. 'better').[3] The exhortations to persevere and warning passages are couched in some of the strongest language in the NT.[4] References to 'leaving the camp' (Heb 13:12–14), for example, may refer to Judaism's protection under the state as a *religio licita*. As the gulf between Jew and Christian widened, there was presumably less protection for the emerging Christian community. Within this context, the authorial intention seems to be twofold: (1) to present a series of warnings on the consequences of abandoning Christ, commonly referred to as the 'warning passages';[5] and (2) to offer positive encouragement to the recipients by focusing on the supremacy of Christ and their status of being in union with him.

The literary context of Hebrews 1:3

The literary structure of Hebrews, like several other critical issues, has eluded scholarly consensus. Indeed, D. E. Aune has noted that 'the structure of Hebrews remains an unsolved problem'.[6] Of all the proposals, one which deserves special attention is

---

Furthermore Hebrews was known relatively early in Rome, and later in the east. Spicq, on the basis of Acts 6:7, and the saturation of priestly language, claimed that the recipients were 'former priests converted to Christianity' (C. Spicq, 'Alexandrinismes dans l'Épître aux Hébreux', *RB* 58 [1951]: 492). Yadin claims that the priestly messiah of the Qumran community assimilates well with the presentation of Jesus's ministry, and therefore suggests that the recipients were 'converts from Qumran' (Y. Yadin, 'The Dead Sea Scrolls and the Epistle to the Hebrews', *Scripta Hierosolymitana* 4 [1958]: 37). And finally Kosmala suggests 'unconverted Jews', due to the severity and content of the letter (H. Kosmala, *Hebräer, Essener, Christen: Studien zur Vorgeschichte der frühchristlichen Verkündigung* [Leiden: Brill, 1959], 18).

[3] 1 Cor 7:9, 38; 11:17; Phil 1:23; Heb 1:4; 6:9; 7:7, 19, 22; 8:6; 9:23; 10:34; 11:16, 35, 40; 12:24; 1 Pet 3:17; 2 Pet 2:21.

[4] See Heb. 3:13; 4:14f; 6:18; 10:32; 12:11ff. cf. 11:1ff. as an illustration of perseverance and hope. The author attacks spiritual lethargy in 2:1–4; 3:7–14; 5:11–14; 6:12; 10:25; 12:3; 12:12–13), this also extends to apostasy.

[5] These warnings are variously identified and divided by the literature: 2:1–4; 3:7–19; 5:11–14; 10:26–31 by F. F. Bruce, *The Epistle to the Hebrews* (Grand Rapids, MI: Eerdmans, 1990), vii–x; 2:1–4; 3:7–19; 5:11–6:12; 10:19–39; 12:14–29 by W. L. Lane, *Hebrews 1–8* (Dallas, TX: Word, 1991); 2:1–4; 3:12–4:2, 11–13; 6:4–8; 10:26–31; 12:13b–17, 25–29 by A. Mugridge, 'Warnings in the Epistle to the Hebrews', *RTR* 46 (1987): 74; 2:1–4; 3:6–4:13; 6:4–6; 10:26–31; 12:25 by W. Grudem, 'Perseverance of the Saints: A Case Study from Hebrews 6: 4–6 and the Other Warning Passages in Hebrews' in *The Grace of God, The Bondage of the Will*, ed. T. Schreiner and B. Ware (Grand Rapids, MI: Baker, 1995), 134; 2:1–4; 3:7–4:13; 5:11–6:12; 10:19–39; 12:1–29 by S. McKnight, 'The Warning Passages of Hebrews: A Formal Analysis and Theological Conclusions', *Trinity Journal* 13 (1992): 22.

[6] D. E. Aune, *The New Testament in Its Literary Environment* (Cambridge: James Clark and Co., 1988), 213.

ΧΑΡΑΚΤΗΡ

Vaganay's structural outline which highlights the thematic symmetry of the work.[7] The verse under discussion, 1:3, 'ὃς ὢν ἀπαύγασμα τῆς δόξης καὶ χαρακτὴρ τῆς ὑποστάσεως αὐτοῦ, φέρων τε τὰ πάντα τῷ ῥήματι τῆς δυνάμεως αὐτοῦ, καθαρισμὸν τῶν ἁμαρτιῶν ποιησάμενος ἐκάθισεν ἐν δεξιᾷ τῆς μεγαλωσύνης ἐν ὑψηλοῖς' (trans. 'And He is the radiance of His glory and the exact representation of His nature, and upholds all things by the word of His power. When He had made purification of sins, He sat down at the right hand of the Majesty on high') falls within the first and shortest section of the epistle (1:1–4, Introduction).

Numismatic material on ΧΑΡΑΚΤΗΡ and related terms

Thrace came under the formal rule of Rome in 168 BCE, after the battle of Pydna during the Third Macedonian War. There was, of course, significant resistance to this transition, exemplified, for example, in the revolt of Andriscus in 149 BCE. After this, however, there was a gradual acceptance of the new political reality of Thrace as a recognized Roman client state. The first century BCE would even see the Thracian king, Rhascuporis, offer willing assistance to Pompey and Caesar, and then to Brutus and Cassius against Antonius and Octavian. Youroukova notes discernible influence of earlier Roman republic coin types on Thracian coins minted during the Roman period (post-168 BCE), no doubt a direct result of being incorporated as a province into the Roman Republic.[8] Ancient sources, including epigraphic evidence suggest the following sequence for the Ordrysian kings of Thrace. The literature however is, at times, admittedly conjectural and often based on circumstantial evidence, but includes Sadalas I, 87–75 BCE; Kotys II, 57–48 BCE; Sadalas II, 48–42 BCE; Kotys III, 38–18 BCE and Raiskouporis II, 18–11 BCE.[9]

The coin of interest for our analysis is a tetradrachm of Kotys II from the Thracian kingdom of Ordrysia. This coin has been catalogued by Moushmov as inv. 5778,[10] Youroukova as inv. 145, Jurukova as inv. 145 and Lukanc as inv. 1924 (Figure 56). The obverse depicts the head of a beardless Dionysos facing to the right, wreathed with ivy and with band across forehead. The reverse portrays Herakles, naked standing facing left, holding a club in his right hand, a lion's skin over his left arm, and an inscription downward to the right and left reading 'ΚΟΤΥΟΣ ΧΑΡΑΚΤΗΡ'. The inscription is relatively clear, 'ΚΟΤΥΟΣ', the name of the ruler 'Kotys' in the genitive case, and 'ΧΑΡΑΚΤΗΡ' in the nominative case. Youroukova suggests that 'ΧΑΡΑΚΤΗΡ'

---

[7] L. Vaganay, 'Le Plan de l'Épître aux Hébreux', in *Mémorial Lagrange*, ed. L.-H. Vincent (Paris: Gabalda, 1940), 269–277.

[8] Y. Youroukova, *Coins of the Ancient Thracians*, trans. V. Athanassov (Oxford: British Archaeological Reports, 1967), 2.

[9] Z. Archibald, *The Odrysian Kingdom of Thrace: Orpheus Unmasked* (Oxford: Clarendon Press, 1998); R. D. Sullivan, *Near Eastern Royalty and Rome, 100–30 BC* (Toronto: Buffalo, 1990); S. Topalov, *The Odrysian Kingdom from the Late 5th to the Mid-4th C. B.C.* (Sofia: K&K Publishers, 1994).

[10] H. Moushmov, *Ancient Coins of the Balkan Peninsula*, trans. Denista Genkova, Dave Surber, and Slavei Theodore Slaveev (Sofia: K&K Publishers, 1912).

Figure 56 Youroukova 145.

'obviously denotes [a] die, or seal'[11] and renders the translation of the inscription as 'die/seal of Kotys'. As we will come to see, there is much greater significance in this inscription than simply distinguishing the coinage of Kotys from those tetradrachms of Thasos that circulated in the same region.

In the extant examples of this coin, it is evident that there were at least three different dies used for the reverse.[12] In a relatively simplistic die study (which included averaging the current life span of dies) Youroukova estimates that upwards of 8,000 tetradrachms of this type were minted with approximately 13.12 kg of silver, a relative minor item of expenditure for an individual who, Cicero informs us, was bribed with 300 talents.[13] This estimated output however, must remain only a tentative possibility given the paucity of extant coins.[14] Youroukova comments, however, 'The limited number of tetradrachmae of Kotys which have reached us could be explained by the possibility that a small part of these coins was kept as bullion. Once reaching the Romans in the form of bribes, aid, etc. the coins were probably melted down and the metal served to mint new series of Republican Roman denarii.'[15]

The word 'χαρακτήρ' does not appear elsewhere on ancient coinage, however is conceptually reminiscent of some early examples. When we turn to the Thracian kings and dynasts some interesting parallels emerge. A tetradrachm of Seuthes II (Youroukova 26) depicts on the obverse a beardless horseman with bare head galloping towards the right with an inflated chlamys. His right hand is throwing a spear, and

---

[11] Youroukova, *Coins*, 43.
[12] Youroukova, *Coins*, 44.
[13] This information is apparent in a speech prosecuting Piso, the governor of Macedonia (*In Pisonem*). See further Youroukova, *Coins*, 42.
[14] In 1976 Youroukova (*Coins*, 44) cited six known examples. Since then up to six more examples have been documented.
[15] Youroukova, *Coins*, 44.

his left hand is holding the reins. The reverse has a shallow incuse square with the inscription ΣΕΥΘΑ ΑΡΓΥΡΙΟΝ (trans. 'silver of Seuthes'). The obverse of Youroukova 27 has ΣΕ with horse prancing right enclosed in a border of dots, and on the reverse has the inscriptions ΣΕΥΘΑ ΚΟΜΜΑ, where κόμμα is presumably derived from κόπτειν (i.e. 'that which is struck by Seuthes'). This undoubtedly indicates that the terms ΑΡΓΥΡΙΟΝ and ΚΟΜΜΑ are simply to be understood as 'coin' without reference to denomination. Also of interest is the inscription ΓΟΡΤΥΝΟΣ ΤΟ ΠΑΙΜΑ on a coin of Gortyna (Central Crete, 480–430 BCE), where παιμα is derived from παίειν (trans. 'the [coin] struck by Gortynos'). Analogous to this usage would be Youroukova 145 ΚΟΤΥΟΣ ΧΑΡΑΚΤΗΡ. Additionally, Weidauer 39 ΦΑΝΟΣ ΕΜΙ ΣΕΜΑ (trans. 'I am the seal Phanos') on an early electrum stater of Ephesus, does seem to refer to a 'type'.

The term 'χαρακτήρ' has a fascinating history and complicated diachronic semantic evolution. Ulrich Wilckens identifies the term as a *nomen agentis* from χαράσσω, which itself derived from χάραξ, and therefore means 'to cut to a point', 'to sharpen'.[16] This is evident in such passages as Hesiod *Works and Days* 385–87 (700 BCE), 'Forty nights and days they are hidden and appear again as the year moves round, when first you sharpen (χαρασσομένοιο) your sickle', or 572–573, 'then it is no longer the season for digging vineyards, but to sharpen (χαρασσέμεναι) your sickles'.[17] At a later point χαρακτήρ appears as a *terminus technicus* for the minting of coins in Aristotle *Politica* 1257a.32–1257b.3 (384–322 BCE):

> ξενικωτέρας γὰρ γενομένης τῆς βοηθείας τῷ εἰσάγεσθαι ὧν ἐνδεεῖς καὶ ἐκπέμπειν ὧν ἐπλεόναζον, ἐξ ἀνάγκης ἡ τοῦ νομίσματος ἐπορίσθη χρῆσις. οὐ γὰρ εὐβάστακτον ἕκαστον τῶν κατὰ φύσιν ἀναγκαίων· διὸ πρὸς τὰς ἀλλαγὰς τοιοῦτόν τι συνέθεντο πρὸς σφᾶς αὐτοὺς διδόναι καὶ λαμβάνειν ὃ τῶν χρησίμων αὐτὸ ὂν εἶχε τὴν χρείαν εὐμεταχείριστον πρὸς τὸ ζῆν, οἷον σίδηρος καὶ ἄργυρος κἂν εἴ τι τοιοῦτον ἕτερον, τὸ μὲν πρῶτον ἁπλῶς ὁρισθὲν μεγέθει καὶ σταθμῷ, τὸ δὲ τελευταῖον καὶ **χαρακτῆρα** ἐπιβαλλόντων ἵνα ἀπολύσῃ τῆς μετρήσεως αὐτούς· ὁ γὰρ **χαρακτὴρ** ἐτέθη τοῦ ποσοῦ σημεῖον. πορισθέντος οὖν ἤδη νομίσματος ἐκ τῆς ἀναγκαίας ἀλλαγῆς ...

> For when they had come to supply themselves more from abroad by importing things in which they were deficient and exporting those of which they had a surplus, the employment of money necessarily came to be devised. For the natural necessaries are not in every case readily portable; hence for the purpose of barter men made a mutual compact to give and accept some substance of such a sort as being itself a useful commodity was easy to handle in use for general life, iron for instance, silver and other metals, at the first stage defined merely by size and weight, but finally also by impressing on it a **stamp** in order that this might relieve them of having to measure it; for the **stamp** was put on as a token of the amount. So when currency had been now invented as an outcome of the necessary interchange of goods ...[18]

---

[16] Werner Kelber, 'χαρακτήρ', *TDNT* 9: 418–423.

[17] G. W. Most, trans. *Hesiod: Theogony, Works and Days, Testimonia* (LCL 57; Cambridge, MA: Harvard University Press, 2006), 223–224.

[18] H. Rackham, trans. *Aristotle. Politics.* (LCL 264; Cambridge, MA: Harvard University Press, 1932), 42–43.

170   *Numismatics and Greek Lexicography*

One distinct contribution of this chapter is to provide a direct and actual example of the often stated etymological derivation of 'χαρακτήρ', as that 'relating to a coin die, image or seal'. Such an oversight in providing evidence is apparent in over fifty lexicons consulted for verifying this phenomenon.[19] Typical in this regard is Abbott-Smith's *A Manual Greek Lexicon of the New Testament* (1922) that simply lists the LXX references (Lev 13:28; 2 Macc 4:10; 4 Mac 15:4 ℵ R*) and provides the twofold definition: (1) a tool for engraving; (2) a stamp or impress: as on a coin or seal, with the addition of Hebrews 1:3 cited as the only example of metaphorical use.[20] The current suggestion of the incorporation of numismatic data broadens the attestation of this term in the first century BCE. Indeed, there is no doubt that such a definition can be extracted from the more ancient epigraphic record (cf. e.g. IG² II/III, 2.1408.11ff. from 385 BCE), yet even at this stage 'χαρακτήρ' could denote a coinage type 'ἦν δ' ὁ ἀρχαῖος χαρακτὴρ δίδραχμον' (Aristot. *Ath. pol. 10.2*). In P. Flor 1.61.21 (first century CE papyrus), the plural form refers to money in general; in BGU 1.88.7 (mid-second century CE), 'χαρακτήρ' refers to branding marks on camels; and in BGU 3.763.7 (early third century CE), it refers to a seal.

In Cicero's *Orator*, written as a summative manifesto and defence of rhetoric (46 BCE), directed particularly towards young Roman men who were reacting against traditional Roman values, he refers twice to 'χαρακτήρ' as a *terminus technicus* (it is after all a Greek word in a Latin text).

CICERO, *Orator* §11[21]

Sed in omni re difficillimum est formam, qui χαρακτήρ Graece dicitur, exponere optimi, quod aliud aliis videtur optimum.

It is always difficult to describe the 'form' or 'pattern' of the 'best' (for which the Greek word is χαρακτήρ) because different people have different notions of what is best.

CICERO, *Orator* §39[22]

Sed iam forma ipsa restat et χαρακτήρ ille qui dicitur. Qui qualis debeat esse ex eis ipsis quae supra dicta sunt intellegi potest.

There now remains the actual type and χαρακτήρ or 'character' as it is called; its ideal form can be recognized from what has been said above.

A similar use is apparent in Cicero's *Topica*, written for his colleague Trebatius Testa, which claims to be a summary of Aristotle's work of the same name.

---

[19] The only example found in all the secondary literature consulted is a passing reference in A. Körte 'Χαρακτήρ', *Hermes* 64, no. 1 (1928): 75.
[20] G. Abbott-Smith, *A Manual Greek Lexicon of the New Testament* (New York: Charles Scribner's Sons, 1922), 479.
[21] G. I. Hendrickson and H. M. Hubbnell, trans. *Cicero. Brutus. Orator* (LCL 342; Cambridge, MA: Harvard University Press, 1939), 330–331.
[22] Hendrickson and Hubbnell, *Cicero*, 406–407.

CICERO, *Topica* §22[23]

Cum autem quid sit quaeritur, notio explicanda est et proprietas et divisio et partitio. Haec enim sunt definitioni attributa; additur etiam descriptio, quam χαρακτῆρα Graeci vocant. Notio sic quaeritur: sitne id aequum quod ei qui plus potest utile est. Proprietas sic: in hominemne solum cadat an etiam in beluas aegritudo. Divisio et eodem pacto partitio sic: triane genera bonorum sint. Descriptio, qualis sit avarus, qualis assentator ceteraque eiusdem generis, in quibus et natura et vita describitur.

When the question concerns what a thing is, one has to explain the concept, and the peculiar or proper quality of the thing, analyze it and enumerate its parts. For these are the essentials of definition. We also include description, which the Greeks call χαρακτήρ. The concept is inquired into in this way: Is justice that which is to the advantage of the stronger? An example of inquiry into the peculiar or proper quality of a thing is the following question: Is grief incidental to man alone, or to the animals as well? Analysis and enumeration are treated in the same fashion: Are there three kinds of 'goods?' Description may be illustrated as follows: What sort of person a miser or a flatterer is, and other cases of the same sort, in which both a person's character and his manner of life are described.

In Cicero's preserved correspondence with his brother Quintus (*Letters to Quintus*) the Greek term is again applied in his Latin text to refer to the style or genre of literature.

CICERO *Letters to Quintus* 20.5[24]

Sed heus tu! celari videor a te. quo modo nam, mi frater, de nostris versibus Caesar? nam primum librum se legisse scripsit ad me ante, et prima sic ut neget se ne Graeca quidem meliora legisse; reliqua ad quendam locum ῥᾳθυμότερα (hoc enim utitur verbo). dic mihi verum: num aut res eum aut χαρακτὴρ non delectat? nihil est quod vereare. ego enim ne pilo quidem minus me amabo. hac de re φιλαλήθως et, ut soles [scribere], fraterne.

But see here, you seem to be keeping me in the dark. Tell me, my dear fellow, how does Caesar react to my verses? He wrote to me before that he read the first Canto and has never read anything better than the earlier part, even in Greek, but finds the rest, down to a certain point a trifle 'languid.' The truth, please! Is it the material or the style he doesn't like? No need for you to be nervous: my self-esteem won't drop a hair's-breadth. Just write to me en ami de la vérité and in your usual fraternal way.

A. Deissmann notes an inscription from Antigonea (Mantinea) dated to shortly after 27 BCE,[25] wherein the phrase 'μέχρι τῶν Σεβαστείων εὐπλόησεν χαρακτήρων'

---

[23] H. M. Hubbnell, trans. *Cicero. On Invention. The Best Kind of Orator. Topics* (LCL 386; Cambridge, MA: Harvard University Press, 1949), 446–447.

[24] D. R. Shackleton Bailey, trans. *Cicero. Letters to Quintus and Brutus. Letter Fragments. Letter to Octavian. Invectives. Handbook of Electioneering* (LCL 462; Cambridge, MA: Harvard University Press, 2002), 142–143.

[25] For the *editio princeps*, see Syll³ 783²³ in W. Dittenberger, *Syllogue Inscriptionum Graecarum* (Leipzig: Lipsiae S. Hirzel, 1977).

172   *Numismatics and Greek Lexicography*

(trans. 'he made a successful voyage to the August Persons' [Augustus and Livia]). This inscription is an example of χαρακτήρ as early evidence of the transferred sense of 'person',[26] an important development in the diachronic sketch of the lexeme. This is a phenomenon completely overlooked by most lexicons. Friberg and Miller simply state that the term is 'used figuratively in the NT of Christ in relation to God, [an] exact representation, precise reproduction, impress'.[27] Similarly, Bloomfield refers only to '"something graven, cut in, stamped," &c. a character, as a letter, mark, sign, stamp on coin'.[28] Lust, Eynikel and Hauspie refer to a physical mark, character or nature.[29]

Louw and Nida's grouping of 'χαρακτήρ' within section 58 (Nature, Class and Example), subsection I (Pattern, Model, Example and Corresponding Representation) as '58.62 χαρακτήρ, ῆρος m: a representation as an exact reproduction of a particular form or structure – "exact representation"',[30] is only partially accurate in designating the semantic possibilities of the lexeme. In addition to the 'representational' function, it was seen above that the meaning of the word could denote: (1) the minting of coinage (Aristotle *Politica* 1257a.32–1257b.3); (2) coinage type (Aristot. *Athēnaīn politeia*, 10.2); (3) money in general (P. Flor 1.61.21); (4) branding marks on camels (BGU 1.88.7); (5) specific reference to a seal (BGU 3.763.7); (6) a pattern (Cicero, *Orator* §36); (7) character (Cicero, *Orator* §134); (8) description (Cicero, *Topica* §83); (9) literary genre (Cicero, *Letters to Quintus* §20.5) and even (10) the transferred sense of 'person' (Syll3 783.23).[31] Ironically then, the attestation of χαρακτήρ on the coinage of Kotys II is not primarily related to the image on the coin but rather to the authority to strike/mint the coin, it is after all, an image of Herakles not Kotys on the coin. It would therefore be appropriate to translate Hebrews 1:3a, given the context of the passage and the background of the term, as 'he is the radiance of God's glory and the *authenticating mark* of God's very being, and he sustains all things by his powerful word'.

It is important to note that the term 'χαρακτήρ' does not imply any deficiency or diminished nature in the stated entity, such as, for example, the inferior difference between a photograph of an object and the object itself, or to complete the analogy, in reference to the camera or the even the operator. This is confirmed by the parallel term 'ἀπαύγασμα' ['radiance' or 'reflection'] in the preceding phrase.[32] Precisely this

---

[26] Adolf Deissmann, *Light from the Ancient East: The New Testament Illustrated by Recently Discovered Texts of the Greco-Roman World*, trans. Lionel R. M. Strachan (New York: Harper & Brothers, 1922), 341 n.1.

[27] Timothy Friberg, Barbara Friberg, and Neva F. Miller, *Analytical Lexicon of the Greek New Testament* (Grand Rapids, MI: Baker Books, 2000), 407.

[28] S. T. Bloomfield, *A Greek and English Lexicon to the New Testament* (London: Longman, Orme, Brown, Green, & Longmans, 1840), 467.

[29] Johan Lust, Erik Eynikel, and Katrin Hauspie, *A Greek-English Lexicon of the Septuagint: Revised Edition* (Deutsche Bibelgesellschaft: Stuttgart, 2003).

[30] L&N, 591–592.

[31] Of the eleven glosses in LSJ, the penultimate entry is that of 'impress, image' for which Hebrew 1:3 is cited as support.

[32] An interesting pairing of 'ἀπαύγασμα' and a term related to 'χαρακτήρ', namely 'εἰκών' occurs in Wisdom 7:26, 'For she is a reflection (ἀπαύγασμα) of eternal light, a spotless mirror of the working of God, and an image (εἰκών) of his goodness.' Lane, *Hebrews 1–8*, 13 states 'The concentration of rare and distinctive vocabulary to describe the relationship of the Son to God has been one factor that has encouraged many interpreters to find in v 3 a hymn-fragment.'

ΧΑΡΑΚΤΗΡ

dimension is captured in Theodore of Mopsuestia's (*c.* 350–428) *Fragments on the Epistle to the Hebrews* 1.2–3, who states that 1:3 'explicates the point of the analogy ... For he says that Christ preserves an accurate representation of God's nature, so that whatever you would think God's nature to be, so you must also think Christ's nature to be, inasmuch as Christ's nature bears the accurate representation of God's nature since Christ's nature does not differ from God's in the least'.[33] This is not to say however, that the 'χαρακτήρ' and 'ἀπαύγασμα' form a hendiadys, such as the claim by Kittel 'they thus intentionally say the same thing ... the same function of the Son is expressed by ἀπαύγασμα and χαρακτήρ'.[34] Rather, the phrases are in synthetic parallelism, where the second adds meaning to the first, insofar as the Son is both the 'ἀπαύγασμα' ('radiance' or 'reflection') and 'χαρακτήρ' ('authenticating mark') of God.

Conclusion

Consideration of the numismatic record has revealed that the term 'χαρακτήρ' on coinage of the Ordrysian kings of Thrace is used in a similar fashion to 'κόπτειν' ('to strike') and 'παίειν' ('to strike'), that is, as the authenticating mark of a ruler, official or superior. This observation, combined with the material from Cicero's technical use of the term as 'authentic character', and the diachronic development in relation to persons in the transferred sense in the inscriptional evidence, together with other sources, demonstrate that the semantic domain of 'χαρακτήρ' is much more complicated, and indeed nuanced, than the current portrayal and English glosses of the term in the lexicons.

---

[33] K. Staab, ed., *Pauluskommentare aus der griechischen Kirche* (Münster: Aschendorff, 1933), 201.
[34] TDNT 9.421.

10

ΚΤΙΣΤΗΣ

Introduction

Κτίστης (1 Pet 4:19) is a New Testament *hapax legomenon*, and is characteristically translated 'creator' in modern English versions. Thus, ASV, CEB, CJB, ESV, GW, GNT, HCSB, KJV, NAS, NCV, NIV, NKJV, NRSV, YLT.[1] As before, attention to the numismatic record is sought to bring greater specificity to the term and clarify its semantic domain. We will explore the possibility that the author of 1 Peter had a particular aspect of κτίστης in view. Coinage assessed below is attested throughout the breadth of the Mediterranean world, including Asia Minor, Greece, Italy, Egypt and Judea.

The historical and literary context of 1 Peter 4:19

The epistle of 1 Peter is addressed παρεπιδήμοις διασπορᾶς (trans. 'to the exiles of the dispersion') in the provinces of Asia (1:1). Διασπορά is used in the Septuagint twelve times in reference to the scattering of the Israelites among the Gentile nations.[2] The author of 1 Peter evidently reinterprets the term in reference to Gentile Christians (1:14, 18; 2:10; 4:3) scattered throughout Asia Minor. Rather than widespread formal persecution, it seems that this environment was socially hostile to Christian belief and practice, in so far as Christians have been λυπηθέντες ἐν ποικίλοις πειρασμοῖς (trans. 'distressed by various trials' [1 Pet 1:6]). The writer has a relatively developed vocabulary for these trials, including forms from δοκιμάζω ('testing' [1 Pet 1:7]); πάθημα/πάσχω ('suffering' [1 Pet 1:11; 2:19–21, 23; 3:14, 17–18; 4:1, 13, 15–16, 19; 5:1, 9–10]); κολαφίζω ('beaten/ harshly treated' [1 Pet 2:20]). These elements of marginalization apparently were experienced as φόβος ('intimidation' [1 Pet 3:14]); καταλαλέω ('slander' [1 Pet 3:16]); and ὀνειδίζω ('vilification' [1 Pet 4:14]), and social marginalization (ἐν ᾧ ξενίζονται μὴ συντρεχόντων ὑμῶν εἰς τὴν αὐτὴν τῆς ἀσωτίας ἀνάχυσιν βλασφημοῦντες, 'They are surprised that you no longer join them in the same excesses of dissipation, and so they malign you [NASB]/heap abuse on you [NIV]' [1 Pet 4:4]). L. T. Johnson astutely

---

[1] Compare, however, 'maker' in BBE, WYC; and 'who made you' in NLT.
[2] Deut 28:25; 30:4; Neh 1:9; Ps 146:2; Isa 49:6; Jer 15:7; 41:17; Dan 12:2; Jdt 5:19; 2 Macc 1:27; Song 8:28; 9:2.

176   *Numismatics and Greek Lexicography*

notes that 'persecution may bring death, but with meaning. Societal scorn can threaten meaning itself, which is a more subtle form of death'.[3]

In this light, 1 Peter's literary intentions appear to be twofold: to encourage and instruct. Encouragement comes primarily through bestowing status upon the believing community, describing them in traditional Jewish nationalistic language (e.g. 1 Peter 2:9–10, '...chosen race, a royal priesthood, a holy nation ... God's people', echoing Exod 19:6; Isa 43:20–21 and Hos 2:25), and referring to the recipients as privileged to exist in such a time (1 Pet 1:10–12). The author assures his readers that the suffering they are encountering should not be regarded as peculiar (4:12), but as the foreseeable experience of believers in an evil society (5:9). Ethical instruction is argued for in light of the responsibility of the previously bestowed status upon the ecclesiastical community.

The literary structure of 1 Peter in its broadest sense is designated by the dual demarcation of the direct address ἀγαπητοί ('beloved brethren') in 2:11 and 4:12. As a result the epistle is divided into three sections. The first section (1:1–2:10) sets the theological foundation for the subsequent discussion, the second section (2:11–4:10) highlights the inevitability of Christian suffering and the third section (4:11–5:14) consists of an exhortation amid the present and imminent future suffering.

The verse under discussion (4:19) falls within the third and shortest section of the epistle. As noted above, κτίστης (4:19) is an NT *hapax legomenon*, and is characteristically translated 'creator' in modern English versions.[4] In a recent article, E. Bons and A. Passoni state that 'it is legitimate to understand [κτίστης] ... against the semantic background of the root κτίζω'.[5] Attention to the numismatic record, however, which is conspicuously lacking in scholarly treatments, broadens the semantic domain of the word beyond this strict category of cosmological creator, especially so in light of the literary and historical context of 1 Peter.

Numismatic material on Κτίστης and related terms

Coinage throughout the breadth of the Mediterranean world, including Asia Minor, Greece, Italy, Egypt and Judea, amply attests to the use of κτίστης, not in the traditional sense of the Judeo-Christian category of 'creator', but rather with reference to political function.

---

[3] L. T. Johnson, *The Writings of the New Testament* (Philadelphia, PA: Fortress, 1986), 435.

[4] Thus, ASV, CEB, CJB, ESV, GW, GNT, HCSB, KJV, NAS, NCV, NIV, NKJV, NRSV, YLT. Cf., however, 'maker' in BBE, WYC; 'who made you' in NLT.

[5] E. Bons and A. Passoni Dell'Acqua, 'A Sample Article: κτίζω – κτίσις – κτίσμα – κτίστης', in *Septuagint Vocabulary: Pre-History, Usage, Reception*, ed. E. Bons and J. Joosten (Atlanta, GA: Society of Biblical Literature, 2011), 173–187 at 186. See also E. Bons, 'Le verbe κτίζω comme terme technique de la création dans la Septante et dans le Nouveau Testament', in *Voces Biblicae: Septuagint Greek and the Significance for the New Testament*, ed. J. Joosten and P. J. Tomson (Louvain: Peeters, 2007), 1–15.

Province of Bithynia and Pontus

Coinage of Bithynia and Pontus uses the term κτίστης in precisely this manner.

Nicaea: RPC 1.2049 (Figure 57) consists of a bronze coin from Nicaea (northwestern Anatolia), minted in 54 CE during the reign of Nero. On the obverse, accompanied by the bare head of the emperor, the inscription reads, ΝΕΡΩΝ ΚΛΑΥΔΙΟΣ ΚΑΙΣΑΡ ΣΕΒΑΣΤ ('Nero Claudius Caesar Augustus'). The reverse has a prominent and detailed depiction of a garlanded altar, around which is inscribed, ΔΙΟΝΥΣΟΥ ΚΤΙΣΤΟΥ ΝΕΙΚΑΙΑΣ ('of Dionysus, founder of Nicaea'). Nicaea had a relatively simple mythological founding. It was generally attributed to Dionysus or Heracles, and named after the nymph Nicaea. Its political history, however, is substantially more complex. The city was established by soldiers of Alexander the Great, was then overtaken by Antigonus I and re-named Antigoneia, only to be secured by Lysimachus in 301 BCE and re-founded as Nicaea, in memory of his recently deceased wife. Roman control of Nicaea was gained in 72 BCE, and the city enjoyed prominence both in political function (the seat of the Roman governor) and as an intersection of trade routes. Strabo goes so far as to refer to Nicaea as the metropolis of Bithynia (12.4.7). The imagery and message of the coin is clear. Nero is legitimate heir to Dionysus's founding of the city.

Caesarea Germanica: RPC 1.2017 (Figure 58) was minted during the reign of Tiberius (*c.* 20 CE) shortly after the foundation of Caesarea Germanica by Germanicus (Germanicus Julius Caesar, 16 BCE–19 CE, nephew of Emperor Tiberius). The obverse has a bare head facing right with the inscription, ΓΕΡΜΑΝΙΚΟΣ ΚΑΙΣΑΡ ΚΤΙΣΤΗΣ ('Germanicos Caesar, founder'). The reverse has ΚΑΙΣΑΡΗΑ ΓΕΡΜΑΝΙΚΗ ('Caesarea Germanica') with a view of the city gate. A. H. M. Jones,[6] following W. Waddington,

Figure 57 RPC 1.2049 (used with permission).

---

[6] A. H. M. Jones, *Cities of the Eastern Roman Provinces* (Oxford: Clarendon Press, 1971), 163.

Figure 58 RPC 1.2017 (used with permission).

E. Babelon and T. Reinach,[7] proposes that this coin commemorates the re-foundation of an Augustan city.

Cius: Four coin types from Cius (RPC 1.2022–2025), issued during the reign of Claudius, refer to Heracles as the legendary founder of the city. The obverse of all four have a bare head facing right, with the inscription ΤΙ ΚΛΑΥΔΙΟΣ ΣΕΒΑΣΤΟΣ ΓΕΡΜΑΝΙΚΟΣ ('Tiberius Claudius Augustus Germanicus'). The obverse of all four have the identical inscription ΗΡΑΚΛΕΟΥΣ ΚΤΙΣΤΟΥ ΚΙΑΝΩΝ ('of Heracles the founder of Cius'),[8] but with varying iconography: 2022 has Heracles standing facing left, with club and lion skin; 2023 has a lion skin draped over a club; 2024 has a quiver and arrows in a case and 2025 has a club. Each of these coins commemorates the foundation of the city.

Province of Archaea

The Roman province of Archaea yields a similarly impressive result of relevant lexicographic data.

Nicopolis: RPC 1.1363 (Figure 59) is a copper coin of from Nicopolis, a city founded by Augustus in celebration of his victory at the nearby battle of Actium. The obverse of 1363 has inscribed ΚΤΙΣΜΑ ΣΕΒΑΣΤΟΥ ('foundation of Augustus') within a wreath. The reverse has ΝΙΚΟΠΟΛΙΣ ΙΕΡΑ ('Nicopolis the sacred'). Similar is RPC 1.1364, a leaded bronze, with identical obverse inscription and similar iconography, the only

---

[7] W. Waddington, E. Babelon and T. Reinach, *Recueil Général des Monnaies Grecques d'Asie Mineure* (Paris: Ernest Leroux, 1912), 281.
[8] This is erroneously listed in RPC I as ΗΡΑΚΛΗΣ ΚΤΙΣΤΗΣ ΚΙΑΝΩΝ.

Figure 59 RPC 1.1363 (used with permission).

variation being the omission of the wreath. When Nero later re-founded the city, it was eponymously entitled Nerononicopolis,[9] as is evident from the inscription on the obverse of RPC 1.1368, 1369, 1370, ΝΕΡΩΝΟΝΙΚΟΠΟΛΙΣ ... ('Nerononicopolis ... '), an issue of Nicopolis coins commemorating Nero's visit to Greece in 66–67 CE. Similarly RPC 1.1373 is a copper coin minted under Nero. On the obverse, accompanied by the laureate head of Nero, is the inscription, ΝΕΡΩΝΙ ΑΠΟΛΛΩΝΙ ΚΤΙΣΤΗ ('for Nero-Apollo, the founder'). The reverse depicts Nike standing facing left with a wreath and palm, with the possessive genitive ΝΕΡΩΝΟΣ ('of Nero'). RPC 1.1374 and 1375 have the same obverse die as 1373, but the reverse depicts Nike either running left (RPC 1.1374), or advancing right (RPC 1.1375). Similarly RPC 1.1376 is a leaded bronze, which on the obverse depicts Nero standing facing right while Apollo plays the lyre, with the inscription ΝΕΡΩΝΙ ΑΠΟΛΛΩΝΙ ΚΤΙΣΤΗ (for Nero-Apollo, the founder). The reverse has Eleutheria standing, holding the pileus and patera, with ΝΕΡΩΝΙ ΔΗΜΟΣΙΩ ΠΑΤΡΩΝΙ ΕΛΛΑΔΟΣ ('for Nero, public patron of Greece').

Province of Asia

The province of Asia also attests to this phenomenon.

Clazomenae: There is a series of coins (41–54 CE) from Clazomenae characterized by the inscription ΣΕΒΑΣΤΟΣ ΚΤΙΣΤΗΣ ('Augustus, founder'). RPC 1.2492 is a leaded bronze with the bare head of Augustus facing right with a star to the right on the obverse, with the inscription ΣΕΒΑΣΤΟΣ ('Augustus'). The reverse depicts Athena, standing facing right holding out her hand below a star and resting her arm

---

[9] B. E. Levy, 'Nero's "Apollonia" Series: The Achaean Context', *Numismatic Chronicle* 149 (1989): 59–68.

on a shield. The reverse inscription reads ΚΛΑΖΟΜΕΝΙΩΝ ΚΤΙΣΤΗΣ ('founder of Clazomenae'). RPC 1.2493 is identical except that the head on the obverse faces left. RPC 1.2494 reads ΣΕΒΑΣΤΟΣ ΚΤΙΣΤΗΣ ('Augustus, founder') with a bare right facing portrait. The obverse depicts an owl facing, with the inscription ΚΛΑΖΟΜΕΝΙΩΝ ('of Clazomenae'). RPC 1.2495 (Figure 60) has the identical inscription as 2494, but replaces the owl on the reverse with a right-facing walking warrior, carrying spear and shield. RPC 1.2492–2495 all commemorate the re-founding of Clazomenae by Augustus, presumably after the earthquake of 12 BCE, as noted by D. Magie[10] and W. H. Gross,[11] although it is possible that it was a result of an earlier earthquake, such as that in 26/25 BCE[12] or 47/46 BCE.[13]

Magnesia: RPC 1.2451 is a coin of Tiberius with laureate head facing right on the obverse, with the inscription ΤΙΒΕΡΙΟΝ ΣΕΒΑΣΤΟΝ ΚΤΙΣΤΗΝ ('Tiberius Augustus, founder'). The reverse has the inscription ΜΑΓΝΗΣΤΩΝ ΑΠΟ ΣΙΠΥΛΟΥ ('Magnesia at Sipylon'). The iconography of the reverse is key to its interpretation. Tiberius raises a turreted figure that Burnett identifies as a 'gesture of restoration' (i.e. the Tyche of Magnesia),[14] and refers to the help provided by Tiberius to Magnesia after the earthquake of 17 CE. Tacitus records that twelve cities were destroyed or severely damaged by the earthquake:

Figure 60 RPC 1.2495.

---

[10] D. Magie, *Roman Rule in Asia Minor* (Princeton, NJ: Princeton University Press, 1950), 479.
[11] W. H. Gross, *Iulia Augusta* (Göttingen: Vandenhoeck & Ruprecht, 1962), 34.
[12] Magie, *Roman Rule*, 469.
[13] A. Davesne, 'Numismatique ct archeologie: Le Temple de Dionysos a Teos', *Revue Numismatique* 29 (1987): 15–20.
[14] Andrew Burnett, Michel Amandry, and Ian Carradice, *Roman Provincial Coinage: Volumes 1–2* (London: British Museum, 1992–1999).

Twelve populous cities of Asia were shattered by an earthquake which happened during the night, so that the blow was all the more abrupt and appalling. And the usual resource in such calamity – flight into some open space – was here of no avail, as the earth yawned and swallowed them up .... Next to them [i.e. Sardis] the largest amount of suffering a relief fell to the Magnesians of Mount Sipylus. (*Ann.* 2.47)

In seeking to maximize political capital Tiberius struck coins commemorating his own generosity in 22–23 CE. The obverses of *British Museum Catalogue*[15] (*BMC* Roman) 70, 71, 72 and 73 depict Tiberius, laureate, togate, seated left on curule chair, his feet resting on a stool, holding a patera (shallow ceramic or metal libation bowl) in his right hand and a long sceptre in his left. The obverse inscription reads CIVITATIBVS ASIAE RESTITVTIS ('cities of Asia restored'). The Asia cities formally responded in varying levels of gratitude. Some changed their names in honour of the emperor (Hierapolis > Hierocaesarea; Kibyra > Kibyra Caesarea; Philadelphia > Neocaesarea; Sardis > Sardis Caesarea). Others issued special coins in commemoration of financial support. The obverse of RPC 1.2991 (Figure 61) depicts a togate figure of the emperor raising the kneeling figure of Tyche of Sardis, with the inscription ΣΕΒΑΣΤΟΣ ΚΑΙΣΑΡΕΩΝ ΣΑΡΔΙΑΝΩΝ ('Augustus, Caesarea Sardis'). In further gratitude Sardis erected a statue (43 CE) in Tiberius's honour, with the accompanying inscription (SEG 36 [1986] 1092) identifying him as ΤΗΣ ΠΟΛΕΩΣ ΚΤΙΣΤΗΣ[16] ('the founder of the city').

Figure 61 RPC 1.2991 (used with permission).

---

[15] H. Mattingly, *Coins of the Roman Empire in the British Museum*, 6 vols. (London: British Museum, 1923–1976), 1.
[16] κτίστης, ου, ὁ is a first declension masculine noun and thus in the genitive should read ΚΤΙΣΤΟΥ, rather than ΚΤΙΣΤΗΣ as per inscription (SEG 36 [1986] 1092).

Teos: RPC 1.2511 (Figure 62) is an Augustan issue (27 BCE–14 CE) which on the obverse depicts a temple with four columns enclosing a bare head which faces to the right, with accompanying inscription which reads ΣΕΒΑΣΤΟΣ ΚΤΙΣΤΗΣ ('Augustus, founder'). RPC 1.2512 (Figure 63) has the identical inscription with the bare head facing right.

Figure 62 RPC 1.2511.

Figure 63 RPC 1.2512.

Figure 64 RPC 1.3601.

Province of Cappadocia

The province of Cappadocia has produced an example of comparative interest from Caesarea. Cappadocia was incorporated into the Roman Empire as a province in 17 CE. Archelaus, Cappadocia's last king, minted silver drachms at Elaeusa. RPC 1.3601 (Figure 64) is an issue from 17/16 BCE and depicts a diademed head of Archelaus on the obverse, with no inscription. The reverse has a depiction of a club, a mint mark (K) and the following inscription: ΒΑΣΙΛΕΩΣ ΑΡΧΕΛΑΟΥ ΦΙΛΟΠΑΤΡΙΔΟΣ ΚΤΙΣΤΟΥ ('of King Archelaus, loving the fatherland, founder').

Province of Judea

The province of Judea also attests to similar terminology employed with reference to the foundation of the city rather than implying necessary characteristics of a cosmological creator. Upon the division of Herod the Great's kingdom by Augustus between his three surviving sons, Philip became tetrarch over Gaulanitis, Trachonitis, Batanea and Paneas (cf. Lk. 3:1). Given the distance from Jerusalem, the epicentre of Jewish religious life in the first century, it is no surprise that Philip is disinterested in the Jewish prohibition of making graven images. Thus, images of both the Caesar and Philip are attested on his coinage. The obverse of RPC 1.4948 (Figure 65) has a bare head of Tiberius facing right, with the inscription, ΤΙΒΕΡΙΟΣ ΣΕΒΑΣΤΟΣ ΚΑΙΣΑΡ ('Tiberius Augustus Caesar'). The reverse has a temple with four columns, with the inscription ΕΠΙ ΦΙΛΙΠΠΟΥ ΤΕΤΡΑΡΧΟΥ ΚΤΙΣ L ΛΔ ('in the time of the founder Philip the tetrarch, year 34'). The circumstances behind this numismatic issue are obviously Philip's re-

Figure 65 RPC 1.4948.

founding of Paneas as Caesarea, and making it his capital. Burnett identifies the temple depicted on the obverse as the temple of Augustus, originally built by Herod.[17]

New Testament lexeme

The verb κτίζω occurs fifteen times in the NT (Mt 19:4; Mk 13:19; Rom 1:25; 1 Cor 11:9; Eph 2:10, 15; 3:9; 4:24; Col 1:16; 3:10; 1 Tim 4:3; Rev 4:11; 10:6 [see Table 18]), specifically in reference to making or creating that which had 'not existed before',[18] exclusively used in reference to God's 'activity in creation'.[19]

The feminine noun κτίσις occurs nineteen times in the NT (Mk 10:6; 13:19; 16:15; Rom 1:20, 25; 8:19–22, 39; 2 Cor 5:17; Gal 6:15; Col 1:15, 23; Heb 4:13; 9:11; 1 Pet 2:13; 2 Pet 3:4; Rev 3:14 [see Table 19]) and again refers exclusively to the act of creation or the result of a creative act. The only exception is 1 Peter 2:13 where the noun refers to 'system of established authority that is the result of some founding action, governance system, authority system'.[20]

---

[17] RPC 1.680.
[18] L&N, §40.35.
[19] L&N, §40.35.
[20] BDAG s.v. κτίσις.

ΚΤΙΣΤΗΣ

185

Table 18 New Testament examples of κτίζω

Mt 19:4	οὐκ ἀνέγνωτε ὅτι ὁ κτίσας ἀπ᾿ ἀρχῆς ἄρσεν ἐποίησεν αὐτούς;
Mk 13:19	ἀπ᾿ ἀρχῆς κτίσεως ἣν ἔκτισεν ὁ θεός
Rom 1:25	τῇ κτίσει παρὰ τὸν κτίσαντα, ὅς ἐστιν εὐλογητός
1 Cor 11:9	καὶ γὰρ οὐκ ἐκτίσθη ἀνὴρ διὰ τὴν γυναῖκα
Eph 2:10	αὐτοῦ γάρ ἐσμεν ποίημα, κτισθέντες ἐν Χριστῷ Ἰησοῦ
Eph 2:15	ἵνα τοὺς δύο κτίσῃ ἐν αὐτῷ εἰς ἕνα καινὸν ἄνθρωπον
Eph 3:9	ἐν τῷ θεῷ τῷ τὰ πάντα κτίσαντι
Eph 4:24	τὸν κατὰ θεὸν κτισθέντα ἐν δικαιοσύνῃ
Col 1:16	ὅτι ἐν αὐτῷ ἐκτίσθη τὰ πάντα
Col 1:16	τὰ πάντα δι᾿ αὐτοῦ καὶ εἰς αὐτὸν ἔκτισται
Col 3:10	εἰς ἐπίγνωσιν κατ᾿ εἰκόνα τοῦ κτίσαντος αὐτόν
1 Tim 4:3	ἃ ὁ θεὸς ἔκτισεν εἰς μετάλημψιν μετὰ εὐχαριστίας
Rev 4:11	ὅτι σὺ ἔκτισας τὰ πάντα
Rev 4:11	διὰ τὸ θέλημά σου ἦσαν καὶ ἐκτίσθησαν
Rev 10:6	ὃς ἔκτισεν τὸν οὐρανὸν καὶ τὰ ἐν αὐτῷ καὶ τὴν γῆν

Table 19 New Testament examples of κτίσις

Mk 10:6	ἀπὸ δὲ ἀρχῆς κτίσεως ἄρσεν καὶ θῆλυ ἐποίησεν αὐτούς
Mk 13:19	ἀπ᾿ ἀρχῆς κτίσεως ἣν ἔκτισεν ὁ θεός
Mk 16:15	κηρύξατε τὸ εὐαγγέλιον πάσῃ τῇ κτίσει
Rom 1:20	τὰ γὰρ ἀόρατα αὐτοῦ ἀπὸ κτίσεως κόσμου
Rom 1:25	καὶ ἐλάτρευσαν τῇ κτίσει παρὰ τὸν κτίσαντα
Rom 8:19	ἡ γὰρ ἀποκαραδοκία τῆς κτίσεως τὴν ἀποκάλυψιν τῶν υἱῶν τοῦ θεοῦ ἀπεκδέχεται
Rom 8:20	τῇ γὰρ ματαιότητι ἡ κτίσις ὑπετάγη
Rom 8:21	καὶ αὐτὴ ἡ κτίσις ἐλευθερωθήσεται ἀπὸ τῆς δουλείας
Rom 8:22	ὅτι πᾶσα ἡ κτίσις συστενάζει καὶ συνωδίνει
Rom 8:39	οὔτε ὕψωμα οὔτε βάθος οὔτε τις κτίσις ἑτέρα δυνήσεται ἡμᾶς χωρίσαι
2 Cor 5:17	εἴ τις ἐν Χριστῷ, καινὴ κτίσις
Gal 6:15	οὔτε γὰρ περιτομή τί ἐστιν οὔτε ἀκροβυστία ἀλλὰ καινὴ κτίσις
Col 1:15	πρωτότοκος πάσης κτίσεως
Col 1:23	τοῦ κηρυχθέντος ἐν πάσῃ κτίσει τῇ ὑπὸ τὸν οὐρανόν
Heb 4:13	καὶ οὐκ ἔστιν κτίσις ἀφανὴς ἐνώπιον αὐτοῦ
Heb 9:11	τοῦτ᾿ ἔστιν οὐ ταύτης τῆς κτίσεως
1 Pet 2:13	ὑποτάγητε πάσῃ ἀνθρωπίνῃ κτίσει διὰ τὸν κύριον
2 Pet 3:4	πάντα οὕτως διαμένει ἀπ᾿ ἀρχῆς κτίσεως
Rev 3:14	ἡ ἀρχὴ τῆς κτίσεως τοῦ θεοῦ

The neuter noun κτίσμα occurs four times in the NT, always in reference to that which is created by God, either specifically present physical creation (1 Tim 4:4; Rev 5:13; 8:9) or with reference to future eschatological new creation (Jas 1:18) (see Table 20).

The final derivative of κτίζω attested in the NT is the single occurrence of κτίστης (1 Pet 4:19) itself (see Table 21).

BDAG lists 'the Creator' as a gloss for κτίστης, providing examples of the word referring to both pagan and Jewish/Christian deities (including a reference to 1 Pet 4:19). However, in all examples provided to support this gloss in BDAG, bar 1 Peter 4:19, the noun has an adjunct, that is, an element not required syntactically, but provided to add additional information about the noun. Such is also the case with seven of the eight occurrences of the term in the LXX. The reference in 2 Kgdms 22:32, where κτίστης lacks an adjunct, is best understood within the context of God founding and continuing David's kingship (cf. MT *tzwr*, masc sing abs = rock). BDAG does, however, also acknowledge that κτίστης is used as a 'designation of rulers and others of high rank',[21] citing predominantly inscriptional evidence in support (SIG 751, 2; 839, 8; I. Priene 229, 4; CIG II 2572). This however has not filtered down into the array of glosses available in the standard lexicons (cf. further references in Table 22).[22]

Table 20 New Testament examples of κτίσμα

1 Tim 4:4	ὅτι πᾶν κτίσμα θεοῦ καλόν
Jas 1:18	εἰς τὸ εἶναι ἡμᾶς ἀπαρχήν τινα τῶν αὐτοῦ κτισμάτων
Rev 5:13	καὶ πᾶν κτίσμα ὃ ἐν τῷ οὐρανῷ
Rev 8:9	τὸ τρίτον τῶν κτισμάτων τῶν ἐν τῇ θαλάσσῃ

Table 21 New Testament example of κτίστης

1 Pet 4:19	πιστῷ κτίστῃ παρατιθέσθωσαν τὰς ψυχάς

Table 22 LXX examples of κτίστης

2 Kgdms 22:32	καὶ τίς κτίστης ἔσται πλὴν τοῦ θεοῦ ἡμῶν;
Jdt 9:12	δέσποτα τῶν οὐρανῶν καὶ τῆς γῆς, κτίστα τῶν ὑδάτων
2 Macc 1:24	ὁ θεός, ὁ πάντων κτίστης
2 Macc 7:23	ὁ τοῦ κόσμου κτίστης ὁ πλάσας ἀνθρώπου
2 Macc 13:14	δοὺς δὲ τὴν ἐπιτροπὴν τῷ κτίστῃ τοῦ κόσμου
4 Macc 5:25	ἡμῖν συμπαθεῖ νομοθετῶν ὁ τοῦ κόσμου κτίστης
4 Macc 11:5	ὅτι τὸν πάντων κτίστην εὐσεβοῦμεν
Sir 24:8	ἐνετείλατό μοι ὁ κτίστης ἁπάντων

---

[21] BDAG, 573.
[22] See further Bons and Dell'Acqua, 'A Sample Article', 183.

ΚΤΙΣΤΗΣ

Given this breadth, one would anticipate that Louw and Nida's *Greek-English Lexicon of the New Testament Based on Semantic Domains* would be sensitive to the elements we have explored thus far. However, this is unfortunately not evident in their classification of NT lexemes.[23] Domain 42, entitled 'Perform, Do' contains five subdomains: A Function (42.1–42.6); B Do, Perform (42.7–42.28); C Make, Create (42.29–42.40); D Work, Toil (42.41–42.50) and E Craft, Trade (42.51–42.53). The entry for 'κτίστης' is grouped exclusively within subdomain C: Make, Create.

42.40 κτίστης, ου *m:* (derivative of κτίζω 'to create,' 42.35) one who creates – 'creator.' πιστῷ κτίστη παρατιθέσθωσαν τὰς ψυχὰς αὐτῶν 'they should entrust themselves completely to their Creator.' 1 Pet 4:19[24]

Louw and Nida seem to be on surer footing with κτίσις, which is grouped both with subdomain D: Rule/Govern within domain 37 (Control, Rule) *and* subdomain C: Make, Create within domain 42 (Perform, Do).

37.43 κτίσις[e], εως *f:* an instituted authority, with the implication that such an authority has been created or formed – 'authority.' ὑποτάγητε πάσῃ ἀνθρωπίνῃ κτίσει διὰ τὸν κύριον 'for the sake of the Lord, submit yourselves to every human authority' 1Pe 2:13. The expression 'human authority' may be rendered as 'every person who has the right to rule.' For another interpretation of κτίσις in 1 Pet 2:13, see 42.39.[25]

42.38 κτίσις[b], εως *f;* κτίσμα, τος *n:* that which has been created – 'creation, creature, what has been created.' κτίσις: ἐλάτρευσαν τῇ κτίσει παρὰ τὸν κτίσαντα 'they worshiped what has been created instead of the one who created' Ro 1:25. κτίσμα: ἀπέθανεν τὸ τρίτον τῶν κτισμάτων τῶν ἐν τῇ θαλάσσῃ 'a third of the creatures of the sea died.' Re 8:9[26]

42.39 κτίσις[d], εως *f:* (derivative of κτίζω 'to create,' 42.35) a human institution or social structure as something which has been created – 'institution, structure.' ὑποτάγητε πάσῃ ἀνθρωπίνῃ κτίσει διὰ τὸν κύριον 'be subject to every human institution on account of the Lord' 1Pe 2:13. It is possible that κτίσις in 1Pe 2:13 may have the implication of 'authorized institution.' It might even be possible to render κτίσις in such a context as 'authority' (compare κτίσις[e] in 37.43).[27]

A similar nuancing is required for κτίστης in further revisions of semantic groupings of NT vocabulary. Namely the distinction needs to be drawn between κτίστης as cosmological creator, and κτίστης as founder, that is, one who securely establishes

---

[23] Hans-Helmut Esser's groups the following together under the same lexeme: κτίζω create, produce; κτίσις creation, creature; κτίσμα created thing, creature; κτίστης originator, creator (H.-H. Esser, 'Creation, Foundation, Creature, Maker', *NIDNNT* 1: 376–389. In specific reference to κτίστης in 1 Pet 4:19, the gloss 'creator' is provided without any further explanation [Esser, *NIDNNT* 1:378]).

[24] L&N, 515.

[25] L&N, 477.

[26] L&N, 414.

[27] L&N, 514–515.

188 Numismatics and Greek Lexicography

a city or people, guaranteeing their safety and well-being.[28] This usage is not only supported by the numismatic material surveyed above, but copious literary sources composed before, during and after the NT period. The selective portion below is listed to nuance and gently challenge Bons and Passoni Dell'Acqua's statement that 'the literary occurrences ... [are] rare'.[29]

Appian, *Roman History 1. The Kings (Fragments)*, 1.2.[30]
ὧν ὁ πρῶτος κτίστης τε Ῥώμης καὶ οἰκιστὴς γεγονώς, ἄρξας τε πατρικῶς μᾶλλον ἢ τυραννικῶς, ὅμως ἐσφάγη, ἢ ὡς ἄλλοι φασίν, ἠφανίσθη

The first of these was the founder and builder of Rome, and although he governed it rather as a father than as an absolute monarch, he was nevertheless slain, or, as some think, translated.

Lucian, *Octogenarians*, §13.[31]
Μιθριδάτης δὲ ὁ Πόντου βασιλεὺς ὁ προσαγορευθεὶς Κτίστης Ἀντίγονον τὸν μονόφθαλμον φεύγων ἐπὶ Πόντου ἐτελεύτησεν βιώσας ἔτη τέσσαρα καὶ ὀγδοήκοντα

Mithridates, king of Pontus, called the Founder, exiled by Antigonus One-eye, died in Pontus at eighty-four,

Plutarch, *Lives. Camillus*, 1.[32]
Περὶ δὲ Φουρίου Καμίλλου πολλῶν καὶ μεγάλων λεγομένων ἴδιον εἶναι δοκεῖ μάλιστα καὶ παράδοξον, ὅτι πλεῖστα μὲν ἐν ἡγεμονίαις καὶ μέγιστα κατορθώσας, δικτάτωρ δὲ πεντάκις αἱρεθείς, θριαμβεύσας δὲ τετράκις, κτίστης δὲ τῆς Ῥώμης ἀναγραφεὶς δεύτερος, οὐδὲ ἅπαξ ὑπάτευσε.

Turning now to Furius Camillus, among the many notable things that are told of him, this seems the most singular and strange, namely, that although in other offices of command he won many and great successes, and although he was five times chosen dictator, four times celebrated a triumph, and was styled a Second Founder of Rome, not even once was he consul.

Plutarch, *Lives. Camillus*, 31.[33]
ὅπως μὴ μόνον ἡγεμὼν Ῥώμης καὶ στρατηγός, ἀλλὰ καὶ κτίστης λέγηται παρώσας Ῥωμύλον.

---

[28] See further *SIG*[3] 751.2; 839.8; R. Merkelbach and S. Şahin 'Inschriften von Perge', *Epigraphica Anatolica* 11 (1988): 97–170.

[29] Bons and Dell'Acqua, 'Sample Article', 183.

[30] Brian McGing, trans. *Appian. Roman History, Volume I* (LCL 2; Cambridge, MA: Harvard University Press, 1912), 32–33.

[31] A. M. Harmon, trans. *Lucian. Phalaris. Hippias or the Bath. Dionysus. Heracles. Amber or the Swans. The Fly. Nigrinus. Demonax. The Hall. My Native Land. Octogenarians. A True Story. Slander. The Consonants at Law. The Carousal (Symposium) or the Lapiths* (LCL 14; Cambridge, MA: Harvard University Press, 1913), 232–33.

[32] Bernadotte Perrin, trans. *Plutarch. Lives, Volume II: Themistocles and Camillus. Aristides and Cato Major. Cimon and Lucullus* (LCL 47; Cambridge, MA: Harvard University Press, 1914), 94–95.

[33] Perrin, trans. *Plutarch. Lives, Volume II*, 170–171.

He wished not merely to be a leader and general of Rome, but to thrust Romulus to one side and be styled its founder.

Plutarch, *Moralia. On Exile*, 15.[34]
ἠδόξει δὲ Κάμιλλος ἐκ τῆς Ῥώμης ἐλαυνόμενος, ἧς δεύτερος κτίστης νῦν ἀναγορεύεται;

Was Camillus deprived of fame when he was banished from Rome, of which he is now acclaimed the second founder?

Plutarch, *Lives. Lucullus*, §511.[35]
ὥστε συνέβη μιᾶς πόλεως διαλυθείσης πολλὰς ἀνοικίζεσθαι πάλιν κομιζομένας τοὺς αὐτῶν οἰκήτορας, ὑφ᾽ ὧν ὡς εὐεργέτης ὁ Λούκουλλος καὶ κτίστης ἠγαπᾶτο.

Thus it came to pass that the dissolution of one city was the restoration of many others, by reason of their recovering their own inhabitants, and they all loved Lucullus as their benefactor and founder.

Josephus, *Against Apion*, 2.39.[36]
καὶ τί δεῖ περὶ τῶν ἄλλων λέγειν; αὐτῶν γὰρ ἡμῶν οἱ τὴν Ἀντιόχειαν κατοικοῦντες Ἀντιοχεῖς ὀνομάζονται· τὴν γὰρ πολιτείαν αὐτοῖς ἔδωκεν ὁ κτίστης Σέλευκος

Our Jewish residents in Antioch are called Antiochenes, having been granted rights of citizenship by its founder, Seleucus.

Appian, *Roman History. The Civil Wars*, 1.13.[37]
Γράκχος δὲ μεγαλαυχούμενος ἐπὶ τῷ νόμῳ ὑπὸ τοῦ πλήθους οἷα δὴ κτίστης οὐ μιᾶς πόλεως οὐδὲ ἑνὸς γένους, ἀλλὰ πάντων, ὅσα ἐν Ἰταλίᾳ ἔθνη, ἐς τὴν οἰκίαν παρεπέμπετο

Gracchus became immensely popular by reason of the law and was escorted home by the multitude as though he were the founder, not of a single city or race, but of all the nations of Italy.

Dionysius of Halicarnassus, *Roman Antiquities*, 1.50.3.[38]
Ζάκυνθόν τε καὶ Ἐριχθόνιον, ὧν ὁ μὲν Αἰνείου πρόγονος ἦν, Ζάκυνθος δὲ τῆς νήσου κτίστης)

Zacynthus and Erichthonius of whom the latter was the ancestor of Aeneas, and Zacynthus was the first settler of the island.

---

[34] Phillip H. De Lacy, trans. *Plutarch. Moralia, Volume VII: On Love of Wealth. On Compliancy. On Envy and Hate. On Praising Oneself Inoffensively. On the Delays of the Divine Vengeance. On Fate. On the Sign of Socrates. On Exile. Consolation to His Wife* (LCL 405; Cambridge, MA: Harvard University Press, 1959), 556–557.

[35] Perrin, trans. *Plutarch. Lives, Volume II*, 566–567.

[36] H. St. J. Thackeray, trans. *Josephus: The Life against Apion* (LCL 186; Cambridge, MA: Harvard University Press, 1926), 306–307.

[37] Horace White, trans. *Appian. Roman History, Volume III: The Civil Wars, Books 1–3.26* (LCL 4; Cambridge, MA: Harvard University Press, 1913), 26–29.

[38] Earnest Cary, trans. *Dionysius of Halicarnassus. Roman Antiquities, Volume I: Books 1–2* (LCL 319; Cambridge, MA: Harvard University Press, 1937), 164–165.

190 *Numismatics and Greek Lexicography*

Josephus, Jewish Antiquities, 1.214.[39]

ὃν εὐθὺς μετ᾽ ὀγδόην ἡμέραν περιτέμνουσι, κἀξ ἐκείνου μετὰ τοσαύτας ἔθος ἔχουσιν οἱ Ἰουδαῖοι ποιεῖσθαι τὰς περιτομάς, Ἄραβες δὲ μετὰ ἔτος τρισκαιδέκατον· Ἰσμάηλος γὰρ ὁ κτίστης αὐτῶν τοῦ ἔθνους Ἀβράμῳ γενόμενος ἐκ τῆς παλλακῆς ἐν τούτῳ περιτέμνεται τῷ χρόνῳ·

Eight days later they promptly circumcised him; and from that time forward the Jewish practice has been to circumcise so many days after birth. The Arabs defer the ceremony to the thirteenth year, because Ishmael, the founder of their race, born of Abraham's concubine, was circumcised at that age.

Diodorus Siculus, *The Library of History*, §4.[40]

Ἱέρων δ᾽ ὁ τῶν Συρακοσίων βασιλεὺς ἐτελεύτησεν ἐν τῇ Κατάνῃ, καὶ τιμῶν ἡρωικῶν ἔτυχεν, ὡς ἂν κτίστης γεγονὼς τῆς πόλεως.

And Hieron, the king of the Syracusans, died in Catana and received the honours which are accorded to heroes, as having been the founder of the city.

In light of this cumulative evidence it is increasingly difficult to maintain that κτίστης exclusively refers to cosmological creation within the Judeo-Christian traditions. Indeed, the second edition of the *New International Dictionary of New Testament Theology and Exegesis* seems already outdated in its recycling of old glosses when it states 'the word group [in the Koine period] is used always of divine creation.'[41] How then does our revised understanding of κτίστης as 'founder' rather than ontological creator function in relation to 1 Peter 4:19 contextually, linguistically and historically?

Contextually, κτίστης in 4:19 recalls κτίσις in 2:13. As noted above, every other use of κτίσις in the NT refers to a created physical entity (e.g. Mk 10:6 ἀπὸ δὲ ἀρχῆς κτίσεως ἄρσεν καὶ θῆλυ ἐποίησεν αὐτούς ['But at the beginning of creation God "made them male and female."']), yet the context of 1 Peter refers to human authorities, be they the emperor (βασιλεύς 2:13) or local magistrates (ἡγεμών 2:14).

Linguistically the use of κτίστης also may be relevant for a hermeneutical employment of empire criticism. That is, attributing to God those titles and honours which typically are employed in Roman and Greek propaganda about state or ruler. 1 Peter 4:19 re-asserts God's providential role and ultimate authority over the inhabitants of cities throughout Asia Minor. There is no real tension between this observation and the command in 2:13 to 'submit yourselves ... to every human institution', as, not only is this qualified with 'for the Lord's sake' (2:13), but is indicative of their precarious circumstances. They are a royal priesthood (2:9), but they also tenuously live within the Roman Empire as 'aliens and strangers' (2:11).

---

[39] H. St. J. Thackeray, trans. *Josephus. Jewish Antiquities, Volume I: Books 1–3* (LCL 242; Cambridge, MA: Harvard University Press, 1930), 106–107.

[40] C. H. Oldfather, trans. *Diodorus Siculus. Library of History, Volume I: Books 1–2.34* (LCL 279; Cambridge, MA: Harvard University Press, 1933), 296–297.

[41] H.-H. Esser, 'κτίζω, κτίσις, κτίσμα, κτίστης', *NIDNTTE* 2: 762.

Historically κτίστης functions to encourage the recipients amid various elements of social marginalization (φόβος ('intimidation' [1 Pet 3:14]); καταλαλέω ('slander' [1 Pet 3:16]), ὀνειδίζω ('vilification' [1 Pet 4:14]), and accusations of retreating from social participation [1 Pet 4:3–6]). In this light, the author reminds the recipients that God himself has founded their community and stands as the supreme authority over their faith and life, irrespective of their current marginalization. Implicit within this encouragement however, there is also an element of exhortation. That is, given this reality, the community must now live up to the status bestowed upon them as a 'chosen race, a royal priesthood, a holy nation … [and] God's people' (1 Pet 2:9–10).

Conclusion

In this chapter we have attempted to temper the NT lexicographic bias of understanding κτίστης as exclusively referring to cosmological creation. In light of the voluminous numismatic material which circulated, before, during and after the period under discussion, it has been suggested that the meaning of κτίστης as 'founder' not 'creator' in 1 Peter 4:19, is not only a potential hypothesis, but a genuine possibility. As we conclude, it may help to rephrase the question from an alternative angle to assist in highlighting the deficiency of the current state of the definition of the word: Κτίστης, understood as 'cosmological creator' is completely unknown in over eight hundred years of the numismatic record throughout the width and breadth of the Mediterranean world. The full lexicographic significance of that singular phenomenon has not yet been appreciated by NT lexicographers who continue to marginalize numismatic material and prefer to derive glosses from outdated lexicons, rather than a fresh assessment of the primary sources.[42]

---

[42] John Lee has astutely noted this phenomenon when he states that 'even the latest lexicons derive their material from their predecessors, and a great deal of it has been passed on uncritically over the course of centuries', John A. L. Lee, 'The Present State of Lexicography of Ancient Greek', in *Biblical Greek Language and Lexicography: Essays in Honor of Frederick W. Danker*, ed. B. A. Taylor, John A. L. Lee, P. R. Burton, and R. E. Whitaker (Grand Rapids, MI: Eerdmans, 2004), 69.

11

ΒΑΣΙΛΕΥΣ ΒΑΣΙΛΕΩΝ

Introduction

Revelation 17:14 and 19:16 apply the title βασιλεὺς βασιλέων (trans. 'king of kings') to Jesus Christ as a victorious epithet, but its significance and meaning have been a subject of much debate. The former passage uses the title within the context of the first act of the judgement on ἡ πόρνη ἡ μεγάλη (trans. 'the Great Whore') and τό θηρίον (trans. 'the Beast') in 17:1–18.[1] The latter passage applies the title to Jesus, presented as riding a white horse defeating the forces of wickedness (Rev 19:11–16). Some commentators suggest that the title derives from the LXX of Daniel 4:37, 'where it is a title for God'.[2] Others suggest that the title is especially apposite during the reign of Domitian of whom it is said 'he dictated the form of a letter to be used by his procurators, he began: "Our lord and god commands so and so."'[3] Still others suggest the title is borrowed from a Babylonian context, and therefore operates as a polemic against Revelation's latter day Babylon, that is Rome.[4] This broad spectrum of scholarly views reveals a fundamental disagreement on the relevant cultural and textual foreground/background of the title in Revelation. The present analysis will explore inscriptions on relevant numismatic evidence and investigate whether the title in Revelation is indebted to a particular cultural context.

---

[1] The historical identification of 'the Great Whore' with Rome in Revelation 17:1 is strengthened by (a) the polysemy of lupa as wolf/whore and the relevant association with the myth of Rome's founding (Dionysius of Halicarnassus, *History of Rome*, 1.79–87; Livy, *Ab Urbe Condita*, 1.4–6; Plutarch, *Life of Romulus*, 2–10; Dio Cassius, *Roman History*, 1), (b) the placement of καθημένης ἐπὶ ὑδάτων πολλῶν (trans. 'sitting on many waters') in Revelation 17:1 (cf. v.15) and Rome's location on the Tiber (Cicero, *On the Republic* 2.5–10; Virgil, *Aeneid* 8.31–35, 62–65; Seutonius, *Augustus*, 37; CIL 6.31542), (c) the reference to seven hills (Claudian, *On the Sixth Consulship 'of Stiicho*, 531–536; Gellius, *Attic Nights* 13.14.1–4, 7), (d) the description in Revelation 17:9 that 'the seven heads [of the beast] are seven mountains on which the woman is seated' recalls Rome's famous location as built on seven hills (Livy, *History*, 5.54.4; Virgil, *Aeneid* 6.783; Cicero, Letters to Atticus 6.5.2; Varro, *Latina* 5.41, 6.24; RIC *Vesp.* 442).

[2] G. K. Beale, *The Book of Revelation: A Commentary on the Greek Text* (Grand Rapids: Eerdmans, 1999), 963.

[3] Suetonius. *Lives of the Caesars, Volume II: Claudius. Nero. Galba, Otho and Vitellius. Vespasian. Titus, Domitian. Lives of Illustrious Men: Grammarians and Rhetoricians. Poets (Terence. Virgil. Horace. Tibullus. Persius. Lucan). Lives of Pliny the Elder and Passienus Crispus.* Trans. J. C. Rolfe. Loeb Classical Library 38 (Cambridge, MA: Harvard University Press, 1914), 350.

[4] T. B. Slater, '"King of Kings and Lord of Lords" Revisited', *NTS* 39 (1993): 159–160.

194   *Numismatics and Greek Lexicography*

The history of ΒΑΣΙΛΕΥΣ ΒΑΣΙΛΕΩΝ

The Greek title βασιλεὺς βασιλέων (trans. 'king of kings') has a long history. Although J. C. Rolfe states that it is 'a title originally applied to the king of Persia and transferred to the king of the Parthians,'[5] Lowell Handy finds earlier attestation. Handy traces the earliest reference of the title 'king of kings' (šar šarrāni) to a royal title for King Tukulti-Ninurta I of Assyria who reigned 1244–1208 BCE.[6] Within the expanding Assyrian Empire, the title was applied literally, that is, the Assyrian ruler installed themselves as rulers over the existing structure of the local city state kings. The Babylonian King Nebuchadnezzar is referred to in Hebrew as מֶלֶךְ מְלָכִים (Ezek 26:7) and in Aramaic as מֶלֶךְ מַלְכַיָּא (Dan 2:37). These and other attestations establish the phrase as derivative of Semitic background.[7] However, the title is also regularly employed in a Persian context, 'Artaxerxes, king of kings (מֶלֶךְ מַלְכַיָּא), to the priest Ezra, the scribe of the law of the God of heaven' (Ezra 7:12).[8] Ernst Fredricksmeyer tabulates thirty-nine occurrences of 'king of kings' within the Persian Achaemenid dynasty inscriptions (553–330 BCE) published by Ronald Kent.[9] The phrase in an Egyptian context is attested by Diodorus of Sicily, the first-century BCE historian, who in description of a monument of Ozymandias (one of the royal names for Ramses)[10] refers to 'ἐπιγεγράφθαι δ᾽ ἐπ᾽ αὐτοῦ "Βασιλεὺς βασιλέων Ὀσυμανδύας εἰμί. εἰ δέ τις εἰδέναι βούλεται πηλίκος εἰμὶ καὶ ποῦ κεῖμαι, νικάτω τι τῶν ἐμῶν ἔργων"' (trans. 'Inscribed upon it is: "King of Kings Ozymandias I am. If anyone wishes to know how great I am and where I lie, let him outdo me in my deeds"').[11]

---

[5]   J. C. Rolfe, trans., *Suetonius. Lives of the Caesars, Volume I: Julius. Augustus. Tiberius. Gaius. Caligula* (LCL 31; Cambridge, MA: Harvard University Press, 1914), 410 note a.

[6]   Lowell K. Handy, *Among the Host of Heaven: The Syro-Palestinian Pantheon as Bureaucracy* (Winona Lake: Eisenbrauns, 1994), 112. See further Ernst Weidner, *Die Inschriften Tukulti-Ninurtas I. und seiner Nachfolger* (Osnabrück: Biblio, 1970), 18.

[7]   Moshe Greenberg, *Ezekiel 21–37: A New Translation with Introduction and Commentary* (London: Yale University Press, 2008), 532.

[8]   See James B. Pritchard, *Ancient Near Eastern Texts Relating to the Old Testament*, 3rd edn. (Princeton: Princeton University Press, 1969), 316 for further Persian references. Cf. Josephus Jewish, Antiquities, Volume IV: Books 9–11, trans. Ralph Marcus. Loeb Classical Library 326. (Cambridge, MA: Harvard University Press, 1937), 11.373, 'ὁ δὲ βασιλεὺς γράφει πρὸς τοὺς σατράπας ἐπιστολὴν τοιάνδε·ο"βασιλεὺς βασιλέων Ξέρξης"Εσδρᾳ ἱερεῖ καὶ ἀναγνώστῃ τῶν τοῦ θεοῦ νόμων χαίρειν"' (trans. 'The king, therefore, wrote the following letter to the satraps, "Xerxes, king of kings, to Ezra, the priest and reader of the laws of God, greeting".')

[9]   Ernst Fredricksmeyer, 'Alexander the Great and the Kingship of Asia', in *Alexander the Great in Fact and Fiction*, ed. A. B. Bosworth and E. J. Baynham (Oxford: Oxford University Press, 2000), 162. Possibly the most famous attestation of the title is in the multilingual Behistun inscription in Old Persian, Elamite and Babylonian by Darius I (522–486 BCE) on a rock relief on the cliff at Mount Behistun (western Iran); see L. W. King and R. C. Thompson, *The Sculptures and Inscription of Darius the Great on the Rock of Behistûn in Persia: A New Collation of the Persian, Susian and Babylonian Texts* (London: British Museum, 1907), 84.

[10]   H. R. Hall, *The Ancient History of the Near East: From the Earliest Times to the Battle of Salamis* (London: Methuen & Co. Ltd., 1913), 317.

[11]   *Diodorus Siculus. Library of History, Volume I: Books 1–2.34*, trans. C. H. Oldfather. Loeb Classical Library 279 (Cambridge, MA: Harvard University Press, 1933), 168–169.

Numismatic evidence

The titulature βασιλεὺς βασιλέων was pervasive in many cultures, including prominent attestation in the Parthian Kingdom. Silver drachms of Mithradates II (123–88 BCE) depict on the obverse the diademed bust of Mithradates II facing left, and on the obverse an archer seated right on a throne holding a bow with the accompanying inscription, ΒΑΣΙΛΕΥΣ ΒΑΣΙΛΕΩΝ ΜΕΓΑΛΟΥ ΑΡΣΑΚΟΥ ΕΠΙΦΑΝΟΥΣ (trans. 'king of kings, great Arsaces, notable') (Figure 66). Example 27.2 in Sellwood's catalogue is notable for being the first use of the title βασιλεὺς βασιλέων on Parthian coinage.[12] Part of the reason he was able to include longer inscriptions on his coinage was the space effective square arrangement of the legend, which all subsequent Arsacid coinage maintained. Mithradates II is also known for his military success in expelling the rebel Hyspaosines and overstriking their coinage with his own.[13]

But this example is the chronological starting point of the most prominently attested legends on the coins of Parthia in the first century BCE. Of the 233 coin-types and variants of Mithradates II (123–88 BCE), 91 have ΒΑΣΙΛΕΥΣ ΒΑΣΙΛΕΩΝ as the first title of the king.[14] Of the 60 coin-types and variants of Mithradates III (57–54 BCE), 25 have ΒΑΣΙΛΕΥΣ ΒΑΣΙΛΕΩΝ. For example, Sellwood 41.8 (Figure 67) is a silver

Figure 66 Sellwood 27.2 (used with permission).

---

[12] David Sellwood, *An Introduction to the Coinage of Parthia* (London: Spink & Son, 1971), §27.2.
[13] Sellwood, *Parthia*, 63.
[14] This and the following statistics for the coins of Parthia were manually compiled and calculated from the following: Sellwood, *Parthia*; David Sellwood, 'New Parthian Coin Types', *Numismatic Chronicle* 19 (1989): 162–168; David Sellwood, 'The End of the Parthian Dynasty', *Spink Numismatic Circular* 98 (1990): 157; David Sellwood, 'The "Victory" Drachms of Phraates IV', *American Journal of Numismatics, Second Series* 7–8 (1995–1996): 75–81; David Sellwood, 'Parthians and Scythians', in *Ex Moneta: Essays on Numismatics, History and Archaeology in Honour of Dr. David W. MacDowall, Vol. 1*, ed. Amal Kumar Jha and Samjay Garg (New Delhi: Harmon, 1998), 97–102.

Figure 67 Sellwood 41.8 (used with permission).

drachm which on the obverse depicts a short-bearded bust facing left, wearing doublebanded diadem and segmented necklace with medallion. The reverse has a beardless archer wearing a hooded cloak seated right holding a bow in his right hand. The Greek inscription reads ΒΑΣΙΛΕΩΣ ΒΑΣΙΛΕΩΝ ΑΡΣΑΚΟΥ ΜΕΓΑΛΟΥ ΔΙΚΑΙΟΥ ΕΠΙΦΑΝΟΥΣ ΘΕΟΥ ΕΥΠΑΤΟΡΟΣ ΚΑΙ ΦΙΛΕΛΛΗΝΟΣ (trans. 'king of kings, great Arsaces, just notable god, well born and friend of the Greek'). Orodes II (57–38 BCE) has 269 types and variants issued, and 206 name him as ΒΑΣΙΛΕΥΣ ΒΑΣΙΛΕΩΝ. For example, Sellwood 42.2 (Figure 68) is a silver drachm which depicts a short-bearded bust facing left wearing diadem, behind the bust Nike is portrayed as flying left with wreath. The reverse is similar to Sellwood 41.8, but the Greek inscription reads ΒΑΣΙΛΕΩΣ ΒΑΣΙΛΕΩΝ ΑΡΣΑΚΟΥ ΦΙΛΟΠΑΤΟΡΟΣ ΔΙΚΑΙΟΥ ΕΠΙΦΑΝΟΥΣ ΦΙΛΕΛΛΗΝΟΣ (trans. 'king of kings, Arsaces, Philopator, just, notable and friend of the Greek'). Of the 26 types and variants Phraates IV (38–2 BCE) issued, 6 include the title ΒΑΣΙΛΕΩΣ ΒΑΣΙΛΕΩΝ. Sellwood 51.9 (Figure 69) is a silver tetradrachm which together with 23 other examples has a (royal) wart on Phraates' brow line,[15] together with a segmented necklace and diadem. The reverse depicts the king seated on the throne receiving a palm branch from Tyche who faces left and also holds cornucopia in her left hand. The inscription reads ΒΑΣΙΛΕΩΣ ΒΑΣΙΛΕΩΝ ΑΡΣΑΚΟΥ ΕΥΕΡΓΕΤΟΥ ΔΙΚΑΙΟΥ ΕΠΙΦΑΝΟΥΣ ΦΙΛΕΛΛΗΝΟΣ (trans. 'king of kings, Arsaces, benefactor,

---

[15] The nodules on the faces on the coins of many of the Parthian kings have attracted much speculation. G. D. Hart, 'Trichoepithelioma and the Kings of Ancient Parthia', *Canadian Medical Association Journal* 92 (2006): 547–549, suggests it could be a trichoepithelioma; K. Liddel, 'Skin Disease in Antiquity', *Journal of the Royal College of Physicians of London* 6 (2006): 81–86, argues that the lesion more likely resembles a basal cell carcinoma; and D. Todman, 'Warts and the Kings of Parthia: An Ancient Representation of Hereditary Neurofibromatosis Depicted in Coins', *Journal of the History of the Neurosciences* 17 (2008): 141–146, expresses a view with much greater specificity, 'The round nodules... are of a size and shape that resemble the cutaneous lesions of Neurofibromatosis Type I (NF-1, von Recklinghausen's Disease)' (141).

ΒΑΣΙΛΕΥΣ ΒΑΣΙΛΕΩΝ

Figure 68 Sellwood 42.2 (used with permission).

Figure 69 Sellwood 51.9 (used with permission).

just, notable and friend of the Greek'). Indeed, each one of the Parthian kings in the principal line of succession in the first century CE, without a single exception, issued coins with the title ΒΑΣΙΛΕΩΣ ΒΑΣΙΛΕΩΝ as part of their self-representation,[16] as did two of the rival claimants.[17]

---

[16] In this and the following footnote I have listed a representative sample of relevant coinage for ΒΑΣΙΛΕΩΣ ΒΑΣΙΛΕΩΝ. Phraataces (2–4 CE), Sellwood 56.1, 57.13, 58.1; Orodes III (6 CE), Sellwood 59.2; Vonones I (8–12 CE), Sellwood 60.2, 60.4; Artabanus II (10–38 CE), Sellwood 61.1, 62.3, 62.8, 62.12; Vardanes I (40–47 CE), Sellwood 64.14, 64.20–27; Gotarzes II (40–51 CE), Sellwood 65.2, 65.4, 65.23; Vonones II (51 CE), Sellwood 67.1; Vologases I (51–78 CE), Sellwood 68.4–8, 68.11; Vologases II (77–80 CE), Sellwood 72.1–2; Pacorus II (78–105 CE), Sellwood 73.2–5, 73.9, 73.10.

[17] Vardanes II (55–58 CE), Sellwood 69.1–6, 69.13; Artabanus III (80–90 CE), Sellwood 74.3, 74.6.

Greeks and Romans were also familiar with the title.[18] Plutarch records that Pompey encountered the title during the campaigns against Mithradates VI. When writing to the king of Parthia, he refused his usual title, βασιλεὺς βασιλέων, 'for many leaders and princes and twelve barbarian kings had come to him. Wherefore, to gratify these other kings, he would not deign, in answering a letter from the king of Parthia, to address him as King of Kings, which was his usual title.'[19] Dio Cassius 37.6 notes another occasion where Pompey also refused Phraates III, king of Parthia's, title by referring to him as only 'king' rather than 'king of kings', 'καὶ προσέτι καὶ πρὸς τὴν ἐπίκλησιν αὐτοῦ ὕβρισεν, ἥπερ πρός τε τοὺς ἄλλους πάντας ἡγάλλετο καὶ πρὸς αὐτοὺς τοὺς Ῥωμαίους, οὗτοί τε αὖ πρὸς ἐκεῖνον ἀεί ποτε ἐκέχρηντο. βασιλέως γὰρ αὐτοῦ βασιλέων καλουμένου, τό τε τῶν βασιλέων ὄνομα περιέκοψε καὶ βασιλεῖ αὐτῷ μόνον ἐπιστέλλων ἔγραψε' (trans. 'he showed contempt for the title of Phraates, in which that ruler delighted before all the world and before the Romans themselves, and by which the latter had always addressed him. For whereas he was called "King of Kings," Pompey clipped off the phrase "of Kings" and addressed his demands merely "to the King" when writing.'[20] In the same passage immediately following, Dio Cassius notes that Pompey gave the title to Tigranes when he had captured him and was celebrating a triumph over him at Rome, no doubt to highlight the greater significance of Pompey's own achievement.[21] Although Appian comes close to affording the title to Pompey when he says, 'αὐτὸς δ᾽, οἷα δὴ βασιλεὺς βασιλέων, αὐτοὺς περιθέοι καὶ ἐφορῴη μένοντας ἐφ᾽ ὧν ἐτάχθησαν' (trans. 'while he, Pompey, like a king of kings, should move to and fro among them to see that they remained where they were stationed'),[22] when referring to his pursuit of the pirates in one episode of the Mithridatic Wars in 67 BCE.

Other sources in the Roman period indicate the widespread knowledge and memory of the title. Cicero refers to the memory of Agamemnon as the 'regnum regi' (trans. 'king of kings') in his correspondence with Dolabella, dated to 3 May 44 CE,[23] as does Velleius Paterculus (19 BCE–31 CE) in recounting, 'Agamemnon, king of kings (rex regum), cast by a tempest upon the island of Crete, founded there three cities, two of which, Mycenae and Tegea.'[24] Quintus Curtius Rufus's *History of Alexander* includes reference to Darius's eventual demise, 'Hunc vitae finem sortitus est ille quem modo contumelia affici putabant,

---

[18] J. G. Griffiths, 'βασιλεὺς βασιλέων: Remarks on the History of a Title', *Classical Philology* 48 (1953): 145–154.

[19] Bernadotte Perrin, trans., *Plutarch. Lives, Volume V: Agesilaus and Pompey. Pelopidas and Marcellus* (LCL 87; Cambridge, MA: Harvard University Press, 1917), 214–215.

[20] Earnest Cary and Herbert B. Foster, trans., *Dio Cassius. Roman History, Volume III: Books 36–40* (LCL 53; Cambridge, MA: Harvard University Press, 1914), 108–109.

[21] Cf. Appian, *Roman History 11: The Syrian War*, §47, 'καὶ βασιλεὺς Ἀρμενίας Τιγράνης ὁ Τιγράνους ἔθνη πολλὰ τῶν περιοίκων ἰδίοις δυνάσταις χρώμενα ἑλών, βασιλεὺς ἀπὸ τοῦδε βασιλέων ἡγεῖτο εἶναι, καὶ τοῖς Σελευκίδαις ἐπεστράτευεν οὐκ ἐθέλουσιν ὑπακούειν' (trans. 'Tigranes, the son of Tigranes conquers Syria Tigranes, king of Armenia, who had subdued many of the neighbouring nations which had kings of their own, and from these exploits had acquired the title of King of Kings, attacked the Seleucidae because they would not acknowledge his supremacy'), Brian McGing, trans., *Appian. Roman History, Volume I* (LCL 2; Cambridge, MA: Harvard University Press, 1912), 196–197.

[22] McGing, trans., *Appian. Roman History, Volume I*, 418–419.

[23] D. R. Shackleton Bailey, trans., *Cicero. Letters to Friends, Volume III: Letters 281–435* (LCL 230; Cambridge, MA: Harvard University Press, 2001), §326.IX.14, 94–95.

[24] Frederick W. Shipley, trans., *Velleius Paterculus. Compendium of Roman History. Res Gestae Divi Augusti* (LCL 152; Cambridge, MA: Harvard University Press, 1924), 1.1, 2–3.

ΒΑΣΙΛΕΥΣ ΒΑΣΙΛΕΩΝ

nisi regem regum et deorum consanguineum salutarent; magnoque denuo experimento comprobatum est neminem magis patere Fortunae quam qui, plurimis eius beneficiis ornatus, iugum eius tota cervice receperit' (trans. 'Such was the end of life allotted to that king whom shortly before men thought to be insulted unless they addressed him as king of kings and kinsman of the gods; and once more it was proved by a striking example, that no one is more exposed to Fortune's changes than one who, having been honoured by very many of her favours, has bowed his neck wholly under her yoke').[25]

Hellenistic Jews were aware of the title as evidenced in Philo of Alexandria's description of God, 'παγγέλοιον γὰρ οἴεσθαι, ὅτι ὁ μὲν νοῦς ὁ ἐν ἡμῖν βραχύτατος ὢν καὶ ἀόρατος ἡγεμὼν τῶν αἰσθητικῶν ὀργάνων ἐστίν, ὁ δὲ τοῦ παντὸς ὁ μέγιστος καὶ τελειότατος οὐχὶ βασιλεὺς βασιλέων εἶναι πέφυκε, βλεπομένων οὐ βλεπόμενος' (trans. 'For it is quite ridiculous to deny that if the mind in us, so exceedingly small and invisible, is yet the ruler of the organs of sense, the mind of the universe, so transcendently great and perfect, must be the King of kings who are seen by Him though He is not seen by them').[26] Strabo's Γεωγραφικά, first published in 7 BCE, makes mention of the title in book 13 which pertains to the northern Aegean region: 'ἔοικε δὲ ὁ ποιητὴς μικρὰν ἀποφαίνειν τὴν πόλιν ἐν τῷ περὶ Ἡρακλέους λόγῳ, εἴπερ ἐξ οἵης σὺν νηυσὶ καὶ ἀνδράσι παυροτέροισιν Ἰλίου ἐξαλάπαξε πόλιν. καὶ φαίνεται ὁ Πρίαμος τῷ τοιούτῳ λόγῳ μέγας ἐκ μικροῦ γεγονὼς καὶ βασιλεὺς βασιλέων, ὡς ἔφαμεν' (trans. 'and it appears that the poet, in what he says about Heracles, represents the city as small, if it be true that "with only six ships and fewer men he sacked the city of Ilium." And it is clearly shown by this statement that Priam became great and king of kings from a small beginning, as I have said before').[27] The title βασιλεὺς βασιλέων is also used in the Roman period for recalling heroes in Greek history. Dio Chysostom (40 CE–115 CE), the Greek orator, used the title in reference to Zeus, 'ὁμοίως δὲ καὶ οἱ θεοὶ καὶ ὁ δὴ μέγας βασιλεὺς βασιλέων, ἅτε κηδεμὼν καὶ πατὴρ κοινὸς ἀνθρώπων καὶ θεῶν, Ζεύς' (trans. 'In like manner do the gods act, and especially the great King of Kings, Zeus, who is the common protector and father of men and gods').[28]

---

[25] J. C. Rolfe, trans., *Quintus Curtius. History of Alexander, Volume I: Books 1–5* (LCL 368; Cambridge, MA: Harvard University Press, 1946), 428–429.

[26] Philo, *On the Special Laws* 214.19, F. H. Colson, trans., *Philo. On the Decalogue. On the Special Laws, Books 1–3* (LCL 320; Cambridge, MA: Harvard University Press, 1937), 108–109. See similar use in reference to God in Philo, *On the Cherubim. The Sacrifices of Abel and Cain. The Worse Attacks the Better. On the Posterity and Exile of Cain. On the Giants*, trans. F. H. Colson and G. H. Whitaker. Loeb Classical Library 227 (Cambridge, MA: Harvard University Press, 1929), 68–69; Philo, *On the Decalogue. On the Special Laws, Books 1–3*, trans F. H. Colson. Loeb Classical Library 320 (Cambridge, MA: Harvard University Press, 1937), 26–27; Philo, *Questions on Genesis*, trans. Ralph Marcus. Loeb Classical Library 380 (Cambridge, MA: Harvard University Press, 1953), 352–353.

[27] Strabo, *Geography* 13.1.32; Horace Leonard Jones, trans., *Strabo. Geography, Volume VI: Books 13–14* (LCL 223; Cambridge, MA: Harvard University Press, 1929), 62–63.

[28] Dio Chrysostom, *The Second Discourse on Kingship* 75, J. W. Cohoon, trans., *Dio Chrysostom. Discourses 1–11* (LCL 257; Cambridge, MA: Harvard University Press, 1932), 98–99. A similar use is found in the Greek tragedian Aeschylus's play *The Suppliants* (dated to 470 BCE) and occurs in the context of Pelasgus's departure from the city as the chorus descends from the mound, 'ἄναξ ἀνάκτων, μακάρων μακάρτατε καὶ τελέων τελειότατον κράτος, ὄλβιε Ζεῦ' (trans. 'O King of Kings, O most blest of the blest, O power most perfect of the perfect, Zeus giver of prosperity'), Aeschylus, *The Suppliants* 524–526, Alan H. Sommerstein, trans., *Aeschylus. Persians. Seven against Thebes. Suppliants. Prometheus Bound* (LCL 145; Cambridge, MA: Harvard University Press, 2009), 358–359.

In further attestation of knowledge and use of the title in the Roman world during the first century BCE, Plutarch *Ant.* 54 has Antony give the title during the *Donations of Alexandria*: ʿδεύτερον δὲ τοὺς ἐξ αὐτοῦ καὶ Κλεοπάτρας υἱοὺς βασιλεῖς βασιλέων ἀναγορεύσας Ἀλεξάνδρῳ μὲν Ἀρμενίαν ἀπένειμε καὶ Μηδίαν καὶ τὰ Πάρθων, ὅταν ὑπαγάγηται, Πτολεμαίῳ δὲ Φοινίκην καὶ Συρίαν καὶ Κιλικίανʾ (trans. 'In the second place, he proclaimed his own sons by Cleopatra Kings of Kings, and to Alexandria he allotted Armenia, Media and Parthia (when he should have subdued it), to Ptolemy Phoenicia, Syria, and Cilicia').[29] This political act by Cleopatra VII and Antony of the division of land among Cleopatra's children in 34 BCE was ultimately a significant catalyst for the deterioration of Antony's relationship with Rome and a cause of the war between Antony and Octavian.[30] Caesarion was honoured above Antony's two sons; in the *Donations of Alexandria* he received the title 'King of Kings' and was recognized as heir to Julius Caesar. A Latin inscription of interest appears on a silver denarius issued after the successful campaign against Armenia in 34 BCE. In Crawford's catalogue of Roman Republican Coinage,[31] item Crawford 543.1 (Figure 70) depicts, on the obverse, the bare head of Mark Antony facing right, an Armenian tiara to the left and the inscription ANTONI ARMENIA DEVICTA (trans. 'Of Antony who conquered Armenia'). The reverse has a diademed and draped bust of Cleopatra facing right, with the inscription CLEOPATRAE REGINAE REGVM FILIORVM REGVM (trans. 'Of Cleopatra, Queen of Kings and of the sons who are kings'). The phrase *filiorum regum* is somewhat ambiguous and could also be rendered 'whose children are kings'. This ambiguity permitted Cleopatra to 'simultaneously tout her illustrious heritage, while also highlighting the fact that she had given birth to children with two of Rome's most powerful generals, Julius Caesar and Mark Antony'.[32] The singular genitive noun

---

[29] Bernadotte Perrin, trans., *Plutarch. Lives, Volume IX: Demetrius and Antony. Pyrrhus and Gaius Marius* (LCL 101; Cambridge, MA: Harvard University Press, 1920), 262–263. On this incident, see Reinhold Meyer, *Studies in Classical History and Society* (Oxford: Oxford University Press, 2002), 57. Further use of the phrase in this regard is evident in Plutarch, *Lives: Lucullus* 14.5, ʿὀλίγων δʾ ἡμερῶν ὁδὸς εἰς Ἀρμενίαν ἐκ Καβείρων, καὶ ὑπὲρ Ἀρμενίας κάθηται Τιγράνης, βασιλεὺς βασιλέων, ἔχων δύναμιν, ᾗ Πάρθους τε περικόπτει τῆς Ἀσίας καὶ πόλεις Ἑλληνίδας εἰς Μηδίαν ἀνακομίζει καὶ Συρίας κρατεῖ καὶ Παλαιστίνης καὶ τοὺς ἀπὸ Σελεύκου βασιλεῖς ἀποκτιννύει, θυγατέρας δʾ αὐτῶν ἄγει καὶ γυναῖκας ὁἀνασπάστουςʾ (trans. 'And it is only a few days' journey from Cabira into Armenia and over Armenia there sits enthroned Tigranes, King of Kings, with forces which enable him to cut the Parthians off from Asia, transplant Greek cities into Media, sway Syria and Palestine, put to death the successors of Seleucus, and carry off their wives and daughters into captivity'), Perrin, *Plutarch. Lives, Volume II*, 512–513.

[30] See further Dio Cassius 49.41, ʿδημηγορήσας τέ τινα ἐκείνην τε βασιλίδα βασιλέων καὶ τὸν Πτολεμαῖον, ὃν Καισαρίωνα ἐπωνόμαζον, βασιλέα βασιλέων καλεῖσθαι ἐκέλευσεʾ (trans. 'also in the course of his address to the people he commanded that she should be called Queen of Kings, and Ptolemy, whom they named Caesarion, King of Kings'), Earnest Cary and Herbert B. Foster, trans., *Dio Cassius. Roman History, Volume V: Books 46–50* (LCL 82; Cambridge, MA: Harvard University Press, 1917), 424–425; cf. 50.3; Plutarch, *Lives, Volume IX: Demetrius and Antony. Pyrrhus and Gaius Marius*, trans. Bernadotte Perrin. Loeb Classical Library 101 (Cambridge, MA: Harvard University Press, 1920), 268–271. Rolf Strootman, 'Queen of Kings: Cleopatra VII and the Donations of Alexandria', in *Kingdoms and Principalities in the Roman Near East*, ed. T. Kaizer and M. Facella (Stuttgart: Franz Steiner Verlag, 2010), 139–158.

[31] Michael H. Crawford, *Roman Republican Coinage* (New York: Cambridge University Press, 1974).

[32] Jason Schulde and Benjamin Reubin, 'Finding Common Ground: Roman Parthian Embassies in the Julio-Claudian Period', in *Arsacids, Romans and Local Elites: Cross-Cultural Interactions of the Parthian Empire*, ed. Jason Schulde and Benjamin Reubin (Oxford: Oxbow Books, 2017), 75.

Figure 70 Crawford 543.1 (used with permission).

(reginae) joined with a genitive plural (regum) of the same root is a well-attested construction in Latin,[33] Greek[34] and Hebrew.[35]

We will now turn our discussion to the phrase βασιλεὺς βασιλέων in the east, with particular attention to the Indo-Greek and Indo-Scythian titular example on coinage. A series of gold Bosporan and Pontic staters of Pharnaces II dated to Pontic Year 245 (53/2 BCE) portray the diademed bust of Pharnaces facing right, with luxuriant hair (Figure 71). The reverse has Apollo enthroned left in relaxed pose, holding in right hand laurel branch over tripod, his left elbow resting on lyre at his side, and the inscription ΒΑΣΙΛΕΩΣ ΒΑΣΙΛΕΩΝ above, and ΜΕΓΑΛΟΥ ΦΑΡΝΑΚΟΥ below, with date ΕΜΣ to the right.[36]

The Scythians were originally a nomadic people from Central Asia who made their way into Bactria in the second century BCE, settling north west of the Bosporan

---

[33] In Guillermo Galán Vioque's commentary on Martial 7.70.1 (tribadum tribas), he provides the following Latin examples: Plautus, Captives 825: regum rex; Plautus, Trinummus 309: victor victorum; Lucretius 3.816: summarum summa; Ovid, Heroides 8.46: dux erat ille ducum; Petronius 37.8: nummorum nummos; Seneca, Agamemnon 39: rex ille regum, ductor Agamemnon ducum; Martial 1.100.2: mammarum maxima mamma; Martial 6.4.1: principumque princeps; Apuleius, Metamorphoses 11.30: deus deum magnorum potior et potiorum summus et summorum maximus et maximorum regnator Osiris. From Guillermo Galán Vioque, Martial, Book VII. A Commentary, trans. J. J. Zoltowsky (Leiden: Brill, 2017).

[34] Lev 16:31, σάββατα σαββάτων; Deut 10:17 ὁ γὰρ κύριος ὁ θεὸς ὑμῶν, οὗτος θεὸς τῶν θεῶν καὶ κύριος τῶν κυρίων; 1 Kings 8:27 ὁ οὐρανὸς τοῦ οὐρανοῦ.

[35] Psalm 136:2–3, לְעוֹלָם חַסְדּוֹ: הוֹדוּ לַאדֹנֵי הָאֲדֹנִים כִּי לְעוֹלָם חַסְדּוֹ: הוֹדוּ לֵאלֹהֵי הָאֱלֹהִים כִּי

[36] K. V. Golenko and J. P. Karyszkowski, 'The Gold Coinage of King Pharnaces of the Bosporus', Numismatic Chronicle 12 (1972): 35; David MacDonald, An Introduction to the History and Coinage of the Kingdom of the Bosporus (London: Classical Numismatic Group, 2005), 182; V. Anokhin, Coins of Ancient Cities of North-Western Black Sea Area (Kiev: Krajina Mriy, 1989).

Figure 71 Pharn 1 (used with permission).

Kingdom. Several distinct groups of Indo-Scythian coin inscriptions preserve multiple attestations and variations of the title βασιλεὺς βασιλέων.[37] Vonones of Indo-Scythia (to be distinguished from Vonones I [8–12 CE], and Vonones II [51 CE] of Parthia) ruled from 75 to 65 BCE and issued several coins from the Arachosian mint in the Arghandab Valley.[38] The Vonones family of coins (Vovones with Splahores, Vonones with Spalagadames, Spaliries with Azes, Azes and Azilises) regularly depict, on the obverse, the king mounted on horseback riding to the right, with a spear and Greek inscription identifying the individual with titles. The reverse depicts radiate Zeus standing facing, leaning on a sceptre on his left hand, carrying a thunderbolt in his

---

[37] See further, John Allen, *Catalogue of the Coins of Ancient India* (London: British Museum, 1967); American Numismatic Society, *Sylloge Nummorum Graecorum: The Collection of the American Numismatic Society, Part 9: Graeco-Bactrian and Indo-Greek Coins* (New York: The American Numismatic Society, 1998); P. L. Gupta and T. R. Hardaker, *Indian Silver Punchmarked Coins: Magadha-Maurya Karshapana Series* (Nashik: Indian Institute of Research in Numismatic Studies, 1985); Robert Göbl, *Münzprägung des Kušnreiches* (Vienna: Verlag der Österreichischen Akademie der Wissenschaften, 1984); Stan Goron and J. P. Goenka, *The Coins of the Indian Sultanates* (New Delhi: Munshiram Manoharlal, 2001); Brian Kritt, *Seleucid Coins of Bactria* (Lancaster: Classical Numismatic Group, 1996); Michael Mitchiner, *Ancient Trade and Early Coinage* (London: Hawkins Publications, 2004); Michael Mitchiner, *Oriental Coins and Their Values: The Ancient & Classical World* (London: Hawkins Publications, 1978); Wilfried Pieper, *Ancient Indian Coins Revisited* (Lancaster: Classical Numismatic Group, 2013); Dilip Rajgor, *Punch-Marked Coins of Early Historic India* (California: Reesha Books International, 2001); E. Rtveladze, *The Ancient Coins of Central Asia* (Tashkent: Uncertain, 1987); Robert C. Senior, *Indo-Scythian Coins and History* (London: Classical Numismatic Group, 2001).

[38] John Hubert Marshall, *Taxilla: An Illustrated Account of Archaeological Excavations Carried Out at Taxila under the Orders of the Government of India between the Years 1913 and 1934* (Cambridge: Cambridge University Press, 2013), 49.

right hand and a monogram indicating the weight standard (Kandahar or Bannu) at either the right or left with Kharoshthi inscription.[39]

Mitchiner's catalogue (MIG)[40] item 5.681 (with three sub-varieties based on varying weight standards) is a silver tetradrachm weighing 9.68 grams with a diameter of 26 mm (Figure 72). The obverse, as noted above, depicts the king holding a spear, mounted on a horse walking right. The inscription reads ΒΑΣΙΛΕΥΣ ΒΑΣΙΛΕΩΝ ΜΕΓΑΛΟΥ ΟΝΩΝΟΥ (trans. 'king of kings, great Vonones'). The reverse depicts Zeus standing facing holding a long sceptre in his left hand and thunderbolt in his right hand, surrounded by an inscription in Kharoshthi which reads *Maharajabhrata dhramikasa Spalahorasa* (trans. 'of Spalahores, the king's brother, the just.'). It is noteworthy that having two names (Vonones on the obverse and Spalahores on the reverse) is somewhat unusual in that the Greek and Kharoshthi inscriptions are not translations of one another as is the case on most examples of Indo-Greek and Indo-Scythian coinage. MIG 5.682 depicts similar iconography and inscriptions as 681 and its sub-variations, but is a silver drachm weighing 2.42 grams.

MIG 5.683 is a rectangular hemi-obol (4 chalkoi) weighing 8.50 grams. It depicts Hercules standing facing holding a club and lion skin on the obverse with the Greek inscription, ΒΑΣΙΛΕΥΣ ΒΑΣΙΛΕΩΝ ΜΕΓΑΛΟΥ ΟΝΩΝΟΥ (trans. 'king of kings, great Vonones'). On the reverse it has Pallas standing left holding spear and shield, with the Kharoshthi inscription, *Maharajabhrata dhramikasa Spalahorasa* (trans. 'of

Figure 72 MIG 5.681 (used with permission).

---

[39] See examples in Alexander Cunningham, *Coins of the Indo-Scythians, Sakas and Kushans* (Delhi: Indological Book House, 1971), plate IV.1–4, 9, 11, 12, plate V.4, 4a; P. Gardner and Reginald S. Poole, *The Coins of the Greeks and Scythic Kings of Bactria and India in the British Museum* (London: British Museum, 1886), plate XXI.7, 8, 10; plate XXII.1, 3; plate XVII.9, 10.

[40] Michael Mitchiner, *Indo-Greek and Indo-Scythian Coinage*, 9 vols. (London: Hawkins Publications, 1975), volume 3, §681a; also, Senior, *Indo-Scythian Coins*, §65.1T.

Spalahores, the king's brother, the just.'). A smaller Di-chalkoi denomination (MIG 5.685) is also attested in rectangular bronze (4.25 grams) has similar inscriptions as 5.683 but an uncertain control mark.

MIG 5.686, varieties a and b, is from a slightly later period within Vonones's reign, depicting Spalagadames, son of Spalahores as viceroy. The obverse has the typical depiction of king mounted on a horse holding spear walking right, with ΒΑΣΙΛΕΥΣ ΒΑΣΙΛΕΩΝ ΜΕΓΑΛΟΥ ΟΝΩΝΟΥ (trans. 'king of kings, great Vonones'). The obverse depicts Zeus standing facing holding long sceptre and thunderbolt, with the inscription, *Spalahora putrasa dhramiasa Spalagadamasa* (trans. 'of the son of Spalahores, Spalagadames the Just'). As with 5.681, 5.686 also has smaller denominations. 5.687(a–c) is a silver drachm with similar inscriptions as 686, and 688(a–b) consists of a bronze rectangular Tri-chalkon (6.38 grams) with similar inscriptions and iconography as 5.683.

Similar titles are attested on the coinage of King Spalirises during the period of 65–40 BCE. MIG 5.694(a–c) is a bronze hemi-obol weighing 8.50 grams and on the obverse depicts the king walking left, holding an ankus (elephant hook) and bow, with a whip over his shoulder. The inscription reads, ΒΑΣΙΛΕΥΣ ΒΑΣΙΛΕΩΝ ΜΕΓΑΛΟΥ ΡΠΑΛΙΡΙΣΟΥ (trans. 'king of kings, great Spalirises') (Figure 73). MIG 5.694 and other coins of Spalirises spell his name in Greek with a Scythian-Yeuh Chi, what looks like a rho, but actually attempts to transliterate the 'sh' phoneme. The reverse depicts Zeus enthroned with his right hand outstretched, the inscription on the reverse reads, *Maharajasa mahatakasa Spalirishasa*.

Coinage of the eastern Bactrian provinces continues the chronological trajectory that we have established thus far. Orodes II, *c*. 57 to 38 BCE, minted MIG 5.642 with sub-varieties a (from Margiana) and b (from Nyssa). MIG 5.642 portrays, on the obverse, a diademed bust of the king facing left with a short beard. The reverse has an archer seated right upon a stool. The inscription on the reverse reads ΒΑΣΙΛΕΥΣ

Figure 73 MIG 5.694 (used with permission).

ΒΑΣΙΛΕΩΝ ΗΝΟΣ ΕΠΙΦΑΙΝΟΥΣ ΚΑΙ ΦΙΛΕΑ ΑΡΣΑΚΟΝ ΦΙΛΟΠΑΤΟΡΟΣ ΔΙΚΑΟΥ (trans. 'king of kings, Inos, notable friend Arsaces, Philopator, just'). Another silver drachm of Orodes 5.643(a-e) of 2.42 grams is similar to 5.642, but adds a star (in front of bust) and a crescent (behind bust) on the obverse. The reverse maintains the seated archer, but has the following inscription, ΒΑΣΙΛΕΥΣ ΒΑΣΙΛΕΩΝ ΑΡΣΑΚΟΥ ΕΥΕΡΓΕΤΟΥ ΔΙΚΑΙΟΥ (trans. 'king of kings, Arsaces, benefactor, just'). MIG 5.644, a coin of Phraates IV, c. 38 to 2 BCE, has the identical Greek inscription as 5.642, but depicts the diademed bust facing left with an eagle behind. It similarly portrays a seated archer with bow on the reverse and includes the following inscription, ΒΑΣΙΛΕΥΣ ΒΑΣΙΛΕΩΝ ΑΡΣΛΚΟΥ (trans. 'king of kings, Arsaces').

The Indo-Scythian dynasty of Azes I and Azilises (57–35 BCE) demonstrates further and widespread use of the title in the first century BCE. MIG 6.737 (Figure 74) is a silver tetradrachm (9.68 grams) and on the obverse depicts Zeus standing left holding a long sceptre with accompanying inscription, ΒΑΣΙΛΕΥΣ ΒΑΣΙΛΕΩΝ ΜΕΓΑΛΟΥ ΑΖΟΥ (trans. 'king of kings great Azes'). The reverse has a winged Nike standing right, holding wreath and palm, with an equivalent inscription in Kharoshthi script. MIG 6.738 has similar iconography and inscription but is the lower denomination of a drachm (2.42 grams). MIG 6.739 (silver tetradrachm, 9.68 grams) has the identical inscription but depicts the king holding a spear mounted on a horse on the obverse. Copper issues are extant in rectangular penta-chalkons, MIG 6.740 (Figure 75) has the same inscriptions but portrays, on the obverse, Poseidon standing facing with right foot on river god and hand on knee, holding a long trident in left hand. The obverse has Yakshi (female pagan nature spirit) standing between vines.[41] MIG 6.742 has the

Figure 74 MIG 6.737 (used with permission).

[41] Fred S. Kleiner, *Gardiner's Art through the Ages: Non-Western Perspectives* (Boston: Wadsworth, 2010), 16; Asha Vishnu, *Material Like of North India: Based on an Archaeological Study, 3rd Century B.C to 1st Century A.D.* (New Delhi: Mittal Publications, 1993), 121.

Figure 75 MIG 6.740 (used with permission).

same inscription and iconography as 6.740 but is issued as a rectangular chalkous (2.42 grams). MIG 6.743 portrays king holding spear, mounted on a horse walking right on the obverse with inscription ΒΑΣΙΛΕΥΣ ΒΑΣΙΛΕΩΝ ΜΕΓΑΛΟΥ ΑΖΟΥ (trans. 'king of kings great Azes'). The reverse has a depiction of the city goddess standing left, holding a palm and lamp with Kharoshthi inscription. In addition, there are twenty further examples, in varying denominations with the obverse inscription ΒΑΣΙΛΕΥΣ ΒΑΣΙΛΕΩΝ ΜΕΓΑΛΟΥ ΑΖΟΥ.[42] The joint coinage of Azes I and Azilises adds to this number over forty-seven distinct issues (with several hundred sub-varieties) with the obverse inscription reading ΒΑΣΙΛΕΥΣ ΒΑΣΙΛΕΩΝ ΜΕΓΑΛΟΥ ΑΖΙΛΙΣΟΥ, and various elements of iconography already discussed.[43]

During the period of the Scythians in the east, in particular throughout the age of the Satraps (1–35 CE), several notable numismatic issues deserve attention. MIG 7.895 is a silver tetradrachm (9.90 grams) issued by Arsakes, ruler of Sakastan (c. 30 CE), and depicts the king, on the obverse, holding a whip, mounted on a horse walking right. The inscription reads ΒΑΣΙΛΕΥΟΝΤΟΣ ΒΑΣΙΛΕΩΝ ΔΙΚΑΙΟΥ ΑΡΣΑΚΟΥ (trans. 'king of kings, Arsakes the just'). The reverse depicts Zeus standing left holding winged Nike on his outstretched right hand, and a long sceptre in his left hand. MIG 7.896 is also a silver tetradrachm (9.90 grams) and has the same obverse iconography and inscription as 7.895, but with a longer Kharoshthi inscription on the reverse. Both these examples are particularly interesting as they preserve the title as a participle plus noun form. As we will see in our discussion below, the only morphological variation

---

[42] MIG 6.743, 744, 745, 746, 747, 748, 749, 750, 751, 752, 753, 754, 755, 756, 757, 758, 759, 760, 761, 762.

[43] MIG 6.763, 766, 767, 768, 769, 770, 771, 772, 773, 774, 775, 776, 777, 778, 779, 780, 781, 782, 783, 784, 785, 786, 787, 788, 789, 790, 791, 792, 793, 794, 795, 796, 797, 798, 799, 800, 801, 802, 803, 804, 805, 806, 807, 808, 809, 810, 811, 812.

in the NT attestation of the title is precisely this, the substitution of a participle for one of the nouns.

Later coins in the period of the first century CE of the Indo-Parthians also attest to similar titulature. From the province of Sakastan there are more than a dozen examples, of which we will highlight only the most salient for our discussion. MIG 8.1067 is a silver Attic drachm (3.7 grams) of Gondophares minted between 20 and 55 CE. MIG 8.1067 is iconographically in the Indo-Parthian style with bust facing left, close fitting undecorated non-radiate cap with posterior cords. The reverse has the king enthroned right, crowned by winged Nike standing behind the throne. The inscription commences, ΒΑΣΙΛΕΥΣ ΒΑΣΙΛΕΩΝ (trans. 'king of kings'). MIG 8.1068 attests similar iconography on the obverse and with only slight variation in the latter part of the reverse inscription, it does however begin identically, ΒΑΣΙΛΕΥΣ ΒΑΣΙΛΕΩΝ, as do MIG 8.1069 and 8.1070 (Figure 76). MIG 8.1072(a–b) is an Arachosian silver tetradrachm countermarked for use in Sakastan. The obverse has a bust of Gondophares facing left, with inscription, ΒΑΣΙΛΕΥΣ ΒΑΣΙΛΕΩΝ ΜΕΓΑΛΟΥ ΥΝΔΥΦΕΡΡΟΥ. The reverse depicts winged Nike standing right holding a wreath and palm.[44] Again there are several dozen relevant examples that support the general picture sketched thus far; that of the widespread Parthian use of the title βασιλεὺς βασιλέων for their rulers. Further evidence is readily available from many other first-century CE Indo-Parthian numismatic inscriptions (see Table 23).[45]

Figure 76 MIG 8.1070 (used with permission).

---

[44] Cf. MIG 4.508, local Balkh coinage of the Kushite King Soter Megas, c. 45/50 CE, which depicts, on the obverse, a diademed bust of the king facing right with pronounced hook at front of nose. The reverse has Zeus standing facing holding thunderbolt and sceptre with inscription, ΒΑΣΙΛΕΥΣ ΒΑΣΙΛΕΩΝ ΣΩΤΗΡ ΜΕΓΑΣ (trans. 'king of kings, great saviour'). The coin is a bronze reduced Attic drachm.

[45] Coinage of Gondophares (25–35 CE) MIG 8.1094, 1095; Coinage of Orthagnes (35–55 CE), MIG 8.1073, 1074, 1075, 1096, 1097, 1098, 1099; Coinage of Otannes III (son of Orthagnes, 35–55 CE), MIG 8.1076; Coinage of Sorpedonus (60 CE), MIG 8.1100; Coinage of Abdagases (55–100/110 CE), MIG 8.1077; Coinage of Pakores (100/110–135 CE), MIG 8.1078, 1102, 1103.

208 Numismatics and Greek Lexicography

Table 23 Selective table of numismatic inscriptional evidence for ΒΑΣΙΛΕΥΣ ΒΑΣΙΛΕΩΝ

Reference	Denomination and weight	Inscription
MIG 5.681a, 681b, 681c	silver tetradrachm, 9.68 grams	ΒΑΣΙΛΕΥΣ ΒΑΣΙΛΕΩΝ ΜΕΓΑΛΟΥ ΟΝΩΝΟΥ
MIG 5.682a, 682b, 682c	silver drachm, 2.42 grams	ΒΑΣΙΛΕΥΣ ΒΑΣΙΛΕΩΝ ΜΕΓΑΛΟΥ ΟΝΩΝΟΥ
MIG 5.683a, 683b, 683c	rectangular bronze hemi-obol (4 chalkoi), 8.50 grams	ΒΑΣΙΛΕΥΣ ΒΑΣΙΛΕΩΝ ΜΕΓΑΛΟΥ ΟΝΩΝΟΥ
MIG 5.684	rectangular bronze Di-chalkon (2 chalkoi), 4.25 grams	ΒΑΣΙΛΕΥΣ ΒΑΣΙΛΕΩΝ ΜΕΓΑΛΟΥ ΟΝΩΝΟΥ
MIG 5.686a, 686b	silver tetradrachm, 9.68 grams	ΒΑΣΙΛΕΥΣ ΒΑΣΙΛΕΩΝ ΜΕΓΑΛΟΥ ΟΝΩΝΟΥ
MIG 5.687a, 687b, 687c	silver drachm, 2.42 grams	ΒΑΣΙΛΕΥΣ ΒΑΣΙΛΕΩΝ ΜΕΓΑΛΟΥ ΟΝΩΝΟΥ
MIG 5.688a, 688b	rectangular bronze Tri-chalkon (3 chalkoi), 6.38 grams	ΒΑΣΙΛΕΥΣ ΒΑΣΙΛΕΩΝ ΜΕΓΑΛΟΥ ΟΝΩΝΟΥ
MIG 5.694a, 694b, 694c	rectangular bronze hemi-obol, 8.50 grams	ΒΑΣΙΛΕΥΣ ΒΑΣΙΛΕΩΝ ΜΕΓΑΛΟΥ ΡΠΑΛΙΡΙΣΟΥ
MIG 5.642a, 642b	silver drachm, 2.42 grams	ΒΑΣΙΛΕΥΣ ΒΑΣΙΛΕΩΝ ΗΝΟΣ ΕΠΙΦΑΙΝΟΥ ΣΚΑΙ ΦΙΛΕΑ ΛΡΣΑΚΟΝ ΦΙΛΟΠΑΤΟΡΟΣ ΔΙΚΑΟΥ
MIG 5.643a, 643b, 643c, 643d, 643e	silver drachm, 2.42 grams	ΒΑΣΙΛΕΥΣ ΒΑΣΙΛΕΩΝ ΑΡΣΑΚΟΥ ΕΥΕΡΓΕΤΟΥ ΔΙΚΑΙΟΥ
MIG 5.644	silver drachm, 2.42 grams	ΒΑΣΙΛΕΥΣ ΒΑΣΙΛΕΩΝ ΑΡΣΑΚΟΥ
MIG 7.895	silver tetradrachm, 9.90 grams	ΒΑΣΙΛΕΥΟΝΤΟΣ ΒΑΣΙΛΕΩΝ ΔΙΚΑΙΟΥ ΑΡΣΑΚΟΥ
MIG 7.896	silver tetradrachm, 9.90 grams	ΒΑΣΙΛΕΥΟΝΤΟΣ ΒΑΣΙΛΕΩΝ ΔΙΚΑΙΟΥ ΑΡΣΑΚΟΥ
MIG 8.1067	silver Attic drachm, 3.70 grams	ΒΑΣΙΛΕΥΣ ΒΑΣΙΛΕΩΝ …
MIG 8.1068a, 1068b	silver Attic drachm, 3.70 grams	ΒΑΣΙΛΕΥΣ ΒΑΣΙΛΕΩΝ …
MIG 8.1069	silver Attic drachm, 3.70 grams	ΒΑΣΙΛΕΥΣ ΒΑΣΙΛΕΩΝ …
MIG 8.1070	silver Attic drachm, 3.70 grams	ΒΑΣΙΛΕΥΣ ΒΑΣΙΛΕΩΝ …
MIG 8.1072a, 1072b	bronze tetradrachm, 8.50 grams	ΒΑΣΙΛΕΥΣ ΒΑΣΙΛΕΩΝ ΜΕΓΑΛΟΥ ΥΝΔΨΦΕΡΡΟΥ
MIG 4.508	bronze reduced Attic drachm, 4.36–3.37 grams	ΒΑΣΙΛΕΥΣ ΒΑΣΙΛΕΩΝ ΣΩΤΗΡ ΜΕΓΑΣ

(Continued)

Reference	Denomination and weight	Inscription
MIG 6.737	silver tetradrachm, 9.68 grams	ΒΑΣΙΛΕΥΣ ΒΑΣΙΛΕΩΝ ΜΕΓΑΛΟΥ ΑΖΟΥ
MIG 6.738	drachm, 2.42 grams	ΒΑΣΙΛΕΥΣ ΒΑΣΙΛΕΩΝ ΜΕΓΑΛΟΥ ΑΖΟΥ
MIG 6.739	silver tetradrachm, 9.68 grams	ΒΑΣΙΛΕΥΣ ΒΑΣΙΛΕΩΝ ΜΕΓΑΛΟΥ ΑΖΟΥ
MIG 6.740	bronze rectangular penta-chalkon	ΒΑΣΙΛΕΥΣ ΒΑΣΙΛΕΩΝ ΜΕΓΑΛΟΥ ΑΖΟΥ
MIG 6.742	bronze rectangular chalkon	ΒΑΣΙΛΕΥΣ ΒΑΣΙΛΕΩΝ ΜΕΓΑΛΟΥ ΑΖΟΥ
MIG 6.743, 744, 745, 746, 747, 748, 749, 750, 751, 752, 753, 754, 755, 756, 757, 758, 759, 760, 761, 762.	various	ΒΑΣΙΛΕΥΣ ΒΑΣΙΛΕΩΝ ΜΕΓΑΛΟΥ ΑΖΟΥ
MIG 6.763, 766, 767, 768, 769, 770, 771, 772, 773, 774, 775, 776, 777, 778, 779, 780, 781, 782, 783, 784, 785, 786, 787, 788, 789, 790, 791, 792, 793, 794, 795, 796, 797, 798, 799, 800, 801, 802, 803, 804, 805, 806, 807, 808, 809, 810, 811, 812.	various	ΒΑΣΙΛΕΥΣ ΒΑΣΙΛΕΩΝ ΜΕΓΑΛΟΥ ΑΖΙΛΙΣΟΥ
MIG 8.1094, 1095	various	ΒΑΣΙΛΕΥΣ ΒΑΣΙΛΕΩΝ ...
MIG 8.1073, 1074, 1075, 1096, 1097, 1098, 1099	various	ΒΑΣΙΛΕΥΣ ΒΑΣΙΛΕΩΝ ...
MIG 8.1076	silver Attic drachm, 3.70 grams	ΒΑΣΙΛΕΥΣ ΒΑΣΙΛΕΩΝ ...
MIG 8.1100	bronze tetradrachm, 8.50 grams	ΒΑΣΙΛΕΥΣ ΒΑΣΙΛΕΩΝ ...
MIG 8.1077	silver Attic drachm, 3.70 grams	ΒΑΣΙΛΕΥΣ ΒΑΣΙΛΕΩΝ ...
MIG 8.1078, 1102, 1103	various	ΒΑΣΙΛΕΥΣ ΒΑΣΙΛΕΩΝ ...

Interpretive implications for the book of Revelation

We now turn our attention to the implications of the above discussion on the interpretation of the NT. Jesus is referred to as the 'king of kings' once in the *Pastorals* and twice in the *Apocalypse*.

1 Timothy 6:15, 'which he will bring about at the right time – he who is the blessed and only Sovereign, the King of kings (ὁ βασιλεὺς τῶν βασιλευόντων) and Lord of lords'.

Revelation 17:14, 'they will make war on the Lamb, and the Lamb will conquer them, for he is Lord of lords and King of kings (βασιλεὺς βασιλέων), and those with him are called and chosen and faithful'

Revelation 19:16, 'On his robe and on his thigh he has a name inscribed, "King of kings (βασιλεὺς βασιλέων) and Lord of lords"'. This title for Jesus then sharply contrasts and critiques the legitimacy of all others in a polemic fashion.

The focus of the current discussion will be on the title in the apocalypse due to the morphological similarity between its use there and with the evidence discussed above.

The book of Revelation is composed as an apocalyptic prophetic circular letter (Rev 1:1–3) addressed to churches in Asia Minor in order to encourage Christians who were suffering persecution under the Roman Empire. A key symbol in the work occurs within the vision of the heavenly throne room in chapters 4–5, where Jesus is portrayed as the slain lamb who defeats his enemies by dying for them.[46] The ultimate and final fall of Babylon in chapters 17:1–19:16 portrays a woman riding a symbol (seven-headed ten-horned beast, Rev 17:3) of the rebellious nations who is intoxicated on the shed blood of the followers of Jesus and all the innocent (Rev 17:6; 18:24). She is referred to as 'Babylon the great, mother of whores and of earth's abominations' (Rev 17:5) and personifies the military and economic power of the Roman Empire. The final battle (19:11–20:15) results in the vindication of the martyrs and leads to the arrival of the οὐρανὸν καινὸν καὶ γῆν καινήν (trans. 'new heaven and new earth'). Within this thematic presentation the author twice uses the title βασιλεὺς βασιλέων (Rev 17:14; 19:16) for the conquering Jesus.

The Roman emperor was not styled or titled as 'king' or its superlative variations.[47] The Romans, at least for the last six centuries BCE, had been defined by their anti-regal stance after the overthrow of King Tarquinius Superbus by Junius Brutus and the founding of the Roman republic in 509 BCE.[48] Most commentators commenting on Revelation 19 therefore view the title βασιλεὺς βασιλέων in light of the OT texts such as Deuteronomy 10:17, Daniel 2:47,[49] 4:37,[50] even though the title does not appear verbatim. J. Massyngberde suggests that the title would be especially appropriate in the time of Domitian, 'our lord and god' (Suetonius, *Domitian* 13).[51] Others interpret

[46] Rev 5:6, 8, 12–13; 6:1, 16, 7:9–10, 14, 17; 12:11; 13:8, 11; 14:1, 4, 10; 15:3; 17:14; 19:7, 9; 21:9, 14, 22–23, 27–22:1; 22:3.

[47] There is no evidence that the Roman emperors 'claimed the title "king of kings"' as stated by Peter S. Williamson, *Revelation* (Grand Rapids, Michigan: Baker Academic, 2015), 281.

[48] Regents in the provinces were sparingly permitted the title 'king' but this was not typical, cf. Jn 19:15; Mt 14:9.

[49] Beale, *Revelation*, 880.

[50] G. K. Beale and Sean M. McDonough, 'Revelation', in *Commentary on the New Testament Use of the Old Testament*, ed. G. K. Beale and D. A. Carson (Grand Rapids: Baker Academic, 2007), 1144; Beale, *Revelation*, 963.

[51] J. Massyngberde Ford, *Revelation: Introduction, Translation, and Commentary* (London: Yale University Press, 2008), 282.

βασιλεὺς βασιλέων in Revelation 19:16 as expressing the generic idea of 'ultimate ruler over all kings',[52] in so far as the genitive functions as a genitive of subordination 'with the idea being that the βασιλεύς is superior over the βασιλέων in the genitive ("king over and above all other kings").'[53] Some, rather dubiously, attempt to retro-translate the phrase Βασιλεὺς βασιλέων καὶ κύριος κυρίων into Aramaic (excluding the word 'and') and calculate via gematria the number of the letters, which is 777, 'the victorious counterpart and antidote to 666'.[54] However, as extensively documented in our above analysis, the title βασιλεὺς βασιλέων was ubiquitous east of the Roman Empire, in particular not only Parthia but also the Indo-Scythians, Indo-Parthians and Indo-Greeks. So much so that there was not a single Parthian ruler in the first century CE who did not use the title on his coinage. Although some commentators do refer to Parthia in their exegetical discussions on Revelation 19, C. R. Koester glosses over the titulature,[55] David A. Thomas focuses on the Parthian iconography of the diadem without any substantive discussion on the inscriptions,[56] and most others (as noted above) focus on the relevant OT passages as background to the phrases interpretation. The interpretation that will be argued presently is that the figure of Christ in both Revelation 17:14 and 19:16 explicitly depicts Christ as symbolic Parthia, that is, the author uses the symbols and titles of Rome's feared enemy to depict the lamb's victory.[57] This identification is supported by four lines of evidence.

---

[52] J. H. Moulton, W. F. Howard, and M. Turner, *A Grammar of New Testament Greek*, 4 vols. (Edinburgh: T&T Clark, 1906–1976), 2:443.

[53] David L. Mathewson, *Revelation: A Handbook on the Greek Text* (Waco, Texas: Baylor University Press, 2016), 268. Daniel B. Wallace, *Greek Grammar beyond the Basics: An Exegetical Syntax of the New Testament* (Grand Rapids: Zondervan, 1996), 136 n.84, further distinguishes between 'genitive of subordination' and a 'par excellence noun', namely 'the class of which the head noun is the supreme member'.

[54] Ben Witherington, *Revelation* (Cambridge: Cambridge University Press, 2003), 244. Also see a similar interpretation in C. H. Giblin, *The Book of Revelation: The Open Book of Prophecy* (Collegeville: Liturgical Press, 1991), 182, and M. Rissi, 'Die Erscheinung Christi nach Off. 19.11–16', *Theologische Zeitschrift* 21 (1965): 81–95.

[55] C. R. Koester, *Revelation* (New Haven: Yale University Press, 2015), 754.

[56] David Andrew Thomas, *Revelation 19 in Historical and Mythological Context* (New York: Peter Lang, 2008), 130–132. Thomas does however provide good evidence in regard to the διαδήματα πολλά (trans. 'many diadems') in Revelation 19:12 which reinforce the picture that emerges from the inscriptional evidence. He states on pages 130–131, that 'the diadem became the permanent symbol of regal power for the Parthian monarch... [it] was an oriental symbol of authority that could not plausibly be associated with the Roman emperor'. See further Fred B. Shore, *Parthian Coins & History: Ten Dragons against Rome* (Quarryville: Classical Numismatic Group, 1993), 141–142.

[57] The location of the name in Revelation 19:16 is ἐπὶ τὸν μηρὸν αὐτοῦ (trans. 'on his thigh'), which may draw on the practice of inscribing one or more names on the thigh of a statue of a deity, as described by, for example, within the sacred precinct of Zeus at Olympia, Pausanius records that he saw a statue which had 'an elegiac couplet is written on its thigh: – To Zeus, king of the gods, as first-fruits was I placed here. By the Mendeans, who reduced Sipte by might of hand' Pausanius, 5.27.12, W. H. S. Jones and H. A. Ormerod, trans., *Pausanias. Description of Greece, Volume II: Books 3–5 (Laconia, Messenia, Elis 1)* (LCL 188; Cambridge, MA: Harvard University Press, 1926), 550–551. The inscription of a name on the rider in chapter 19 contrasts sharply with the representation of the whore riding the beast, who also has names and titles written on her body (Rev 17:3–5). Beale, *Revelation*, 963, notes that the location at the thigh recalls the typical location of the warrior's sword, based on passages such as Exodus 32:27, Judges 3:16, 21, and Psalm 45:3. This effectively replaces the military sword with the sword of his mouth (Rev 19:15).

First, the Parthians were Rome's most notorious military enemy during the first century BCE and first century CE. The Roman-Parthian wars stretched from 53 BCE to 217 CE. The Battle of Carrhae in 53 BCE saw the Parthian General Surena decisively defeat Marcus Licinius Crassus's seven Roman legions in upper Mesopotamia. Plutarch recounts the encounter in considerable detail, 'Οἱ δὲ Πάρθοι διαστάντες ἐκ μήκους ἤρξαντο τοξεύειν ἅμα πανταχόθεν' (trans. 'but the Parthians now stood at long intervals from one another and began to shoot their arrows from all sides at once').[58] Plutarch offers further vivid descriptions of the Parthian archers, 'making vigorous and powerful shots from bows which were large and mighty and curved so as to discharge their missiles with great force.'[59] The only hope the Romans had was that eventually the missiles would be exhausted, 'but when they perceived that many camels laden with arrows were at hand, from which the Parthians who first encircled them took a fresh supply, then Crassus, seeing no end to this, began to lose heart.'[60] The result was a devastating loss for the Romans, with over 20,000 killed and 10,000 captured,[61] one of the most catastrophic defeats in Roman military history. Other significant defeats of the Roman forces by Parthian armies occurred in the Syrian invasion of 40 BCE in which all the cities of the coast were taken (except Tyre), the Roman client Hyrcanus II was overthrown and Antigonus was installed in his place (40–37 BCE). Despite a compromise between Caesar and Phraataces in 1 CE over the Roman control of Armenia, much of the region continued to be contested by both for decades.[62] In 36 CE Artabanus II installed his son Arsaces on the vacant Armenian throne, an action which triggered a war. A similar incident occurred in the installation of Tiridates on the Armenian throne by the Parthian king (and his brother) Vologases I in 58 CE.[63] Roman forces replaced Tiridates with a Cappadocian prince, which in turn led to a series of Parthian invasions over five years until an agreement was settled on which allowed the Parthian control of Armenia on the condition that the kingship was granted by the Roman emperor. Despite this in principle agreement, there continued to be significant conflict between the two states well into the second century, culminating in Trajan's Parthian campaign (115–117 CE).

Second, two specific geographic references within the apocalypse support the identification of Parthia as the (symbolic) threat.[64] After the sixth angel's trumpet blast instructions are given to 'release the four angels who are bound at the great river Euphrates' (Rev 9:14). Similarly, the outpouring of the sixth bowl is described as follows, 'The sixth angel poured his bowl on the great river Euphrates, and its water

---

[58] Plutarch, *Lives: Crassus* 24.5; Bernadotte Perrin, *Plutarch. Lives, Volume III: Pericles and Fabius Maximus. Nicias and Crassus* (LCL 65; Cambridge, MA: Harvard University Press, 1916), 388–389.

[59] Perrin, *Plutarch. Lives, Volume III*, 388–389.

[60] Perrin, *Plutarch. Lives, Volume III*, 390–391.

[61] Plutarch, *Life of Crassus*, 31.7; Perrin, *Plutarch. Lives, Volume III*, 412–417.

[62] Martin Sicker, *The Pre-Islamic Middle East* (London: Praeger, 2000), 162.

[63] Sicker, *The Pre-Islamic*, 163.

[64] M. E. Boring, *Revelation* (Louisville: Westminster John Knox, 1989); R. H. Charles, *A Critical and Exegetical Commentary on the Revelation of St. John*, 2 vols. (Edinburgh: T. & T. Clark, 1920); Wilfrid J. Harrington, *Revelation* (Collegeville: Liturgical, 1993); Frederick J. Murphy, *Fallen Is Babylon: The Revelation to John* (Harrisburg: Trinity, 1998); Grant R. Osborne, *Revelation* (Grand Rapids: Baker Academic, 2002).

was dried up in order to prepare the way for the kings from the east' (Rev 16:12). Historical memory is preserved by Herodotus who records that when Babylon was overtaken by the Persians in 539 BCE, they diverted the Euphrates River and marched into the city on the river bed:

> He (Cyrus) posted his army at the place where the river enters the city, and another part of it where the stream issues from the city ... Having so arrayed them ... [he drew] off the river by a canal into the lake, which was till now a marsh, he made the stream to sink till its former channel could be forded. When this happened, the Persians who were posted with this intent made their way into Babylon by the channel of the Euphrates, which had now sunk about to the height of the middle of a man's thigh.[65]

Strabo confirms that the Euphrates marked the eastern boundary of the Roman Empire, 'The Euphrates and the land beyond it constitute the boundary of the Parthian empire. But the parts this side the river are held by the Romans.'[66] The specific motif of eastern forces crossing the Euphrates boundary in attack is attested in earlier apocalyptic literature. 1 Enoch 56:5–6, composed in the period of 105–64 BCE,[67] has the following in description of the struggle of Israel with her enemies:

> In those days, the angels will assemble and thrust themselves to the east at the Parthians and Medes. They will shake up the kings (so that) a spirit of unrest shall come upon them, and stir them up from their thrones; and they will break forth from their beds like lions and like hungry hyenas among their own flocks. And they will go up and trample upon the land of my elect ones and the land of my elect ones will be before them like a threshing floor or a highway.

Revelation too has angels letting foreign forces loose at the Euphrates's eastern border. Whereas in Revelation 9:14 the hostile forces gather at a ford on the Euphrates, now (16:12) that river bed is dried up, and the eastern Parthian forces can cross the mighty Euphrates bed at any point of their choosing.

Third, other descriptive features also enhance this symbolic Parthian threat. The first of the four riders in Revelation 6:2 has been variously understood, including as Christ himself and the conquering as the spreading gospel.[68] One of several issues with this identification is that the rider holds a bow whereas Christ does war with the sword of his

---

[65] A. D. Godley, *Herodotus. The Persian Wars*, Volume I: Books 1–2 (LCL 117; Cambridge, MA: Harvard University Press, 1920), 238–241.

[66] Strabo, *Geography* 16.1.28, Horace Leonard Jones, *Strabo. Geography, Volume VII: Books 15–16* (LCL 241; Cambridge, MA: Harvard University Press, 1930), 237.

[67] E. Isaac, '1 (Ethiopic Apocalypse of) Enoch', in *The Old Testament Pseudepigrapha: Volume One, Apocalyptic Literature and Testament*, ed. J. H. Charlesworth (Peabody: Hendrickson Publishers, 1983), 7.

[68] Edmundo F. Lupieri, *A Commentary on the Apocalypse of John*, trans. Maria Poggi Johnson and Adam Kamesar (Grand Rapids: Eerdmans, 1999); Christopher Rowland, *Revelation* (Nashville: Abingdon, 1998), 82; John Sweet, *Revelation* (London: SCM, 1990), 139 states 'the witness of the church is the means of Christ's reign on earth'.

214   *Numismatics and Greek Lexicography*

mouth (1:16; 2:16; 19:15, 21), or indeed that the riders are best taken as a group, and no interpreter in the major commentaries has seen the plausibility of identifying the other three as Christlike. More probable is the view that all four horses represent the threat of human war and conquest.[69] Adding to this portrayal is that the rider of the white horse has a bow and crown (Rev 6:2). As is evident from historical accounts of Parthian military activity, the favoured form of offence was mounted bowmen, although they obviously did not limit themselves to this single form of attack.[70] The iconography of the king mounted on a horse in the Parthian coins surveyed above also confirms this symbolic image, as do the multiple examples of bowmen on the reverse of coins above.[71]

Fourth, after Nero's demise in 68 CE, there arose speculation as to whether he was actually dead or had departed to the east to raise an army and return to reclaim his throne. Suetonius, *Nero* 57 records:

> He met his death in the thirty-second year of his age, on the anniversary of the murder of Octavia, and such was the public rejoicing that the people put on liberty caps and ran about all over the city. Yet there were some who for a long time decorated his tomb with spring and summer flowers, and now produced his statues on the rostra in the fringed toga, and now his edicts, as if he were still alive and would shortly return and deal destruction to his enemies. Nay more, Vologaesus, king of the Parthians, when he sent envoys to the senate to renew his alliance, earnestly begged this too, that honour be paid to the memory of Nero. In fact, twenty years later, when I was a young man, a person of obscure origin appeared, who gave out that he was Nero, and the name was still in such favour with the Parthians that they supported him vigorously and surrendered him with great reluctance.[72]

Ian Boxall observes that 'this would not have been lost on Roman hearers of the Apocalypse ... Nero was about to return, backed by his Parthian allies.'[73]

Conclusion

We began by noting the variegated ways in which the titular phrase βασιλεὺς βασιλέων has been understood by the secondary literature, governed primarily by differing views of the proposed textual foreground and background (LXX, Babylonian, Roman etc.).

---

[69] Robert Mounce, *The Book of Revelation* (Grand Rapids: Eerdmans, 1998), 152–154; Jürgen Roloff, *Revelation*, trans. John E. Alsup (Minneapolis: Fortress, 1993), 133.

[70] Plutarch, *Luc.* 28.2–4; Plutarch, *Crass.* 25.8.

[71] See above discussion on Sellwood 27.2; 41.8; 42.2, cf. MIG 694(a–c); 644.

[72] Suetonius, *Nero* 57, J. C. Rolfe, trans. *Suetonius. Lives of the Caesars, Volume II: Claudius. Nero. Galba, Otho, and Vitellius. Vespasian. Titus, Domitian. Lives of Illustrious Men: Grammarians and Rhetoricians. Poets (Terence. Virgil. Horace. Tibullus. Persius. Lucan). Lives of Pliny the Elder and Passienus Crispus* (LCL 38; Cambridge, MA: Harvard University Press, 1914), 178–181. Cf. Tacitus, *Hist.* 1.2; 2.8f; Sib. Or. 4:119–124, 137–139; 5:137–152, 361–385.

[73] Ian Boxall, *The Revelation of St. John* (London: Continuum, 2006), 108.

ΒΑΣΙΛΕΥΣ ΒΑΣΙΛΕΩΝ

Although it was acknowledged that the origin of the phrase was derived, according to the earliest primary sources, from a Semitic context (possibly Akkadian), the title was more regularly used for kings from the 'east'. This was demonstrably the case for Babylonia, Persia, Indo-Greek, Indo-Scythian and Bactrian states. The title was, however, overwhelming most regularly attested on the coins of Parthia, in terms of both numerical attestations and consistency of application to the rulers in the first century BCE to first century CE. As was highlighted in our above analysis, in the first century CE there was not a single Parthian ruler who did not use the title βασιλεὺς βασιλέων on his coinage. It was also seen that although Greeks, Romans and Hellenistic Jews were familiar with the title, as evidenced in the usage with Zeus and the children of Cleopatra and Antony, the phrase was never adopted and applied to a human ruler.

Within the book of Revelation Jesus is thus presented triumphantly conquering Rome in the image of Rome's feared enemy; he shares both the title and form of transport. Ironically, or perhaps quite suitably, the ultimate conqueror of Rome is portrayed in the form of her historic enemy. Koester states that 'the Roman fear of Parthia is often overstated'[74] citing the occasion of the brother of the Parthian king formally submitted to Nero in 66 CE as support. However, Koester (a) underestimates the volatile nature of the Roman/Parthian relations in the final decades of the first century (after all the Parthian conflict in 115 CE under Hadrian did not occur in a vacuum), and (b) seems to overlook that the image in Revelation is drawing on the historic memory of the Parthians rather than being an imminent threat, although this should not necessarily be ruled out. In sum, the title and figure of Jesus in Revelation 17:14 and 19:16 play on the historic fears and anxieties of a Parthian invasion through memory of multiple points of reference, but in particular the title given to Jesus is βασιλεὺς βασιλέων.

[74] Koester, *Revelation*, 395.

12

Conclusion

The celebrated ancient Roman historian Livy (59 BCE–17 CE) recorded the following words in the preface of his *Ab Urbe Condita* (trans. 'from the founding of the city') 1.10:

> What chiefly makes the study of history wholesome and profitable is this, that you behold the lessons of every kind of experience set forth as on a conspicuous monument; from these you may choose for yourself and for your own state what to imitate, from these mark for avoidance what is shameful in the conception and shameful in the result.[1]

Livy's observations on the value of paying close attention to and studying ancient history metaphorically refer to this as a 'monument' recording the deeds of the nation, from which one can derive much benefit. Nowhere else is this observation more evident than the numismatic record, wherein there is preserved a wealth of cultural, social, political and, most importantly for our purposes, linguistic material illustrating and contextualizing the Greek language of the first century CE. As noted throughout, the modest aim of this volume has been to encourage conversation between two, traditionally distant, academic fields: numismatics and Greek lexicography. Such an attempt is, unfortunately, fraught with difficulty due to the highly nuanced, specialist and often introspective nature of each discipline. In the current study we have been predominantly concerned with implications of this interdisciplinary enquiry of numismatics and lexicography for insights into New Testament studies, but the application could, with further research, be broadened to adjacent fields in Septuagint studies or Hellenistic Greek.

Within the last century, there have been significant shifts in the endeavour to incorporate a broader array and fuller dataset in the composition of Greek lexicons, evidenced for instance in the consideration of the documentary papyri in attesting usage of the language. Throughout this study, we have sought to highlight a specific lacuna in the evidence used for Hellenistic Greek lexicography, not to the exclusion of any others, but the inclusion of numismatic material alongside other traditional evidence.

---

[1] Livy, *History of Rome* 1.10, B. O. Foster, trans., *Livy: History of Rome, Volume I: Books 1–2* (LCL 114; Cambridge, MA: Harvard University Press, 1919), 7.

The study was structured into two distinct parts to facilitate initial methodological reflection (Part I: Chapters 1–4), and applied examples of the approach to New Testament studies that sought to demonstrate the cogency of the method (Part II: Chapters 5–11). More specifically, however, Chapter 1, *Introduction*, sketched a high-level vision for the inclusion of numismatic material not merely for iconographic contributions, but specifically for philological contributions. It was seen that the incorporation of previously neglected Greek lexical data was not only methodologically desirable, but had the potential to open new interpretive vistas for both lexicography in general, and New Testament studies in particular.

In order to contextualize the particular material culture under discussion, a historical survey of coinage was provided in Chapter 2, *The History of Coinage*. This chapter sought not only to demonstrate the great variety of coinage produced in antiquity, but also to provide a diachronic framework for the evolution of coinage from its earliest adoption in Asia Minor in the seventh century BCE through to its prolific use in the thousands of varieties attested on Roman provincial examples.

Chapter 3, *The Study of Coinage*, was primarily written for colleagues who desire to utilize numismatic material in philological or lexical analysis, but do not have the relevant training in numismatics to identify the most profitable primary and secondary sources. While it was readily acknowledged that no survey can do justice to the breadth of relevant source material, nor the detail that will satisfy every enquiry, the material introduced in this chapter provides, at the very least, a starting point of departure for investigation of the numismatic material.

Incorporating one long-standing field of study (numismatics) into another long-standing field of study (lexicography) raises several methodological questions about how the material can and should be used. Chapter 4, *Critical Issues in the Appeal to Coinage*, addresses some of the most important concerns relating to the use of coinage for lexicographic purposes. Three questions were addressed. First, it was seen that the propagandistic tendencies did not necessarily detract from coinage as a source for discerning imperial ideology and the use of specific terminology. Second, it was found that inhabitants of the ancient world were, as far as can be ascertained, aware of the significance of the inscribed surface of a coin. Third, despite the narrow cultural window represented on a coin, it was found that this evidence could be profitably used, if one was careful to nuance the implications of this limitation in a mature manner.

Chapters 5 through 11 offered specific case studies of the method for New Testament interpretation. Chapter 5 noted that commentators regularly highlighted the alleged tension in John 15 between 'friendship' and 'obedience'. Chapter 5 employed numismatic inscriptional evidence to explore the ΦΙΛ–lexeme and more carefully denote the semantic domains of relevant terminology. The analysis confirmed that no such tension existed within the sociopolitical context in which the Gospel of John was written. The inclusion of specific political terminology on Roman coins (e.g. ΦΙΛΙΑ; ΦΙΛΟΚΑΙΣΑΡ; ΦΙΛΟΚΛΑΥΔΙΟΣ; ΦΙΛΟΡΩΜΑΙΟΣ; ΦΙΛΟΣΕΒΑΣΤΩΝ) was one way in which elite concepts of political friendship, evidenced in Cicero and Seneca, were communicated to the masses. In light of the numismatic evidence, the ΦΙΛ–lexeme was seen to refer to not only the emotional bond of friendship, but also the dimension of obligation.

Chapter 6 argued that the meaning of the ΚΑΡΠΟΦΟΡΟΣ in Acts 14:17 is significantly enhanced through analysis of the inscription and iconography on relevant coinage. The term ΚΑΡΠΟΦΟΡΟΣ displayed a wide semantic domain, including fruitfulness of trees, fertility of land and as a regular label and epithet for Demeter/ Ceres, including the coinage of tetrarch Philip in 30/31 CE. Analysis of the coinage of Lystra revealed an interest in the depiction of Ceres/Demeter on local coinage. Motivation in Acts 14:17 in employing the relatively rare term ΚΑΡΠΟΦΟΡΟΣ was to identify the true source of such seasonal provision in a manner the inhabitants of Lystra would readily recognize.

Chapter 7 investigated the New Testament *hapax legomenon* νεωκόρος (Acts 19:35). It was discovered that several commentators had been too hasty in accepting some ΝΕΩΚΟΡΟΣ coinage when there was good reason to doubt their authenticity. This case study highlighted the potential methodological problem of uncritically accepting the authenticity of coins for the sake of historical argumentation. The problem persists in many New Testament commentaries and derivative discussions. What is needed is a fresh analysis of the primary source documents (coins) by those with sufficient experience in numismatics. Although the term ΝΕΩΚΟΡΟΣ is unattested on coinage in the first century, the reference in Acts should be understood in light of Ephesus's long devotion to Artemis.

Chapter 8 assessed the provincial coinage of Thessalonica for contributions to linguistic and cultural insights specifically for the purpose of contextualizing Paul at Thessalonica within the matrix of the Roman political world. Three case studies were considered and included divine honours for Caesar through the numismatic inscriptional epithet ΘΕΟΣ, evidence of a favoured political relationship with Rome through the city's status as ΕΛΕΥΘΕΡΙΑ, and the religious identity of the city which was shaped by its historic interest in ΚΑΒΕΙΡΟΣ.

Chapter 9 explored the lexeme ΧΑΡΑΚΤΗΡ and considered the implications for its usage in Hebrews 1:3. Based on the attestation and similar usages of the ΧΑΡΑΚΤΗΡ, ΚΟΠΤΕΙΝ, and ΠΑΕΙΝ on Mediterranean coinage, a semantic overlap was proposed. The implication drawn was that in Hebrews 1:3 ΧΑΡΑΚΤΗΡ was to be understood as the authenticating mark of a ruler, official or superior, rather than a secondary 'representation'. Although not extrapolated further, this has obvious Christological implications for the author of Hebrews.

Chapter 10 examined the term ΚΤΙΣΤΗΣ in 1 Peter 4:19. Despite the apparent translational and lexicographic bias as identify the term as cosmological creator, the numismatic material evidenced a broader attestation of the term being employed with reference to the founding of a city or state. Contextually, in 1 Peter, this understanding was seen to enhance the overall message of the author, and allowed one to appreciate more fully the link between 1 Peter 4:19 and 2:13. Linguistically, ΚΤΙΣΤΗΣ understood in the fashion contributes to understanding 1 Peter as resistance literature, in that it attributes to God certain titles and honours which were typically reserved for the human ruler of the state. Historically, the term was seen to more clearly offer encouragement to the recipients amid various forms of social marginalization.

Chapter 11 considered the title ΒΑΣΙΛΕΥΣ ΒΑΣΙΛΕΩΝ in the Apocalypse (Rev 17:14; 19:16). It was noted that the phrase has generated a variety of interpretations in regards to its identification, symbolism and background. It was seen that commentators

220   *Numismatics and Greek Lexicography*

regularly noted that joining a singular noun with its genitive plural is a common way to express the superlative in Hebrew. Others, however, found special relevance of the phrase to the time of Domitian when it is said 'he dictated the form of a letter to be used by his procurators, he began: "Our lord and god commands so and so"' (Suetonius, *Domitian* 13). Our own analysis argued that inscriptions on relevant coinage confirm that the title was a clear allusion to the tradition of the Parthian kings, Rome's historic enemy. Within the context of the Apocalypse, the title is applied to Jesus Christ, presented triumphantly conquering Rome in the image of Rome's feared Parthian enemy.

One positive and unexpected consequence of the study was the perspective that the numismatic material provided. On several occasions, after the numismatic inscriptions had been collated and assessed, precisely the same distinctive meaning was evident in literary examples, yet these had frequently been overlooked by lexicographers in the evidence presented in the lexicons. The case studies concerning ΚΤΙΣΤΗΣ and ΧΑΡΑΚΤΗΡ were particularly striking in this fashion. This was a reminder of the needed corrective for scholars to simply assume that not only the definition but also supporting evidence in a lexical entry is only *part* of the evidence for the use and meaning of the term.

Further avenues for research in this area abound. First, there is much opportunity for further exploration for contributions in the manner of case studies explored in Part 2 of the volume, namely specific focus on a single lexeme that seeks to fully investigate the lexical implications of the attestation of the word on the numismatic inscriptional evidence. Second, in light of these opportunities, lexicographers have a responsibility to include relevant numismatic material in lexical entries. This material could be incorporated as illustrative of well-documented semantic categories, or lesser known and attested nuances. Third, from our initial study in this area there appears to be some benefit to consider a specialist numismatic lexicon which, as far as possible, tabulates and fully documents the inscriptional Greek linguistic evidence on coinage. The time period under investigation could, initially, reasonably be set to 700 BCE to 400 CE. This could take the promising, but incomplete and deficient, model of a volume like Leschhorn's *Lexikon der Aufschriften auf griechischen Münzen*,[2] but provide an exhaustive documentation, dating and categorization of material. The immense benefit of this proposed volume would be accessibility, documentation of specifically dated numismatic inscriptions, linked, where possible, to a specific geographical location. This, it seems, would be the realistic precursor for broader academic engagement for individual case studies and incorporation into the standard array of lexicons. The proposed numismatic lexicon could also benefit from scholia, glosses and explanatory notes which are found in the margins of ancient texts for the purposes of clarification. Although later, post-Byzantine examples are attested,[3] one which could profitably be employed in this task is Harpocration's *Lexicon of the Ten (Attic) Orators* from the second century CE.

---

[2]   W. Leschhorn, *Lexikon der Aufschriften auf griechischen Münzen* (Wien: Verlag der Österreichischen Akademie der Wissenschaften, 2002).

[3]   *Collection of All Words and Expressions* by Hesychius (fifth century CE), lexicon of *Orion of Thebes* (fifth century CE), the *Lexicon* of Photius (ninth century CE), the *Suda* (tenth century CE), the *Etymologicum Magnum* (twelfth century CE), etc.

The aim of this present volume was to bring together two fields of professional academia, numismatics and post-classical Greek lexicography, in a manner which covered new methodological ground. In the present volume, this interdisciplinary pursuit applied the theory to New Testament Studies, with what seems to be fruitful and encouraging results. The focus was not upon the symbolic or iconographic world of Roman or Greek religion, economics or political propaganda, which, it was acknowledged, can be profitably employed for interpretive cruxes. Rather our analysis was upon the specific contribution of coinage to our understanding of post-classical Greek lexicography. The study was undertaken in the hope that it might act as a catalyst for further scholarly attention to this neglected, yet rich source, of documentary material within Greek lexicography. It is also hoped that the present discussion goes some way to contribute to the scholarly interest in the material culture of the ancient world, and provide specific guidance as to where and how scholars could employ numismatic data for their area of interest and expertise.

This work is my attempt to open a formal dialogue with colleagues and suggest that there is much profitable numismatic lexical material that has largely been overlooked, the reasons for which were explored in the chapter on method. It is hoped that the discussion, especially as this method is illustrated through the applied case studies, will encourage the redefinition of the boundaries of relevant evidence for the lexicographer, that is, the serious attention to the incorporation of coinage within the purview of material covered.

Bibliography

Abbott, Frank Frost. *A History and Description of Roman Political Institutions*. Boston: Ginn & Co., 1911.

Abbott, Lyman. *The Acts of the Apostles: With Notes, Comments, Maps, and Illustrations*. New York: A. S. Barnes, 1876.

Abbott-Smith, G. *A Manual Greek Lexicon of the New Testament*. New York: Charles Scribner's Sons, 1922.

Abrams, B. L., and N. G. Waterman. 'Dirty Money'. *Journal of the American Medical Association* 219.9 (1972): 1202–1203.

Akurgal, E. *Ancient Civilizations and Ruins of Turkey*. Ankara: Haşet Kitabevi, 1985.

Alfaro, A. C. *Sylloge Nummorum Graecorum: España. Museo Arqueológico Nacional, Madrid: Volumen I. Hispania; Ciudades Feno-púnicas. Parte 1: Gadir y Ebusus*. Madrid: Museo Arqueológico Nacional, 1994.

Alfaro, A. C. *Sylloge Nummorum Graecorum: España. Museo Arqueológico Nacional, Madrid: Volumen I. Hispania; Ciudades Feno-púnicas. Parte 2: Acuñaciones cartaginesas en Iberia y emisiones ciudadanas*. Madrid: Museo Arqueológico Nacional, 2004.

Alfaro, A. C., and G. A. Arévalo. *Sylloge Nummorum Graecorum: España. Museo Arqueológico Nacional, Madrid: Volumen 2. Hispania; ciudades del área meridional. Acuñaciones con escritura indígena*. Madrid: Artegraf, 2005.

Alfaro, Carmen, and Andrew Burnett. *A Survey of Numismatic Research, 1996–2001*. Madrid: Madrid International Numismatic Commission, 2003.

Alföldi, A. 'The Main Aspects of Political Propaganda on the Coinage of the Roman Republic'. Pages 63–95 in *Essays in Roman Coinage Presented to Harold Mattingly*. Edited by R. A. G. Carson and C. H. V. Sutherland. Oxford: Oxford University Press, 1956.

Alföldi, Andreas. *Caesar in 44 v. Chr. Vol. 2, Das Zeugnis der Münzen. Antiquitas 3.17*. Bonn: R. Habelt, 1974.

Allen, John. *Catalogue of the Coins of Ancient India*. London: British Museum, 1967.

Amandry, Michel, Andrew Burnett, Jerome Mairat, William E. Metcalf and Laurent Bricaul. *Roman Provincial Coinage*, vol. 3. London: British Museum Press, 2015.

Amandry, Michel, and Philip Attwood. *A Survey of Numismatic Research, 2002–2007*. Glasgow: International Association of Professional Numismatists, 2009.

Andreau, J. *Banking and Business in the Roman World*. Cambridge: Cambridge University Press, 1999.

Angelakis, Emmanouil, Esam I. Azhar, Fehmida Bibi, Muhammad Yasir, Ahmed K. Al-Ghamdi, Ahmad M. Ashshi, Adel G. Elshemi and Didier Raoult. 'Paper Money and Coins as Potential Vectors of Transmissible Disease'. *Future Microbiology* 9.2 (2014): 249–261.

Anokhin, V. *Coins of Ancient Cities of North-Western Black Sea Area*. Kiev: Krajina Mriy, 1989.

Archibald, Z. *The Odrysian Kingdom of Thrace: Orpheus Unmasked*. Oxford: Clarendon Press, 1998.

Arnold, C. E. 'Ephesians'. Pages 300–341 in *Zondervan Illustrated Bible Backgrounds Commentary, Vol. 3: Romans to Philemon*. Edited by Clinton E. Arnold and Steven M. Baugh. Grand Rapids, MI: Zondervan, 2002.

Arnold-Biucchi, Carmen, and Maria Caccamo-Caltabiano. *A Survey of Numismatic Research, 2008–2013*. Taormina: International Association of Professional Numismatists, 2015.

Arslan, E. A. *Sylloge Nummorum Graecorum: Italia. Catanzaro, Museo Provinciale: Part II. Bruttium*. Catanzaro: Amministrazione provinciale di Catanzaro, Ufficio cultura. Agrigento, 1999.

Ashton, R., and S. Ireland. *Sylloge Nummorum Graecorum: Great Britain 5. Ashmolean Museum (Oxford): Pt. 9, Bosporus-Aeolis*. London: Oxford University Press, 2007.

Ashton, R., and S. Ireland. *Sylloge Nummorum Graecorum: Great Britain 5. Ashmolean Museum (Oxford): Pt. 11, Caria to Commagene*. London: Oxford University Press, 2013.

Ashton, R. H. J. *Sylloge Nummorum Graecorum: Finland. The Erkki Keckman Collection in the Skopbank, Helsinki. Part 2. Asia Minor except Karia*. Helsinki: Finnish Society of Sciences and Letters, 1999.

Aune, D. E. *The New Testament in Its Literary Environment*. Cambridge: James Clark and Co., 1988.

Babelon, Ernest. *Description Historique et Chronologique de monnaies de la République Romaine*. Paris: Rollin et Feuardent, 1885.

Babelon, Ernest. *Traité de Monnaies Grecques et Romaines*, 4 vols. Paris: E. Leroux, 1901–1933.

Bagwell-Purefoy, P., and A. R. Meadows, *Sylloge Nummorum Graecorum: Great Britain 9. The British Museum: Part 2. Spain*. London: The British Museum, 2001.

Bailey, D. R. Shackleton., trans. *Cicero. Letters to Friends, Volume III: Letters 281–435*. LCL 230; Cambridge, MA: Harvard University Press, 2001.

Baker, Richard. 'The Countermarks Found on Ancient Roman Coins: A Brief Introduction'. *Journal for the Society of Ancient Numismatics* 15.3 (1984): 52–58.

Bakhoum, S. *Sylloge Nummorum Graecorum: France 4. Bibliothèque Nationale de France: Alexandrie 1, Auguste-Trajan*. Paris and Zurich: Bibliothèque Nationale de France and Numismatica Ars Classica, 1998.

Bakos, M. *Sylloge Nummorum Graecorum: Hungary. Budapest, Magyar Nemzeti Múzeum: Part 2. Dacia – Moesia Superior*. Milan: Ed. Ennerre, 1994.

Baldus, H. R. *Sylloge Nummorum Graecorum: Deutschland. Staatliche Münzsammlung München: Heft 19. Troas – Lesbos*. Berlin: Gebrüder Mann, 1991.

Baldus, H. R. *Sylloge Nummorum Graecorum: Deutschland. Staatliche Münzsammlung München: Heft 28. Syrien: Nicht-königliche Prägungen*. Berlin: Gebrüder Mann, 2001.

Baldus, H. R. *Sylloge Nummorum Graecorum: Deutschland. Staatliche Münzsammlung München: Heft 22. Karien*. Berlin: Gebrüder Mann, 2006.

Bammel, E. 'Syrian Coinage and Pilate'. *JJS* 2 (1950/1): 108–110.

Bammel, E. 'Ein Beitrag zur paulinishen Staatsanschauung'. *TLZ* 85 (1960): 837–840.

Bar, M. *Sylloge Nummorum Graecorum: Belgique 1. Bibliothèque Royale de Belgique: La collection de bronzes grecs de Marc Bar*. Bruxelles: Bibliothèque Royale de Belgique, 2007.

Barag, D. 'The Countermarks of the Legio Decima Fretensis'. Pages 117–125 in *Proceedings of the International Numismatic Convention (Jerusalem, 26–31 December, 1963)*. Edited by A. Kindler. Tel Aviv: Schocken, 1967.

224 *Bibliography*

Barag, D., and S. Qedar. 'A Countermark of the Legio Quinta Scytica from the Jewish War'. *Israel Numismatic Journal* 13 (1994): 66–69.

Barello, F. *Sylloge Nummorum Graecorum: Italia. Cremona, Museo civico Ala Ponzone.* Cremona: Museo civico Ala Ponzone, 2006.

Barney, Stephen A., W. J. Lewis, J. A. Beach and Oliver Berghof. *The 'Etymologies' of Isidore of Seville.* Cambridge: Cambridge University Press, 2006.

Barrett, C. K. *The Gospel According to St. John*, 2nd ed. Cambridge: SPCK, 1978.

Barrett, C. K. *A Critical and Exegetical Commentary on the Acts of the Apostles.* Edinburgh: T&T Clark, 2002.

Bastien, Pierre. *Le buste monétaire des empereurs romains.* Wetteren: Editions numismatiques romaines, 1992.

Beale, G. K. *The Book of Revelation: A Commentary on the Greek Text.* Grand Rapids, MI: Eerdmans, 1999.

Beale, G. K., and Sean M. McDonough. 'Revelation'. Pages 1081–1116 in *Commentary on the New Testament Use of the Old Testament.* Edited by G. K. Beale and D. A. Carson. Grand Rapids: Baker Academic, 2007.

Bellinger, A. R. *Essays in the Coinage of Alexander the Great.* New York: S.J. Durst, 1963.

Benson, Frank Sherman. *Ancient Greek Coins.* Self published. 1901–1902.

Bérend, D. *Sylloge Nummorum Graecorum: The Collection of the American Numismatic Society. Part 5. Sicily 3 (Syracuse-Siceliotes).* New York: The American Numismatic Society, 1988.

Berghaus, Peter, Robert A. G. Carson and Nicholas M. Lowick. *A Survey of Numismatic Research, 1972–1977.* Berne: International Association of Professional Numismatists, 1979.

Bloomfield, S. T. *A Greek and English Lexicon to the New Testament.* London: Longman, Orme, Brown, Green, & Longmans, 1840.

Bodzek, J. *Sylloge Nummorum Graecorum: Poland 3. The National Museum in Cracow: Part 4. Sarmatia – Bosporus.* Kraków: The Polish Academy of Arts and Sciences, 2006.

Boehringer, C., W. Schwabacher and E. von Post. *Sylloge Nummorum Graecorum: Sweden: 1.2. Sammlung Eric von Post.* Stockholm: The Royal Academy of Letters, History and Antiquities, 1995.

Boers, H. Review of *Greek-English Lexicon of the New Testament: Based on Semantic Domains.* Edited by Johannes P. Louw and Eugene A. Nida. *JBL* 108 (1989): 705–707.

Bonner, C. 'A Reminiscence of Paul on a Coin Amulet'. *HTR* 43 (1950): 165–168.

Bons, E. 'Le verbe κτίζω comme terme technique de la création dans la Septante et dans le Nouveau Testament'. Pages 1–15 in *Voces Biblicae: Septuagint Greek and the Significance for the New Testament.* Edited by J. Joosten and P. J. Tomson. Louvain: Peeters, 2007.

Bons, E., and A. Passoni Dell'Acqua. 'A Sample Article: κτίζω – κτίσις – κτίσμα – κτίστης'. Pages 173–187 in *Septuagint Vocabulary: Pre-History, Usage, Reception.* Edited by E. Bons and J. Joosten. Atlanta, GA: Society of Biblical Literature, 2011.

Bopearachchi, O. *Sylloge Nummorum Graecorum: The Collection of the American Numismatic Society. Part 9. Graeco-Bactrian and Indo-Greek Coins.* New York: The American Numismatic Society, 1998.

Boring, M. E. *Revelation.* Louisville: Westminster John Knox, 1989.

Boxall, Ian. *The Revelation of St. John.* London: Continuum, 2006.

Bratcher, Robert G., and William David Reyburn. *A Translator's Handbook on the Book of Psalms.* New York: United Bible Societies, 1991.

Braund, David. *Rome and the Friendly King: The Character of Client Kingship.* New York: St. Martin's Press, 1984.

Breitenbach, Alfred. 'Lexikon II (lateinisch)'. Pages 1–29 in *Reallexikon für Antike und Christentum, volume 23*. Edited by Georg SchöLlgen, Heinzgerd Brakmann, Sible de Blaauw, Therese Fuhrer, Karl Hoheisel, Winrich LöHr, Wolfgang Speyer and Klaus Thraede. Stuttgart: Anton Hiersemann, 2008.

Breitenstein, N. *Sylloge Nummorum Graecorum: Denmark. The Royal Collection of Coins and Medals, Danish National Museum. Part 4. Sicily 1: Abacaenum-Petra*. Copenhagen: Munksgaard, 1942.

Breitenstein, N. *Sylloge Nummorum Graecorum: Denmark. The Royal Collection of Coins and Medals, Danish National Museum. Part 5. Sicily 2: Segesta-Sardinia*. Copenhagen: Munksgaard, 1942.

Breitenstein, N. *Sylloge Nummorum Graecorum: Denmark. The Royal Collection of Coins and Medals, Danish National Museum. Part 8. Macedonia 1: Acanthus-Uranopolis. Dynasts*. Copenhagen: Munksgaard, 1943.

Breitenstein, N. *Sylloge Nummorum Graecorum: Denmark. The Royal Collection of Coins and Medals, Danish National Museum. Part 9. Macedonia 2: Alexander I–Alexander III*. Copenhagen: Munksgaard, 1943.

Breitenstein, N. *Sylloge Nummorum Graecorum: Denmark. The Royal Collection of Coins and Medals, Danish National Museum. Part 10. Macedonia 3: Philip III-Philip VI. Macedonia under the Romans. Kings of Paeonia*. Copenhagen: Munksgaard, 1943.

Breitenstein, N. *Sylloge Nummorum Graecorum: Denmark. The Royal Collection of Coins and Medals, Danish National Museum. Part 17. Argolis-Aegean Islands*. Copenhagen: Munksgaard, 1944.

Breitenstein, N. *Sylloge Nummorum Graecorum: Denmark. The Royal Collection of Coins and Medals, Danish National Museum. Part 18. Bosporus-Bithynia*. Copenhagen: Munksgaard, 1944.

Breitenstein, N. *Sylloge Nummorum Graecorum: Denmark. The Royal Collection of Coins and Medals, Danish National Museum. Part 19. Mysia*. Copenhagen: Munksgaard, 1945.

Breitenstein, N. *Sylloge Nummorum Graecorum: Denmark. The Royal Collection of Coins and Medals, Danish National Museum. Part 20. Troas*. Copenhagen: Munksgaard, 1945.

Breitenstein, N. *Sylloge Nummorum Graecorum: Denmark. The Royal Collection of Coins and Medals, Danish National Museum. Part 21. Aeolis-Lesbos*. Copenhagen: Munksgaard, 1945.

Breitenstein, N. *Sylloge Nummorum Graecorum: Denmark. The Royal Collection of Coins and Medals, Danish National Museum. Part 22. Ionia 1: (Clazomenae-Ephesus)*. Copenhagen: Munksgaard, 1946.

Breitenstein, N. *Sylloge Nummorum Graecorum: Denmark. The Royal Collection of Coins and Medals, Danish National Museum. Part 23. Ionia 2: (Erythrae-Priene)*. Copenhagen: Munksgaard, 1946.

Breitenstein, N. *Sylloge Nummorum Graecorum: Denmark. The Royal Collection of Coins and Medals, Danish National Museum. Part 24. Ionia 3: (Smyrna-Teos. Islands)*. Copenhagen: Munksgaard, 1946.

Breitenstein, N. *Sylloge Nummorum Graecorum: Denmark. The Royal Collection of Coins and Medals, Danish National Museum. Part 25. Caria 1: (Alabanda-Orthosia)*. Copenhagen: Munksgaard, 1947.

Breitenstein, N. *Sylloge Nummorum Graecorum: Denmark. The Royal Collection of Coins and Medals, Danish National Museum. Part 26. Caria 2: (Sebastopolis-Trapezopolis). Satraps. Islands*. Copenhagen: Munksgaard, 1947.

Breitenstein, N. *Sylloge Nummorum Graecorum: Denmark. The Royal Collection of Coins and Medals, Danish National Museum. Part 27. Lydia 1: (Acrasus-Saïtta).* Copenhagen: Munksgaard, 1947.

Breitenstein, N. *Sylloge Nummorum Graecorum: Denmark. The Royal Collection of Coins and Medals, Danish National Museum. Part 28. Lydia 2: (Sala-Tripolis).* Copenhagen: Munksgaard, 1947.

Breitenstein, N. *Sylloge Nummorum Graecorum: Denmark. The Royal Collection of Coins and Medals, Danish National Museum. Part 29. Phrygia 1: (Abbaïtis-Eumeneia).* Copenhagen: Munksgaard, 1948.

Breitenstein, N. *Sylloge Nummorum Graecorum: Denmark. The Royal Collection of Coins and Medals, Danish National Museum. Part 30. Phrygia 2: (Grimenothyrae-Trajanopolis).* Copenhagen: Munksgaard, 1948.

Breitenstein, N., and O. Mørkholm. *Sylloge Nummorum Graecorum: Denmark. The Royal Collection of Coins and Medals, Danish National Museum. Part 31. Lycia. Pamphylia.* Copenhagen: Munksgaard, 1955.

Breitenstein, N., and O. Mørkholm. *Sylloge Nummorum Graecorum: Denmark. The Royal Collection of Coins and Medals, Danish National Museum. Part 32. Pisidia.* Copenhagen: Munksgaard, 1956.

Breitenstein, N., and O. Mørkholm. *Sylloge Nummorum Graecorum: Denmark. The Royal Collection of Coins and Medals, Danish National Museum. Part 33. Lycaonia-Cilicia.* Copenhagen: Munksgaard, 1956.

Brennan, P., M. Turner and N. L. Wright. *Faces of Power: Imperial Portraiture on Roman Coins.* Sydney: Nicholson Museum, 2007.

Broughton, T. R. S. 'Roman Asia'. Pages 499–918 in *An Economic Survey of Ancient Rome,* vol. 4. Edited by T. Frank. Baltimore, MD: John Hopkins Press, 1938.

Brown, Raymond E. *The Gospel According to John xiii–xxi.* New York: Doubleday & Company Inc., 1970.

Bruce, F. F. *The Acts of the Apostles: Greek Text with Introduction and Commentary.* Grand Rapids, MI: Eerdmans, 1990.

Bruce, F. F. *The Epistle to the Hebrews.* Grand Rapids, MI: Eerdmans, 1990.

Brumfield, A. C. *The Attic Festivals of Demeter and Their Relation to the Agricultural Year.* New York: Arno Press, 1981.

Brunt, P. A., and J. M. Moore. *Res Gestae Divi Augusti: The Achievements of Divine Augustus.* Oxford: Oxford University Press, 1983.

Buechner, W. *De Neocoria.* Gissae: Typis Guilelmi Keller, 1888.

Bultmann, Rudolf. *The Gospel of John: A Commentary.* Translated by G. R. Beasley Murray. Philadelphia, PA: Westminster Press, 1971.

Burnett, Andrew. 'The Iconography of Roman Coin Types in the Third Century BC'. *Numismatic Chronicle* 146 (1986): 67–75.

Burnett, Andrew. *Coinage in the Roman World.* London: Seaby, 1987.

Burnett, Andrew. *Coins: Interpreting the Past.* Berkeley: University of California Press, 1991.

Burnett, Andrew, Michel Amandry and Ian Carradice. *Roman Provincial Coinage: Volumes 1–2.* London: British Museum, 1992–1999.

Burnett, A. 'Buildings and Monuments on Roman Coins'. Pages 137–164 in *Roman Coins and Public Life under the Empire.* Edited by G. Paul. Ann Arbor: University of Michigan Press, 1999.

Burrell, B. *Neokoroi: Greek Cities and Roman Emperors.* Leiden: Brill, 2004.

Burrell, B. 'Neokoros'. *EAH* 9 (2013): 4743.

Butcher, Kevin. *Roman Provincial Coins: An Introduction to the 'Greek Imperials'*. London: Seaby, 1988.

Butcher, Kevin. *Small Change in Ancient Beirut: The Coin Finds from Bey 006 and Bey 045, Persian, Hellenistic, Roman, and Byzantine Periods*. Beirut: American University, 2002.

Butcher, Kevin. *Coinage in Roman Syria: Northern Syria, 64 BC–AD 253*. London: Royal Numismatic Society, 2004.

Butcher, Marguerite Spoerri. *Roman Provincial Coinage*, vol. 7. London: British Museum, 2006.

Butcher, M. Spoerri, and D. Calomino. 'Provincial Coinages: Eastern Provinces'. Pages 228–243 in *A Survey of Numismatic Research 2008–2013*. Edited by C. Arnold-Biucchi and M. Caccamo-Caltabiano. Taormina: International Numismatic Commission and International Association of Professional Numismatists, 2015.

Buttrey, Theodore V. *The Triumviral Portrait Gold of the Quattuorviri Monetales of 42 B.C.* New York: American Numismatic Society, 1956.

Buttrey, Theodore V. *Greek, Roman, and Islamic Coins from Sardis*. Cambridge: Harvard University Press, 1981.

Buttrey, T., and S. Buttrey. 'Calculating Ancient Coin Production Again'. *American Journal of Numismatics* 9 (1997): 113–135.

Caccamo-Caltabiano, M. *Sylloge Nummorum Graecorum: Italia. Agrigento, Museo archeologico regionale: fondo dell'ex Museo civico e altre raccolte del Medagliere*. Palermo: Regione siciliana assessorato regionale dei beni culturali e ambientali e della P.I. Cremona, 1999.

Caccamo-Caltabiano, M., L. Campagna and A. Pinzone, eds. *Nuove prospspettive della ricerca sulla Sicilia del III sec. a.C.: archeologia, numismatica, storia*. Messina: Dipartimento di Scienze dell' Antichita dell'Università degli Studi di Messina, 2004.

Carradice, I. 'The "Regal" Coinage of the Persian Empire'. Pages 73–108 in *Coinage and Administration in the Athenian and Persian Empires*. Edited by I. Carradice. Oxford: BAR Publishing, 1987.

Carradice, I., and M. Price. *Coinage in the Greek World*. London: Seaby, 1988.

Carradice, I. A. *Sylloge Nummorum Graecorum: Great Britain 6. The Lewis Collection in Corpus Christi College, Cambridge. Pt 2, The Greek Imperial Coins*. London: Oxford University Press, 1992.

Carson, D. A. *The Gospel According to John*. Grand Rapids, MI: Inter-Varsity Press, 1991.

Carter, W. *Matthew and the Margins*. Sheffield: Sheffield Academic Press, 2000.

Carter, W. *Empire and John*. London: T&T Clark, 2008.

Cary, Earnest, and Herbert B. Foster, trans. *Dio Cassius. Roman History, Volume III: Books 36–40*. LCL 53; Cambridge, MA: Harvard University Press, 1914.

Cary, Earnest, and Herbert B. Foster, trans. *Dio Cassius. Roman History, Volume V: Books 46–50*. LCL 82; Cambridge, MA: Harvard University Press, 1917.

Cary, Earnest, trans. *Dionysius of Halicarnassus. Roman Antiquities, Volume I: Books 1–2*. LCL 319; Cambridge, MA: Harvard University Press, 1937.

Casey, John, and Richard Reece. *Coins and the Archaeologist*. Oxford: British Archaeological Reports, 1974.

Casey, P. J. *Understanding Ancient Coins: An Introduction for Archaeologists*. London: Batsford, 1986

Casey, P. J. and R. Reece. *Coins and the Archaeologist*. London: Seaby, 1988.

Catalli, F. *Sylloge Nummorum Graecorum: Italia. Firenze, Museo Archeologico Nazionale: Part 2, Etruria*. Rome, Florence and Zurich: Istituto central per il catalogo e la documentazione, Ministero per i Beni e le Attività Culturali, Soprintendenza per i Beni Archeologici della Toscana, Numismatica Ars Classica, 2007.

Chadwick, John. 'The Semantic History of Greek ἐσχάρα'. Pages 515–523 in *O-o-pe-ro-si: Festschrift für Ernst Risch zum 75. Geburtstag*. Edited by Annemarie Etter. Berlin: De Gruyter, 1986.

Chadwick, John. 'Semantic History and Greek Lexicography'. Pages 281–288 in *La langue et les textes en grec ancien: Actes du Colloque Pierre Chantraine (Grenoble, 5–8 Septembre 1989)*. Edited by Françoise Létoublon. Amsterdam: J. C. Gieben, 1992.

Chadwick, John. 'The Case for Replacing Liddell and Scott'. *Bulletin of the Institute of Classical Studies* 39 (1994): 1–11.

Chadwick, John. *Lexicographica Graeca: Contributions to the Lexicography of Ancient Greek*. Oxford: Clarendon, 1996.

Chancey, Mark A. 'The Epigraphic Habit of Hellenistic and Roman Galilee'. Pages 83–98 in *Religion, Ethnicity, and Identity in Ancient Galilee: A Region in Transition*. Edited by J. Zangenberg, H. W. Attridge and D. B. Martin. Tübingen: Mohr Siebeck, 2007.

Chantraine, P. *Dictionnaire étymologique de la langue grecque*. Paris: Klincksieck, 1968–1980.

Charles, R. H. *A Critical and Exegetical Commentary on the Revelation of St. John*, 2 vols. Edinburgh: T. & T. Clark, 1920.

Christesen, Paul, and Sarah Murray. 'Macedonian Religion'. Pages 428–445 in *A Companion to Ancient Macedonia*. Edited by Joseph Roisman and Ian Worthington. Oxford: Wiley-Blackwell, 2010.

Christiansen, E., and A. Kromann. *Sylloge Nummorum Graecorum: Denmark. The Royal Collection of Coins and Medals, Danish National Museum. Part 41. Alexandria-Cyrenaica*. Copenhagen: Munksgaard, 1974.

Clain-Stefanelli, E. E. 'Numismatics – An Ancient Science. A Survey of Its History'. Pages 1–102 in *Contributions from the Museum of History and Technology*. Edited by Vladimir Clain-Stefanelli and E. F Clain-Stefanelli. Washington, DC: Smithsonian Institution, 1970.

Clain-Stefanelli, E. E. *Numismatic Bibliography*. Munich: Battenberg, 1985.

Cohen, Henry. *Description Historique des Monnaies Frappées sous L'empire Romaine*, 2nd ed. Paris: Rollin and Feuardent, 1890–1892.

Cohoon, J. W., trans. *Dio Chrysostom. Discourses 1–11*. LCL 257; Cambridge, MA: Harvard University Press, 1932.

Cole, S. G. 'Demeter in the Greek City and Its Countryside'. Pages 133–154 in *Oxford Readings in Greek Religion*. Edited by R. Buxton. Oxford: Oxford University Press, 2000.

Collison, Robert Lewis. *A History of Foreign-Language Dictionaries*. London: André Deutsch, 1982.

Consani, Carlo. 'La koiné et les dialectes grecs dans la documentation linguistique et la réflexion métalinguistique des premiers siècles de notre ère'. Pages 23–39 in *La koiné grecque antique*. Edited by Claude Brixhe (Nancy: Presses universitaires de Nancy, 1993.

Conzelmann, Hans. *A Commentary on the Acts of the Apostles*. Translated by James Limburg, A. Thomas Kraabel and Donald H. Juel. Philadelphia, PA: Fortress, 1987.

Crawford, Michael H. 'Money and Exchange in the Roman World'. *JRS* 60 (1970): 40–46.

Crawford, Michael H. *Roman Republican Coinage*, 2 vols. New York: Cambridge University Press, 1974.

Crawford, M. 'Trade and Movement of Coinage across the Adriatic in the Hellenistic Period'. Pages 1–11 in *Scripta Nummaria Romana: Essays Presented to Humphrey Sutherland*. Edited by R. A. G. Carson and C. M. Kraay. London: Spink, 1978.

Crawford, Michael H. 'Roman Imperial Coin Types and the Formation of Public Opinion'. Pages 47–64 in *Studies in Numismatic Method Presented to Philip Grierson*. Edited by C. Brooke, B. Steward, J. Pollard and T. Volk. Cambridge: Cambridge University Press, 1983.

Crawford, Michael H. 'Numismatics'. Pages 185–234 in *Sources for Ancient History*. Edited by M. Crawford. Cambridge: Cambridge University Press, 1983.

Crawford, Michael H. *Coinage and Money under the Roman Republic: Italy and the Mediterranean Economy*. Berkeley: University of California Press, 1985.

Cribb, J. *Money: From Cowrie Shells to Credit Cards*. London: British Museum, 1986.

Crook, John. *Consilium Principis: Imperial Councils and Counsellors from Augustus to Diocletian*. Cambridge: Cambridge University Press, 1955.

Crönert, Wilhelm. *Passow's Wörterbuch der griechischen Sprache*. Göttingen: Vandenhoeck and Ruprecht, 1912–1914.

Cunningham, Alexander. *Coins of the Indo-Scythians, Sakas and Kushans*. Delhi: Indological Book House, 1971.

Daehn, William E. *Ancient Greek Numismatics: A Guide to Reading and Research; A Bibliography of Works Written in English with Summaries of Their Contents*. London: Classical Numismatic Group Inc., 2012.

Dalaison, J. *Sylloge Nummorum Graecorum, France 7, Bibliothèque Nationale de France: Paphlagonie, Pont, Arménie Mineure*. Bordeaux: Ausonius, 2015.

Danker, Frederick William, and Kathryn Krug. *The Concise Greek-English Lexicon of the New Testament*. Chicago: University of Chicago Press, 2009.

Davesne, A. 'Numismatique ct archeologie: Le Temple de Dionysos a Teos'. *Revue Numismatique* 29 (1987): 15–20.

De Callataÿ, Françoise. *L'histoire des Guerres Mithridatiques vue par les Monnaies*. Louvain-la-Neuve: Département d'archéologie et d'histoire de l'art, Séminaire de numismatique Marcel Hoc, 1997.

Deissmann, Adolf. *Light from the Ancient East: The New Testament Illustrated by Recently Discovered Texts of the Greco-Roman World*. Translated by Lionel R. M. Strachan. New York: Harper & Brothers, 1922.

Dillard, James Price. 'Persuasion'. Pages 203–218 in *Handbook of Communication and Science*. Edited by C. R. Berger, M. E. Roloff and D. R. Roskos-Ewoldsen. London: Sage Publishers, 1987.

Dimitrov, D., I. Prokopov and B. Kolev. *Modern Forgeries of Greek and Roman Coins*. Sofia: K&K Publishers, 1997.

Dittenberger, W. *Syllogue Inscriptionum Graecarum*. Leipzig: Lipsiae S. Hirzel, 1977.

Dilts, R. *Heraclidis Lembi excerpta Politiarum*. Durham, NC: Duke University, 1971.

Döderlein, Ludwig. *Lateinische Synonyme und Etymologieen: Dritter Theil*, 6 vols. Leipzig: F. C. W. Vogel, 1829.

Donfried, Karl P. 'The Cults of Thessalonica and the Thessalonian Correspondence'. *NTS* 31 (1985): 336–356.

Doob, L. *Public Opinion and Propaganda*, 2nd ed. Hambden: Archon Books, 1966.

Draganov, D. *Sylloge Nummorum Graecorum: Bulgaria. Ruse. Bobokov Brothers Collection: Thrace & Moesia Inferior. Part 1. Deultum*. Ruse: Bobokov Brothers Foundation, 2005.

Dräger, M. *Die Stiidte der Provinz Asia in der Flavierzeit. Studien zur kleinasiatischen Stadt- und Regionalgeschichte*. Frankfurt: Peter Lang, 1993.

Bibliography

Drexhage, Hans-Joachim. *Preise, Mieten/Pachten,Kosten und Lohne im romischen Agypten bis zum Regierungsantritt Diokletians.* St. Katharinen: Scripta Mercaturae, 1991.

Drew-Bear, T. 'Representations of Temples on the Greek Imperial Coinage'. *American Numismatic Society Museum Notes* 19 (1974): 27–63.

Ducat, J. 'La confédération béotienne et l'expansion thébaine à l'époque archaïque'. *BCH* 97 (1973): 59–73.

Dumesnil, M. J. B. Gardin. *Latin Synonyms with Their Different Significations: And Examples Taken from the Best Latin Authors.* Translated by J. M. Gosset. London: Richard Taylor, 1888.

Duncan-Jones, R. *The Economy of the Roman Empire: Quantitative Studies.* Cambridge: Cambridge University Press, 1982.

Duncan-Jones, R. 'Mobility and Immobility of Coin in the Roman Empire'. *Annali* 36 (1989): 121–137.

Duncan-Jones, R. *Structure and Scale in the Roman Economy.* Cambridge: Cambridge University Press, 1990.

Duncan-Jones, R. *Money and Government in the Roman Empire.* Cambridge: Cambridge University Press, 1994.

Duncan-Jones, R. 'The Denarii of Septimus Severus and the Mobility of Roman Coin'. *Numismatic Chronicle* 161 (2001): 75–89.

Dyer, K. D. '"But Concerning That Day … " (Mark 13:32). "Prophetic" and "Apocalyptic" Eschatology in Mark 13'. Pages 104–122 in *Society of Biblical Literature 1999 Seminar Papers.* Atlanta, GA: Society of Biblical Literature, 1999.

Eckhel, J. *Doctrina numorum veterum,* 8 vols. Vienna: Sumptibus J.V. Degen, 1792–1839.

Editor. 'Literature'. *The Expository Times* 30.11 (1919): 491–503.

Edson, C. 'Cults of Thessalonica'. *HTR* 41 (1948): 188–204.

Edson, C. *IG X, 2 1 Inscriptiones Graecae, X: Inscriptiones Epiri, Macedoniae, Thraciae, Scythiae Pars II, fasc. 1: Inscriptiones Thessalonicae et viciniae.* Berlin: de Gruyter, 1972.

Ehrhardt, C. 'Roman Coin Types and the Roman Public'. *JNG* 34 (1984): 41–54.

Elkins, Nathan T. 'The Trade in Fresh Supplies of Ancient Coins: Scale, Organisation, and Politics'. Pages 91–107 in *All the King's Horses: Essays on the Impact of Looting and the Illicit Trade on Our Knowledge of the Past.* Edited by P. K. Lazarus and A. W. Baker. Washington, DC: Society for American Archaeology Press, 2012.

Elliott, J. K. Review of *Greek-English Lexicon of the New Testament: Based on Semantic Domains,* by Johannes P. Louw and Eugene A. Nida. *NovT* 31 (1989): 379–380.

Ellul, J. *Propaganda: The Formation of Men's Attitudes.* New York: Vintage Books, 1973.

Elsen, J. 'La Stabilité Du Système Pondéral et Monétaire Attique (Vie-IIe s. avant notre ére)'. *RBN* 148 (2002): 1–32.

Erdkamp, P. 'Agriculture, Underemployment, and the Cost of Rural Labour in the Roman World'. *CQ* 49.2 (1999): 556–572.

Esser, H.-H. 'Creation, Foundation, Creature, Maker'. *NIDNNT* 1: 376–389.

Esser, H.-H., 'κτίζω, κτίσις, κτίσμα, κτίστης'. *NIDNTTE* 2: 762.

Étienne, R., and Denis Knoepfler. 'Le monnayage d'Hyettos à l'époque archaïque'. *BCH Suppl.* 3 (1976): 383–390, 400.

Evans, C. S. '"On This Rock I will Build My Church" (Matthew 16.18): Was the Promise to Peter a Response to Tetrarch Philip's Proclamation?' Pages 20–32 in *The Earliest Perceptions of Jesus in Context: Essays in Honor of John Nolland.* Edited by Aaron White, David Wenham and Craig A. Evans. London: Bloomsbury, 2018.

Evans, Jane DeRose. *The Art of Persuasion: Political Propaganda from Aeneas to Brutus.* Ann Arbor: University of Michigan Press, 1992.

Fava, Anna Serena. *I Simboli Nelle Monete Argentee Repubblicane e la Vita dei Romani*. Turin, Italy: Museo Civico, 1969.

Fears, J. Rufus. 'The Cult of Virtues and Roman Imperial Ideology'. *ANRW* 17.2 (1981): 827–948.

Ferguson, J. *The Religions of the Roman Empire*. London: Thames and Hudson, 1970.

Finley, M. I. *The Ancient Economy*. Berkeley: University of California Press, 1973.

Fischer, J. E. *Sylloge Nummorum Graecorum: The Collection of the American Numismatic Society. Part 1. Etruria-Calabria*. New York: The American Numismatic Society, 1969.

Fishlake, J. R. 'Article VII'. *Quarterly Review* 51 (1834): 144–177.

Fishlake, J. R. 'Article I'. *Quarterly Review* 75 (1845): 293–324.

Fishwick, Duncan. *The Imperial Cult in the Latin West*. Leiden: Brill, 1993.

Fitzmyer, Joseph A. *The Acts of the Apostles: A New Translation with Introduction and Commentary*. New Haven, CT: Yale University Press, 2008.

Flower, H. *Ancestor Marks and Aristocratic Power in Roman Culture*. Oxford: Clarendon Press, 1996.

Foakes-Jackson, F. J., and Kirsopp Lake, eds. *The Beginnings o' Christianity: The Acts of the Apostles*, 5 vols. London: Macmillan, 1933.

Foley, H. *The Homeric Hymn to Demeter: Translation, Commentary and Interpretive Essays*. Princeton, NJ: Princeton University Press, 1994.

Ford, J. Massyngberde. *Revelation: Introduction, Translation, and Commentary*. London: Yale University Press, 2008.

Foster, B. O., trans. *Livy: History of Rome, Volume I: Books 1–2*. LCL 114; Cambridge, MA: Harvard University Press, 1919.

Frank, Tenney. *An Economic Survey of Ancient Rome*, 6 vols. Paterson, NJ: Pageant Books, 1933–1940.

Franke, P. R. 'Zu den Homonoia-Münzen Kleinasiens'. Pages 81–102 in *Stuttgarter Kolloquium zur Historische Geographie des Altertums I, 1980*. Edited by Eckart Olshausen. Bonn: Habelt, 1987.

Franke, P. R., and H. Küthmann. *Sylloge Nummorum Graecorum: Deutschland. Staatliche Münzsammlung München: Heft 1. Hispania – Gallia Narbonensis*. Berlin: Gebrüder Mann, 1968.

Franke, P. R., and H. Küthmann. *Sylloge Nummorum Graecorum: Deutschland. Staatliche Münzsammlung München: Heft 2. Etruria – Umbria – Picenum – Latium – Samnium – Frentani – Campania – Apulia*. Berlin: Gebrüder Mann, 1970.

Franke, P. R., and H. Küthmann. *Sylloge Nummorum Graecorum: Deutschland. Staatliche Münzsammlung München: Heft 3. Kalabrien – Lukanien*. Berlin: Gebrüder Mann, 1973.

Franke, P. R., and H. Küthmann. *Sylloge Nummorum Graecorum: Deutschland. Staatliche Münzsammlung München: Heft 4. Bruttium – Karthager in Italien*. Berlin: Gebrüder Mann, 1974.

Franke, P. R., and S. Grunauer von Hoerschelmann. *Sylloge Nummorum Graecorum: Deutschland. Staatliche Münzsammlung München: Heft 5. Sikelia*. Berlin: Gebrüder Mann, 1977.

Franke, P. R., W. Leschhorn and A. U. Stylow. *Sylloge Nummorum Graecorum: Deutschland. Sammlung v. Aulock: Index*. Berlin: Gebrüder Mann, 1981.

Fraser, B. L. 'Beyond Definition: Organising Semantic Information in Bilingual Dictionaries'. *International Journal of Lexicography* 21 (2008): 69–93.

Fraser, B. L. 'Lexicographic Slips: Gathering and Organising Contextual Data for Dictionary Entries'. Pages 53–72 in *Lexicografia e semântica lexical: Caminhos para a*

232 Bibliography

feitura de um dicionário de Grego: Colóquio Internacional – ACTAS (Lisboa, 24–25 de Novembro de 2006). Edited by Manuel Alexander Júnior. Lisbon: Centro de Estudos Clássicos, 2008.

Fredricksmeyer, Ernst. 'Alexander the Great and the Kingship of Asia'. Pages 136–166 in Alexander the Great in Fact and Fiction. Edited by A. B. Bosworth and E. J. Baynham. Oxford: Oxford University Press, 2000.

Friberg, Timothy, Barbara Friberg and Neva F. Miller. Analytical Lexicon of the Greek New Testament. Grand Rapids, MI: Baker Books, 2000.

Friesen, S. J. Twice Neokoros: Ephesus, Asia, and the Cult of the Falvian Imperial Family. Leiden: Brill, 1993.

Furtwängler, A. 'Neue Beobachtungen zur frühesten Munzprägung'. Schweizerische Numismatische Rundschau 65 (1986): 153–165.

Gaebler, H. Die antiken Münzen von Makedonia und Paionia, Die antiken Münzen Nord-Griechenlands Vol. III. Berlin: De Gruyter, 1935.

Gaffiot, F. Dictionnaire. Paris: Hachette, 1934.

Gardner, P. A History of Ancient Coinage. Oxford: Clarendon Press, 1918.

Gardner, P., and Reginald S. Poole. The Coins of the Greeks and Scythic Kings of Bactria and India in the British Museum. London: British Museum, 1886.

Garnsey, Peter, and Richard Saller. The Roman Empire: Economy, Society and Culture. London: Bloomsbury, 2014.

Giard, Jean-Baptiste. Bibliothèque Nationale: Catalogue des Monnaies de l'empire Romaine, 3 vols. Paris: Bibliothèque Nationale de France, 1976–2008.

Giblin, C. H. The Book of Revelation: The Open Book of Prophecy. Collegeville: Liturgical Press, 1991.

Göbl, Robert. Münzprägung des Kušnreiches. Vienna: Verlag der Österreichischen Akademie der Wissenschaften, 1984.

Goddard, J., and I. A. Carradice. Sylloge Nummorum Graecorum: Great Britain 12. The Hunterian Museum University of Glasgow: Part 1. Roman Provincial Coins, Spain – Kingdoms of Asia Minor. London: Oxford University Press, 2004.

Goddard, J., and I. A. Carradice. Sylloge Nummorum Graecorum: Great Britain 12. The Hunterian Museum University of Glasgow: Part 2. Roman Provincial Coins, Cyprus – Egypt. London: Oxford University Press, 2007.

Godley, A. D., trans. Herodotus. The Persian Wars, Volume I: Books 1–2. LCL 117; Cambridge, MA: Harvard University Press, 1920.

Goetz, Georg. 'Differentiae Scriptores'. Pages 481–484 in Real-encyclopädie der classischen Altertumswissenschaft, volume 5. Edited by Georg Wissowa. Stuttgart: Metzler, 1903.

Goetz, Georg. 'Glossographie'. Pages 1433–1466 in Real-encyclopädie der classischen Altertumswissenschaft, volume 7. Edited by Georg Wissowa and Wilhelm Kroll. Stuttgart: Metzler, 1910.

Golenko, K. V., and J. P. Karyszkowski. 'The Gold Coinage of King Pharnaces of the Bosporus'. Numismatic Chronicle 12 (1972): 25–38.

Gorini, Giovanni. I ritrovamenti monetali nel mondo antico: Problemi e metodi. Padua, Italy: Esedra, 2003.

Goron, Stan, and J. P. Goenka. The Coins of the Indian Sultanates. New Delhi: Munshiram Manoharlal, 2001.

Grant, M. From Imperium to Auctoritas. Cambridge: Cambridge University Press, 1946.

Green, Gene L. The Letters to the Thessalonians. Grand Rapids, MI: Eerdmans, 2002.

Greenberg, Moshe. Ezekiel 21–37: A New Translation with Introduction and Commentary. London: Yale University Press, 2008.

Greene, Kevin. *The Archaeology of the Roman Economy*. Berkely: University of California Press, 1986.

Greenwood, L. H. G., trans. *Cicero. The Verrine Orations, Volume II: Against Verres, Part 2, Books 3–5*. LCL 293; Cambridge, MA: Harvard University Press, 1935.

Grether, Gertrude. 'Livia and the Roman Imperial Cult'. *AJP* 67 (1946): 222–252.

Grierson, Philip. *Bibliographie Numismatique*, 2nd ed. Brussels: Cercle d'Études Numismatiques, 2001.

Griffiths, J. G. 'βασιλεὺς βασιλέων: Remarks on the History of a Title'. *Classical Philology* 48 (1953): 145–154.

Grudem, W. 'Perseverance of the Saints: A Case Study from Hebrews 6: 4-6 and the Other Warning Passages in Hebrews'. Pages 133–182 in *The Grace of God, The Bondage of the Will*. Edited by T. Schreiner and B. Ware. Grand Rapids: Baker, 1995.

Guido, F. *Sylloge Nummorum Graecorum: Italia. Sassari. Museo Archeologico 'G.A. Sanna': Part 14 1. Sicilia – Numidia*. Milano: Ed. Ennerre Catanzaro, 1994.

Gupta, P. L., and T. R. Hardaker, *Indian Silver Punchmarked Coins: Magadha-Maurya Karshapana Series*. Nashik: Indian Institute of Research in Numismatic Studies, 1985.

Hackens, T. *Sylloge Nummorum Graecorum: Grèce 1.1. Collection Réna H. Evelpidis, Athènes: Italie, Sicilie, Thrace*. Louvain: Institut supérieur d'archéologie et d'histoire de l'art, 1970.

Hackens, T. *Sylloge Nummorum Graecorum: Grèce 1.2. Collection Réna H. Evelpidis, Athènes: 12 Macédoine, Thessalie, Illyrie, Epire, Corcyre*. Louvain: Institut supérieur d'archéologie et d'histoire de l'art, 1975.

Hackens, Tony. *A Survey of Numismatic Research, 1985–1990*. Brussels: International Numismatic Commission, 1991.

Haenchen, Ernst. *John: Volume 2*. Translated by R. W. Funk and U. Busse. Philadelphia, PA: Fortress Press, 1984.

Hagner, D. A. 'Lystra'. *ISBE* 3 (1988): 192–193.

Hall, H. R. *The Ancient History of the Near East: From the Earliest Times to the Battle of Salamis*. London: Methuen & Co. Ltd., 1913.

Handy, Lowell K. *Among the Host of Heaven: The Syro-Palestinian Pantheon as Bureaucracy*. Winona Lake: Eisenbrauns, 1994.

Hannestad, N. *Roman Art and Imperial Policy*. Arhus: University Press, 1986.

Hans, L. M. 'Der Kaiser mit dem Schwert'. *JNG* 33 (1983): 57–66.

Hardin, J. 'Decrees and Drachmas at Thessalonica: An Illegal Assembly in Jason's House (Acts 17.1–10a)'. *NTS* 52 (2006): 29–49.

Harl, Kenneth W. *Civic Coins and Civic Politics in the Roman East*. Berkeley: University of California Press, 1987.

Harl, Kenneth W. *Coinage in the Roman Economy*. Baltimore, MD: Johns Hopkins University Press, 1996.

Harmon, A. M., trans. *Lucian. Phalaris. Hippias or the Bath. Dionysus. Heracles. Amber or the Swans. The Fly. Nigrinus. Demonax. The Hall. My Native Land. Octogenarians. A True Story. Slander. The Consonants at Law. The Carousal (Symposium) or the Lapiths*. LCL 14; Cambridge, MA: Harvard University Press, 1913.

Harrington, Wilfrid J. *Revelation*. Collegeville: Liturgical, 1993.

Harris, W. V. 'A Revisionist View of Roman Money'. *JRS* 96 (2006): 1–24.

Harrison, James R. 'Paul and the Imperial Gospel at Thessaloniki'. *JSNT* 25.1 (2002): 71–96.

Harrison, James R. '"The Fading Crown": Divine Honour and the Early Christians'. *JTS* 54.2 (2003): 493–529.

234 *Bibliography*

Harrison, James R. *Paul and the Imperial Authorities at Thessalonica and Rome: A Study in the Conflict of Ideology*. Tübingen: Mohr Siebeck, 2011.

Harrison, James R. 'Paul and Empire II: Negotiating the Seduction of Imperial "Peace and Security" in Galatians, Thessalonians and Philippians'. Pages 165–184 in *New Testament and Empire*. Edited by A. Winn. Atlanta, GA: SBL Press, 2015.

Hart, G. D. 'Trichoepithelioma and the Kings of Ancient Parthia'. *Canadian Medical Association Journal* 92 (2006): 547–549.

Hausmann, E. *Sylloge Nummorum Graecorum: Deutschland. Sammlung der Universitätsbibliothek Leipzig: 2 Römische Provinzialprägungen, Addenda und Corrigenda zum 1. Band*. München: Hirmer, 2008.

Hazzard, R. A. *Ptolemaic Coins: An Introduction for Collectors*. Toronto: Kirk and Bentley, 1995.

Head, B. V. *Catalogue of Greek Coins in the British Museum: Attica, Megaris, Aegina*. London: British Museum, 1888.

Head, B. V. *On the Chronological Sequence of the Coins of Boeotia*. Cambridge: Cambridge University Press, 1895.

Head, B. V. *Historia Numorum*, 2nd ed. London: Clarendon, 1911.

Healy, J. F. *Sylloge Nummorum Graecorum: Great Britain 7. Manchester University Museum. The Raby and Güterbock Collections*. London: Oxford University Press, 1986.

Heichelheim, F. M. *Sylloge Nummorum Graecorum: Great Britain 4. Fitzwilliam Museum: Leake and General Collections: Part 1. Spain (Emporiae, Rhoda)-Italy*. London: Oxford University Press, 1940.

Heichelheim, F. M. *Sylloge Nummorum Graecorum: Great Britain 4. Fitzwilliam Museum: Leake and General Collections: Part 2. Sicily-Thrace*. London: Oxford University Press, 1947.

Heichelheim, F. M. *Sylloge Nummorum Graecorum: Great Britain 4. Fitzwilliam Museum: Leake and General Collections: Part 3. Macedonia-Acarnania (Anactorium)*. London: Oxford University Press, 1951.

Heichelheim, F. M., and E. S. G. Robinson. *Sylloge Nummorum Graecorum: Great Britain 4. Fitzwilliam Museum: Leake and General Collections: Part 4. Acarnania (Argos Amphilochicum) – Phliasia*. London: Oxford University Press, 1956.

Heichelheim, F. M., and E. S. G. Robinson. *Sylloge Nummorum Graecorum: Great Britain 4. Fitzwilliam Museum: Leake and General Collections: Part 5. Sicyon-Thera*. London: Oxford University Press, 1958.

Heichelheim, F. M., E. S. G. Robinson. *Sylloge Nummorum Graecorum: Great Britain 4. Fitzwilliam Museum: Leake and General Collections: Part 6. Asia Minor: Pontus-Phrygia*. London: Oxford University Press, 1965.

Heilig, Christoph. *Hidden Criticism?: The Methodology and Plausibility of the Search for a Counter-Imperial Subtext in Paul*. Tübingen: Mohr Siebeck, 2015.

Hekster, Olivier. 'Coins and Messages: Audience Targeting on Coins of Different Denominations?' Pages 20–35 in *Representation and Perception of Roman Imperial Power*. Edited by Paul Erdkamp, O. Hekster, G. de Kleijn, Stephan T.A.M. Mols and Lukas de Blois. Leiden: Brill, 2003.

Helly, Bruno. 'Le groupe des monnaies fédérales thessaliennes avec Athéna "aux pompons"'. *Revue Numismatique* 6 (1966): 7–32.

Hemberg, B. *Die Kabiren*. Uppsala: Almquist & Wiksells, 1950.

Hemer, C. J. 'Towards a New Moulton and Milligan'. *NovT* 24 (1982): 97–123.

Hemer, C. J. *The Book of Acts in the Setting of Hellenistic History*. Edited by Conrad H. Gempf. Tübingen: Mohr Siebeck, 1989.

Henderson, Jeffrey, trans. *Aristophanes. Frogs. Assemblywomen. Wealth*. LCL 180; Cambridge, MA: Harvard University Press, 2002.

Hendin, D. *Not Kosher: Forgeries of Ancient Jewish and Biblical Coins*. New York: Amphora, 2005.

Hendin, D. *Guide to Biblical Coins*, 5th ed. Jerusalem: Amphora, 2010.

Hendrickson, G. I., and H. M. Hubbnell, trans. *Cicero. Brutus. Orator*. LCL 342; Cambridge, MA: Harvard University Press, 1939.

Hendrix, Holland Lee. 'Thessalonicans Honor Romans'. ThD diss., Harvard University, 1984.

Hendrix, Holand Lee. 'Archaeology and Eschatology at Thessalonica'. Pages 107–118 in *The Future of Early Christianity: Essays in Honor of Helmut Koester*. Edited by Birger A. Pearson. Minneapolis, MN: Fortress Press, 1991.

Heuchert, V. 'Roman Provincial Coinage'. Pages 313–343 in *A Survey of Numismatic Research 1996 – 2001*. Edited by C. Alfaro and A. Burnett. Madrid: International Numismatic Commission and International Association of Professional Numismatists, 2003.

Heuchert, Volker. 'The Chronological Development of Roman Provincial Coin Iconography'. Pages 29–56 in *Coinage and Identity in the Roman Provinces*. Edited by Christopher Howgego, Volker Heuchert and Andrew Burnett. Oxford: Oxford University Press, 2005.

Hicks, E. L. *The Collection of Ancient Greek Inscriptions in the British Museum: Ephesos*. Oxford: Clarendon, 1890.

Hill, P. V. 'Coin Symbolism and Propaganda during the Wars of Vengeance (44–36 B.C.)'. *Quaderni Ticinese* 4 (1975): 157–207.

Hiorth, F. 'Arrangements of Meanings in Lexicography'. *Lingua* 4 (1954–55): 413–424.

Hire, Pauline. 'The Cambridge New Greek Lexicon Project'. *Classical World* 98 (2005): 179–185.

Hollander, David B. *Money in the Late Roman Republic*. Leiden: Brill, 2007.

Hölscher, T. *Staatsdenkmal und Publikum: vom Untergang der Republik bis zur Festigung des Kaisertums in Rom*. Konstanz: Konstanzer althistorische Vorträge und Forschungen 9, 1984.

Hoover, Oliver D. *Greek and Roman Numismatics*. Oxford: Oxford University Press, 2011.

Hopkins, K. 'Taxes and Trade in the Roman Empire (200 B.C.–A.D. 400)'. *JRS* 70 (1980): 101–125.

Horsley, G. H. R. *New Documents Illustrating Early Christianity, Volume 1: A Review of the Greek Inscriptions and Papyri Published in 1976*. North Ryde: Ancient History Documentary Research Centre, 1981.

Horsley, G. H. R. *New Documents Illustrating Early Christianity, Volume 2: A Review of the Greek Inscriptions and Papyri Published in 1977*. North Ryde: Ancient History Documentary Research Centre, 1982.

Horsley, G. H. R. *New Documents Illustrating Early Christianity, Volume 3: A Review of the Greek Inscriptions and Papyri Published in 1978*. North Ryde: Ancient History Documentary Research Centre, 1983.

Horsley, G. H. R. *New Documents Illustrating Early Christianity, Volume 4: A Review of the Greek Inscriptions and Papyri Published in 1979*. North Ryde: Ancient History Documentary Research Centre, 1987.

Horsley, G. H. R. *New Documents Illustrating Early Christianity, Volume 5: Linguistic Essays*. North Ryde: Ancient History Documentary Research Centre, 1989.

Horsley, G. H. R. 'The Inscriptions of Ephesos and the New Testament'. *Novum Testamentum* 34 (1992): 105–168.

Horsley, G. H. R. 'The Politarchs'. Pages 419–431 in *The Book of Acts in Its First Century Setting, Volume 2, Greco-Roman Setting*. Edited by David W. J. Gill and Conrad Gempf. Grand Rapids, MI: Eerdmans, 1994.

Horsley, G. H. R., and John A. L. Lee. 'A Lexicon of the New Testament with Documentary Parallels: Some Interim Entries, 1'. *Filología Neotestamentaria* 10 (1997): 55–84.

Horsley, G. H. R., and John A. L. Lee. 'A Lexicon of the New Testament with Documentary Parallels: Some Interim Entries, 2'. *Filología Neotestamentaria* 11 (1998): 57–84.

Horsley, Richard A. *Paul and the Roman Imperial Order*. New York: Trinity Press International, 2004.

Hort, Arthur F., trans. *Theophrastus. Enquiry into Plants, Volume I: Books 1–5*. LCL 70; Cambridge, MA: Harvard University Press, 1916.

Hostein, Antony, and Jerome Mairat. *Roman Provincial Coinage*, vol. 9. London: British Museum Press, 2016.

Houghton, A., A. Spaer and C. Lorber. *Sylloge Nummorum Graecorum: Israel 1. The Arnold Spaer Collection of Seleucid Coins*. London: I. Vecchi Ltd., 1998.

Houghton, Arthur, Catharine Lorber and O. Hoover, *Seleucid Coins: A Comprehensive Catalogue*, 2 vols. New York: American Numismatic Society, 2002–2008.

Houston, G. W. 'Roman Imperial Administrative Personnel during the Principates of Vespasian and Titus'. Ph.D. diss., University of North Carolina, Chapel Hill, 1971.

Howgego, C. J. *Greek Imperial Countermarks: Studies in the Provincial Coinage of the Roman Empire*. London: Royal Numismatic Society, 1985.

Howgego, C. J. 'Why Did Ancient States Strike Coins?' *NC* 150 (1990): 1–27.

Howgego, C. 'The Supply and Use of Money in the Roman World 200 B.C. to A.D. 300'. *JRS* 82 (1992): 1–31.

Howgego, C. 'Coin Circulation and the Integration of the Roman Economy'. *JRA* 7 (1994): 5–21.

Howgego, C. *Ancient History from Coins*. London: Routledge, 1995.

Howgego, C. 'Coinage and Identity in the Roman Provinces'. Pages 1–17 in *Coinage and Identity in the Roman Provinces*. Edited by Christopher Howgego, Volker Heuchert and Andrew Burnett. Oxford: Oxford University Press, 2005.

Howgego, C., Volker Heuchert and Andrew Burnett. *Coinage and Identity in the Roman Provinces*. Oxford: Oxford University Press, 2005.

Hubbnell, H. M., trans. *Cicero. On Invention. The Best Kind of Orator. Topics*. LCL 386; Cambridge, MA: Harvard University Press, 1949.

Hurter, S. 'The Black Sea Hoard: The Cache of an Ancient Counterfeit Mint'. *Bulletin on Counterfeits* 15.1 (1990): 2–4.

Hurter, Silvia, and Leo Mildenberg. *The Arthur S. Dewing Collection of Greek Coins*. New York: American Numismatic Society, 1985.

Imholtz Jr., August A. '"Liddell and Scott": Precursors, Nineteenth-Century Editions, and the American Contributions'. Pages 117–134 in *Oxford Classics: Teaching and Learning 1800–2000*. Edited by Christopher Stray. London: Duckworth, 2007.

Isaac, E. '1 (Ethiopic Apocalypse of) Enoch'. Pages 5–89 in *The Old Testament Pseudepigrapha: Volume One, Apocalyptic Literature and Testament*. Edited by J. H. Charlesworth. Peabody: Hendrickson Publishers, 1983.

Jackson, John, trans. *Tacitus, Annals: Books 4–6, 11–12*. LCL 312; Cambridge: Harvard University Press, 1937.

Jacobsen, A., and O. Mørkholm, *Sylloge Nummorum Graecorum: Denmark. The Royal Collection of Coins and Medals, Danish National Museum. Part 39. Parthia-India.* Copenhagen: Munksgaard, 1965.

Jaunzems, E. *Sylloge Nummorum Graecorum: The Collection of the American Numismatic Society. Part 4. Sicily 2 (Galaria-Styella).* New York: The American Numismatic Society, 1977.

Jenkins, G. K. *Sylloge Nummorum Graecorum: Denmark. The Royal Collection of Coins and Medals, Danish National Museum. Part 42. North Africa. Syrtica-Mauretania.* Copenhagen: Munksgaard, 1969.

Jenkins, G. K., and A. Kromann, *Sylloge Nummorum Graecorum: Denmark. The Royal Collection of Coins and Medals, Danish National Museum. Part 43. Spain-Gaul.* Copenhagen: Munksgaard, 1979.

Jewett, R. *The Thessalonian Correspondence: Pauline Rhetoric and Millenarian Piety.* Philadelphia, PA: Fortress, 1986.

Johnson, L. T. *The Writings of the New Testament.* Philadelphia, PA: Fortress, 1986.

Johnson, L. T. *The Acts of the Apostles.* Collegeville: Liturgical Press, 1992.

Johnston, Ann. *Greek Imperial Denominations, ca. 200–275: A Study of the Roman Provincial Coinages of Asia Minor.* London: Royal Numismatic Society, 2007.

Jones, A. H. M. 'Numismatics and History'. Pages 61–81 in *The Roman Economy: Studies in Ancient Economic and Administrative History.* Edited by P. Brunt. Oxford: Blackwell, 1974.

Jones, Horace Leonard, trans. *Strabo. Geography, Volume V: Books 10–12.* LCL 211; Cambridge, MA: Harvard University Press, 1928.

Jones, Horace Leonard, trans. *Strabo. Geography, Volume VI: Books 13–14.* LCL 223; Cambridge, MA: Harvard University Press, 1929.

Jones, Horace Leonard. *Strabo. Geography, Volume VII: Books 15–16.* LCL 241; Cambridge, MA: Harvard University Press, 1930.

Jones, W. H. S., and H. A. Ormerod, trans. *Pausanias. Description of Greece, Volume II: Books 3–5 (Laconia, Messenia, Elis 1).* LCL 188; Cambridge, MA: Harvard University Press, 1926.

Jones, W. H. S., trans. *Pausanias. Description of Greece, Volume IV: Books 8.22–10.* LCL 297; Cambridge, MA: Harvard University Press, 1935.

Judge, E. A. 'Setting the Record Straight: Alternative Documents of a Protest in the Roman Army of Egypt'. Pages 378–384 in *The First Christians in the Roman World: Augustan and New Testament Essays.* Edited by James R. Harrison. Tübingen: Mohr Siebeck, 2008.

Kapossy, B. *Sylloge Nummorum Graecorum: Switzerland 2. Katalog der Sammlung Jean-Pierre Righetti im Bernischen Historischen Museum.* Bern: P. Haupt, 1993.

Katsari, Constantina. *The Roman Monetary System: Eastern Provinces from the First to Third Century AD.* Cambridge: Cambridge University Press, 2011.

Kearsley, R. A. 'Ephesus: Neokoros of Artemis'. Pages 203–206 in *New Documents Illustrating Early Christianity: A Review of the Greek Inscriptions and Papyri Published in 1980–1981,* vol. 6. Edited by S. R. Llewelyn. Sydney: Macquarie University, 1992.

Keener, Craig S. *Acts. Volume 2, 3: 1–14:28: An Exegetical Commentary.* Grand Rapids, MI: Baker Academic, 2013.

Keener, Craig S. *Acts. Volume 3, 15: 1–23:35: An Exegetical Commentary.* Grand Rapids, MI: Baker Academic, 2013.

Keep, Robert P. *A Homeric Dictionary for Schools and Colleges.* New York: Harper and Brothers, 1895.

Keil, Josef. 'Die erste Kaiserneokorie von Ephesos'. *Numismatische Zeitschrift N.F.* 12 (1919): 118–120.

Kelber, Werner. 'χαρακτήρ'. *TDNT* 9: 418–423.

Kessler, David, and Peter Temin. *Money and Prices in the Early Roman Empire.* Massachusetts Institute of Technology, Department of Economics, Working Paper Series, 2005.

Kiessling, Emil. *Wörterbuch der griechischen Papyrusurkunden mit Einschluss der griechischen Inschriften, Ausschriften, Ostraka, Mumienschilder usw. aus Ägypten, Bande IV.* Berlin: Bersasser, 1944–1971.

Kiessling, Emil. *Wörterbuch der griechischen Papyrusurkunden mit Einschluss der griechischen Inschriften, Ausschriften, Ostraka, Mumienschilder usw. aus Ägypten, Supplement 1 (1940–1966).* Amsterdam: Hakkert, 1971.

King, C. E., and C. M. Kraay. *Sylloge Nummorum Graecorum: Great Britain 5. Ashmolean Museum (Oxford): Pt. 4, Paeonia-Thessaly.* London: Oxford University Press, 1981.

King, L. W., and R. C. Thompson. *The Sculptures and Inscription of Darius the Great on the Rock of Behistûn in Persia: A New Collation of the Persian, Susian and Babylonian Texts.* London: British Museum, 1907.

Kleeberg, John, Hermann Maué, Lutz Ilisch, Bernd Kluge, Wolfgang Steguweit, Andrew Burnett and Cécile Morrisson. *A Survey of Numismatic Research, 1990–1995.* Berlin: International Association of Professional Numismatists, 1997.

Kleiner, Fred S. *Gardiner's Art through the Ages: Non-Western Perspectives.* Boston: Wadsworth, 2010.

Kleiner, G. *Sylloge Nummorum Graecorum: Deutschland. Sammlung v. Aulock: Hefte 1.-3. Pontus, Paphlagonien, Bithynien.* Berlin: Gebrüder Mann, 1957.

Kleiner, G. *Sylloge Nummorum Graecorum: Deutschland. Sammlung v. Aulock: Heft 4. Mysien.* Berlin: Gebrüder Mann, 1957.

Kleiner, G. *Sylloge Nummorum Graecorum: Deutschland. Sammlung v. Aulock: Heft 5. 5. Troas, Aeolis, Lesbos.* Berlin: Gebrüder Mann, 1959.

Klose, D. O. A. *Die Münzprägung von Smyrna in der römischen Kaiserzeit.* Berlin: de Gruyter, 1987.

Klose, D. O. A. *Sylloge Nummorum Graecorum: Deutschland. Staatliche Münzsammlung München: Heft 20. Ionien 1: Frühes Elektron–Priene.* Berlin: Gebrüder Mann, 1995.

Klose, D. "Münz – oder Gruselkabinett?" Pages 253–264 in *Internationales Kolloquium zur kaiserzeitlichen Münzprägung Kleinasiens.* Edited by J. Nollé, B. Overbeck and P. Weiss. Milan: Ennerre, 1997.

Koester, C. R. *Revelation.* New Haven, CT: Yale University Press, 2015.

Koester, Helmut. 'From Paul's Eschatology to the Apocalyptic Schemata of 2 Thessalonians'. Pages 441–458 in *The Thessalonian Correspondence.* Edited by R. F. Collins. Leuven: Leuven University Press, 1990.

Koester, Helmut. 'Ephesos in Early Christian Literature'. Pages 119–140 in *Ephesos, Metropolis of Asia: An Interdisciplinary Approach to Its Archaeology, Religion, and Culture.* Edited by Helmut Koester. Valley Forge: Trinity Press International, 1995.

Köker, H. *Sylloge Nummorum Graecorum: Turkey 6. Burdur Museum.* Istanbul: Turkish Institute of Archaeology, 2012.

Körte, A. 'Χαρακτήρ'. *Hermes* 64.1 (1928): 75.

Konuk, K. *Sylloge Nummorum Graecorum: Turkey 1. The Muharrem Kayhan collection.* Istanbul and Bordeaux: Ausonius Publications, 2002.

Konuk, Koray. 'The Electrum Coinage of Samos in Light of a Recent Hoard'. Pages 44–53 in *Neue forschungen zu Ionien.* Edited by E. Schwertheim and E. Winter. Bonn: Habelt, 2005.

Konuk, Koray. 'Asia Minor to the Ionian Revolt'. Pages 43–60 in *The Oxford Handbook of Greek and Roman Coinage*. Edited by William E. Metcalf. Oxford: Oxford University Press, 2012.

Konuk, K., O. Tekin and A. E. Özdizbay. *Sylloge Nummorum Graecorum. Turkey 1, The Muharrem Kayhan Collection Part 2*. Istanbul: Turkish Institute of Archaeology, 2015.

Kos, P., and A. Šemrov. *Sylloge Nummorum Graecorum: Slovenia. Ljubljana, Narodni Muzej. Volume 3. Moesia Superior. Part 1. Viminacium*. Milano: Ed. Ennerre, 1996.

Kosmala, H. *Hebräer, Essener, Christen: Studien zur Vorgeschichte der frühchristlichen Verkündigung*. Leiden: Brill, 1959.

Kovacs, David. *Euripides. Helen. Phoenician Women. Orestes*. LCL 11; Cambridge, MA: Harvard University Press, 2002.

Kovalenko, S. *Sylloge Nummorum Graecorum: Russia. State Pushkin Museum of Fine Arts, Volume I. Coins of the Black Sea Region: Part 1 Ancient Coins from the Northern Black Sea Littoral*. Leuven: Peeters, 2011.

Kovalenko, S. *Sylloge Nummorum Graecorum: Russia. State Pushkin Museum of Fine Arts, Volume I. Coins of the Black Sea Region: Part 2 Ancient Coins of the Black Sea Littoral*. Leuven: Peeters, 2014.

Kovalenko, S. *Sylloge Nummorum Graecorum: Russia. State Pushkin Museum of Fine Arts: Volume II. Greek Coins of Italy and Sicily*. Rome, L'Erma di Bretschneider, 2017.

Kraay, C. M. *Sylloge Nummorum Graecorum: Great Britain 5. Ashmolean Museum (Oxford): Pt. 1A, Etruria-Lucania (Thurium)*. London: Oxford University Press, 1962.

Kraay, C. M. *Sylloge Nummorum Graecorum: Great Britain 5. Ashmolean Museum (Oxford): Pt. 2, Italy: Lucania (Thurium) – Bruttium, Sicily, Carthage*. London: Oxford University Press, 1969.

Kraay, C. M. *Archaic and Classical Greek Coins*. London: Methuen, 1976.

Kraay, C. M. *Sylloge Nummorum Graecorum: Great Britain 5. Ashmolean Museum (Oxford): Pt. 3, Macedonia*. London: Oxford University Press, 1976.

Kraft, K. 'Der goldene Kranz Caesars und der Kampf um die Entlarvung des "'Tyrannen'"'. *JRS* 3.4 (1952–53): 7–97.

Kraft, K. *Das System der kaiserzeitlichen Münzprägung in Kleinasien*. Berlin: Mann, 1972.

Kraft, K., and D. Kienast. *Sylloge Nummorum Graecorum: Deutschland. Sammlung v. Aulock: Heft 7. Karien*. Berlin: Gebrüder Mann, 1962.

Kreitzer, Larry J. *Striking New Images: Roman Imperial Coinage and the New Testament World*. JSNTSup 134. Sheffield: Sheffield Academic, 1996.

Kremydi, S. 'Roman Provincial Coinage'. Pages 182–195 in *A Survey of Numismatic Research 2002-2007*. Edited by D. Bateson and M. Amandry. Glasgow: International Numismatic Commission and International Association of Professional Numismatists, 2009.

Kremydi-Sicilianou, S. *Sylloge Nummorum Graecorum: Greece 2. The Alpha Bank Collection: Macedonia I, Alexander I – Perseus*. Athens: Alpha Bank, 2000.

Kritt, Brian. *Seleucid Coins of Bactria*. Lancaster: Classical Numismatic Group, 1996.

Krmnicek, Stefan. 'Das Konzept der Objektbiographie in der antiken Numismatik'. Pages 47–59 in *Coins in Context 1: New Perspectives for the Interpretation of Coin Finds*. Edited by H. V. Kaenel and F. Kemmers. Mainz: Philipp Von Zabern, 2009.

Kroll, J. H. *Sylloge Nummorum Graecorum: Deutschland. Staatliche Münzsammlung München: Heft 14. Attika – Megaris – Ägina*. Berlin: Gebrüder Mann, 2002.

240   *Bibliography*

Kromann, A., and O. Mørkholm, *Sylloge Nummorum Graecorum: Denmark. The Royal Collection of Coins and Medals, Danish National Museum. Part 40. Egypt: The Ptolemies*. Copenhagen: Munksgaard, 1977.

Küthmann, H., and K. Kraft. *Sylloge Nummorum Graecorum: Deutschland. Sammlung v. Aulock: Heft 6. Ionien*. Berlin: Gebrüder Mann, 1960.

Küthmann, H., and U. Pause-Dreyer. *Sylloge Nummorum Graecorum: Deutschland. Staatliche Münzsammlung München: Heft 6. Sikelia – Punier in Sizilien – Lipara – Sardinia – Punier in Sardinien – Nachträge*. Berlin: Gebrüder Mann, 1980.

Küthmann, H., U. Pause-Dreyer, *Sylloge Nummorum Graecorum: Deutschland. Staatliche Münzsammlung München: Heft 7. Taurische Chersones – Sarmatien – Dacia – Moesia superior – Moesia inferior*. Berlin: Gebrüder Mann, 1985.

Kysar, R. *John*. Minneapolis, MN: Augsburg Publishing House, 1986.

Lake, Kirsopp, and Henry J. Cadbury. *English Translation and Commentary. Vol. 4 of The Beginnings of Christianity: The Acts of the Apostles*. Edited by F. J. Foakes-Jackson and Kirsopp Lake. London: Macmillan, 1933.

Lane, W. L. *Hebrews 1–8*. Dallas: Word, 1991.

Langslow, D. R. *Medical Latin in the Roman Empire*. Oxford: Oxford University Press, 2000.

Larfeld, W. *Handbuch der griechischen Epigraphik*. Leipzig: O. R. Reisland, Hildashelm, 1898–1907.

Le Rider, Georges, and Françoise de Callataÿ. *Les Séleucides et les Ptolémées* (Paris: Éd. du Rocher, 2006.

Lee, John A. L. 'A Note on Septuagint Material in the Supplement to Liddell and Scott'. *Glossa* 47 (1969): 234–242.

Lee, John A. L. 'Hebrews 5:14 and ἕξις: A History of Misunderstanding'. *Novum Testamentum* 39 (1997): 151–176.

Lee, John A. L. *A History of New Testament Lexicography*. New York: Peter Lang, 2003.

Lee, John A. L. 'The Present State of Lexicography of Ancient Greek'. Pages 66–74 in *Biblical Greek Language and Lexicography: Essays in Honor of Frederick W. Danker*. Edited by B. A. Taylor, John A. L. Lee, P. R. Burton and R. E. Whitaker. Grand Rapids: Eerdmans, 2004.

Leschhorn, W. *Sylloge Nummorum Graecorum: Deutschland. Staatliche Münzsammlung München: Heft 23. Lydien*. Berlin: Gebrüder Mann, 1997.

Leschhorn, W. *Sylloge Nummorum Graecorum: Deutschland. Staatliche Münzsammlung München: Heft 24. Phrygien*. Berlin: Gebrüder Mann, 1989.

Leschhorn, W. *Sylloge Nummorum Graecorum: Deutschland. Herzog Anton Ulrich-Museum Braunschweig, Kunstmuseum des Landes Niedersachsen*. München: Hirmer, 1998.

Leschhorn, W. *Lexikon der Aufschriften auf griechischen Münzen*. Wien: Verlag der Österreichischen Akademie der Wissenschaften, 2002.

Lesquier, J. *Papyrus de Magdola being Papyrus Grecs de Lille II*. Paris: Leroux, 1912.

Levante, E. *Sylloge Nummorum Graecorum: Switzerland 1. Levante – Cilicia*. Berne: Credit Suisse, 1986.

Levante, E. *Sylloge Nummorum Graecorum: Switzerland 1. Levante – Cilicia. Supplement 1*. Zurich: Numismatica Ars Classica, 1993.

Levante, E. *Sylloge Nummorum Graecorum: France 2. Bibliothèque Nationale de France: Cilicie*. Paris and Zurich: Bibliothèque Nationale de France and Numismatica Ars Classica, 1993.

Levante, E. *Sylloge Nummorum Graecorum: France 3*. Bibliothèque Nationale de France: Pamphylie, Pisidie, Lycaonie, Galatie. Paris and Zurich: Bibliothèque Nationale de France and Numismatica Ars Classica, 1994.

Levante, E. *Sylloge Nummorum Graecorum: France 5. Bibliothèque Nationale de France: Mysie*. Paris and Zurich: Bibliothèque Nationale de France and Numismatica Ars Classica, 2001.

Levick, B. *Roman Colonies in Southern Asia Minor*. Oxford: Clarendon Press, 1967.

Levick, B. 'Propaganda and the Imperial Coinage'. *Antichthon* 16 (1982): 104–116.

Lewis, P., and Ron Bolden. *The Pocket Guide to Saint Paul: Coins Encountered by the Apostle on His Travels*. Kent Town: Wakefield Press, 2002.

Levy, B. E. 'Nero's "Apollonia" Series: The Achaean Context'. *Numismatic Chronicle* 149 (1989): 59–68.

Liampi, K. *Sylloge Nummorum Graecorum: Deutschland. Staatliche Münzsammlung München: Heft 10/11. Makedonien: Könige*. Berlin: Gebrüder Mann, 2001.

Liampi, K. *Sylloge Nummorum Graecorum: Deutschland. Staatliche Münzsammlung München: Heft 12. Thessalien – Illyrien – Epirus – Korkyra*. Berlin: Gebrüder Mann, 2007.

Liddel, K. 'Skin Disease in Antiquity'. *Journal of the Royal College of Physicians of London* 6 (2006): 81–86.

Lindars, B. *The Gospel of John*. Grand Rapids, MI: Eerdmans, 1982.

Lindsay, W. M. *Isidori Hispalensis episcope etymologiarum sive originum libri XX*, 2 vols. Oxford: Clarendon, 1911.

Llewelyn, S. R. *New Documents Illustrating Early Christianity, Volume 6: A Review of the Greek Inscriptions and Papyri Published in 1980–81*. North Ryde: Ancient History Documentary Research Centre, 1992.

Llewelyn, S. R. *New Documents Illustrating Early Christianity, Volume 7: A Review of the Greek Inscriptions and Papyri Published in 1982–83*. North Ryde: Ancient History Documentary Research Centre, 1994.

Llewelyn, S. R. *New Documents Illustrating Early Christianity, Volume 8: A Review of the Greek Inscriptions and Papyri Published 1984–85*. Grand Rapids, MI: Eerdmans, 1998.

Llewelyn, S. R. *New Documents Illustrating Early Christianity, Volume 9: A Review of the Greek Inscriptions and Papyri Published in 1986 and 1987*. Grand Rapids, MI: Eerdmans, 2002.

Llewelyn, S. R., and J. R. Harrison. *New Documents Illustrating Early Christianity, Volume 10: A Review of the Greek and Other Inscriptions and Papyri Published between 1988 and 1992*. Grand Rapids, MI: Eerdmans, 2012.

Lo Cascio, E. 'State and Coinage in the Late Republic and Early Empire'. *JRS* 71 (1981): 76–86.

Louw, Johannes P., and Eugene A. Nida, eds. *Greek-English Lexicon of the New Testament: Based on Semantic Domains*, 2nd ed.; 2 vols. New York: United Bible Societies, 1988–1989.

Lubetski, Meir, and Edith Lubetski, eds. *New Inscriptions and Seals Relating to the Biblical World*. ABS 19. Atlanta, GA: SBL Press, 2012.

Luckensmeyer, David. *The Eschatology of First Thessalonians*. Göttingen: Vandenhoeck & Ruprecht, 2009.

Lupieri, Edmundo F. *A Commentary on the Apocalypse of John*. Translated by Maria Poggi Johnson and Adam Kamesar. Grand Rapids: Eerdmans, 1999.

Lust, Johan, Erik Eynikel and Katrin Hauspie. *A Greek-English Lexicon of the Septuagint: Revised Edition*. Deutsche Bibelgesellschaft: Stuttgart, 2003.

Luz, U. *Matthew 21–28: A Commentary*. Translated by J. E. Crouch. Minneapolis, MN: Fortress Press, 2005.

Mabbott, T. O. 'Epictetus and Nero's Coinage'. *Classical Philology* 36.4 (1941): 398–399.

242   *Bibliography*

MacDonald, David. *The Coinage of Aphrodisias*. London: Royal Numismatic Society, 1992.
MacDonald, David. *An Introduction to the History and Coinage of the Kingdom of the Bosporus*. London: Classical Numismatic Group, 2005.
Magalhães, M. M. *Sylloge Nummorum Graecorum: Brasil. Museu Histórico Nacional: Moedas gregas e provinciais romanas*. Rio de Janeiro: Museu Histórico Nacional, 2011.
Magie, D. *Roman Rule in Asia Minor*. Princeton, NJ: Princeton University Press, 1950.
Magness, Jodi. *The Archaeology of Qumran and the Dead Sea Scrolls*. Grand Rapids, MI: Eerdmans, 2002.
Malina, Bruce J., and Ricard L. Rohrbaugh. *Social Science Commentary on the Gospel of John*. Minneapolis, MN: Fortress, 1998.
Maltiel-Gerstenfeld, Jacob. *260 Years of Ancient Jewish Coins: A Catalogue*. Tel Aviv: Kol Print Service, 1982.
Maltiel-Gerstenfeld, Jacob. *New Catalogue of Ancient Jewish Coins*. Tel Aviv: Minerva, 1987.
Manders, Erika. *Coining Images of Power: Patterns in the Representation of Roman Emperors on Imperial Coinage, AD 193–284*. Leiden: Brill, 2012.
Mannsperger, D. *Sylloge Nummorum Graecorum: Deutschland. Münzsammlung der Universität Tübingen: Heft 1. Hispania – Sikelia*. Berlin: Gebrüder Mann, 1981.
Mannsperger, D. *Sylloge Nummorum Graecorum: Deutschland. Münzsammlung der Universität Tübingen: Heft 2. Taurische Chersones – Korkyra*. Berlin: Gebrüder Mann, 1982.
Mannsperger, D., and G. Fischer-Heetfeld. *Sylloge Nummorum Graecorum: Deutschland. Münzsammlung der Universität Tübingen: Heft 3 Akarnanien – Bithynien*. Berlin: Gebrüder Mann, 1985.
Mannsperger, D. *Sylloge Nummorum Graecorum: Deutschland. Münzsammlung der Universität Tübingen: Heft 4. Mysien – Ionien*. Berlin: Gebrüder Mann, 1989.
Mannsperger, D. *Sylloge Nummorum Graecorum: Deutschland. Münzsammlung der Universität Tübingen: Heft 5. Karien und Lydien*. Berlin: Gebrüder Mann, 1994.
Mannsperger, D., and M. Matzke. *Sylloge Nummorum Graecorum: Deutschland. Münzsammlungder Universität Tübingen: Heft 6. Phrygien – Kappadokien, Römische Provinzprägungen in Kleinasien*. Berlin: Gebrüder Mann, 1998.
Manson, T. W. 'The Problem of the Epistle to the Hebrews'. *BJRL* 32 (1949–50): 1–17.
Marinescu, C. A. 'Modem Imitations of Ancient Coins from Bulgaria'. *Minerva* 9.5 (1998): 46–48.
Marshall, I. H. *Acts*. Grand Rapids, MI: Eerdmans, 1980.
Marshall, John Hubert. *Taxilla: An Illustrated Account of Archaeological Excavations Carried out at Taxila under the Orders of the Government of India between the Years 1913 and 1934*. Cambridge: Cambridge University Press, 2013.
Martin, T. R. 'Why Did the Greek Polis Originally Need Coins?' *Historia* 45 (1996): 257–283.
Martini, R., B. Fischer and N. Vismara. *Sylloge Nummorum Graecorum: Italia. Milano. Civiche Raccolte Numismatiche: Part 1. Hispania-Gallia anellenica*. Milano: Ed. Ennerre, 1988.
Martini, R. *Sylloge Nummorum Graecorum: Italia. Milano. Civiche Raccolte Numismatiche: Part 13. Aegyptus. Fasc. 1. Ptolemaei*. Milano: Ed. Ennerre, 1989.
Martini, R. *Sylloge Nummorum Graecorum: Italia. Milano. Civiche Raccolte Numismatiche: Part 13. Aegyptus. Fasc. 2. Octavianus Augustus-Lucius Verus*. Milano: Ed. Ennerre, 1991.
Martini, R. *Sylloge Nummorum Graecorum: Italia. Milano. Civiche Raccolte Numismatiche: Part 13. Aegyptus. Fasc. 3. Commodus-Galerius Caesar*. Milano: Ed. Ennerre, 1992.

Martini, R. *Sylloge Nummorum Graecorum: Italia. Milano. Civiche Raccolte Numismatiche: Part 14. Cyrenaica-Mauretania.* Milano: Ed. Ennerre, 1989.

Martini, R. *The Pangerl Collection Catalog and Commentary on the Countermarked Roman Imperial Coins.* Milan: Ennerre, 2003.

Martini, Rodolfo, and N. Vismara. *Sylloge Nummorum Romanorum Italia: Milano; Civiche Raccolte Numismatiche.* Milan: Civiche Raccolte Numismatiche, 1990–1994.

Mathewson, David L. *Revelation: A Handbook on the Greek Text.* Waco, TX: Baylor University Press, 2016.

Mathiesen, H. E. *Sylloge Nummorum Graecorum: Denmark. Aarhus University Part 1. Aarhus University collection.* Copenhagen: Munksgaard, 1986.

Mathiesen, H. E. *Sylloge Nummorum Graecorum: Denmark. Aarhus University Part 2. The Fabricius Collection (Collections of Aarhus University and the Danish National Museum).* Copenhagen: Munksgaard, 1987.

Mattingly, H. *Coins of the Roman Empire in the British Museum*, 6 vols. London: British Museum, 1923–1976.

Mattingly, H. 'A Mithraic Tessera from Verulam'. *Numismatic Chronicle* 12 (1932): 54–57.

Mattingly, H. *The Roman Imperial Coinage*, 10 vols. London: Spink, 1923–2007.

Mattingly, H. *Roman Coins from the Earliest Times to the Fall of the Western Empire*, 2nd ed. London: Methuen, 1960.

May, David M. 'The Empire Strikes Back: The Mark of the Beast in Revelation'. *Review and Expositor* 106 (2009): 83–97.

May, David. 'Interpreting Revelation with Roman Coins: A Test Case, Revelation 6:9-11'. *Review & Expositor* 106 (2009): 445–465.

McGing, Brian, trans. *Appian. Roman History, Volume I.* LCL 2; Cambridge, MA: Harvard University Press, 1912.

McKnight, S. 'The Warning Passages of Hebrews: A Formal Analysis and Theological Conclusions'. *Trinity Journal* 13 (1992), 21–59.

Meadows, A. 'The Eras of Pamphylia and the Seleucid Invasions of Asia Minor'. *American Journal of Numismatics* 21 (2009): 51–88.

Meadows, A. 'The Spread of Coins in the Hellenistic World'. Pages 169–194 in *Explaining Money and Financial Innovation: A Historical Analysis*. Edited by P. Bernholz and R. Vaubel. New York: Springer, 2014.

Meadows, A., and J. Williams. 'Moneta and the Monuments: Coinage and Politics in Republican Rome'. *JRS* 91 (2001): 27–49.

Meinardus, O. F. A. *St. Paul in Ephesus and the Cities of Galatia and Cyprus.* New Rochelle: Caratzas Brothers, 1979.

Mellink, M. J. 'Archaeology in Asia Minor'. *AJA* 63 (1959): 73–85.

Melville Jones, J. *Testimonia Numaria, Greek and Latin Texts Concerning Ancient Greek Coinage, Volume I: Texts and Translations.* London: Spink and Son, 1993.

Melville Jones, J. *Testimonia Numaria, Greek and Latin Texts Concerning Ancient Greek Coinage, Volume II: Addenda and Commentary.* London: Spink and Son, 2007.

Merkelbach, R., and S. Şahin. 'Inschriften von Perge'. *Epigraphica Anatolica* 11 (1988): 97–170.

Meshorer, Y. *Jewish Coins of the Second Temple Period.* Tel-Aviv: Am Hassefer, 1967.

Meshorer, Y. *Sylloge Nummorum Graecorum: The Collection of the American Numismatic Society. Part 6. Palestine-South Arabia.* New York: The American Numismatic Society, 1981.

Meshorer, Y. *A Treasury of Jewish Coins.* Jerusalem: Amphora Books, 2001.

Metcalf, William. *Oxford Handbook of Greek and Roman Coinage.* Oxford: Oxford University Press, 2012.

244   *Bibliography*

Meyer, Reinhold. *Studies in Classical History and Society*. Oxford: Oxford University Press, 2002.

Michaels, J. R. *The Gospel of John*. Grand Rapids, Michigan: Eerdmans, 2010.

Mielczarek, M. *Sylloge Nummorum graecorum: Poland 1. The Archaeological and Ethnographical Museum in Łódź: Part 4. Galatia – Zeugitana*. Kraków: The Polish Academy of Arts and Sciences, 1998.

Militký, J. *Sylloge Nummorum Graecorum: Czech Republic 1. The National Museum, Prague. Part 3. Macedonia and Paeonia*. Prague: The National Museum, 2016.

Millar, Fergus. *The Emperor in the Roman World*. London: Duckworth, 1992.

Millar, Fergus. *The Roman Near East 31 BC–AD 337*. London: Harvard University Press, 1993.

Miller, Frank Justus, trans. *Ovid. Metamorphoses, Volume I: Books 1–8*. LCL 42; Cambridge, MA: Harvard University Press, 1916.

Miller, H. H. *Greece through the Ages, as Seen by Travelers from Herodotus to Byron*. New York: Funk & Wagnalls, 1972.

Milne, J. G. *Sylloge Nummorum Graecorum: Great Britain 5. Ashmolean Museum (Oxford): Pt. 1, Evans Collection. Italy*. London: Oxford University Press, 1951.

Minns, Ellis H. 'Parchments of the Parthian Period from Avroman in Kurdistan'. *JHS* 35 (1915): 22–65.

Mionnet, T. *Description des médailles antiques*. Paris: Toulouse, 1806–1808.

Mirnik, I. *Sylloge Nummorum Graecorum: Croatia. Zagreb. The Archaeological Museum Numismatic Collection. Part 8. Aegyptus. Ptolemaei–Roman Provincial Coinage*. Zagreb: Archaeological Museum of Zagreb, 2017.

Mitchell, Stephen. *Anatolia: Land, Men, and Gods in Asia Minor*, 2 vols. Oxford: Clarendon, 1993.

Mitchiner, Michael. *Indo-Greek and Indo-Scythian Coinage*, 9 vols. London: Hawkins Publications, 1975.

Mitchiner, Michael. *Oriental Coins and Their Values: The Ancient & Classical World*. London: Hawkins Publications, 1978.

Mitchiner, Michael. *Ancient Trade and Early Coinage*. London: Hawkins Publications, 2004.

Mitsopoulos-Leon, Veronika. 'Ephesus'. Pages 306–310 in *The Princeton Encyclopedia of Classical Sites*. Edited by Richard Stillwell, William L. MacDonald and Marian Holland McAllister. Princeton, NJ: Princeton University Press, 1976.

Moffatt, James. *A Critical and Exegetical Commentary on the Epistle to the Hebrews*. Edinburgh: T&T Clark International, 1924.

Mommsen, Theodor. *Geschichte des römischen Münzwesens*. Berlin: Weidmann, 1860.

Morcom, J., and M. J. Price. *Sylloge Nummorum Graecorum: Great Britain 10. The John Morcom Collection of Western Greek Bronze Coins*. London: Oxford University Press, 1995.

Morgenstern, Matthew. 'Mandaic Magic Bowls in the Moussaie Collection: A Preliminary Survey'. Pages 165–169 in *New Inscriptions and Seals Relating to the Biblical World*. Edited by Meir Lubetski and Edith Lubetski. Atlanta, GA: SBL Press, 2012.

Mørkholm, O. *Sylloge Nummorum Graecorum: Denmark. The Royal Collection of Coins and Medals, Danish National Museum. Part 34. Cyprus-Cappadocia. Uncertain Coins. Imperial cistophori*. Copenhagen: Munksgaard, 1956.

Mørkholm, O. *Sylloge Nummorum Graecorum: Denmark. The Royal Collection of Coins and Medals, Danish National Museum. Part 35. Syria: Seleucid Kings*. Copenhagen: Munksgaard, 1959.

Mørkholm, O. *Sylloge Nummorum Graecorum: Denmark. The Royal Collection of Coins and Medals, Danish National Museum. Part 36. Syria: Cities*. Copenhagen: Munksgaard, 1959.

Mørkholm, O. *Sylloge Nummorum Graecorum: Denmark. The Royal Collection of Coins and Medals, Danish National Museum. Part 37. Phoenicia*. Copenhagen: Munksgaard, 1961.

Mørkholm, O. *Sylloge Nummorum Graecorum: Denmark. The Royal Collection of Coins and Medals, Danish National Museum. Part 38. Palestine-Characene*. Copenhagen: Munksgaard, 1961.

Mørkholm, O. *Sylloge Nummorum Graecorum: Deutschland. Sammlung v. Aulock: Heft 10. Lykien*. Berlin: Gebrüder Mann, 1964.

Mørkholm, O. *Sylloge Nummorum Graecorum: Deutschland. Sammlung v. Aulock: Heft 11. Pamphylien*. Berlin: Gebrüder Mann, 1965.

Mørkholm, Otto. *Early Hellenistic Coinage: From the Accession of Alexander to the Peace of Apamea (336-188 B.C.)*. Cambridge: Cambridge University Press, 1991.

Most, Glenn W., trans. *Hesiod. Theogony. Works and Days. Testimonia*. LCL 57; Cambridge, MA: Harvard University Press, 2007.

Moulton, J. H., W. F. Howard and M. Turner. *A Grammar of New Testament Greek*, 4 vols. Edinburgh: T&T Clark, 1906-1976.

Moulton, J. H. 'Notes from the Papyri. I'. *Expositor* 6.3.4 (1901): 271-282.

Moulton, J. H. 'Notes from the Papyri. II'. *Expositor* 6.7.2 (1903): 104-121.

Moulton, J. H. 'Notes from the Papyri. III'. *Expositor* 6.8.6 (1903): 423-439.

Moulton, J. H., and G. Milligan. 'Lexical Notes from the Papyri. IV'. *Expositor* 7.5.1 (1908): 51-60.

Moulton, J. H., and G. Milligan. 'Lexical Notes from the Papyri. V'. *Expositor* 7.5.2 (1908): 170-185.

Moulton, J. H., and G. Milligan. 'Lexical Notes from the Papyri. VI'. *Expositor* 7.5.3 (1908): 262-277.

Moulton, J. H., and G. Milligan. 'Lexical Notes from the Papyri. VII'. *Expositor* 7.6.1 (1908): 84-93.

Moulton, J. H., and G. Milligan. 'Lexical Notes from the Papyri. VIII'. *Expositor* 7.6.2 (1908): 183-192.

Moulton, J. H., and G. Milligan. 'Lexical Notes from the Papyri. IX'. *Expositor* 7.6.3 (1908): 273-281.

Moulton, J. H. and G. Milligan. 'Lexical Notes from the Papyri. X'. *Expositor* 7.6.4 (1908): 370-384.

Moulton, J. H., and G. Milligan. 'Lexical Notes from the Papyri. XI'. *Expositor* 7.6.6 (1908): 562-568.

Moulton, J. H., and G. Milligan. 'Lexical Notes from the Papyri. XII'. *Expositor* 7.7.1 (1909): 88-95.

Moulton, J. H., and G. Milligan. 'Lexical Notes from the Papyri. XIII'. *Expositor* 7.7.3 (1909): 282-285.

Moulton, J. H., and G. Milligan. 'Lexical Notes from the Papyri. XIV'. *Expositor* 7.7.4 (1909): 375-384.

Moulton, J. H., and G. Milligan. 'Lexical Notes from the Papyri. XV'. *Expositor* 7.7.5 (1909): 470-480.

Moulton, J. H., and G. Milligan. 'Lexical Notes from the Papyri. XVI'. *Expositor* 7.7.6 (1909): 559-568.

Moulton, J. H., and G. Milligan. 'Lexical Notes from the Papyri. XVII'. *Expositor* 7.9.3 (1910): 284-288.

Moulton, J. H., and G. Milligan. 'Lexical Notes from the Papyri. XVIII'. *Expositor* 7.10.1 (1910): 89–96.

Moulton, J. H., and G. Milligan. 'Lexical Notes from the Papyri. XVIII'. *Expositor* 7.10.3 (1910): 282–288.

Moulton, J. H., and G. Milligan. 'Lexical Notes from the Papyri. XIX'. *Expositor* 7.10.5 (1910): 477–480.

Moulton, J. H., and G. Milligan. 'Lexical Notes from the Papyri. XX'. *Expositor* 7.10.6 (1910): 563–568.

Moulton, J. H., and G. Milligan. 'Lexical Notes from the Papyri. XXI'. *Expositor* 8.1.3 (1911): 284–288.

Moulton, J. H., and G. Milligan. 'Lexical Notes from the Papyri. XXI'. *Expositor* 8.1.4 (1911): 380–384.

Moulton, J. H., and G. Milligan. 'Lexical Notes from the Papyri. XXII'. *Expositor* 8.1.5 (1911): 475–480.

Moulton, J. H., and G. Milligan. 'Lexical Notes from the Papyri. XXIII'. *Expositor* 8.1.6 (1911): 561–568.

Moulton, J. H., and G. Milligan. 'Lexical Notes from the Papyri. XXIV'. *Expositor* 8.2.3 (1911): 275–288.

Moulton, J. H., and G. Milligan. 'Lexical Notes from the Papyri. XXV'. *Expositor* 8.4.6 (1912): 561–568.

Moulton, J. H., and G. Milligan. *Vocabulary of the Greek Testament: Illustrated from the Papyri and Other Non-Literary Sources*. London: Hodder and Stoughton, 1930.

Mounce, Robert. *The Book of Revelation*. Grand Rapids, MI: Eerdmans, 1998.

Moushmov, H. *Ancient Coins of the Balkan Peninsula*. Translated by Denista Genkova, Dave Surber and Slavei Theodore Slaveev. Sofia: K&K Publishers, 1912.

Mugridge, A. 'Warnings in the Epistle to the Hebrews'. *RTR* 46 (1987): 74–82.

Murphy, Catherine M. *Wealth in the Dead Sea Scrolls and in the Qumran Community*. Leiden: Brill, 2001.

Murphy, Frederick J. *Fallen Is Babylon: The Revelation to John*. Harrisburg: Trinity, 1998.

Murphy-O'Connor, J. *Paul: A Critical Life*. Oxford: Oxford University Press, 1996.

Naster, Paul, J.-B. Colbert de Beaulieu, Joan M. Fagerlie, Jacques Yvon and Helen W. Mitchell Brown. *A Survey of Numismatic Research, 1966–1971*. New York: International Numismatic Commission, 1973.

Nicholl, Colin R. *From Hope to Despair in Thessalonica*. Cambridge: Cambridge University Press, 2004.

Nicolet-Pierre, H., J. Delepierre, M. Delepierre and G. Le Rider. *Sylloge Nummorum Graecorum: France 1. Bibliothèque Nationale de France: Collection Jeanet Marie Delepierre*. Paris: Bibliothèque nationale de France, 1983.

Nicole-Pierre, H., and J.-N. Barrandon. 'Monnaies d'électrum archaïques. Le trésor de Samos de 1894 (IGCH 1158) conservé à Paris'. *RN* 152 (1997): 121–135.

Nollé, J. *Sylloge Nummorum Graecorum: Deutschland. Pfälzer Privatsammlungen: 4. Pamphylien*. München: Hirmer, 1993.

Nollé, J. *Sylloge Nummorum Graecorum: Deutschland. Pfälzer Privatsammlungen: 5. Pisidien und Lykaonien*. München: Hirmer, 1999.

Nollé, J. 'Zur neueren Forschungsgeschichte der kaiser- zeitliche Stadtprägungen Kleinasiens'. Pages 11–26 in *Internationales Kolloquium zur kaiserzeitlichen Münzprägung Kleinasiens*. Edited by J. Nollé, B. Overbeck and P. Weiss. Milan: Ennerre, 1997.

Oakes, P. 'Re-Mapping the Universe: Paul and the Emperor in 1 Thessalonians and Philippians'. *JSNT* 27 (2005): 301–322.

Oikonomídou-Karamesíni, M. *Sylloge Nummorum Graecorum: Grèce. 3, Musée numismatique d'Athènes: Collection Antoine Christomanos. Première partie, Italie-Eubée*. Athens: Academy of Athens, 2004.

Oldfather, C. H., trans. *Diodorus Siculus. Library of History, Volume III: Books 4.59–8*. LCL 340; Cambridge, MA: Harvard University Press, 1939.

Oldfather, W. A., trans. *Epictetus. Discourses, Books 3–4. Fragments. The Encheiridion*. LCL 218; Cambridge, MA: Harvard University Press, 1928.

Orwell, George. *All Propaganda Is Lies, 1941–1942*. Edited by P. Davison. London: Secker and Warburg, 1998.

Osborne, Grant R. *Revelation*. Grand Rapids, MI: Baker Academic, 2002.

Oster, Richard. 'Numismatic Windows into the Social World of Early Christianity'. *JBL* 101 (1982): 195–223.

Oster, R. 'Acts 19: 23-41and an Ephesian Inscription'. *HTR* 77.2 (1984): 233–237.

Oster, Richard. '"Show Me a Denarius": Symbolism of Roman Coinage and Christian Beliefs'. *ResQ* 28 (1986): 107–115.

Özdizbay, A. E., and O. Tekin. *Sylloge Nummorum Graecorum: Turkey 8. Muğla Museum 1. Caria*. Istanbul: Turkish Institute of Archaeology, 2013.

Parente, A. R. *Sylloge Nummorum Graecorum: France 6. Bibliothèque Nationale de France: Italie 1, Étrurie, Calabre*. Paris and Zurich: Bibliothèque Nationale de France and Numismatica Ars Classica, 2003.

Passow, Franz. *Handwörterbuch der griechischen Sprache*. Leipzig: F. C. W. Vogel, 1825–1831.

Paton, W. R., trans. *Polybius. The Histories, Volume I: Books 1–2*. LCL 128; Cambridge, MA: Harvard University Press, 2010.

Penna, V., and Y. Stoyas. *Sylloge Nummorum Graecorum: Greece 7, Volume 1. The KIKPE Collection of Bronze Coins*. Athens: Academy of Athens, 2012.

Perrin, Bernadotte, trans. *Plutarch. Lives, Volume II: Themistocles and Camillus. Aristides and Cato Major. Cimon and Lucullus*. LCL 47; Cambridge, MA: Harvard University Press, 1914.

Perrin, Bernadotte. *Plutarch. Lives, Volume III: Pericles and Fabius Maximus. Nicias and Crassus*. LCL 65; Cambridge, MA: Harvard University Press, 1916.

Perrin, Bernadotte, trans. *Plutarch. Lives, Volume V: Agesilaus and Pompey. Pelopidas and Marcellus*. LCL 87; Cambridge, MA: Harvard University Press.

Perrin, Bernadotte, trans. *Plutarch. Lives, Volume VII: Demosthenes and Cicero. Alexander and Caesar*. LCL 99; Cambridge, MA: Harvard University Press, 1919.

Pervo, Richard I. *Acts: A Commentary*. Minneapolis: Fortress, 2009.

Petrusevki, M. 'Aukewa damokoro'. *Ziva Antika* 15 (1965): 12.

Pick, B. 'Die Neokorien von Ephesos'. Pages 234–244 in *Corolla Numismatica: Numismatic Essays in Honour of Barclay V. Head*. Edited by G. F. Hill. Oxford: Oxford University Press, 1906.

Pieper, Wilfried. *Ancient Indian Coins Revisited*. Lancaster: Classical Numismatic Group, 2013.

Porter, S. E. *Paul in Acts*. Peabody, MA: Hendrickson, 2001.

Preisigke, Friedrich. *Girowesen im griechischen Ägypten, enthaltend Korngiro, Geldgiro, Girobanknotariat mit Einschluss des Archivwesens: ein Beitrag zur Geschichte des Verwaltungsdienstes im Altertume*. Strassburg im Elsass: Schlesier & Schweikhardt, 1910.

Preisigke F., and Emil Kiessling. *Wörterbuch der griechischen Papyrusurkunden mit Einschluss der griechischen Inschriften, Ausschriften, Ostraka, Mumienschilder usw. aus Ägypten*, 3 vols. Berlin: Erbe, 1925–1931.

Price, M. J. 'Thoughts on the Beginnings of Coinage'. Pages 1–10 in *Studies in Numismatic Method Presented to Philip Grierson*. Edited by B. H. I. Stewart, Christopher N. L. Brooke, J. G. Pollard and T. R. Volk. Cambridge: Cambridge University Press, 1983.

Price, M. J. *Sylloge Nummorum Graecorum: Great Britain 4. Fitzwilliam Museum: Leake and General Collections: Part 7. Asia Minor: Lycia-Cappadocia*. London: Oxford University Press, 1967.

Price, M. J. *Sylloge Nummorum Graecorum: Great Britain 4. Fitzwilliam Museum: Leake and General Collections: Part 8. Syria-Nabathaea*. London: Oxford University Press, 1971.

Price, M. J. *Sylloge Nummorum Graecorum: Great Britain 6. The Lewis Collection in Corpus Christi College, Cambridge. Pt 1, The Greek and Hellenistic Coins (with Britain and Parthia)*. London: Oxford University Press, 1972.

Price, Martin. *A Survey of Numismatic Research, 1978–1984*. London: International Numismatic Commission, 1986.

Price, M. J. *The Coinage in the Name of Alexander the Great and Philip Arrhidaeus: A British Museum Catalogue*. London: British Museum Press, 1991.

Price, M. J. *Sylloge Nummorum Graecorum: Great Britain 9. The British Museum: Part 1. The Black Sea*. London: The British Museum, 1993.

Price, M., and B. Trell. *Coins and Their Cities*. London: Vecchi, 1977.

Price, S. R. F. *Rituals and Power: The Roman Imperial Cult in Asia Minor*. Cambridge: Cambridge University Press, 1984.

Pritchard, James B. *Ancient Near Eastern Texts Relating to the Old Testament*, 3rd ed. Princeton, NJ: Princeton University Press, 1969.

Prokopov, I. *Contemporary Coin Engravers and Coin Masters from Bulgaria* (Sofia: K&K Publishers, 2004.

Prokopov, I., K. Kissyov and E. Paunov. *Modem Counterfeits of Ancient Greek and Roman Coins from Bulgaria*. Sofia: K&K Publishers, 2003.

Prokopov, I., and E. Paunov. *Cast Forgeries of Classical Coins from Bulgaria*. Sofia: K&K Publishers, 2004.

Psoma, S., and G. Touratsoglou. *Sylloge Nummorum Graecorum: Greece 4. National Numismatic Museum: The Petros Z. Saroglos Collection, Use-loan by the Club of the Officers of the Armed Forces. Part 1. Macedonia*. Athens: KERA, Academy of Athens, 2005.

Race, William H., trans. *Pindar. Olympian Odes*. LCL 56; Cambridge, MA: Harvard University Press, 1997.

Rackham, H., trans. *Aristotle. Politics*. LCL 264; Cambridge, MA: Harvard University Press, 1932.

Raffety, W. E. 'Crown'. *ISBE* 1 (1979): 831–832.

Rajgor, Dilip. *Punch-Marked Coins of Early Historic India*. California: Reesha Books International, 2001.

Ramage, A. 'Golden Sardis'. Pages 14–26 in *King Croesus' Gold: Excavations at Sardis and the History of Gold Refining*. Edited by A. Ramage and P. Craddock. Cambridge, MA: Harvard University Arts Museums, 2000.

Ramsay, William Mitchell. *The Church in the Roman Empire before A.D. 170*. London: Hodder, 1903.

Ramsay, William Mitchell. *The Cities of St Paul: Their Influence on His Life and Thought*. New York: Armstrong and Son, 1908.

Ramsay, William Mitchell. *The Bearing of Recent Discovery on the Trustworthiness of the New Testament*. London: Hodder & Stoughton, 1915.

Ramsay, William Mitchell. 'Studies in the "Roman Province Galatia" VI—Some Inscriptions of Colonial Caesarea Antiochea'. *JRS* 14 (1924): 172–205.

Rasmusson, Nils L., Carsten Svarstad and Lars O. Lagerqvist. *A Survey of Numismatic Research, 1960–1965*. Copenhagen: International Numismatic Commission, 1967.

Rathbone, Dominic. 'Prices and Price Formation in Roman Egypt'. Pages 183–244 in *Economic antique. Prix et formation des prix dans les economies antiques*. Edited by Jean Andreau, Pierre Briant and Raymond Descat. Saint-Bertrand-de-Comminges: Musee archeologique departmental, 1997.

Rebuffat, F. *La Monnaie dans l'antiquité*. Paris: Picard, 1996.

Reiser, Marius. 'Numismatik und Neues Testament'. *Biblica* 81 (2000): 457–488.

Richardson, N. J. *The Homeric Hymn to Demeter*. Oxford: Clarendon Press, 1974.

Rickman, Geoffrey. *The Corn Supply of Ancient Rome*. Oxford: Oxford University Press, 1980.

Ripollès, P. P., and H. Nilsson. *Sylloge Nummorum Graecorum: Sweden 2. The Collection of the Royal Coin Cabinet National Museum of Monetary History: Part 6. The G. D. Lorichs Collection*. Stockholm: The Royal Academy of Letters, History and Antiquities, 2003.

Rissi, M. 'Die Erscheinung Christi nach Off. 19.11-16'. *Theologische Zeitschrift* 21 (1965): 81–95.

Ritter, H.-W. *Sylloge Nummorum Graecorum: Deutschland. Sammlung v. Aulock: Heft 9. Phrygien*. Berlin: Gebrüder Mann, 1964.

Robertson, Anne S. *Roman Imperial Coins in the Hunter Coin Cabinet*. Oxford: Oxford University Press, 1962–1982.

Robinson, E. S. G. *Sylloge Nummorum Graecorum: Great Britain 1. Part 1: The Collection of Capt. E.G. Spencer-Churchill, M.C., of Northwick Park and The Salting Collection in the Victoria and Albert Museum*. London: Oxford University Press, 1931.

Robinson, E. S. G. *Sylloge Nummorum Graecorum: Great Britain 1. Part 2: The Newnham Davis Coins in the Wilson Collection of Classical and Eastern Antiquities. Marischal College, Aberdeen*. London: Oxford University Press, 1936.

Robinson, E. S. G. *Sylloge Nummorum Graecorum: Great Britain 2. The Lloyd Collection: Part 1. Etruria to Lucania (Thurium)*. London: Oxford University Press, 1933.

Robinson, E. S. G. *Sylloge Nummorum Graecorum: Great Britain 2. The Lloyd Collection: Part 2. Bruttium (Caulonia)-Sicily (Eryx)*. London: Oxford University Press, 1934.

Robinson, E. S. G. *Sylloge Nummorum Graecorum: Great Britain 2. The Lloyd Collection: Part 3. Sicily (Galaria- Selinus)*. London: Oxford University Press, 1935.

Robinson, E. S. G. *Sylloge Nummorum Graecorum: Great Britain 2. The Lloyd Collection: Part 4. Sicily (Syracuse-Lipara)*. London: Oxford University Press, 1937.

Robinson, E. S. G. *Sylloge Nummorum Graecorum: Great Britain 3. The Lockett Collection: Part 1. Spain-Italy (Gold and Silver)*. London: Oxford University Press, 1938.

Robinson, E. S. G. *Sylloge Nummorum Graecorum: Great Britain 3. The Lockett Collection: Part 2. Sicily-Thrace (Gold and Silver)*. London: Oxford University Press, 1939.

Robinson, E. S. G. *Sylloge Nummorum Graecorum: Great Britain 3. The Lockett Collection: Part 3. Macedonia-Aegina (Gold and Silver)*. London: Oxford University Press, 1942.

Robinson, E. S. G. *Sylloge Nummorum Graecorum: Great Britain 3. The Lockett Collection: Part 4. Peloponnese-Aeolis (Gold and Silver)*. London: Oxford University Press, 1945.

Robinson, E. S. G. *Sylloge Nummorum Graecorum: Great Britain 3. The Lockett Collection: Part 5. Lesbos-Cyrenaica. Addenda (Gold and Silver)*. London: Oxford University Press, 1949.

Robinson, E. S. G. 'The Coins from the Ephesian Artemision Reconsidered'. *JHS* 71 (1951): 156–167.

Rogers, E. *The Copper Coinage of Thessaly*. London: Spink & Son Ltd., 1932.

Rolfe, J. C., trans. *Suetonius. Lives of the Caesars, Volume I: Julius. Augustus. Tiberius. Gaius. Caligula* (LCL 31; Cambridge, MA: Harvard University Press, 1914.

Rolfe, J. C., trans. *Suetonius. Lives of the Caesars, Volume II: Claudius. Nero. Galba, Otho, and Vitellius. Vespasian. Titus, Domitian. Lives of Illustrious Men: Grammarians and Rhetoricians. Poets (Terence. Virgil. Horace. Tibullus. Persius. Lucan). Lives of Pliny the Elder and Passienus Crispus.* LCL 38; Cambridge, MA: Harvard University Press, 1914.

Rolfe, J. C., trans. *Quintus Curtius. History of Alexander, Volume I: Books 1–5.* LCL 368; Cambridge, MA: Harvard University Press, 1946.

Roloff, Jürgen. *Revelation.* Translated by John E. Alsup. Minneapolis, MN: Fortress, 1993.

Rosenberger, M. *The Coinage of Eastern Palestine, and Legionary Countermarks, Bar-Kochba Overstrucks.* Jerusalem: Rosenberger, 1978.

Rowland, Christopher. *Revelation.* Nashville: Abingdon, 1998.

Rtveladze, E. *The Ancient Coins of Central Asia.* Tashkent: Uncertain, 1987.

Rudd, Niall, trans. *Horace. Odes and Epodes.* LCL 33; Cambridge, MA: Harvard University Press, 2004.

Ruijgh, C. 'Observations sur κορέσαι, κορέω, myc. da-ko-ro δακόρος, etc.' Pages 376–392 in *O-o-pe-ro-si: Festschrift für Ernst Risch zum 75 Geburtstag.* Edited by A. Etter. Berlin: de Gruyter, 1986.

Rupprecht, Hans-Albert, and Andrea Jördens. *Wörterbuch der griechischen Papyrusurkunden mit Einschluss der griechischen Inschriften, Ausschriften, Ostraka, Mumienschilder usw. aus Ägypten, Supplement 2 (1967–1976).* Wiesbaden: Otto Harrassowitz, 1991.

Rupprecht, Hans-Albert, and Andrea Jördens. *Wörterbuch der griechischen Papyrusurkunden mit Einschluss der griechischen Inschriften, Ausschriften, Ostraka, Mumienschilder usw. aus Ägypten, Supplement 3 (1977–1988).* Wiesbaden: Otto Harrassowitz, 2000.

Savio, Adriano. *Catalogo Completo Della Collezione Dattari: Numi augg. Alexandrini.* Trieste: G. Bernardi, 1999.

Sayles, W. G. *Classical Deception. Counterfeits, Forgeries and Reproductions of Ancient Coins.* Iola: Krause Publications, 2001.

Schaps, D. *The Invention of Coinage and the Monetization of Ancient Greece.* Ann Arbor: University of Michigan Press, 2004.

Schaps, David M. *Handbook for Classical Research.* London: Routledge, 2011.

Schmidt, Peter. 'Differentiarum Scriptores'. Pages 558–559 in *Der neue Pauly, volume 3.* Edited by Hubert Cancik and Helmuth Schneider. Munich: Druckenmüller, 1997.

Schulde, Jason, and Benjamin Reubin. 'Finding Common Ground: Roman Parthian Embassies in the Julio-Claudian Period'. Pages 65–92 in *Arsacids, Romans and Local Elites: Cross-Cultural Interactions of the Parthian Empire.* Edited by Jason Schulde and Benjamin Reubin. Oxford: Oxbow Books, 2017.

Schnackenburg, Rudolf. *The Gospel According to Saint John: Volume Three.* Translated by David Smith and G.A. Kon. New York: Crossroad, 1982.

Schultz, H.-D. 'Falschungen ephesischer Münzen'. *Mitteilungen der Österreichischen Numismatischen Gesellschaft* 35.1 (1995): 7–14.

Schultz, H.-D. 'Römische Provinzialprägung'. Pages 219–239 in *A Survey of Numismatic Research 1990–1995.* Edited by C. Morrison and B. Kluge. Berlin: International Numismatic Commission and International Association of Professional Numismatists, 1997.

Schultz, S. *Sylloge Nummorum Graecorum: Deutschland. Sammlungder Universitätsbibliothek Leipzig: 1 Autonome griechische Münzen.* München: Hirmer, 1993.

Schultz, S., and J. Zahle. *Sylloge Nummorum Graecorum: Denmark. The Royal Collection of Coins and Medals, Danish National Museum. Supplement. Acquisitions 1942–1996.* Copenhagen: Munksgaard, 2002.

Schürer, E. *The History of the Jewish People in the Age of Jesus Christ (175 BCE–AD135),* revised G. Vermes and F. Millar, vol. 1. Edinburgh: T&T Clark, 1973.

Schwabacher, W., and C. Jørgenstein. *Sylloge Nummorum Graecorum: Denmark. The Royal Collection of Coins and Medals, Danish National Museum. Part 1. Italy 1: Etruria-Campania.* Copenhagen: Munksgaard, 1942.

Schwabacher, W., and C. Jørgenstein. *Sylloge Nummorum Graecorum: Denmark. The Royal Collection of Coins and Medals, Danish National Museum. Part 2. Italy 2: Apulia-Lucania (Metapontum).* Copenhagen: Munksgaard, 1942.

Schwabacher, W., and C. Jørgenstein. *Sylloge Nummorum Graecorum: Denmark. The Royal Collection of Coins and Medals, Danish National Museum. Part 3. Italy 3: Lucania (Poseidonia)-Bruttium.* Copenhagen: Munksgaard, 1942.

Schwabacher, W. *Sylloge Nummorum Graecorum: Denmark. The Royal Collection of Coins and Medals, Danish National Museum. Part 6. Thrace 1: The Tauric Chersonese-Thrace (Mesembria).* Copenhagen: Munksgaard, 1942.

Schwabacher, W. *Sylloge Nummorum Graecorum: Denmark. The Royal Collection of Coins and Medals, Danish National Museum. Part 7. Thrace 2: Odessus-Sestos. Islands. Kings and Dynasts.* Copenhagen: Munksgaard, 1943.

Schwabacher, W. *Sylloge Nummorum Graecorum: Denmark. The Royal Collection of Coins and Medals, Danish National Museum. Part 11. Thessaly-Illyricum.* Copenhagen: Munksgaard, 1943.

Schwabacher, W. *Sylloge Nummorum Graecorum: Denmark. The Royal Collection of Coins and Medals, Danish National Museum. Part 12. Epirus-Acarnania.* Copenhagen: Munksgaard, 1943.

Schwabacher, W., and N. Breitenstein. *Sylloge Nummorum Graecorum: Denmark. The Royal Collection of Coins and Medals, Danish National Museum. Part 13. Aetolia-Euboea.* Copenhagen: Munksgaard, 1944.

Schwabacher W., and N. Breitenstein. *Sylloge Nummorum Graecorum: Denmark. The Royal Collection of Coins and Medals, Danish National Museum. Part 14. Attica-Aegina.* Copenhagen: Munksgaard, 1944.

Schwabacher W., and N. Breitenstein. *Sylloge Nummorum Graecorum: Denmark. The Royal Collection of Coins and Medals, Danish National Museum. Part 15. Corinth.* Copenhagen: Munksgaard, 1944.

Schwabacher, W., and N. Breitenstein. *Sylloge Nummorum Graecorum: Denmark. The Royal Collection of Coins and Medals, Danish National Museum. Part 16. Phliasia-Laconia.* Copenhagen: Munksgaard, 1944.

Sellwood, David. *An Introduction to the Coinage of Parthia.* London: Spink & Son, 1971.

Sellwood, David. 'New Parthian Coin Types'. *Numismatic Chronicle* 19 (1989): 162–168.

Sellwood, David. 'The End of the Parthian Dynasty'. *Spink Numismatic Circular* 98 (1990): 157.

Sellwood, David. 'The "Victory" Drachms of Phraates IV'. *American Journal of Numismatics Second Series* 7–8 (1995–1996): 75–81.

Sellwood, David. 'Parthians and Scythians'. Pages 97–102 in *Ex Moneta: Essays on Numismatics, History and Archaeology in Honour of Dr. David W. MacDowall, Vol. 1.* Edited by Amal Kumar Jha and Samjay Garg. New Delhi: Harmon, 1998.

Senior, Robert C. *Indo-Scythian Coins and History.* London: Classical Numismatic Group, 2001.

Shackleton Bailey, D. R., trans. *Cicero. Letters to Quintus and Brutus. Letter Fragments. Letter to Octavian. Invectives. Handbook of Electioneering.* LCL 462; Cambridge, MA: Harvard University Press, 2002.

Sheedy, K. A. *Sylloge Nummorum Graecorum: Australia 1. Australian Centre for Ancient Numismatic Studies: The Gale Collection of South Italian Coins.* Sydney: Numismatic Association of Australia, 2008.

Sherwin-White, A. N. *Roman Society and Roman Law in the New Testament.* Oxford: Clarendon Press, 1963.

Shipley, Frederick W., trans. *Velleius Paterculus. Compendium of Roman History. Res Gestae Divi Augusti.* LCL 152; Cambridge, MA: Harvard University Press, 1924.

Shipton, K., and A. Meadows, eds. *Money and Its Uses in the Ancient Greek World.* Oxford: Oxford University Press, 2001.

Shore, Fred B. *Parthian Coins & History: Ten Dragons against Rome.* Quarryville: Classical Numismatic Group, 1993.

Sicker, Martin. *The Pre-Islamic Middle East.* London: Praeger, 2000.

Silva, M. Review of *Greek-English Lexicon of the New Testament: Based on Semantic Domains*, by Johannes P. Louw and Eugene A. Nida. *WTJ* 5 (1989): 163–167.

Simon, E. *Die Götter der Römer.* Munich: Hirmer, 1990.

Sjöqvist, Eric, and Theodore V. Buttrey. *Morgantina Studies: Results of the Princeton University Archaeological Expedition to Sicily, Vol. 2: The Coins.* Princeton, NJ: Princeton University Press, 1989.

Slater, T. B. "'King of Kings and Lord of Lords' Revisited'. *NTS* 39 (1993): 159–160.

Sommerstein, Alan H., trans. *Aeschylus. Persians. Seven against Thebes. Suppliants. Prometheus Bound.* LCL 145; Cambridge, MA: Harvard University Press, 2009.

Spaeth, B. S. 'The Goddess Ceres in the Ara Pacis Augustae and the Carthage Relief'. *AJA* 98.1 (1994): 65–100.

Spaeth, B. S. *The Roman Goddess Ceres.* Austin: University of Texas Press, 1996.

Spaeth, B. S. 'Ceres'. *EAH* 3 (2013): 1418–1419.

Spicq, C. 'Alexandrinismes dans l'Épître aux Hébreux'. *RB* 58 (1951): 481–502.

Spinelli, Marianna. 'The "Soma" of the God: Subtypes as Qualification of the Corporal Gestures of the Main Subject on the Kaulonia Coins'. Pages 793–800 in *Identity and Connectivity: Proceedings of the 16th Symposium on Mediterranean Archaeology.* Edited by Luca Bombardieri, Anacleto D'Agostino, Guido Guarducci, Valentina Orsi and Stefano Valentini. Oxford: Aracheopress, 2013.

Springschitz, L. *Sylloge Nummorum Graecorum [: Österreich].Sammlung Dreer, Klagenfurt, im Landesmuseum für Kärnten: Teil 1. Italien, Sizilien.* Klagenfurt: Geschichtsverein für Kärnten, 1967.

Springschitz, L. *Sylloge Nummorum Graecorum [: Österreich].Sammlung Dreer, Klagenfurt, im Landesmuseum für Kärnten: 2. Spanien, Gallien, Keltenländer.* Klagenfurt: Geschichtsverein für Kärnten, 1984.

Springschitz, L. *Sylloge Nummorum Graecorum [: Österreich].Sammlung Dreer, Klagenfurt, im Landesmuseum für Kärnten: Teil 3. Thracien - Macedonien, Päonien.* Klagenfurt: Geschichtsverein für Kärnten, 1999.

Spufford, P. *Money and Its Uses in Medieval Europe.* Cambridge: Cambridge University Press, 1988.

Staab, K., ed. *Pauluskommentare aus der griechischen Kirche.* Münster: Aschendorff, 1933.

Stancomb, W., A. M. Burnett, A. R. Meadows, K. Sheedy, and U. Wartenberg. *Sylloge Nummorum Graecorum: Great Britain 11. The William Stancomb Collection of Coins of the Black Sea Region.* London: Oxford University Press, 2000.

Sterrett, J. R. S. *The Wolfe Expedition to Asia Minor*. Boston: Damrell and Upham, 1888.

Still, T. D. *Conflict at Thessalonica: A Pauline Church and Its Neighbours*. Sheffield: Sheffield Academic, 1999.

Stone, Michael. *Ancient Judaism: New Visions and Views*. Grand Rapids, MI: Eerdmans, 2011.

Strickert, Frederick M. 'The Coins of Philip'. Volume 1. Pages 165–189 in *Bethsaida: A City by the North Shore of the Sea of Galilee*, 4 vols. Edited by Rami Arav and Richard A. Freund. Kirksville: Truman State University Press, 1995–2009.

Strickert, Frederick M. 'The Dying Grain Which Bears Much Fruit: John 12:24, the Livia Cult, and Bethsaida'. Volume 3. Pages 149–182 in *Bethsaida: A City by the North Shore of the Sea of Galilee*, 4 vols. Edited by Rami Arav and Richard A. Freund. Kirksville: Truman State University Press, 1995–2009.

Strickert, Frederick M. 'The First Woman to Be Portrayed on a Jewish Coin: Julia Sebaste'. *JSJ* 33.1 (2002): 65–91.

Strootman, Rolf. 'Queen of Kings: Cleopatra VII and the Donations of Alexandria'. Pages 139–158 in *Kingdoms and Principalities in the Roman Near East*. Edited by T. Kaizer and M. Facella. Stuttgart: Franz Steiner Verlag, 2010.

Stuard, S. M. Review of *Money and Its Uses in Medieval Europe*, by P. Spufford. *Journal of Economic History* 49 (1989): 207.

Sugden, K. F. *Sylloge Nummorum Graecorum: Great Britain 8. The Hart collection, Blackburn Museum*. London: Oxford University Press, 1989.

Sullivan, R. D. 'The Dynasty of Cappadocia'. *ANRW* 7.2 (1980): 1125–1168.

Sullivan, R. D. *Near Eastern Royalty and Rome, 100–30 BC*. Toronto: Buffalo, 1990.

Sutherland, C. H. V. *Coinage in Roman Imperial Policy 31 B.C–A.D. 68*. London: Methuen, 1951.

Sutherland, C. H. V. 'The Intelligibility of Roman Imperial Coin Types'. *JRS* 49 (1959): 46–55.

Sutherland, C. H. V., and C. M. Kraay. *Coins of the Roman Empire in the Ashmolean Museum. Vol. 1, Augustus, c. 31 B.C.–A.D. 14*. Oxford: Clarendon, 1975.

Svoronos, J. N. *Τα Νομίσματα του Κράτους τον Πτολεμαῖον*. Athens, Greece: P. D. Sakellarios, 1904.

Sweet, John. *Revelation*. London: SCM, 1990.

Sydenham, Edward Allen. *Coinage of the Roman Republic*. London: Spink, 1952.

Szaivert W., and C. Daburon. *Sylloge Nummorum Graecorum: Österreich. Sammlung Leypold, Wiener Neustadt: Kleinasiatische Münzender Kaiserzeit. 1 Pontus – Lydien.* Vienna: Institutfür Numismatik und Geldgeschichte, 2000.

Szaivert, W., and C. Daburon, *Sylloge Nummorum Graecorum: Österreich. Sammlung Leypold, Wiener Neustadt: Kleinasiatische Münzen der Kaiserzeit. 2 Phrygien – Kommagene: mit Nachträgen, Korrekturen und Indizes zu beiden Bänden*. Wien: Institut für Numismatik und Geldgeschichte, 2004.

Tekin, O., and S. Altinoluk. *Sylloge Nummorum Graecorum: Turkey 2. Anamur Museum. 1. Roman Provincial Coins*. Istanbul: Turkish Institute of Archaeology, 2007.

Tekin, O., S. Altınoluk and F. Körpe. *Sylloge Nummorum Graecorum: Turkey 3. Çanakkale Museum. 1. Roman Provincial Coins of Mysia, Troas etc*. Istanbul: Turkish Institute of Archaeology, 2009.

Tekin, O., and A. E. Özdizbay. *Sylloge Nummorum Graecorum: Turkey 4. Ancient Coins from Mysia, Troad and Aeolis in the Collection of Selçuk Tanrikulu*. Istanbul: Turkish Institute of Archaeology, 2010.

Tekin, O., S. Altınoluk and E. Sağir. *Sylloge Nummorum Graecorum: Turkey 5. Tire Museum. 1. Roman Provincial Coins from Ionia, Lydia, Phrygia and, etc*. Istanbul: Turkish Institute of Archaeology, 2011.

Tekin, O., and S. Altınoluk. *Sylloge Nummorum Graecorum: Turkey 7. Ö demiş Museum.* Istanbul: Turkish Institute of Archaeology, 2012.

Tekin, O., and A. E. Özdizbay. *Sylloge Nummorum Graecorum Turkey 9.1 The Ozkan Arikanturk Collection Volume 1 Troas.* Istanbul: Turkish Institute of Archaeology, 2015.

Tekin, O., and A. E. Özdizbay. *Sylloge Nummorum Graecorum Turkey 9.2 The Ozkan Arikanturk Collection Volume 1 Aeolis.* Istanbul: Turkish Institute of Archaeology, 2017.

Tekin, O. *Sylloge Nummorum Graecorum Turkey 10. The Yavuz Tatis Collection Part 1. Ionia and Lydia.* Istanbul: Turkish Institute of Archaeology, 2016.

Thackeray, H. St. J., trans. *Josephus. The Life. Against Apion.* LCL 186; Cambridge, MA: Harvard University Press, 1926.

Thackeray, H. St. J., trans. *Josephus. Jewish Antiquities, Volume I: Books 1-3.* LCL 242; Cambridge, MA: Harvard University Press, 1930.

Theophilos, Michael P. *The Abomination of Desolation in Matthew 24:15.* London: T&T Clark International, 2012.

Thielman, Frank. 'God's Righteousness as God's Fairness in Romans 1:17: An Ancient Perspective on a Significant Phrase'. *JETS* 54 (2011): 35–48.

Thomas, David Andrew. *Revelation 19 in Historical and Mythological Context.* New York: Peter Lang, 2008.

Thompson, M. 'The Mints of Lysimachus'. Pages 163–182 in *Essays in Greek Coinage presented to Stanley Robinson.* Edited by C. M. Kraay and G. K. Jenkins. Oxford: Clarendon, 1968.

Thompson, M., and R. R. Holloway. *Sylloge Nummorum Graecorum, the Burton Y. Berry collection: Part 1. Macedonia to Attica.* New York: The American Numismatic Society, 1961.

Thompson, M., and I. L. Merker. *Sylloge Nummorum Graecorum, the Burton Y. Berry collection: Part 2. Megaris to Egypt.* New York: The American Numismatic Society, 1962.

Thomson, Cynthia L. 'Hairstyles, Head-Coverings, and St. Paul: Portraits from Roman Corinth'. *BA* 51.2 (1988): 99–115.

Todman, D. 'Warts and the Kings of Parthia: An Ancient Representation of Hereditary Neurofibromatosis Depicted in Coins'. *Journal of the History of the Neurosciences* 17 (2008): 141–146.

Topalov, S. *The Odrysian Kingdom from the Late 5th to the Mid-4th C. B.C.* Sofia: K&K Publishers, 1994.

Topalov, S. *Novi prinosi kŭm prouchvane kontramarkiraneto na moneti v raĭona na zapadnopontiĭskite gradove prez III – I v. pr. n. e.: = New Contributions to the Study of the Countermarking of the Coins in the Area of the West Pontic Cities 3rd-1st c. B.C.* Sofia: Nasko, 2002.

Torbágyi, M. *Sylloge Nummorum Graecorum: Hungary. Budapest, Magyar Nemzeti Múzeum: Part 1 Hispania – Sicilia: fasc. 1 Hispania – Apulia.* Milan: Ed. Ennerre, 1992.

Torbágyi, M. *Sylloge Nummorum Graecorum: Hungary. Budapest, Magyar Nemzeti Múzeum: Part 1 Hispania - Sicilia: fasc. 2 Calabria-Bruttium.* Milan: Ed. Ennerre, 1992.

Torbágyi, M. *Sylloge Nummorum Graecorum: Hungary. Budapest, Magyar Nemzeti Múzeum: Part 1 Hispania - Sicilia: fasc. 3 Sicilia.* Milan: Ed. Ennerre, 1993.

Touratsoglou, Ioannis. *Die Münzstätte von Thessaloniki in der römischen Kaiserzeit: 32/31 v. Chr. bis 268 n. Chr.* Berlin: De Gruyter, 1988.

Trebilco, Paul R. 'Asia'. Pages 291–362 in *The Book of Acts in Its Graeco-Roman Setting.* Edited by D. W. J. Gill and C. Gempf. Grand Rapids, MI: Eerdmans, 1994.

Trebilco, Paul R. *The Early Christians in Ephesus from Paul to Ignatius*. Tübingen: Mohr Siebeck, 2004.

Tribulato, Olga. *Ancient Greek Verb-Initial Compounds: Their Diachronic Development within the Greek Compound System*. Berlin: de Gruyter, 2015.

Troxell, H. A. *Sylloge Nummorum Graecorum: The Collection of the American Numismatic Society. Part 2. Lucania*. New York: The American Numismatic Society, 1972.

Troxell, H. A. *Sylloge Nummorum Graecorum: The Collection of the American Numismatic Society. Part 3. Bruttium-Sicily 1 (Abacaenum-Eryx)*. New York: The American Numismatic Society, 1975.

Troxell, H. A. *Sylloge Nummorum Graecorum: The Collection of the American Numismatic Society. Part 8. Macedonia 2 (Alexander I-Philip II)*. New York: The American Numismatic Society, 1994.

Tsourti, E., and M. D. Trifiró. *Sylloge Nummorum Graecorum: Greece 5. National Numismatic Museum: The A.G. Soutzos Collection*. Athens: Academy of Athens, 2007.

Tsangari, D. I. *Sylloge Nummorum Graecorum: Greece 6. The Alpha Bank Collection: From Thessaly to Euboea*. Athens: Academy of Athens, 2011.

Turgenev, Ivan Sergeevich. *Fathers and Sons*. Translated by Richard Freeborn. Oxford: Oxford University Press, 1998.

Vaganay, L. 'Le Plan de l'Épître aux Hébreux'. Pages 269–277 in *Mémorial Lagrange*. Edited by L.-H. Vincent. Paris: Gabalda, 1940.

Van der Horst, Peter W. *Philo's Flaccus: The First Pogrom*. Leiden: Brill, 2003.

Verboven, K. *The Economy of Friends: Economic Aspects of Amicitia and Patronage in the Late Republic*. Brussels: Latomus, 2002.

Vermeule, C. *The Cult Images of Imperial Rome*. Rome: Bretschneider, 1987.

Vida, I. *Sylloge Nummorum Graecorum: Hungary. Budapest, Magyar Nemzeti Múzeum: Part 3. Moesia Inferior: Callatis, Dionysopolis, Istrus, Marcianopolis, Nicopolis ad Istrum, Odessus, Tomis*. Milan: Ed. Ennerre, 2000.

Vioque, Guillermo Galán. *Martial, Book VII. A Commentary*. Translated by J. J. Zoltowsky. Leiden: Brill, 2017.

Vishnu, Asha. *Material Like of North India: Based on an Archaeological Study, 3rd Century B.C to 1st Century A.D*. New Delhi: Mittal Publications, 1993.

Vismara, N. *Sylloge Nummorum Graecorum: Italia. Milano. Civiche Raccolte Numismatiche: Part 2. Gallia ellenica-Guerra Sociale*. Milano: Ed. Ennerre, 1990.

Vismara, N. *Sylloge Nummorum Graecorum: Italia. Milano. Civiche Raccolte Numismatiche: Part 3. Campania-Calabria*. Milano: Ed. Ennerre, 1989.

Vismara, N. *Sylloge Nummorum Graecorum: Italia. Milano. Civiche Raccolte Numismatiche: Part 4. Lucania-Bruttium. Fasc. 1: Lucania*. Milano: Ed. Ennerre, 1997.

Vismara, N. *Sylloge Nummorum Graecorum: Italia. Milano. Civiche Raccolte Numismatiche: Part 4. Lucania-Bruttium. Fasc. 2: Bruttium*. Milano: Ed. Ennerre, 1998.

Vismara, N. *Sylloge Nummorum Graecorum: Italia. Milano. Civiche Raccolte Numismatiche: Part 6. Macedonia – Thracia. Fasc. 1: Macedonia greca, Paeonia, Emisssioni di area celtica*. Milano: Ed. Ennerre, 1999.

Vismara, N. *Sylloge Nummorum Graecorum: Italia. Milano. Civiche Raccolte Numismatiche: Part 6. Macedonia – Thracia. Fasc. 3: Chersonesus Tauricus – Sarmatia – Thracia – Chersonesus Thraciae – Isole della Thracia*. Milano: Ed. Ennerre, 2000.

Vismara, N. *Sylloge Nummorum Graecorum: Italia. Milano. Civiche Raccolte Numismatiche: Part 12. Syria-Bactria et India. Fasc. 1. Seleucides (reges) – Chalcidice*. Milano: Ed. Ennerre, 1992.

Vismara, N. *Sylloge Nummorum Graecorum: Italia. Milano. Civiche Raccolte Numismatiche: Part 12. Syria-Bactria et India. Fasc. 4. Iudaea-Bactria et India*. Milano: Ed. Ennerre, 1991.

Von Aulock, H. *Sylloge Nummorum Graecorum: Deutschland. Sammlung v. Aulock: Heft 8. Lydien*. Berlin: Gebrüder Mann, 1963.

Von Aulock, H. *Sylloge Nummorum Graecorum: Deutschland. Sammlung v. Aulock: Heft 12. Pisidien, Lykaonien, Isaurien*. Berlin: Gebrüder Mann, 1964.

Von Aulock, H. *Sylloge Nummorum Graecorum: Deutschland. Sammlung v. Aulock: Heft 13. Kilikien*. Berlin: Gebrüder Mann, 1966.

Von Aulock, H., and P. R. Franke. *Sylloge Nummorum Graecorum: Deutschland. Sammlung v. Aulock: Heft 14. Galatien, Kappadokien, kaiserzeitliche Kistophoren, posthume Lysimachus- und Alexander-tetradrachmen, Incerti*. Berlin: Gebrüder Mann, 1967.

Von Aulock, H., and P. R. Franke. *Sylloge Nummorum Graecorum: Deutschland. Sammlung v. Aulock: Heft 15. Nachträge 1. Pontus, Armenia Minor, Paphlagonien, Bithynien*. Berlin: Gebrüder Mann, 1967.

Von Aulock, H., and P. R. Franke. *Sylloge Nummorum Graecorum: Deutschland. Sammlung v. Aulock: Heft 16. Nachträge 2. Mysien,Troas, Aeolis, Lesbos*. Berlin: Gebrüder Mann, 1967.

Von Aulock, H., and P. R. Franke. *Sylloge Nummorum Graecorum: Deutschland. Sammlung v. Aulock: Heft 17. Nachträge 3. Ionien, Karien, Lydien*. Berlin: Gebrüder Mann, 1968.

Von Aulock, H., and P. R. Franke. *Sylloge Nummorum Graecorum: Deutschland. Sammlung v. Aulock: Heft 18. Nachträge 4. Phrygien, Lykien, Pamphylien, Pisidien, Lykaonien, Isaurien, Kilikien, Galatien, Kappadokien, kaiserzeitl. Kistophoren, Incerti*. Berlin: Gebrüder Mann, 1968.

Von Aulock, H. 'Die römische Kolonie Lystra und ihre Münzen'. *Chiron* 2 (1972): 509–518.

Von Wahlde, Urban C. *The Gospel and Letters of John: Volume 2*. Grand Rapids, MI: Eerdmans, 2010.

Waggoner, N. *Sylloge Nummorum Graecorum: The Collection of the American Numismatic Society. Part 7. Macedonia 1 (Cities, Thraco-Macedonian Tribes, Paeonian kings)*. New York: The American Numismatic Society, 1987.

Wagner, Franz. *Lexicon Latinum Universae Phraseologiae Corpus Congestum*. Translated by Augustin Borgnet. Ridgwood: Gregg Press, 1878.

Walczak, E. *Sylloge Nummorum Graecorum, Poland, Vol. 2. The National Museum in Warsaw, Part 1 – The Northern Black Sea Coast Chersonesus – Bosporus*. Kraków: The Polish Academy of Arts and Sciences, 2015.

Walker, D. R. *The Metrology of the Roman Silver Coinage: Part I, From Augustus to Domitian*. Oxford: British Archaeological Reports, 1976.

Wallace, Daniel B. *Greek Grammar beyond the Basics: An Exegetical Syntax of the New Testament*. Grand Rapids, MI: Zondervan, 1996.

Wallace, R. W. 'The Origin of Electrum Coinage'. *AJA* 91 (1987): 385–397.

Wallace-Hadrill, A. 'The Emperor and His Virtues'. *Historia* 30 (1981): 298–323.

Wallace-Hadrill, A. 'Image and Authority in the Coinage of Augustus'. *JRS* 76 (1986): 66–87.

Wanamaker, C. A. *The Epistles to the Thessalonians: A Commentary on the Greek Text*. Grand Rapids, MI: Eerdmans, 1990.

Weber, M. *General Economic History*. New York: Greenberg, 1927.

Weidauer, L. *Probleme der Frühen Elektronprägung*. Freiburg: Office du livre, 1975.

Weidner, Ernst. *Die Inschriften Tukulti-Ninurtas I. und seiner Nachfolger*. Osnabrück: Biblio, 1970.

Weima, Jeffrey A. D. '1–2 Thessalonians'. Pages 871–890 in *Commentary on the New Testament Use of the Old Testament*. Edited by G. K. Beale and D. A. Carson. Grand Rapids, MI: Baker Academic, 2007.

Weima, Jeffrey A. D. '"Peace and Security" (1 Thess. 5.3): Prophetic Warning or Political Propaganda?' *NTS* 58 (2012): 331–359.

Weima, Jeffrey A. D. *1–2 Thessalonians*. Grand Rapids, MI: Baker Academic, 2014.

Weinstock, S. *Divus Julius*. Oxford: Oxford University Press, 1971.

Weissenrieder, Annette, and Friederike Wendt. 'He Is a God! Acts 28: 1–9 in the Light of Iconographical and Textual Sources Related to Medicine'. Pages 127–156 in *Picturing the New Testament: Studies in Ancient Visual Images*. Edited by A. Weissenrieder, F. Wendt and P. von Gemünden. Tübingen: Mohr Siebeck, 2005.

Weissenrieder, Annette, and Friederike Wendt. 'Images as Communication: The Methods of Iconography'. Pages 3–49 in *Picturing the New Testament: Studies in Ancient Visual Images*. Edited by Annette Weissenrieder, Friederike Wendt and P. von Gemünden. Tübingen: Mohr Siebeck, 2005.

Wengst, K. *Pax Romana and the Peace of Jesus Christ*. Philadelphia: Fortress, 1987.

Wenkel, David H. *Coins as Cultural Texts in the World of the New Testament*. London: Bloomsbury, 2017.

West, Louis C. 'The Cost of Living in Roman Egypt'. *Classical Philology* 11.3 (1916): 293–314.

Westcott, B. F. *The Gospel According to St. John*. London: Buttler and Tanner, 1882.

Westcott, B. F. *The Epistle to the Hebrews: The Greek Text with Notes and Essays*. New York: Macmillan, 1903.

Westermark, U. *Sylloge Nummorum Graecorum: Sweden: 1.1 The collection of His late Majesty King Gustav VI Adolf. The Fred Forbat Collection*. Stockholm: The Royal Academy of Letters, History and Antiquities, 1974.

Westermark, U. *Sylloge Nummorum Graecorum: Sweden 2. The Collection of the Royal Coin Cabinet National Museum of Monetary History: Part 1. Gallia - Sicily*. Stockholm: The Royal Academy of Letters, History and Antiquities, 1976.

Westermark, U. *Sylloge Nummorum Graecorum: Sweden 2. The Collection of the Royal Coin Cabinet National Museum of Monetary History: Part 2. Thrace – Euboia*. Stockholm: The Royal Academy of Letters, History and Antiquities, 1980.

Westermark, U., and H. Nilsson. *Sylloge Nummorum Graecorum: Sweden 2. The Collection of the Royal Coin Cabinet National Museum of Monetary History: Part 3. Attica – Lesbos*. Stockholm: The Royal Academy of Letters, History and Antiquities, 1991.

Westermark, U., and R. H. J. Ashton. *Sylloge Nummorum Graecorum: Finland. The Erkki Keckman Collection in the Skopbank, Helsinki. Part 1. Karia*. Helsinki: Finnish Society of Sciences and Letters, 1994.

White, Horace, trans. *Appian. Roman History, Volume III: The Civil Wars, Books 1-3.26*. LCL 4; Cambridge, MA: Harvard University Press, 1913.

White, J. R. '"Peace and Security" (1 Thessalonians 5.3): Is It Really a Slogan?' *NTS* 59 (2013): 382–385.

White, J. R. '"Peace" and "Security" (1 Thess. 5.3): Roman Ideology and Greek Aspiration'. *NTS* 60 (2014): 499–510.

White, Michael L. 'Urban Development and Social Change'. Pages 27–79 in *Ephesos, Metropolis of Asia: An Interdisciplinary Approach to Its Archaeology, Religion, and Culture*. Edited by Helmut Koester. Valley Forge: Trinity Press International, 1995.

Williams, D. 'The Pot Hoard from the Archaic Artemision of Ephesus'. *BICS* 38 (1991–1993): 98–103.

Williams, Jonathan. 'Religion and Roman Coins'. Pages 143–163 in *A Companion to Roman Religion*. Edited by J. Rüpke. Oxford: Blackwell, 2007.

Williams, R. T., and A. R. Meadows. *Sylloge Nummorum Graecorum: Great Britain 13. The Collection of the Society of Antiquaries, Newcastle upon Tyne*. London: Oxford University Press, 2005.

Williamson, Peter S. *Revelation*. Grand Rapids, MI: Baker Academic, 2015.

Witetschek, Stephan. 'Artemis and Asiarchs: Some Remarks on Ephesian Local Colour in Acts 19'. *Biblica* 90.3 (2009): 334–355.

Witherington, Ben. *The Acts of the Apostles: A Socio-Rhetorical Commentary*. Grand Rapids, MI: Eerdmans, 1998.

Witherington, Ben. *Revelation*. Cambridge: Cambridge University Press, 2003.

Yadin, Y. 'The Dead Sea Scrolls and the Epistle to the Hebrews'. *Scripta Hierosolymitana* 4 (1958): 36–55.

Yamauchi, Edwin. *The Stones and the Scriptures*. New York: Holman, 1972.

Youroukova, Y. *Coins of the Ancient Thracians*. Translated by V. Athanassov. Oxford: British Archaeological Reports, 1967.

Zanker, Paul. *The Power of Images in the Age of Augustus*. Translated by Alan Shapiro. Ann Arbor: University of Michigan Press, 1988.

Ziegler, R. *Sylloge Nummorum Graecorum: Deutschland. Pfälzer Privatsammlungen: 6. Isaurien und Kilikien*. München: Hirmer, 2001.

Zgusta, Ladislav. *Lexicography Then and Now: Selected Essays*. Tübingen: Niemeyer, 2006.

Zupko, Ronald Edward. *British Weights and Measures: A History from Antiquity to the Seventeenth Century*. Madison: University of Wisconsin Press, 1977.

Index of Modern Authors

Abbott, F. F. 153
Abbott, L. 126
Abbott-Smith, G. 170
Abrams, B. L. 20
Akurgal, E. 128
Alfaro, A. C. 44, 61, 69
Alföldi, A. 39, 72
Allen, J. 46, 202
Altınoluk, S. 62
Amandry, M. 44, 64–5, 67, 70, 89, 110,
    122, 138–9, 146, 151, 154–5, 180
Andreau, J. 73, 92
Angelakis, E. 20
Anokhin, V. 201
Archibald, Z. 167
Arévalo, G. A. 61
Arnold-Biucchi, C. 44, 70
Arnold, C. E. 128
Arslan, E. A. 60
Ashshi, A. M. 20
Ashton, R. 52, 57
Attwood, P. 44
Aune, D. E. 166
Azhar, E. I. 20

Babelon, E. 45–6, 178
Bagwell-Purefoy, P. 58
Bailey, D. R. S. 171, 198
Baker, A. W. 6, 92
Baker, R. 89, 124
Bakhoum, S. 52
Bakos, M. 59
Baldus, H. R. 54–5
Bammel, E. 9, 155
Bar, M. 48, 90
Barag, D. 90
Barello, F. 60
Barney, S. A. 157
Barrandon, J. -N. 22
Barrett, C. K. 106, 117
Bastien, P. 72

Beale, G. K. 160, 193, 210–11
Bellinger, A. R. 34
Benson, F. S. 42
Bérend, D. 63
Berghaus, P. 44
Bibi, F. 20
Bloomfield, S. T. A. 118, 172
Bodzek, J. 61
Boehringer, C. W. 61
Boers, H. 13
Bolden, R. 78, 124–5
Bonner, C. 9–11
Bons, E. 176, 186, 188
Bopearachchi, O. 63
Boring, M. E. 212
Boxall, I. 214
Bratcher, R. G. 118
Braund, D. 107–8
Breitenbach, A. 157
Breitenstein, N. 49–51
Brennan, P. 74
Bricaul, L. 67
Broughton, T. R. S. 128
Brown, R. E. 106
Bruce, F. F. 109, 115, 131, 166
Brumfield, A. C. 121
Brunt, P. A. 71, 152
Buechner, W. 129, 133
Bultmann, R. 106–7
Burnett, A. 41–2, 44–6, 58, 64–5, 67, 69,
    72, 74, 89, 110, 122, 134, 138–9, 146,
    151, 154–5, 180, 184
Burrell, B. 78, 129–31, 133–4, 136, 139, 141
Butcher, K. 45, 65, 69
Butcher, M. S. 67, 70
Buttrey, S. 24, 37, 39, 46
Buttrey, T. 24, 37, 39, 46

Caccamo-Caltabiano, M. 44, 60, 70–1
Cadbury, H. J. 123
Calomino, D. 65, 70

Index of Modern Authors

Carradice, I. 23–7, 57–8, 65, 67, 89, 110, 122, 138–9, 146, 151, 154–5, 180
Carson, D. A. 44, 72, 91, 106–7, 160, 210
Carter, W. 73, 107, 113
Cary, E. 189, 198, 200
Casey, J. 44
Casey, P. J. 6
Catalli, F. 60
Chadwick, J. 12
Chancey, M. A. 74
Chantraine, P. 12, 129
Charles, R. H. 170, 212
Christiansen, E. 51
Clain-Stefanelli, E. E. 43–5
Cohen, H. 47
Cohoon, J. W. 199
Colbert, J. de -B. 44
Cole, S. G. 121
Collison, R. L. 7
Consani, C. 126
Conzelmann, H. 123
Crawford, M. H. 36–9, 45–6, 72–3, 76, 91, 94, 138, 151, 200
Cribb, J. 19
Crönert, W. 5
Crook, J. 108, 112, 140
Cunningham, A. 203

Daburon, C. 48
Daehn, W. E. 44
Dalaison, J. 53, 65
Danker, F. W. 13, 191
Davesne, A. 180
David 8–9, 19, 43, 69, 90, 95, 106–7, 114, 118, 120, 153, 160, 186, 195, 201, 211
De Callataÿ, F. 36, 46
Deissmann, A. 9, 106–7, 171–2
Delepierre, J. 25, 52
Delepierre, M. 25, 52
Dilts, R. 21
Dimitrov, D. 138
Dittenberger, W. 171
Döderlein, L. 157–8
Donfried, K. P. 155, 160
Draganov, D. 48
Dräger, M. 139
Drew-Bear, T. 133
Drexhage, H.-J. 92
Ducat, J. 31

Dumesnil, M. J. B. 157–8
Duncan-Jones, R. 73, 77
Dyer, K. 73

Eckhel, J. 78
Edson, C. 154, 159–60
Ehrhardt, C. 72
Elkins, N. T. 6, 92
Elliott, J. K. 13
Ellul, J. 72
Elsen, J. 28
Elshemi, A. G. 20
Erdkamp, P. 77, 125
Esser, H. -H. 187, 190
Étienne, R. 31
Evans, C. S. 120
Evans, J. D. 72
Eynikel, E. 172

Fagerlie, J. M. 44
Fava, A. S. 38
Fears, J. R. 73, 143
Ferguson, J. 125
Finley, M. I. 20
Fischer, B. 55, 59, 63
Fischer, J. E. 55, 59, 63
Fishlake, J. R. 7
Fitzmeyer, J. A. 126
Flower, H. 72
Foakes-Jackson, F. J. 123, 133
Foley, H. 121
Foster, H. B. 198, 200, 217
Frank, T. 97, 128
Franke, P. R. 53–4, 155
Fraser, B. L. 12
Fredricksmeyer, E. 194
Friberg, B. 172
Friberg, T. 172
Friesen, S. J. 133, 139
Furtwängler, A. 23

Gaebler, H. 146–8
Gaffiot, F. 11
Gardner, P. 21, 203
Garnsey, P. 125
Giard, J. -B. 47
Giblin, C. H. 211
Göbl, R. 202
Goddard, J. 58

Godley, A. D. 117, 213
Goenka, J. P. 202
Goetz, G. 157
Golenko, K. V. 201
Gorini, G. 44
Goron, S. 202
Grant, M. 88, 146
Green, G. L. 118, 153, 172
Greenberg, M. 19, 194
Greene, K. 92, 96
Greenwood, L. H. G. 96
Grether, G. 120
Grierson, P. 23, 44, 72
Griffiths, J. G. 198
Grudem, W. 166
Guido, F. 60, 71
Gupta, P. L. 202

Hackens, T. 44, 58
Haenchen, E. 106
Hagner, D. A. 124
Hall, H. R. 188, 194
Handy, L. K. 194
Hannestad, N. 72
Hans, L. M. 76
Hardaker, T. R. 202
Hardin, J. 161
Harl, K. W. 46, 69
Harmon, A. M. 188, 195
Harrington, W. J. 212
Harris, W. V. 20
Harrison, J. R. 15, 74, 146, 152, 156
Hart, G. D. 58, 196
Hausmann, E. 55
Hauspie, K. 172
Hazzard, R. A. 36
Head, B.V. 31, 89, 148
Healy, J. F. 57
Heichelheim, F. M. 56–7
Heilig, C. 146
Hekster, O. 77
Helly, B. 151
Hemberg, B. 160
Hemer, C. J. 15, 142
Henderson, J. 13, 119
Hendin, D. 111, 138
Hendrickson, G. I. 126, 170, 213
Hendrix, H. L. 151, 153–4, 156
Heuchert, V. 41–2, 65, 69

Hicks, E. L. 133
Hill, P. V. 25, 72
Hiorth, F. 12
Hire, P. 12
Hollander, D. 19
Hölscher, T. 72, 77
Hoover, O. 36, 43
Hopkins, K. 46, 73, 92, 128
Horsley, G. H. R. 15, 109, 131, 153, 163
Hort, A. F. 118
Hostein, A. 65–7
Houghton, A. 35, 59
Houston, G. W. 140
Howard, W. F. 211
Howgego, C. 19–20, 41–2, 45, 64–5, 69, 71, 73, 75–7, 89–91, 148
Hubbnell, H. M. 170–1
Hurter, S. 30, 138

Ilisch, L. 44
Imholtz, A. A. 7
Ireland, S. 57
Isaac, E. 213

Jackson, J. 123, 132–3
Jacobsen, A. 51
Jaunzems, E. 63
Jenkins, G. K. 35, 52
Jewett, R. 153, 160
Johnson, L. T. 142, 175–6, 213
Johnston, A. 69
Jones, A. H. M. 71, 74–5, 177
Jones, H. L. 122, 128, 199, 213
Jones, W. H. S. 119, 211
Jørgenstein, C. 49
Judge, E. 74

Kapossy, B. 62
Karyszkowski, J. P. 201
Katsari, C. 94–5
Kearsley R. A. 141
Keckman 30, 52
Keener, C. S. 124, 141
Keep, R. P. 11
Keil, J. 139
Kelber, W. 169
Kessler, D. 95–6
Kiessling, E. 5, 13–14
King, C. E. 57, 143

King, L. W. 194
Kleeberg, J. 44
Kleiner, F. S. 205
Kleiner, G. 53, 134
Klose, D. O. 54, 134, 136, 139, 155
Kluge, B. 44, 69
Knoepfler, D. 31
Koester, C. R. 211, 215
Koester, H. 142, 156, 160
Köker, H. 62
Kolev, K. 138
Konuk, K. 22–4, 62
Körte, A. 170
Kos, P. 61
Kosmala, H. 165–6
Kovacs, D. 118
Kovalenko, S. 61
Kraay, C. M. 23, 31, 35, 45, 47, 57, 91, 143
Kraft, K. 41, 53, 69, 152
Kreitzer, L. J. 4, 113
Kremydi-Sicilianou, S. 58, 65, 70
Kritt, B. 202
Krmnicek, S. 89
Kroll, J. H. 54, 157
Kromann, A. 51–2
Krug, K. 13
Küthmann, H. 53–4
Kysar, R. 105

Lake, K. 123, 133, 194
Lane, W. L. 166, 172
Langslow, D. R. 117
Larfeld, W. 10
Lee, J. A. L. 8, 11–12, 15, 151, 153, 191
Le Rider, G. 25, 36, 52
Leschhorn, W. 54–5, 134, 220
Lesquier, J. 129
Levante, E. 52, 62
Levick, E. 72, 121–3, 125
Levy, B. E. 179
Lewis, P. 78, 124–5
Liampi, K. 54
Liddel, K. 196
Lindars, B. 105
Lindsay, W. M. 157
Llewelyn, S. R. 15, 141
Lo Cascio, E. 20
Lorber, C. 36, 59
Louw, J. P. 13, 116–17, 172, 187

Lubetski, E. 3
Lubetski, M. 3
Luckensmeyer, D. 160
Lupieri, E. F. 213
Lust, J. 172
Luz, U. 4–5

Mabbott, T. O. 90
MacDonald, D. 69, 128, 201
Magalhães, M. M. 48
Magie, D. 180
Magness, J. 89
Mairat, J. 64–7
Malina, B. 109
Maltiel-Gerstenfeld, J. 119
Manders, E. 71
Mannsperger, D. 55
Manson, T. W. 165
Marinescu, C. A. 138
Marshall, I. H. 127, 141
Marshall, J. H. 202
Martin, T. R. 19
Martini, R. 47, 59–60, 90
Mathewson, D. L. 211
Mathiesen, H. E. 52
Mattingly, H. 10–11, 46–7, 67, 72–3, 181
Maué, H. 44
May, D. M. 90, 114
McGing, B. 188, 198
McKnight, S. 166
Meadows, A. 19, 36, 41, 58, 72–3
Meinardus, O. F. A. 128
Meir 3
Mellink, J. J. 128
Melville 21–2
Merkelbach, R. 188
Meshorer, Y. 63, 76, 110–11, 119
Metcalf, W. 22, 45, 65–7
Metcalf, W. E. 22, 45, 65–7
Meyer, R. 200
Michaels, J. 107
Mielczarek, M. 60
Militký, J. 49
Millar, F. 41, 108–9
Miller, F. J. 124
Miller, H. H. 28
Miller, N. F. 172
Milligan, G. 14–15, 119
Milne, J. G. 57

Minns, E. H. 118
Mionnet, T. 78
Mirnik, I. 48
Mitchell, S. 44, 98, 122, 124–6
Mitchiner, M. 202–3
Mitsopoulos-Leon, V. 128
Moffatt, J. 165
Mommsen, T. 8, 46
Moore, J. M. 153
Morcom, J. 58
Morgenstern, M. 3
Mørkholm, O. 34–5, 45, 51, 53
Morrisson, C. 44
Most, G. W. 121, 169
Moulton, J. H. 14–15, 119, 211
Mounce, R. 214
Moushmov, H. 146, 167
Mugridge, A. 166
Murphy, C. M. 74
Murphy-O'Connor, J. 140
Murphy, F. J. 212

Naster, P. 44
Nicholl, C. R. 159
Nicolet-Pierre, H. 25, 52
Nida, E. A. 13, 116–17, 172, 187
Nilsson, H. 62
Nollé, J. 55, 65, 133–4, 136

Oakes, P. 6, 156
Oikonomídou-Karamesíni, M. 58
Oldfather, C. H. 118, 190, 194
Oldfather, W. A. 76
Orwell, G. 72
Osborne, G. R. 212
Oster, R. 3–4, 73–5, 113, 128, 133
Özdizbay, A. E. 62–3

Parente, A. R. 52
Passow, F. 5, 11
Paton, W. R. 96
Pause-Dreyer, U. 54
Penna, V. 59
Perrin, B. 40, 159, 188–9, 198, 200, 212
Pervo, R. I. 140–1
Petrusevski, M. 129
Pick, B. 139
Pieper, W. 202
Porter, S. E. 126

Preisigke, F. 5, 10, 13–14
Price, M. J. 23, 34, 44, 57–8, 72, 90, 133
Price, S. R. F. 133
Pritchard, J. B. 194
Prokopov, I. 138
Psoma, S. 58

Qedar, S. 90

Race, W. H. 118
Rackham, H. 152, 169
Raffety, W. E. 152
Rajgor, D. 202
Ramage, A. 22
Ramsay, W. M. 98, 122, 124, 126
Raoult, D. 20
Rasmusson, N. L. 44
Rathbone, D. 92, 95
Rebuffat, F. 45
Reece, R. 6, 44
Reiser, M. 4, 113
Reyburn, W. D. 118
Richardson, N. J. 121
Rickman, G. 95
Ripollès, P. P. 62, 65, 89
Rissi, M. 211
Ritter, H. -W. 53
Robertson, A. S. 47
Robinson, E. S. G. 10, 23, 35, 56–7
Rogers, E. 151
Rohrbaugh, R. L. 109
Rolfe, J. C. 193–4, 199, 214
Rosenberger, M. 90
Rowland, C. 213
Rtveladze, E. 202
Rudd, N. 122
Ruijgh, C. 129
Rupprecht, H. -A. 5, 14

Sağir, E 62
Şahin, S 188
Savio, A. 69
Sayles, W. G. 138
Schaps, D. 8, 11, 19, 92
Schmidt, P. 157
Schnackenburg, R. 106
Schultz, H. -D. 69, 136, 138
Schultz, S. 52, 55
Schürer, E. 100, 108

Schwabacher, S. 49–50, 61
Schwabacher, W. 49–50, 61
Sellwood, D. 195–7, 214
Šemrov, A. 61
Senior, R. C. 202–3
Shackleton Bailey, D. R. 171, 198
Sheedy, K. A. 7, 48, 58
Sherwin-White, A. N. 127, 141
Shipley, F. 198
Shipton, K. 19
Shore, F. B. 211
Sicker, M. 212
Silva, M. 13, 129
Simon, E. 121
Sjöqvist, E. 37
Slater, T. B. 193
Sommerstein, A. H. 199
Spaer, A. 59
Spaeth, B. S. 121
Spicq, C. 166
Spinelli, M. 71
Springschitz, L. 48
Spufford, P. 19
Staab, K. 173
Stancomb, W. 58
Steguweit, W. 44
Sterrett, J. R. S. 123–4
Still, T. D. 155–6, 193
Stone, M. 3
Stoyas, Y. 59
Strickert, F. M. 119–20
Strootman, R. 200
Stuard, S. M. 19
Sugden, K. F. 58
Sullivan, R. D. 108, 167
Sutherland, C. H. V. 47, 72, 75, 91
Svarstad, C. 44
Svoronos, J. N. 36
Sweet, J. 213
Sydenham, E. A. 46
Szaivert, W. 48

Tekin, O. 62–3
Temin, P. 95–6
Thackeray, H. St. J. 189–90
Theophilos, M. P. 4
Thielman, F. 114
Thomas, D. A. 72, 123, 211

Thompson, M. 35, 63, 129, 194
Thomson, C. L. 6, 9
Todman, D. 196
Topalov, S. 90, 167
Torbágyi, M. 59
Touratsoglou, G. 58, 146, 148–50
Touratsoglou, I. 58, 146, 148–50
Trebilco, P. R. 127, 139, 141
Tribulato, O. 117
Trifiró, M. D. 58
Troxell, H. A. 63
Tsangari, D. I. 59
Tsourti, E. 58
Turgenev, I. S. 3
Turner, M. 74, 211

Vaganay, L. 167
Van der Horst, P. W. 108
Verboven, K. 20
Vermeule, C. 133
Vida, I. 59
Vioque, G. G. 201
Vishnu, A. 205
Vismara, N. 47, 59–60
Von Aulock, H. 53–4, 121–2, 134
Von Post, E. 61
Von Wahlde, U. C. 106

Waggoner, N. 63
Wagner, F. 157–8
Walczak, E. 60
Walker, D. R. 41
Wallace, D. B. 211
Wallace, R.W. 23
Wallace-Hadrill, A. 72
Wanamaker, C. A. 152–3
Wartenberg, U. 58
Waterman, N. G. 20
Weber, M. 19
Weidauer, L. 23, 169
Weidner, E. 194
Weima, J. A. D. 146, 154, 156, 160
Weinstock, S. 152
Weissenrieder, A. 71, 113–14
Wendt, F. 71, 113–14
Wengst, K. 155
Wenkel, D. H. 9, 43
West, L. C. 90, 96, 158

Westcott, B. F. 106, 165
Westermark, U. 52, 61–2
White, J. R. 97, 120, 127, 140–1, 156, 189
Williams, D. 23, 41
Williams, J. 72, 75–6
Williams, R. T. 58, 72
Williamson, P. S. 210
Witetschek, S. 140–1
Witherington, B. 142, 211
Wright, N. L. 74

Yadin, Y. 166
Yamauchi, E. 78
Yasir, M. 20
Youroukova, Y. 167–9
Yvon, J. 44

Zanker, P. 72, 77
Zgusta, L. 7
Ziegler, R. 55
Zupko, R. E. 36

Index of Scripture References and Other Ancient Sources

OLD TESTAMENT / HEBREW BIBLE

Exodus
19:6	176
20:11	124
23:27	211
33:11	107

Leviticus
13:28	169
16:31	201

Deuteronomy
10:17	210
28:25	175
30:4	175

Judges
3:16	211
3:21	211

2 Kingdoms (LXX)
22:32	186

2 Chronicles
20:7	107

Ezra
7:12	194

Nehemiah
1:9	175
9:6	124

Psalms
45:3	211
107:34	118
136:2–3	201
146:2	175
146:6	124
148:9	118

Song of Solomon
8:28	175
9:2	175

Isaiah
41:8	107
43:20–21	176
49:6	175

Jeremiah
2:21	118
15:7	175
42:17	175

Ezekiel
26:7	194

Daniel
2:37	194
2:47	210
4:37	193, 210
12:2	175

Hosea
2:25	176

Amos
9:6	124

APOCRYPHA / DEUTEROCANONICAL WORKS

Tobit
5:15	99

Judith
5:19	175
9:12	186

Wisdom
5:17–18 160
7:26 172

Sirach
24:8 186

2 Maccabees
1:24 186
1:27 175
4:10 169
7:23 186
13:14 186

4 Maccabees
5:25 186
11:5 186
15:4 170

PSEUDEPIGRAPHA

1 Enoch
56:5–6 213

Psalms of Solomon
8:8 156

Sibylline Oracles
4:119–124 214
4:137–139 214
5:137–152 214
5:361–385 214

ANCIENT JEWISH WRITERS

Josephus
Antiquities
1.214 190
11.373 194
14.223–227 128
14.226 128
14.262–264 128
15.363 119
17.151–152 5
17.155 5
17.206 5
19.274–279 110
19.339 111

War
1.153 130
1.648–655 5
2.5 5
9.4 130

Against Apion
2.39 189

Philo
De congressu eruditionis gratia
64 8

In Flaccum
36–40 107

Leg. Ad Gai.
302 112

Moses
1.316 130
1.318 130
2.72 130
2.159 130
2.174 130
2.276 130–1

On Flight and Finding
1.90 130
1.93–94 130

Quaestiones et solutiones in Genesin
2.17 130

Spec. Laws
2.120 130
214.19 199

Rewards
1.74 130
QG 2:17 130

NEW TESTAMENT

Matthew
2:1–12 4
2:11 101
3:8 117
3:10 117

7:17–19	117	14:5	99–100
10:9	101	14:11	101
10:29	97, 100	16:15	184–5
12:33	117		
13:23	116	Luke	
13:26	117	3:1	183
14:9	210	3:8–9	117
17:27	100	6:43	117
18:24	100	7:41	99–100
18:28	99–100	8:8	117
19:4	184–5	8:15	116
20:2	97–100	9:3	101
20:9	99–100	10:35	97, 99–100
20:9–10	100	12:6	97, 100
20:10	99–100	12:17	117
20:13	99–100	18:24	101
21:43	117	19:13	100
22:15–22	76	19:15	101
22:17b-21	76	19:16	100
22:19	99–101	19:18	100
23:16–17	101	19:20	100
24	4	19:23	101
24:15	4	19:24–25	100
24:28	4	20:20–26	76
25:15–16	100	20:24	99–100
25:18	101	22:5	101
25:20	100		
25:22	100	John	
25:24–25	100	2:15	101
25:27	101	3:2	107
25:28	100	6:7	99–100
26:15	101	7:51	107
27:3	101	9:19	107
27:5–6	101	11:5	114
27:9	101	12:5	99–100
28:12	101	15	105
28:15	101	15:4	105
		15:5	117
Mark		15:7	105
4:20	116	15:8	100
4:28	116	15:14	105–7, 112
6:8	101	15:15	106
6:37	99–100	15:18–26	105
10:6	184–5	19:12	112
10:29	100	19:15	210
12:13–17	76		
12:15	99–100	Acts	
12:41	101	3:6	101
12:42	100	4:24	124
13:19	184–5	4:37	101

Index of Scripture References and Other Ancient Sources

269

6:7	166	**Galatians**	
7:16	101	6:15	184–5
8:18	101		
8:20	101	**Ephesians**	
14:8	115	2:10	184–5
14:11	125	2:15	184–5
14:12	115, 124	3:9	184–5
14:13	124	4:24	184–5
14:15	115, 124		
14:17	115, 117, 120, 122,	**Philippians**	
	125–6, 219	1:23	166
17:1–10	161		
17:6	146	**Colossians**	
17:7	146	1:6	116
17:22–33	115	1:10	116
17:30	115	1:15	184–5
17:29	101	1:16	184–5
19	141, 161	1:23	184–5
19:19	101	2:9	165
19:21–41	127, 142	3:10	184–5
19:26	127		
19:27	127	**1 Thessalonians**	
19:28	127	2:9	161–2
19:35	127, 133, 140–1,	2:17	152
	219	2:19	152
20:33	101	2:17–3:10	152
24:26	101	2:19	152
25:23	8	4:9–12	161
25:26	8	4:11	161
		4:15	146
Romans		4:15–17	163
1:20	184–5	4:17	146
1:25	184–5, 187	5:1–9	163
7:4	116	5:3	146, 156
7:5	116	5:8	160
8:19–22	184–5		
8:28	10	**2 Thessalonians**	
8:39	184–5	2:1–3	163
		2:8	146
1 Corinthians			
3:12	101	**1 Timothy**	
4:3	10	4:3	184–5
7:9	166	4:4	186
7:38	166	6:15	210
11:9	184–5		
11:17	166	**Hebrews**	
		1:3	165–7, 170, 173, 219
2 Corinthians		1:3a	172
5:17	184–5	1:4	166
		2:1–4	166

3:6–4:13	166	James	
3:7–14	166	1:18	186
3:7–19	166	5:3	101
3:7–4:13	166		
3:12–4:2	166	1 Peter	
3:13	166	1:1	175
4:13	184–5	1:6	175
4:14	166	1:7	175
5:11–13	166	1:10–12	176
5:11–14	166	1:11	175
5:11–6:12	166	1:14	175
5:14	11	1:18	101, 175
6:1	165	2:9	190
6:4–6	166	2:9–10	176, 191
6:9	166	2:10	175
6:12	166	2:11	176, 190
6:18	166	2:13	184–5, 187, 190, 219
7:7	166	2:14	190
7:19	166	2:19–21	175
7:22	166	2:20	175
8:6	166	2:23	175
9:11	184–5	3:14	175, 190
9:14	165	3:16	191
9:23	166	3:17	166
10:19–39	166	3:17–18	175
10:23	166	4:1	175
10:25	166	4:2	176
10:26	166	4:3	175
10:26–31	166	4:3–6	191
10:32	166	4:4	175
10:34	166	4:12	176
11:1	166	4:13	175
11:16	166	4:14	191
11:35	166	4:15–16	175
11:40	166	4:19	175–6, 186–7, 190–1, 219
12:1–29	166		
12:3	166	5:1	175
12:11	166	5:9	176
12:12–13	166	5:9–10	175
12:13b-17	166		
12:14–29	166	2 Peter	
12:24	166	2:21	166
12:25	166	3:4	184–5
12:25–29	166		
13:9	165	Revelation	
13:12–14	166	1:1–3	210
13:22	165	1:16	214

Index of Scripture References and Other Ancient Sources

2:16	214
3:14	184–5
4–5	210
4:11	184–5
5:6	210
5:8	210
5:12–13	210
5:13	186
6:1	210
6:2	213–14
6:6	99–100
6:16	210
7:9–10	210
7:14	210
7:17	210
8:9	186
9:7	101
9:14	211–13
10:6	184–5
12:11	210
13:8	210
13:11	210
14:1	210
14:4	210
14:10	210
15:3	210
16:12	212
17:1	193
17:1–18	193
17:1–19:16	210
17:3	210
17:3–5	211
17:5	210
17:6	210
17:14	193, 210–11, 219
17:15	193
17:19	193
18:12	101
18:24	210
19	210–11
19:7	210
19:9	210
19:11–16	193
19:11–20:15	210
19:15	211, 214
19:16	193, 210–11, 219
19:21	214

21:9	210
21:14	210
21:22–23	210
21:27–22:1	210
22:2	117
22:3	210

EARLY CHRISTIAN WRITINGS

Ambrose of Milan
Duties of the Clergy

3.135	106

Eusebius
Historia ecclesiastica

III, 17	76
VI, 25.14	165

Theodore of Mopsuestia
Fragments on the Epistle to the Hebrews

1.2–3	173

GRECO-ROMAN LITERATURE

Aeschylus
The Suppliants

524–526	199

Aristophanes
Ecclesiazusae

1169–75	12–13

Frogs

383–384	119

Appian
Roman History

1	198
1.2	188
1.13	189

Aristotle
Politica

1257a.32-1257b.3	169, 172

Economics

1345.b20	22

Rhetorica
1.5.4   114

Athēnaïn politeia
10.2   170

Augustus
Res Gestae
34   152

Callimachus
Hymn to Ceres/Demeter
1   121

Cicero
Verrine Orations
2.3.189   96

Rhetorica ad Herennium
4.59.62   125

Orator (De oratore)
11   170
36   172
39   170
83   172
134   172

Topica
22   171
83   172
Letters to Atticus
6.5.2   193
Letters to Quintus
20.5   171–2
On the Republic
2.5–10   193

Claudian
On the Sixth Consulship of Stiicho
531–536   193

Dio Cassius
Historia Romana
1   193
37.6   198
39.41   200
50.3   200

57.8.1   81
53.16.4   152

Dio Chrysostom
The Second Discourse on Kingship
75   199

Diodorus Siculus
Library of History
4   190
5.10   118
5.56.3   30
31.9.7–8   143

Dionysius of Halicarnassus
Antiquitates romanae
1.50.3   189
1.79–87   193
6.94.2   121

Epictetus
Discourses of Epictetus
4.5.16–17   76

Euripides
Helen
1485   118

Ion
54–55   129

Bacchae
58–59   124
79   125

Gellus
Attic Nights
13.14.1–4   193
13.14.7   193

Herodotus
Historiae
1.94   21
1.178–216   212
1.193   117
2.193   117
4.172   117
4.183   117

Index of Scripture References and Other Ancient Sources

Hesiod
Theogony
319   30
912–914   121

Catalogues of Women
Fragment 7   30

Works and Days
385–387   169
572–573   169

Homer
Iliad
6.144–221   30
16.327   30

Odyssey
1.96–324   124
1.405–419   124

Horace
Odes
1.1213–18   124
2.12.22   122

Isocrates
Panegyricus
28   121

Livy
History
5.54.4   193
6–10   39
29.5–11   143
45.18.3–7   143

Ad Urbe Condita
1.4–6   193
1.10   217

Lucian
Octogenarians
13   188

Lucretius
De rerum natura
2.6.11   125

Ovid
Metamorphoses
1.177–180   124
7. 365   30
8.612–727   124

Fasti
1.659–74   121

Pausanias
Description of Greece
2.4.1   29
5.27.12   211
8.53.7   118

Pindar
Isthmian Ode
7.44   30

Olympian Ode
7.54   30
7.54–74   30
13.60   30

Pythian Ode
4.6   118

Plato
Laws
XI 918a-b   22

Pliny
Natural History
33.13.43   36
34.7.17   30

Plutarch
Alexander
2   159

Antoninus
54   200

Caesar
66   40

Camillus
1   188

31	188–9
Crassus	
24.5	212
31.7	212
25.8	214
Lucullus	
14.5	200
28.2–4	214
511	189
Moralia. On Exile	
15	189
Pompey	
5	198
Romulus	
2–10	193
Polybius	
Histories	
2.15.1	96
Quintus Curtius Rufus	
History of Alexander	
5	198–9
Seneca	
De clementia	
1.14.2	81
Strabo	
Geographica	
7.47	143
8.5.5	107
12.4.7	177
12.6.1	122
13.132	199
14.1.24	128
16.1.28	212
Suetonius	
Augustus	
37	193
Tiberius	
26	81

Nero	
8	81
57	214
Vespasian	
12	81
Domitian	
13	210, 220
Tacitus	
Annales	
1.72	81
2.47	181
2.87	81, 98
4.55	131–2
6.8	109
Historiae	
1.2	214
2.8	214
Theophrastus	
Enquiry	
1.3.5	118
Varro	
Latina	
5.41	193
6.24	193
Virgil	
Aeneid	
6.783	193
8.31–35	193
8.62–65	193
Xenophon	
Ways and Means	
1.3	117
Hellenica	
6.3.6	121

PAPYRI & OSTRACA

O. Ber 2.210	95
BGU 1.88.7	170, 172
BGU 3.763.7	170, 172

Index of Scripture References and Other Ancient Sources

P. Flor 1.61.21	170, 172
P. Magd 35	129
P. Mich 2.1271	97
P.Oxy 263	98
P. Oxy 264	97
P. Oxy 267	97
P. Oxy 285	97
P. Oxy 375	98
P. Oxy 390	98
P. Oxy 520	98
P. Oxy 731	97
P. Oxy 736	96
P. Oxy 737	96–7, 99
P. Oxy 739	96
P. Oxy 742	96
P. Oxy 745	96
P. Oxy 819	96–7
P. Oxy 985	98
P. Oxy 1188	97
P. Oxy 1281	97
P. Teb 474	98
P. Wisc 2.38	95
PBM 131	98
PBM 701	98
PBM 1171	96
PBM 1177	98

INSCRIPTIONS

AEpigr.126b	98
CIL 4.3340	98
CIL 6.31542	193
CIG II 2572	186
I. Eph III 647	141
I. Eph III 857	141
I. Eph VII 3005	141
I. Priene 229	186
I. Priene 231	141
IG [X] II/I 31	151
IG XII.8.195	160
IG^2 II/III, 2.1408	170
IT 31	156
IT 32	154, 156
IT 33	156
IT 132	154
IT 133	154
SEG 30.1314.5	119
SEG 36.1092	181
SEG 46.1565	156

SIG^3 751	186
SIG^3 839	186
Syll 6555	119
Syll^3 783[23]	171–2

COINAGE

Alram 166	110
Alram 248	110
AMNG III/2, 41	144–5
BMC 70	181
BMC 71	181
BMC 72	181
BMC 73	181
BMC 223	134
BMC 227	134
BMC 228	134
BMC 233–236	134
BMC 235	135
BMC 242	135
BMC 243	135
BMC 247	135
BMC 254	135
BMC 255	135
BMC 259	135
BMC 260	135
BMC 263	135
BMC 265	135
BMC 266	136
BMC 267	136
BMC 269	136
BMC 271–275	135
BMC 276–279	136
BMC 281	135
BMC 282	135
BMC 292	135
BMC 300	136
BMC 302–305	136
BMC 307	136
BMC 308	136
BMC 309	136
BMC 310	136
BMC 311	136
BMC 312	136
BMC 314	136
BMC 318	136
BMC 328	136
BMC 329	137
BMC 330	137

BMC 331	137	MIG 6.744	206, 209
BMC 342	137	MIG 6.745	206, 209
BMC 343	137	MIG 6.746	206, 209
BMC 350–358	137	MIG 6.747	206, 209
BMC 359–363	137	MIG 6.748	206, 209
BMC 370–376	137	MIG 6.749	206, 209
BMC 377–379	137	MIG 6.750	206, 209
BMC 380	138	MIG 6.751	206, 209
BMC 381–384	137	MIG 6.752	206, 209
BMC 384	138	MIG 6.753	206, 209
BMC 390–391	137	MIG 6.754	206, 209
BMC 392	138	MIG 6.755	206, 209
BMC 393–394	137	MIG 6.756	206, 209
BMC 395	138	MIG 6.757	206, 209
Carradice I	24	MIG 6.758	206, 209
Carradice II	24–5	MIG 6.759	206, 209
Carradice IIIa	25–6	MIG 6.760	206, 209
Carradice IIIb (early)	25–6	MIG 6.761	206, 209
Carradice IIIb (late)	25–6	MIG 6.762	206, 209
Carradice IVa	25, 27	MIG 6.763	206, 209
Carradice IVb	25, 27	MIG 6.766	206, 209
Carradice IVc	25, 27	MIG 6.767	206, 209
CNG 75.2007.798	149–50	MIG 6.768	206, 209
Crawford 20.1	36–7	MIG 6.769	206, 209
Crawford 295.1	38–9	MIG 6.770	206, 209
Crawford 480.13	39	MIG 6.771	206, 209
Crawford 543.1	200–1	MIG 6.772	206, 209
Crawford 72.3	37–8	MIG 6.773	206, 209
Dewing 1508	31	MIG 6.774	206, 209
Jurukova 145	145	MIG 6.775	206, 209
Lukanc 1924	167	MIG 6.776	206, 209
MIG 4.508	207–8	MIG 6.777	206, 209
MIG 5.642	204–5, 208	MIG 6.778	206, 209
MIG 5.643	205, 208	MIG 6.779	206, 209
MIG 5.644	205, 208, 214	MIG 6.780	206, 209
MIG 5.681	203, 208	MIG 6.781	206, 209
MIG 5.682	203, 208	MIG 6.782	206, 209
MIG 5.683	203–4, 208	MIG 6.783	206, 209
MIG 5.684	203–4, 208	MIG 6.784	206, 209
MIG 5.686	203–4, 208	MIG 6.785	206, 208–9
MIG 5.687	204, 208	MIG 6.786	206, 208
MIG 5.688	208	MIG 6.787	206, 209
MIG 5.694	204, 208, 214	MIG 6.788	206, 209
MIG 6.737	205, 209	MIG 6.789	206, 209
MIG 6.738	205, 209	MIG 6.790	206, 209
MIG 6.739	205, 209	MIG 6.791	206, 209
MIG 6.740	205–6, 209	MIG 6.792	206, 209
MIG 6.742	205, 209	MIG 6.793	206, 209
MIG 6.743	206, 209	MIG 6.794	206, 209

Index of Scripture References and Other Ancient Sources   277

MIG 6.795	206, 209	RIC *Claud.* 15	158
MIG 6.796	206, 209	RIC *Claud.* 16	158
MIG 6.797	206, 209	RIC *Claud.* 21	157
MIG 6.798	206, 209	RIC *Claud.* 22	157
MIG 6.799	206, 209	RIC *Claud.* 27	157
MIG 6.800	206, 209	RIC *Claud.* 28	157
MIG 6.801	206, 209	RIC *Claud.* 38	157
MIG 6.802	206, 209	RIC *Claud.* 39	157
MIG 6.803	206, 209	RIC *Claud.* 46	157
MIG 6.804	206, 209	RIC *Claud.* 47	157
MIG 6.805	206, 209	RIC *Claud.* 51	157
MIG 6.806	206, 209	RIC *Claud.* 52	157
MIG 6.807	206, 209	RIC *Claud.* 57	157
MIG 6.808	206, 209	RIC *Claud.* 58	157
MIG 6.809	206, 209	RIC *Claud.* 61	157
MIG 6.810	206, 209	RIC *Claud.* 62	157
MIG 6.811	206, 209	RIC *Claud.* 96	158–9
MIG 6.812	206, 209	RIC *Nero* 181	79
MIG 7.895	206	RIC *Vesp.* 442	193
MIG 7.896	206	RPC 1.76	88–9
MIG 8.1067	207, 208	RPC 1.77	81
MIG 8.1068	207, 208	RPC 1.78	81
MIG 8.1069	207, 208	RPC 1.185	81
MIG 8.1070	207, 208	RPC 1.278	81
MIG 8.1072	207, 208	RPC 1.300	81
MIG 8.1073	207, 209	RPC 1.301	81
MIG 8.1074	207, 209	RPC 1.680	184
MIG 8.1075	207, 209	RPC 1.1363	178–9
MIG 8.1076	207, 209	RPC 1.1364	178
MIG 8.1077	207, 209	RPC 1.1368	179
MIG 8.1078	207, 209	RPC 1.1369	179
MIG 8.1094	207, 209	RPC 1.1370	179
MIG 8.1095	207, 209	RPC 1.1373	179
MIG 8.1096	207, 209	RPC 1.1374	179
MIG 8.1097	207, 209	RPC 1.1375	179
MIG 8.1098	207, 209	RPC 1.1427	150–1
MIG 8.1099	207, 209	RPC 1.1551	152–3
MIG 8.1100	207, 209	RPC 1.1552	147, 153–4
MIG 8.1102	207, 209	RPC 1.1553	154–5
MIG 8.1003	207, 209	RPC 1.1554	147–8
Moushmov 5778	167	RPC 1.1555	148–9
Moushmov 6594	146	RPC 1.1563	149–50
Pharn 1	202	RPC 1.2017	177–8
Ravel 619	28–9	RPC 1.2022	178
RIC *Aug.* 210	40	RPC 1.2023	178
RIC *Claud.* 5	158	RPC 1.2024	178
RIC *Claud.* 6	158	RPC 1.2025	178
RIC *Claud.* 9	157	RPC 1.2049	177
RIC *Claud.* 10	157	RPC 1.2143	155

RPC 1.2293	180	RPC 2.F1064	138–9
RPC 1.2294	180	RPC 2.F1065	139
RPC 1.2295	180	Sellwood 27.2	195, 214
RPC 1.2379	68	Sellwood 41.8	195–6, 214
RPC 1.2451	180	Sellwood 42.2	196–7, 214
RPC 1.2492	179	Sellwood 51.9	196–7
RPC 1.2495	180	Sellwood 56.1	197
RPC 1.2511	182	Sellwood 57.13	197
RPC 1.2512	182	Sellwood 58.1	197
RPC 1.2620	138	Sellwood 59.2	197
RPC 1.2912	155	Sellwood 60.2	197
RPC 1.2928	155	Sellwood 60.4	197
RPC 1.2988	155	Sellwood 61.1	197
RPC 1.2991	181	Sellwood 62.3	197
RPC 1.3027	109	Sellwood 62.12	197
RPC 1.3028	110	Sellwood 64.14	197
RPC 1.3029	110	Sellwood 64.20	197
RPC 1.3030	110	Sellwood 65.2	197
RPC 1.3031	110, 112	Sellwood 65.4	197
RPC 1.3054	110	Sellwood 65.23	197
RPC 1.3055	110	Sellwood 67.1	197
RPC 1.3056	110, 112–13	Sellwood 68.4	197
RPC 1.3057	110	Sellwood 68.5	197
RPC 1.3538	122–4	Sellwood 68.6	197
RPC 1.3539	122	Sellwood 68.7	197
RPC 1.3540	122–3, 125	Sellwood 68.8	197
RPC 1.3601	183	Sellwood 68.11	197
RPC 1.4778	110	Sellwood 69.1	197
RPC 1.4948	120, 183–4	Sellwood 69.2	197
RPC 1.4949	119–21, 125	Sellwood 69.3	197
RPC 1.4950	120	Sellwood 69.4	197
RPC 1.4967	86–7	Sellwood 69.5	197
RPC 1.4968	87–8	Sellwood 69.6	197
RPC 1.4969	87–8	Sellwood 69.13	197
RPC 1.4979	109	Sellwood 72.1	197
RPC 1.4982	109–11	Sellwood 73.2	197
RPC 1.4983	109, 111	Sellwood 73.3	197
RPC 1.4985	109	Sellwood 73.4	197
RPC 1.5421	149	Sellwood 73.5	197
RPC 1.5445	155	Sellwood 73.9	197
RPC 1.5446	155	Sellwood 73.10	197
RPC 2.327	160–1	Sellwood 74.3	197
RPC 2.328	161–2	Sellwood 74.6	197
RPC 2.329	161	Senior 65.1.T	203
RPC 2.330	161–2	SNG ANS 807	33
RPC 2.1070	139	SNG Ashmolean 648	31–2
RPC 2.1196	110–11	SNG Ashmolean 728	31–2
RPC 2.2626	139	SNG Ashmolean 760	23
RPC 2.2627	139	SNG Ashmolean 1671	32–3

Index of Scripture References and Other Ancient Sources

SNG Ashmolean 2891	33–4
SNG Ashmolean 3300	143–4
SNG Ashmolean 3301	145
SNG Ashmolean 3756	34–5
SNG Cop 32	28–9
SNG Cop 70	34–5
SNG Cop 369	144–5
SNG Cop 397	134
SNG Cop 400	135
SNG Cop 402	135
SNG Cop 409	135
SNG Cop 411	135
SNG Cop 415	135
SNG Cop 416	135
SNG Cop 417	136
SNG Cop 419–423	135
SNG Cop 425	135
SNG Cop 431	135
SNG Cop 436	135
SNG Cop 442–448	136
SNG Cop 453	136
SNG Cop 454	136
SNG Cop 460–462	136
SNG Cop 472	137
SNG Cop 473	137
SNG Cop 486	137
SNG Cop 488	137
SNG Cop 489	137
SNG Cop 494	138
SNG Cop 496–500	137
SNG Cop 501–503	137
SNG Cop 510–512	137
SNG Cop 513–520	137
SNG Cop 521	138
SNG Cop 532–534	137
SNG Cop 535	138
SNG Cop 536	138
SNG Cop 538	138
SNG Cop 541	137
SNG Keckman 544	30
SNG Lewis 1448	135
SNG Lewis 1449	135
SNG Lewis 1450	136
SNG Lewis 1453	136
SNG Lewis 1454	137
SNG Lewis 1457	137
SNG Lewis 1459	137
SNG Lewis 1461	137
SNG Lewis 1463	137

SNG Mün 127	134
SNG Mün 132	134
SNG Mün 133	134
SNG Mün 141–145	135
SNG Mün 152–155	135
SNG Mün 158	135
SNG Mün 160	135
SNG Mün 161	135
SNG Mün 162	136
SNG Mün 163	135
SNG Mün 164	135
SNG Mün 165	136
SNG Mün 166	136
SNG Mün 168	135
SNG Mün 173	135
SNG Mün 184	136
SNG Mün 187	136
SNG Mün 189	136
SNG Mün 190	136
SNG Mün 193	136
SNG Mün 196	136
SNG Mün 208	137
SNG Mün 209	137
SNG Mün 212	137
SNG Mün 213–215	137
SNG Mün 224	137
SNG Mün 234–238	137
SNG Mün 240	137
SNG Mün 241	137
SNG Mün 243	137
SNG Mün 249–254	137
SNG Mün 257–260	137
SNG Mün 263	137
SNG Mün 266–268	137
SNG Mün 270	137
SNG Mün 275	138
SNG Mün 276	137
SNG Paris 1.1544	25, 28
SNG Righetti 853	135
SNG Righetti 854	136
SNG Righetti 856	136
SNG Righetti 857	136
SNG Righetti 860	137
SNG Righetti 861–863	137
SNG Righetti 864	137
SNG Righetti 867	138
SNG Righetti 868	137
SNG Righetti 869	138
SNG vA 1884	134

SNG vA 1888	134	SNG vA 1924	137
SNG vA 1890	135	SNG vA 1925	137
SNG vA 1891	135	SNG vA 1928–1930	137
SNG vA 1893	135	SNG vA 1931	137
SNG vA 1895	135	SNG vA 1933	137
SNG vA 1896–1898	135	SNG vA 1934	137
SNG vA 1899	136	SNG vA 7863	134, 139
SNG vA 1900	136	SNG vA 7869	135
SNG vA 1902	135	SNG vA 7871	135
SNG vA 1903	135	SNG vA 7872	136
SNG vA 1904	136	SNG vA 7873	136
SNG vA 1905	136	SNG vA 7874	135
SNG vA 1906	136	SNG vA 7877	135
SNG vA 1907	136	SNG vA 7880	136
SNG vA 1908	136	SNG vA 7887	137
SNG vA 1912	137	SNG vA 7888	137
SNG vA 1913	137	SNG vA 7889	137
SNG vA 1914	137	Weidauer 39	169
SNG vA 1916	137	Youroukova 26	168
SNG vA 1921–1923	137	Youroukova 145	167–9

CPSIA information can be obtained
at www.ICGtesting.com
Printed in the USA
LVHW051927080122
708050LV00018B/1585